The Architecture of European Codes and Contract Law

Private Law in European Context Series

VOLUME 8

Series Editors:
Martijn Hesselink
Ugo Mattei
Horatia Muir Watt

For the
Society of European Contract Law (SECOLA)

Massimo Bianca *Hugh Collins* *Stefan Grundman (President)*
Ewoud Hondius *Sophie Stijns*

Contract law is probably the most dynamic area of European Private Law and also the fundamental private law discipline in all national legal systems. SECOLA was founded to assist the study of European contract law and to enhance its quality. SECOLA organises an open, truly international and interdisciplinary discussion platform. The focus of the Society is upon newly enacted European Community legal measures, on core concepts in the field of European contract law, and on proposals for further legislation. The Society organises one or two international conferences each year, arranges for the publication of scholarly discussions in the filed including books to be published in this series, and assists with other network activities. In addition, SECOLA has created a journal dedicated to the same aims (see www.secola.org and www.degruyter.de/rs/280_7944_DEU_h.htm).

A list of previous titles in the series may be found at the end of this volume.

The Architecture of European Codes and Contract Law

Edited by

Stefan Grundmann and Martin Schauer

KLUWER LAW INTERNATIONAL

A C.I.P. catalogue record for this book is available from the Library of Congress

ISBN 90 411 2530 2

Published by:
Kluwer Law International
P.O. Box 316
2400 AH Alphen aan den Rijn
The Netherlands

Sold and distributed in North, Central and South America by:
Aspen Publishers, Inc.
7201 McKinney Circle
Frederick, MD 21704
USA

Sold and distributed in all other countries by:
Turpin Distribution Services Ltd.
Stratton Business Park
Pegasus Drive
Biggleswade
Bedfordshire SG18 8TQ
United Kingdom

Table of Contents

Chapter 12
The Greek Consumer Law **219**
Elisa Alexandridou

Chapter 13
Verbrauchervertragsrecht im tschechischen Recht **235**
Luboš Tichý

Part IV
Formation of Contract and Precontractual Information **281**

Chapter 16
Formation of Contract and Pre-Contractual Information from an Italian Perspective (Final Remarks from the Perspective of European Contract Law) **283**
Vincenzo Roppo

Part I
Introduction and Overview

Chapter 1
The Architecture of European Codes and Contract Law – A Survey of Structures and Contents

Stefan Grundmann

I. THE OVERALL DESIGN OF THE INQUIRY

1. The Importance of Architecture and Codes

The core advantages of codification are typically seen as being that the system is made explicit and that rules can more easily be found.[1] Nowadays, both ideas seem to be even more important for emerging European private and contract law than for national contract law.

The first reason for this is that European legal science needs cross-border discussion and is nowhere near as developed as national legal communities are. Discussion – not just by comparative law specialists, but by

---

[1] For a discussion of the advantages of codification see, for instance, Lurger, *Grundfragen der Vereinheitlichung des Vertragsrechts in der Europäischen Union* (2002) p. 36 *et seq.*; Schreckenburger, '*Die Gesetzgebung der Aufklärung und die Europäische Kodifikationsidee*', in Merten and Schreckenburger, *Kodifikation gestern und heute* (1995) p. 89 *et seq.*; Schmidt, *Die Zukunft der Kodifikationsidee* (1995); Münch, '*Strukturprobleme der Kodifikation*' in Behrends and Sellert (eds.), *Der Kodifikationsgedanke und das Modell des Bürgerlichen Gesetzbuches (BGB)*, (2000) p. 147; Canaris, *Systemdenken und Systembegriff in der Jurisprudenz entwickelt am Beispiel des deutschen Privatrechts* (1969); Zimmermann, 'Codification: history and present significance of an idea' (1995) 3 *European Review of Private Law*, 95.

S. Grundmann, M. Schauer (eds), *The Architecture of European Codes and Contract Law*, 3–30

all interested circles and in the grand domestic dogmatic traditions – is needed and it is possible only (or is at least largely facilitated) if solutions can easily be compared. And this means there must be a common Cardesian system of legal ideas. It might even be that forming the basis of a common European discussion is what matters most in the process towards a European optional code, a common frame of reference or a European restatement of contract law(s).[2] It is easier to discuss this in terms like: 'In Austria, our solution to rule 5:107 is the following', than to specify the problem in long descriptions.

On the other hand, there are strong reasons not to write a European system – or architecture – just for system's sake and on the basis of what codes present so far, but rather to reconsider and extensively rewrite what is known as system in traditional codes. This is the second reason why, in emerging European private and contract law, it may be even more important to discuss the 'architecture' than in national laws. The idea would be that in the process of European codification, a fundamentally new systematic concept should be the aim. The reason for this is that over the last three to five decades, contract law, and the world which contract law has to reflect, has changed so radically. A system created now should really reflect the current status of contract law and the problems it has to approach. Among the most radical changes are: the paradigm of individual transactions is supplemented if not largely substituted by that of mass transactions, i.e. standard contract terms are the normal type of contract drafting today; consumer law has become much more important and, more generally, the idea of regulating markets and contracts, not just providing facilitative law in the form of default rules (the so-called '*Reservevertragsordnung*'); contracts nowadays come very often not as individual contracts, but in chains and networks (including hybrids between contracts and companies); the information society has shaped contract law probably more than any other field of law; sales law, which was the paradigm of national contract law and of international unification over decades, has got its companion in importance, the service and long-term contracts, probably today even more important in terms of gross income than sales, but certainly more complex and a core modern problem in a service society. With all these changes, it would be astonishing if the system, if the architecture of codes did not have to change as well. The architecture of codes matters – old and new, already invented and still to be developed – if one does not just want to stick to traditional models created for other times and a different world and if one takes the starting point seriously that codes and system should reflect the inherent nature of substantive law solutions (at the time when the code is enacted).

---

2 In this sense, for instance, Th. Wilhelmsson, 'The Design of an Optional (Re)Statement of European Contract Law – Real Life Instead of Dead Concepts', in S. Grundmann and J. Stuyck (eds.), *An Academic Green Paper on European Contract Law* (2002) pp. 353, 361.

2. Which Architectural Questions?

In this book, three basic 'architectural' questions are dealt with.

The first is about the level of abstraction. This question is discussed at least with respect to one point, i.e. whether the core concept should be juristic act, obligation or contract. This is largely a question addressed to (the report on) Germany, where the two first named, more abstract, concepts have been developed and primarily discussed. The question is, however, a more general one. Any Code discussed gives, albeit implicitly, answers to the question of which level of abstraction is appropriate. The first section is therefore more generally about how Codes deal, in their systematic arrangement, with some core questions of formation and performance or breach of contract, namely mistake and misrepresentation, standard contract terms and remedies in the case of breach of contract.

The second question is about the relationship between consumer contract law and 'other' contract law. From the perspective of national law, the 'other' contract law constitutes the 'normal' contract law, and consumer contract law rather the 'outsider'. From an EC Law perspective, the contrary would rather seem to be the case. Consumer contract law has been a powerful – if not the most powerful – driving force in the development of the *Acquis Communautaire* in contract law. Keeping both areas separate would create an obvious impediment in a process where EC Contract Law might be generalized and where national and EC contract law influence each other mutually in order to help in finally bringing about a Common Frame of Reference or a European Optional Code. The core question would, however, seem to be whether consumer contract law and other contract law are not too diverse to be treated jointly.

A third question in the architecture of (European) contract law would be of substance. Indeed, discussing architecture has also to include, at least in one instance, an area of substantive contract law. The pre-contractual phase is of particular interest here. From the chronological order, it seems plausible to start here (especially if later on, the study might continue). Moreover, from a substantive law perspective, the topic is particularly interesting because the borderlines between 'inside' and 'outside' the contract are at issue. And from an EC Law perspective, the area is of utmost importance because virtually all legal measures contain – in many cases even primarily – information duties applying to the pre-contractual phase. Thus the architecture of both national codes, which should at least transpose these rules but often also contain other rules for this phase, and of EC Contract Law can be studied in a particularly close relationship.

3. Comparative Law, EC Law and European Confidication as Integrated Perspectives

The question as to why architectural questions matter is closely related to what levels have to be considered as a 'European Contract Law'.

One would first look to comparative law. The architecture of codes is today mainly the architecture of national codes. On the other hand, there are also substantive law questions and the question of whether to extend consumer law. And the comparative law approach itself may be declining in importance. It would seem quite clear that European Contract Law today must be comparative contract law. It cannot be so, however, because[3] the *Acquis Communautaire*, the body of harmonized contract law, has already passed a political and democratic process. Comparative law would also be difficult to implement because often it is necessary to deal with all the modern evolutions and problems mentioned above: with consumer law; with regulation (as in competition law) and enabling law, because such a market order is typically also the prerequisite for contracts fulfilling their scope, i.e. free and meaningful planning by the parties; with regulation of core sectors, for instance financial services and more generally long-term relationships which are so important in a (new) service society. The action plan of 2003[4] rather clearly takes a decision in this sense: The future will be based on the *Acquis Communautaire*, not mainly on a comparative law approach, which will be supplementary only.

Therefore one should look secondly, and just as intensively, to the *Acquis Communautaire* as a basis of European Contract Law. In the context of this book this is mainly the background to Parts 2 and 3. Consumer contract law is basically of EC Law origin, and pre-contractual duties are as well, at least in large part. European Contract Law can, however, not be exclusively focussed on the *Acquis Communautaire* either. Not only does it depend on national laws as its source of inspiration and still today also as its tool for transposition, but there is a second reason as well: The European Parliament and the EC Commission have pronounced themselves very clearly in favour of a European Code which, if adopted at all, would 'only' be optional. This is much in line with many authors on the SECOLA interim conference in Leuven in 2001.[5] The European Code would thus always compete with national laws, not substitute them.

---

[3] On the following more extensively S. Grundmann, 'The Optional European Code on the Basis of the Acquis Communautaire – Starting Point and Trends', (2004) 10 *European Law Journal* 698.

[4] Communication of the Commission to the Council and the European Parliament – a more coherent European Contract Law, Action Plan of 12 Feb. 2003, COM(2003) 68 final, OJ C 63/1, 2003, esp. nn 55–64.

[5] S. Grundmann and J. Stuyck (eds.), *An Academic Green Paper on European Contract Law* (2002) Part IV.

In fact, the perspective of a European Code is a third level to be taken into consideration. The time has now come in which a new common instrument – if one does not want to speak of European Code[6] – is probably a realistic scenario already. Therefore, even if there were no good economic or cultural arguments in favour of such an (Optional) European Code, one could not close one's eyes to such a process without loosing influence on its contents. One would have to discuss it anyway – however, this needs to be repeated, as an optional instrument only. And it is perhaps even for this level primarily that the question which architectural design is preferable is asked.

It is exactly in this integrative spirit – comparative law, European Law, *Acquis Communautaire*, two-level system and European Code – that this book is conceived: starting from the Member States and a comparison of the different architectural designs to be found in this basis of European Contract Law (mainly in Part II); passing then on to a core question which is very much inspired by existing EC Contract Law, the question of how to conceive the relationship between consumer contract law and 'other' contract law (Part III); finally reaching the area where national contract and EC Contract Law are most intimately intertwined, the (information duties in the) pre-contractual phase (Part IV); and all this from the perspective of a coming Common Frame of Reference and of an Optional European Code, i.e. considerations on the immediate future. The approach is integrative also in so far as legal scholarship meets economic approaches and as more formal considerations are combined with substantive law questions.

II. THE OVERALL ARCHITECTURE AND THE LEVEL OF ABSTRACTION: STARTING FROM CONTRACT, OBLIGATION AND JURISTIC ACT? (PART II)

Part II is devoted to the overall architecture, namely the level of abstraction: The German Code, as the most abstract example, uses mainly the concepts of juristic act and obligation. Other jurisdictions followed partly or at least in doctrinal discussion, such as Austria. Contracts would be an obvious alternative starting point. In this part, the traditional old European Codes and the Dutch Code are examined with respect to the core question of 'level of abstraction'. This is just one of several such questions related to the level of abstraction. The main questions asked of the authors are related to the formation of contracts (legal arrangements for mistake and misrepresentation, nullity for violation of the law or bona mores), to standard contract

[6] See H. Collins, 'The "Common Frame of Reference" for EC Contract Law: A Common Lawyer's Perspective', in: Meli and Maugeri (eds.), *L'Armonizzazione del Diritto Europeo* (2004) pp. 107, 124: 'Let's just call it a code' (with respect to the 'Common Frame of Reference').

terms as a particularly important phenomenon, and to the regime and remedies for breach of contract (namely rescission and damages). The results are then contrasted with the current codification process in central Europe. Five contributions cover this field pretty comprehensively.

1. The French *Code Civil*

The first contribution is devoted to the *French Code Civil* (1804) which shares with the Austrian Civil Code (1811, in parts in force in West Galicia already in 1798) the privilege of forming the first great Code in Europe. This characterization is mainly due to the fact that in these instances a coherent (Code) system was paramount for the first time.[7] This distinguishes the French (and the Austrian) Civil Code from the slightly earlier *Allgemeines Preußisches Landrecht* which was the most modern compilation of the 18th century – in spirit a product of the enlightened state of Prussia, but not yet following the coherent system so important for the age of enlightenment more generally and for the slightly younger Civil Codes.[8]

In her contribution on the French *Code Civil*, Prof. Remy-Corlay, deals with the contract law parts of it. In its third book of three, devoted to different means of acquiring property, the French Civil Code (in its famous title III) deals with contract law. This title is very much inspired by the Iustinian Digests and Institutes and has remained virtually unchanged for over 200 years. Prof. Remy-Corlay states that, while there are important parts of contract law outside the Code (insurance, labour and consumer contracts), the Code is still an integral part of contract law, but has never been perfect. The first deficiency would seem to be that contract law is hidden away (one of 20 titles in book III!). Even within the title, important parts are missing: namely performance and breach of contract as a whole system. The title distinguishes: formation, effect of obligations, different kinds of obligations, extinction of obligations and evidence. Prof. Remy-Corlay then describes in two sections formation and performance/breach of contract.

---

7 On the spirit of the *Code Civil* see: Halperin, *Le Code Civil* (1996) pp. 101–121; Martin, *Mythologie du Code Napoléon – aux soubassements de la France moderne* (2003); Seignac, *La législation civile dans la revolution francaise* (1895). For this Code and all Codes of the age of enlightenment: Schreckenberger, '*Die Gesetzgebung der Aufklärung und die europäische Kodifikationsidee*', in Merten and Schreckenberger (ed.), *Kodifikation gestern und heute* (1995) p. 87; Wieacker, *Privatrechtsgeschichte der Neuzeit – unter besonderer Berücksichtigung der deutschen Entwicklung* (1967) pp. 322–347.

8 On the *Allgemeines Preußisches Landrecht*: Conrad, *Rechtsstaatliche Bestrebungen im Absolutismus Preußens und Österreichs am Ende des 18. Jahrhunderts* (1961); Gose and Würtenberger (eds.) *Zur Ideen- und Rezeptionsgeschichte des Preußischen Allgemeinen Landrechts* (1999); see also n. 7.

With respect to formation, the level of abstraction seems lower than in German law. 'Juristic act' is not a category as such (and trends to introduce such concepts have been rebutted). The starting point is rather the contract and consent (and these rules can be applied by analogy to minor phenomena such as unilateral promises). The rules read beautifully; however, in the text as a whole, important bits seem to be missing (e.g. binding force of declaration of wills, revocation, meeting of minds, etc.) and it does not appear to be as systematic as the German '*Rechtsgeschäftslehre*'. Important concepts such as representation are missing completely; the author discusses a suitable place for it at some length. Remarkable progress has been made in case law, namely with respect to pre-contractual duties (partly using also article 1382 *Code Civil* on torts). Prof. Remy-Corlay pays particular attention to the integration of standard contract terms into the contract – a question dealt with outside the Code, exclusively in the *Code de la Consommation*! Even in France, the integration of such terms is, however, a disputed issue, also in commercial contracts, and therefore, according to Prof. Remy-Corlay, should rather be dealt with in a part on formation. A second specific focus in this contribution is on the treatment of mistake, fraud and duress in the Civil Code; mistake would seem to be accepted as an excuse more often in case law than in the Code, and fraud has been extended to fraudulent silence.

With respect to performance and breach, Prof. Remy-Corlay is still more critical. While the part on formation as a whole is seen quite positively, the rules on performance and breach, scattered over Chapters 2 and 3 of title III, are not. The basic distinction between obligations to give and obligations to do is seen as the consequence of contracts having real effect (transfer of property); this effect is debatable in French Law today. The author deplores important lacunae: nothing on the right to withhold performance, on the *clausula rebus sic stantibus*, and on *mora creditoris*. The author then deals in particular with the concepts of performance and breach. The concept of performance, also in France, has changed from a concept in which the execution of the will of the parties was paramount to one in which 'solidarity' would seem to be an important issue (Jamin, Mazeaud). The author discusses at some length '*objet*' and '*cause*' of the contract. The concept of breach is a uniform concept: no distinction of different types of breach of contracts is made, not even between 'obligations of means' and 'obligations of result', which is such an important distinction in French Law. The last part on sanctions is interesting in so far as the three remedies – damages, rescission, and specific performance – are seen in this sequence, i.e. that performance *in natura* is rather seen as an exceptional remedy, not the rule. Damages are an area which is typically studied for contracts in conjunction with torts. Under French Law, a combination of damages and the other remedies has already been possible for quite some time (a modern trend, it would seem).

2. The German *Bürgerliches Gesetzbuch* (BGB)

The German Civil Code, the *Bürgerliches Gesetzbuch* (BGB), differs considerably from the French Civil Code. It has always been considered as the opposite extreme insofar as it uses much more abstract, scholarly categories. It is considered not to be the fruit of a strong popular stream of feelings and thought, but rather of one century of scholarly debate, namely the Pandectist school of thinking.[9]

Grundmann, in his contribution on the *Bürgerliches Gesetzbuch*, briefly describes this spirit of the BGB, the struggle of one century, mainly in legal science, and points out that there are in fact good reasons to hail the technical arrangement of the Code. The overall order in five books (Family Law (book 4); Wills and Estates (book 5); Property Law (book 3); Contracts and Torts (the Law of Obligations, book 2, partly book 1)) is clearer than in the Codes of the century before in that they represent areas of the law as we know them today and even the sequence is 'modern': contract and then property, i.e. the transactions come first, family and wills and estates (the 'status') come only afterwards ('from status to contract'). The other sections of the contribution are devoted to contract law in particular, and in this respect the author is more critical. In three sections, he treats formation of contract (mainly book 1), then performance and breach of contract (book 2) and then the many questions raised.

With respect to formation, the author concentrates on book 1 which in its section 3 contains rules on legal capacity, legally binding declaration of intentions (i.e. offer and acceptance), consent, conditions precedent and subsequent, representation and validation by the person concerned (and then in section 4 and 5 on prescription and computation of terms). The author holds that as such, this is quite a logical order, but that starting from juristic act does not have a lot of advantages: the German Civil Code does not consider the two declarations of intention together, but each one separately. This may be important for instance for wills and estates, but there is little common ground really between family law and wills and estates on the one hand and contracts on the other (questions of formality, of mistake, of the possibility of representation and others all differ considerably). The author would therefore rather start from the paradigm of contract only, especially because con-

9 Markesinis, Lorenz and Dannemann, *The German Law of Obligations*, Vol. 1 (1997) p. 13; Wassermann (ed.), *Kommentar zum Bürgerlichen Gesetzbuch (Alternativkommentar)*, Vol. 1 (1987), Introduction, para. 53 (p. 23); Wieacker (n. 7), 479. For a particularly favourable view of these qualities of the German Civil Code see, for instance, Maitland, 'The Making of the German Civil Code', in: Fisher (ed.), *The Collected Papers of Frederic William Maitland*, Vol. 3 (1911) p. 484. For a comparison between the French and the German Civil Code: Lasserre-Kiesow, *La technique législative – étude sur les codes civils français et allemand* (2002).

tract law in itself has become so complex. He would argue for this approach at least on the European level. Moreover, he criticizes that the fact that the German Civil Code has in general led the German legislature to regulate questions of formation of contract in different places, far from each other, and that this created the difficulty that connected problems, for instance for individually bargained for contracts and for standard contract terms, cannot easily be compared. Having rules on the formation of contracts also in book 2, for instance with respect to standard contracts terms, is seen as being less than ideal. The author agrees, however, that formation can be regulated for all types of contracts jointly (as in German Law) as Codes rather than distinguishing types of contracts according to contents and performance and not according to modes and questions of formation. He sees some lacunae – mainly a general part on information duties, the specific ones forming nowadays a large bulk of rules – and some instances in which sets of rules should be relocated (mainly on standard contract terms and on the right of revocation in cases where particular marketing techniques are used).

With respect to performance and breach, the author concentrates on book 2 which contains a general part on contract law (or rather obligations (§§ 214–432 BGB)), a part on specific contracts (§§ 433–810 BGB), and rules on restitution and torts (§§ 811–853 BGB). Here the author discusses whether the concept of obligation is needed and finds that, in fact, only very few rules of the 'general law of obligations' apply in the same way to torts and contracts. Again, he argues for starting from the concept of contracts only, at least on the European level, for the reasons already mentioned above. He then discusses the architecture of the general part more in detail which contains sections 1–4 on: obligations, standard contract terms, contracts and extinction of obligations (via proper performance), while sections 5–7 deal with particular questions going beyond one simple contract, i.e. assignment of claims, assignment of debts and multitude of creditors and debtors. The author is very critical about regulating content, performance and breach – each one of them – in several sets of rules, for instance distinguishing between a breach which occurred in a contract which creates duties only for one party or in a contract which creates (as in most cases) duties for both parties. Moreover prerequisites and legal consequences are often separated from one another (for instance in the case of rescission). In the last reform of German Law, the differences in the regimes on breach of contract in the different types of contracts have been considerably reduced. As this is welcomed by the author, it is not surprising that he finds that a considerable amount of general rules on performance and breach (for all types of contracts) can be formulated. Thus, the author is in favour of a general part on performance and breach, but criticizes the large number of distinctions which are based mainly on theory and not on practical relevance (for instance between contracts which create duties only for one party or which create duties for both) and which considerably exclude closely related rules from one another. Finally, the author sees two major lacunae: the absence of rules on networks of contracts, and the importance of rules on long-term and service relationships.

The author then exemplifies all these ideas with respect to formation of contracts (legal arrangements for mistake and misrepresentation, nullity for violation of the law or bona mores), to standard contract terms, and to the regime and remedies for breach of contract (namely rescission and damages). In his concluding remarks, he proposes a less complicated order in which the modern problems of contract law would all find their place.

3. The Austrian *Allgemeines Bürgerliches Gesetzbuch* (ABGB)

The Austrian Code, the *Allgemeines Bürgerliches Gesetzbuch* (ABGB), while not being the fruit of a revolutionary movement, shares with the French Code the clarity, the more down-to-earth language, and it is certainly a law written for the Austrian people at the insistence of an emperor deeply inspired by the ideals of the age of enlightenment.[10]

Schauer, in his contribution on the ABGB, explains some of the characteristics of the ABGB. It has been strongly influenced by natural law and is much shorter than the Prussian '*Allgemeines Landrecht*' (ALR), which had been prepared only two decades earlier. The reason for that is that the drafters of the law focused more on the creation of basic principles than on rules which cover every detail. Despite its indisputable quality, the ABGB, having reached an age of almost two centuries, no longer fully meets modern demands. Another reason why it has lost some of its relevance is the fact that that legislation created a number of special acts which apply apart from the ABGB.

The system of the ABGB is inspired by the Roman law 'institutions system'. This is why the ABGB does not have a Section Dealing with 'General Issues' (*Allgemeiner Teil*). Therefore, the 'starting point' is not the legal transaction but the contract. Nevertheless, this fact does not create any serious problems. Insofar as there are no special provisions for unilateral legal transactions, the gaps are filled by the analogous application of the provision for contracts.

The author then emphasizes another characteristic feature of the Austrian Contract Law which he describes as 'trialism'. Provisions about contracts cannot only be found in the ABGB but also in the Commercial Code (*Handelsgesetzbuch* (HGB)) and in the Consumer Protection Act

10 On the spirit of the ABGB see, Swoboda, *Das ABGB im Lichte der Lehren Kants* (1926); and also n. 7. On the potential of reform see M. Schauer and C. Fischer-Czermak (eds.), *Das ABGB auf dem Weg ins 3. Jahrtausend* (2003). For a comparison between the French and the Austrian Civil Code: Dezza, *Lezioni di storia della codificazione civile – Il Code Civil (1804) e l'Allgemeines Bürgerliches Gesetzbuch* (ABGB, 1812), 2nd ed. (2000).

(*Konsumentenschutzgesetz* (KSchG)). The author does not recommend this system as a model for a European Code and is strongly in favour of a 'monistic codification' which includes not only general law but also special provisions for businesses and consumers.

Then Schauer explains that the provisions on the conclusion of contracts apply to all contracts, including those in the areas of family law and inheritance law, if there are no special rules for certain kinds of contracts. In his opinion, however, the provisions on the conclusion of contracts in Austrian law contain several gaps and deficits. The first one is that there is no general provision on obligations in the pre-contractual phase, in particular on information duties. Doctrine and courts agree however, that a general principle may be derived from some rules on pre-contractual duties which apply in special cases. The second deficit is the numerous kinds of consumer rights to terminate the contract, which in a European codification should be simplified and harmonized. Another deficit of the Austrian law lies in the fact that in the chapter on the conclusion of contracts there are no provisions on agency (they can be found in the chapter on the Power of Attorney Agreement (*Auftragsvertrag*)). For a European codification the author recommends an agency section whose scope should depend on the scope of the codification itself.

As for the General Terms and Conditions, the author is strongly in favour of a concept of providing rules on the inclusion and the legality of the General Terms together with the provisions on the conclusion of contracts in general and not in connection with the special provisions on different kinds of contracts.

Then the author explains the system of breach of contract law in the ABGB. The Austrian law distinguishes between certain types of breach of contract, such as delay, impossibility, breach of warranty and *laesio enormis*. This does not correspond with a uniform breach of contract system which can be found in the CISG, the Principles of European Contract Law and others. The author argues in favour of the uniform model which he thinks is clearer and simpler. If the breach of contract is due to the fault of the obligor then the obligee may claim damages. This right remains unaffected even if the obligee terminates the contract. In most cases the obligee may claim his interest in the fulfilment of the contract ('*Erfüllungsinteresse*').

Schauer agrees with Grundmann that the special characteristics of long-term legal relationships must be given attention. In his opinion however, special rules for network contracts have not yet been elaborated clearly enough to allow their codification. On the other hand, the author supports the idea that contracts without a consideration should not be ignored in a European codification.

In his final remarks the author repeats that European contract would not require a Section Dealing with General Issues. The ABGB is an example that such a model works. Finally, the author raises the question of whether national laws will really be of great influence in the creation of a European uniform law, since so much of the fundamental preparatory work has already been done. The question will be which subjects should be included in a European code and where to draw the line between this code and the national laws. CISG and the European Principles of Contract Law give different answers to that question – the CISG leaving more subjects to the national laws and the PECL including more within its scope. The author argues in favour of the latter model because it comes closer to the goal to provide the market participants with a uniform and transparent framework.

4. The Dutch Civil Code (*Nieuwe Burgerlijk Wetboek*)

Prof. Verschraegen, in her contribution on the *Burgerlijke Wetboek*, starts out with a survey on the history of the Dutch Code: the close relationship of the Code of 1837 to the French Code, despite some differences (contracts not causing transfer of title and development of a general part on obligations); the increasing impact of modern developments both inside and outside this code, also in case law; and the will, just after World War II, to build a new coherent Code which was gradually enacted from the late 1950s to the end of the 20th century (and beyond), also with a coherent contract law or rather: law of obligations. This new Code is definitely integrative in spirit, integrating also the old Commercial Code, consumer law and also case law, very similar to what happened later in Germany (see above (b)). The author then speaks of the style of the Dutch Code as a whole, of the Parts on Patrimonial Law and General Law of Obligations and in a third section illustrates all this with some contract law examples.

The new Dutch Code as a whole is seen to be more detailed than the French Civil Code and less abstract than the German Code, thus maintaining, at least theoretically, the style of a readable book (like the French Civil Code), but approaching nevertheless the complexity of modern times and reflecting two more centuries of intensive private law scholarship. As far as style goes, all the methods of modern legislation should be used by the reader (examples, commentaries, etc.), and it should be clear that, with its general part (book 3), the new Code is much closer to the German model than the Code of 1837 and perhaps even belongs more to the Germanic world than the Romance world. Huber's decision against a general part (in the Swiss Code) has not been followed. In other instances, however, concepts are developed for the most important instances and then applied by analogy in other contexts.

The law of obligations is divided between book 3 (general part) and book 6 (law of obligations). The general part is again divided up into two sections. The first contains definitions only and some principles (good faith and the like), but not substantive law (as is the case in its German counterpart). This general part, first section, also differs from its German counterpart in so far as it includes not only (some basic) rules on formation

(*Rechtsgeschäftslehre*), but also on performance and breach. In the second section of the general part, the rules on formation of contracts can be found in more detail, and indeed, the concept of juristic act is prominent here. Here, a true law of formation of obligations can be found. This would mean that abstraction is carried even further than in the German Code. The law of obligations (book 6) is surprising in so far as contracts come only in title five, more specific issues such as transfer of obligations much earlier. Considering the whole picture, the interplay between many sets of rules seems no less complex than in the German Civil Code.

In the last section, Prof. Verschraegen illustrates all this by a set of key examples: contract and tort, seen (in conjunction with unjust enrichment) as a common category under the heading of 'obligations'; quasi-contracts, a common category for obligations outside contracts and torts (*negotiorum gestio*, undue payment, unjust enrichment); good faith, being used rather broadly in the Netherlands;[11] express and implied terms, the most important problem being that of standard contract terms (integration into the contract and substantive legal control); and breach of contract, the remedies being a claim to specific performance, damages besides performance, damages instead of performance, rescission and rescission combined with damages (exactly like under German Law). In some of these examples, the author is critical and questions whether the choices made were always those most suited to coherent system building in contract law (doubting, for instance, the importance of a category such as 'obligations' with respect to the remedy of damages).

5. The Endeavours in Central Europe

Prof. Vékas, in his contribution on Central Europe, starts out by stressing the rather secondary importance of traditional private law codification in Central European states, privatization coming first, then business law, mainly market regulation and company law, in part also commercial law. He then turns to private law codification. Hungary in particular had traditionally been more influenced by German, Austrian and Swiss than by French models. Prof. Vékas then details the key developments in the major countries before he turns to a more analytical part. A first dilemma for Central European states was Europeanization: Was it worth entering into a thorough national codification process at all? The next dilemma was whether to use a monist or dualist approach. Prof. Vékas stresses that this relates less to the question of whether a Commercial Code with special rules for commercial contracts should be developed – only the still united Czechoslovachia opted

11 For a comparative law survey see Grundmann and Mazeaud (eds.), *General Clauses and Standards in European Contract Law*, (2006).

for this road – than to the question of how to deal with consumer law: piecemeal transposition in single (modest) acts was the starting point, some countries later on opting for a Consumer Code in which to concentrate the transposition of several directives. Prof. Vékas analyses the advantages (gathering all EC Law material in one act) and disadvantages (disintegration of private law) of this approach and pronounces himself clearly in favour of integration into one Civil Code. In his conclusions, he shows that Central European states opted to follow western Member States rather than codifying independently, understandable given the time restraints. With respect to questions of interplay between national and EC Law, however, he sees more potential for mutual learning.

Prof. Vékas' contribution is supplemented by Prof. Josipovíc for the particular case of Croatia. She mainly describes the already existing Consumer Contract Code. Most directives have been transposed into this Code. Its systematic order is discussed in quite some detail. The author sees at least some potential for finding inspiration here also for the task of systemizing parts of consumer related directives on the EC level. Prof. Josipovíc also analyses the legislative reform steps taken in 2004 which lead to a Civil Code, into which the Consumer Code material is not integrated. This Civil Code does, however, contain the core directive – the Sales Directive – although this directive is, formally, a consumer directive. It also contains directives such as the Product Liability and the Sales Agent Directives. Croatia thus opts for a dualist approach but with some effort to build coherent sub-systems of private law.

III. CONSUMER LAW – AREA APART OR FORERUNNER OF A EUROPEAN CODE? (PART III)

1. Questions

The second part deals with the relationship between consumer contract law and other contract law. From the perspective of national law, as has been mentioned, the 'other' contract law constitutes the traditional contract law, consumer contract law rather the 'outsider', but from the EC Law perspective, consumer contract law would seem to be one of, if not the most, powerful driving force. Bringing consumer and other contract law together, would in fact considerably facilitate the task of generalizing EC Contract Law and encourage a cross-fertilisation between national and EC contract law which might finally bring about a Common Frame of Reference or a European Optional Code.

The core question is whether consumer contract law and other contract law are not so diverse in character that any joint regulation – or codification – would either be impossible or carry the risk that coherent value judgements are unfeasible in such a construct. The question raised about the relationship between consumer contract law and other contract law and about the potential for EC Contract Law to be generalized has, in fact, many aspects. One is the question of coherence within the *Acquis Communautaire*, the only body of the law which can be termed as EC Consumer Contract Law.[12] The second aspect is whether this body of law can be generalized for the whole of contract law or whether consumer contract law is too idiosyncratic for transposing rules and value judgements from here to other contract relationships. Yet another aspect is how far rules created for specific contracts (and EC Law rules are often such!) can be generalized also for other specific contracts or for general contract law (applying to all types of contracts).

2. Law and Economics

The first contribution, by Hatzis, deals with one set of fundamentals which require consideration in order to answer the question(s) raised: what law and economics theory proposes as the foundations of contract law, and in particular of consumer contract law, and whether they are too important, or can even be defined.

Hatzis treats these questions indirectly, in five sections: on economic theory of contract law generally, on the question how contract law on the continent, mostly codified law based on Roman law, can be seen in this perspective, on whether consumer contract law should be seen as an integral part of general contract law, and then on two examples which address the core issue of contract freedom on the one hand and (paternalistic) mandatory rules on the other. These two examples should illustrate one core contention, i.e. that contract law on the continent is even more efficient than common law in core controversial cases.

In his short description of the economic model of contract law, Hatzis stresses that contract law is certainly primarily about enforcing promises and strengthening this basic tool of individual planning, but that good economic theory is of course also very much about the question in which instances contract freedom needs complementary rules limiting and regulating it

[12] This is the question raised by the Communication of the Commission to the Council and the European Parliament on European Contract Law, COM(2001) p. 398, OJ C 255/1, 2001; the four directorates general which took part in the elaboration of this communication are DG Sanco, DG Internal Market, DG Justice and Internal Affairs and DG Enterprise, as well as the Legal Service; the international discussion can be found in a condensed form in: S. Grundmann and J. Stuyck (ed.), *An Academic Green Paper on European Contract Law* (2002); equally important for this question Communication of the Commission of 12 Feb. 2003 (above n. 4); a thorough first answer in: K. Riesenhuber, *System und Prinzipien des Europäischen Vertragsrechts* (2003); see also the plea for system building in: S. Grundmann (ed.), *Systembildung und Systemlücken in Kerngebieten des Europäischen Privatrechts* (2000); English summary in 1 (2005) ERCL 297.

('caring about the weak parties in transactions'). He then mentions the most important cases where the negotiation mechanism is imperfect or even fails. Hatzis stresses, however, that the mechanism is already superior to alternatives in many cases, where not all preconditions for perfect negotiation are totally met, even imperfect markets and negotiations can to a certain extent be the 'reflection' of the idea of perfect markets. Slightly imperfect negotiations are better than abandoning the mechanism totally (because then judges have to step in, knowing typically less about the situation than the parties, not bearing the consequences etc.). In two lists, Hatzis details the conditions of perfect contracts and then the defects possible – and the traditional answers in different areas of the law (from consumer law to competition law). Consumer law in this list is but one instance of information problems. Intervention should only lead to the restoration of the best possible conditions of perfect markets.

In his second section Hatzis describes how contract law on the continent comes, in principle, closer to economic efficiency than common law. He holds that the lack of 'grand' theories on the continent – so well known in the common law world – stems from the fact that contract law is running more smoothly, that centuries of expertise and of continuous amendment have shaped a very sound contract law, based on Roman law which already was rather pragmatic, and a law where legal security is high (predictability for the parties who want to use this planning device). Common law has rather adopted continental solutions, where it is efficient, than developed itself. The grand theories on the continent are therefore already inherent in the Codes. At the end of this section, Hatzis names five cases that, in his opinion, exemplify this superiority (with reference to research already done). He takes up two in the last two sections.

First, he briefly returns to consumer contract law. He stresses that the two examples described, while being general, are of particular importance in consumer contracts and that consumer contract law in fact requires particular considerations in some cases.

Hatzis' first example is efficient breach and is related to the second, i.e. penalty clauses and their enforceability. Hatzis starts from the idea (universally accepted in economics) that in some instances breach of contract can be more efficient than performance. On the other hand, the remedy of damages has the weakness that not all damages can easily be quantified and proved, which is a problem for any mechanism based just on allowing breach and granting damages. Hatzis then stresses that under continental law, the problem is not solved at the expense of third parties: they are not bound and are not liable for the breach by the promisor. Under some laws, such as German Law, the segregation of the promise from the performance (transfer of the good) even strengthens this position. Common law is more reluctant, puts burdens on third parties and thus reduces the potential of efficient breach. On the other hand, common law does not enforce penalty clauses and can be unpredictable with respect to liquidated damages – whereas continental law strikes down (or reduces) only grossly disproportionate penalties. Hatzis argues that the solution under continental law is preferable, also the one proviso named because it catches the few abusive and indeed inefficient penalty clauses (which typically are not based on consensus and can be found mainly in standard contract terms in relationships with consumers). Otherwise, however, penalty clauses (and liquidated damages) are seen to be efficient because they allow the parties to really 'plan' the breach and the sharing of the net gain of a breach, moreover they circumvent the problem that damages can be difficult to quantify. Hatzis mentions several more reasons in favour of penalty clauses, unless abusive, among them market related arguments (newcomers can commit themselves in a credible form and thus quickly build up an equivalent to the reputation of existing competitors).

All this is relevant also for the codification process: Hatzis would advise reliance on the civilian tradition and on a codified system based on it. On the other hand, he argues for the inclusion of law and economics expertise, because Europeanization 'present(s) a golden opportunity for modernization based on economic analysis.'

3. Specific Consumer Contract Legislation to be Found in Member States

In a second set of contributions, those countries which have a Consumer Contract Code are discussed more thoroughly, partly also on a comparative law basis. These are France, Austria, and Greece in particular, but also the Czech Republic, because a formerly communist country is probably in a unique situation with respect to the relationship between professionals and the so-called weaker party in a market economy. This experience is even richer today with the very recent Italian Consumer Law Code.[13]

Prof. Rochfeld, in her contribution on the French *Code de la consommation* of 1993, is very critical of the French Code, which she covers in the first section. Her second section is devoted to what can be learnt from this experience for Europe. Her criticism of the French Law is based primarily on the fact that it is only a compilation, with large lacunae and no coherent order, and not a real codification in the sense of system building as had been initially intended. The Code is divided into five parts (information, product safety, consumer debts and insolvency, consumer associations and institutions). It put consumer law material together, thus making it more accessible. Large lacunae have, however, been left: all law on specific contracts has been left out (distance teaching, package travels, pharmaceuticals and others);

13 *Decreto legislativo recante Codice del Consumo, a norma dell'articolo 7 della Legge 29 Luglio 2003, n. 229, Gazetta Ufficiale 2005*; on this law, for instance, de Cristofaro, *Il 'Codice del Consumo' – un'occasione perduta?*, Studium iuris (2005) p. 1137.

similarly all rules of general contract law which protect the weaker party without being formally restricted to consumers (for instance implied warranties and many others); and as well all international and European sources (an annex at least reproducing all the Directives has often been requested). Also product liability is missing here. Moreover, a coherent order is missing, there is no definition of consumer contracts, three different definitions of consumers or weaker parties (partly also extending the scope of application beyond consumers). In the second section, Rochfeld raises the question what can be learned from this. She considers the possibility of separating consumer law from 'other' contract law altogether. Technically, a Consumer Code would need to integrate large parts of general contract law; it is not autonomous enough to be complete otherwise. What is more, consumer law largely become general contract law or is just an imitation of it, for example with respect to pre-contractual duties, revocation rights and information rules. It is often a major stimulus for 'other' contract law. In fact, the author identifies two opposing views: those for whom liberal party autonomy is more important are happier with the *Code Civil*; those for whom trends to materialize contract law are of greater consequence favour the *Code de la consommation*. An examples of this is the discussion about unfair contract terms law, now partially extended to commercial contracts also under French Law, and the dispute on where to transpose the Sales Directive (in the *Code Civil* or in the *Code de la consommation*). The conclusion is evident: consumer law is too large a part of contract law and influences it too much to segregate one from the other.

Lurger, in her contribution on the Austrian Consumer Law Code, poses very similar questions and draws basically the same conclusions. She divides the subject into three sections. In the first, on Austria, she considers whether only consumers need protection and what can be learnt for the European codification process. The separate *Konsumentenschutzgesetz* (consumer code) came into force as early as 1979 and until 1995 it contained virtually all consumer specific law.[14] However it did not include general contract law as applied for consumer protection purposes and was not laid out in a strict order (it was merely a compilation). At times, the directives have been taken as a model and then generalized; in other instances this has not happened. In the case of sales law, Austria basically transposed the model (new for Austria) in the Civil Code for all sales contracts. The same was already true – to a somewhat lesser extent – for unfair contract terms. The author sees in these two last examples the strongest integrative success while many other transpositions in the *Konsumentenschutzgesetz* seem unsystematic and do not guarantee coherence with general contract law. She criticizes, however, the (sometimes) intrusive ECJ case law (*Simone Leitner*) which forced Austria to

[14] After 1995 this is different with respect to several directives and their transposition, among them time sharing, credit transfers and distance selling of financial products, and partially to package holidays and consumer credits.

rewrite all the law on immaterial damages. In a second section, she questions an approach which identifies only consumers as in need of protection. Many legal measures do indeed also protect businesses and should do so (such as those on advertising, amongst others). Many authors point to the fact that the protective need is basically one of information and information is always needed in all parts of markets; from consumer protection to general party protection, also under the heading of good faith! Certainly this is particularly important for non-professionals. Thus Lurger (and many others) see materialization of contract law as a major general trend in the last few decades. She sees a partial conflict (or potential equilibrium) between party autonomy and party protection and illustrates this with mandatory information rules which, while they restrict freedom, also restore the material basis of the consensus principle and its legitimacy. If then a European Code is on the agenda, what is the role of consumer law? This question is briefly discussed in the third section. She concludes that Austria is not a good example; consumer law is marginal and unsystematic, and its potential to be integrated and even to serve as a driving force has not been exploited. Freedom of contract is seen as paramount in Austria, while party protection of less importance. This creates an imbalance. This is also her main criticism of the existing endeavours of private groups of scholars such as the Lando, Gandolfi and Study Groups. Lurger argues for integration, both on the level of principles and of rules.

Alexandridou, in her contribution on the Greek Consumer Law Code, starts from the assumption that 'corrective justice' is needed in any legal system, for consumers in particular, but in fact to some extent for all players. She draws the attention to the existence of a specific consumer law code in Greece, but as well to the fact that the Sales Directive has finally been transposed into the Civil Code with the express intention of avoiding fragmentation (however, contrary to what happened in Germany, only sales law, not general contract law, was reformed). On this basis, Alexandridou discusses the Consumer Code and then unfair contract terms, doorstep and distance selling, sales and advertising. The Code contains three chapters: on definitions (consumer and supplier), on substantive law (mainly transposition of directives, among them all those mentioned above apart from sales law) and on organizational questions. While Austria, Germany and Scandinavia had strong consumer protection law anyhow, Greece had not. The notion of consumer is clear insofar as legal persons are included, but not with respect to the question whether the term 'final recipient' also includes professional clients. The transposition of the Unfair Contract Terms Directive adds some rules on (prerequisites for the) integration of such terms, gives in an annex a (binding) blacklist (not, however, apparently fully integrated) and subjects the main subject matter of the contract to a fairness test (going thus beyond the directive). There is additionally case law which applies the standards also to commercial contracts (bank loans). The directives on doorstep and distance selling have been transposed rather literally, but the sanctions are particularly harsh (failure to give the information prescribed or to give the contract in writing leads to nullity, not just extension of the revocation right and unsolicited delivery leads to complete loss of the goods). Moreover, all unsolicited means of communication are conditional on an opting in of the consumer (in the directive only fax and voice-mail systems) and there is an express provision about respecting the consumer's privacy. Sales law (except for commercial guarantees) has been integrated into the Civil Code, applying to all clients. Some economically sound limits to the client's rights contained in the directive have been abandoned (even where the client could very well have known the defect, he keeps his rights and he is basically free to choose between the four remedies).[15] The duty to give notice of defects once they have been detected has not been introduced, nor has a direct action against the producer. Among the major changes for Greek law are: the binding force of advertising; the new limitation period of two years, also for used goods (formerly six months); the four remedies (formerly no right of repair); and the possibility to cumulate damages with these four remedies. Advertising is regulated in the law against unfair competition (mainly transposing the directive, but adding an indicative list and particular rules on protection of minors), but also in Consumer Law with respect to means of communication (see above) and some rather strict rules on sales promotions. Alexandridou's conclusion is that, in Greece, the (external sales law) integration of consumer law into general contract law is not really under discussion and is not necessary anyway because of the trend to broadly define the term consumer.

Finally Tichy, in his contribution on the Czech Republic, discusses consumer law in three sections: the general background of Czech private law, Czech consumer law and what could be a desirable solution in the future. His report seems to be quite representative of the difficulties of central Euro-

---

15 For some responsibility also of the purchaser see: G. de Cristofaro, *Difetto di conformità al contratto e diritti del consumatore – l'ordinamento italiano e la direttiva 99/44/CE sulla vendita e le garanzie dei beni di consumo* (2000) pp. 169–171; S. Grundmann, in: C. Bianca and S. Grundmann (eds.), *EU Sales Directive – Commentary* (2002), art. 2 para. 51 *et seq.*; similarly for art. 35 (3) CISG which uses the same terminology: J. Heilmann, *Mängelgewährleistung im UN-Kaufrecht – Voraussetzungen und Rechtsfolgen im Vergleich zum deutschen internen Kaufrecht und zu den Haager Einheitlichen Kaufgesetzen* (1994) pp. 208, 410. According to J. Honnold (*Uniform Law for International Sales* (1999) para. 229) the main aim is even only to lighten the onus of proof for knowledge; see also Ch. Twigg-Flesner, 'Network liability for manufacturers' guarantees – remedying legislative shortcomings with a legal jigsaw' (1999) J.B.L. pp. 177, 180. The rule imposing a certain order between the remedies really is about reducing costs of remedies: S. Grundmann, 'Consumer Law, Commercial Law, Private Law – How can the Sales Directive and the Sales Convention be so similar?' (2003) 14 *European Business Law Review* pp. 237, 243 *et seq.*; M. Wolf, '*Reform des Kaufrechts durch EG-Richtlinie – ein Vorteil für die Wirtschaft? Die möglichen Auswirkungen einer Richtlinie über den Verbrauchsgüterkauf und -garantien auf das deutsche Kaufrecht und die Wirtschaft*', *Recht der internationalen Wirtschaft* (1997) pp. 899, 902; indirectly also COM(95) 520 final, p. 14.

pean countries. Czech private law has formerly been based on the Austrian ABGB and HGB (Civil and Commercial Code). The communist Civil Code first made much shorter (1951) and later largely eliminated institutions like private property and contract freedom (1963–1964), with an exception for foreign trade. In 1992 a major reform reintroduced most of contract freedom and – besides the Civil Code – a Commercial Code (at the same time, the old State Business Law was abolished). Today, mandatory law is said to exist mainly to protect third party interests, but many rules in fact also aim to protect one of the two parties. Despite this, consumer law continues to be marginal. In communist times, the state which largely met the demand of consumers was supposed to treat them fairly. Nowadays, it seems marginal for several reasons: Transposition of EC consumer law had to take place too quickly to really work on the fundamentals of consumer law, and today a true codification seems much more interesting to private law scholars than this particular area. Like private law, consumer law, divided into two Codes, appears to be rather fragmented in the Czech Republic. Formally, it is integrated into the Civil Code. In many instances there are special laws mainly for consumer credits and product liability. In the future, a large special law is planned. Legal persons are included in the list of potential consumers. Where there are particular laws, transposition would often seem to be more extensive. While doorstep and distance selling largely follow the model of the directives, the protection of package travel law seems not to apply to professional clients (contrary to what the directive prescribes), but the rules seem to be very demanding for the catalogue which has to be handed over to the client. And standard contract terms law also fails to specify the criteria which the directive contains in its article 4. Moreover, it goes very far in prescribing a nullity sanction (too far, at times to the detriment of consumers). Finally, Tichy addresses the core question of whether consumers should be treated separately at all or whether protection of the weaker party is not rather a general private law issue.

4. The EC Law and the European Codification Dimension of Consumer Contract Law

The last set of contributions discusses the EC level more directly, namely the question how far the *Acquis Communautaire* can serve as a starting point for more generalization and perhaps even for the elaboration of a Common Frame of Reference or Codification.

Schmid, on the basis of his major monograph on related issues,[16] asks the question of whether the *Acquis* can be the basis for a future European

[16] Ch. Schmid, *Die Instrumentalisierung des Privatrechts durch die Europäische Union: Privatrecht und Privatrechtskonzeptionen in der Entwicklung der Europäischen Integrationsverfassung* (2005); English summary in 1 (2005) ERCL 211.

Contract Law Code – given the ever increasing density of the *Acquis Communautaire* and despite its inconsistencies. In his answer, he starts out with an explanation of private law aims, from enlightenment (freedom, equal access to private law institutions and justice) and 19th century liberalism to the materialisation of private law in the second half of the 20th century, in all cases, however, with a clear basis in commutative justice, i.e. that 'the party relationship must not be instrumentalized by external collective goals'. When then comparing this with European private law, Schmidt finds that these goals are also fostered to a great extent on the EC level – because freedom now reaches across borders, external regulation by the nation state can be questioned more effectively and deregulation gives private parties more freedom to regulate themselves. Yet, even today it is clear that, in principle, contract law and consumer protection are not an aim in themselves on the EC level, but only tools for market integration. Schmid then approaches what he calls the 'dark sides' of this instrumentalist approach, examples of 'excessive instrumentalization': he finds that information duties are paramount in EC Contract Law and are well developed, but that information duties in national laws which are equally well developed may risk being struck down because they might form an obstacle for cross-border trade. With respect to the *GB-Inno BM* case, Schmid even thinks that the consumer protection argument put forward by the ECJ (national law forbidding comparative advertising restricts the possibility of consumer information) was misleading and that the case was really about balancing market integration with protection of small enterprises. In the Axa Royal Belge case, the ECJ struck down a rule obliging insurance companies to warn the client that any later change of company could be costly, because such a rule was not precise enough and therefore not strictly necessary – again for market integration purposes. And also the abolition of a minimum harmonization approach (for instance with respect to the Product Liability Directive) is criticized for being motivated only by market integration motives (and without taking into account opposing interests and values, namely strong and, in the case decided, even vital consumer interests). The conclusions are as follows: In Schmid's view, the European Code cannot in principle just be an extension of the *Acquis Communautaire*, which is instrumentalist. The Code would need to be more justice oriented, like traditional codes. And in this case, even the case law on the EC level is likely to be no longer instrumentalist. The European Principles of Contract Law are probably not sensitive enough to trends of commutative justice, but not instrumentalist either and thus much closer to traditional codes. Even if assuming that the *Acquis* thus changed in character, a European Code would be legitimate in Schmid's view only if it were to integrate consumer and general contract law (also in spirit), if it developed in a democratically, more accountable way and if applicable on an optional basis only.

In his answer to Schmid, Howells deals with three issues: the dominant role of information rules, the maximum harmonization approach and the

Codification perspective, each of them critically. While accepting that information can be of use and that the paradigm of the informed and confident consumer may have been used to strike down over-protective rules (as in Germany), Howells expresses his concerns with a tendency in ECJ case law to strike down national rules which try to handle a genuine concern too easily (example: *Axa Royal Belge* case). Howells sees the maximum harmonization approach mainly rooted in ECJ case law (based on fundamental freedoms) and therefore important also whenever the EC Commission could not impose such an approach in its legislative measures (as for distance marketing of financial services and unfair trade practices). Rooting the approach in ECJ case law means, however, that it applies only to cross-border cases. Quite a few authors argue in favour of this approach because this is the only way really to test different national rules in a process of competition.[17] Howells is concerned with maximum harmonization (generally) because national laws may strike a different – and possibly more convincing – balance between freedom and protective needs. He stresses that EC rules may have a bias for a solution just because it fosters integration, that they are often based on (unsound) compromises, and that it would be astounding if the EC legislature really (always!) knew better than the national legislatures. With respect to a European Code, Howells asks the question of what process would be sufficient: to invent anew (like the Lando principles and the Study Group, who have done so in a 19th century spirit rather than really taking into account social values and consumer protection ideas), to systemize the *Acquis*, or to argue for a mixture in which the *Acquis* plays an important role and where its scope would be to create a system for our times, including modern trends and values (and this, of course, seems to be Howells' preference). He finally asks the question of whether an optional instrument should be a set of rules to be chosen by the parties or rather a model code for which Member States opt. In any case, Howells is more concerned about getting a conservative document and about stagnation. His (almost) last word is: 'The law is not owned by the lawyers, but merely entrusted to them to serve the needs of the community.' And (not only for Howells) it should be clear that consumer law of the 20th century should play a prominent role here.

IV. FORMATION OF CONTRACT AND PRE-CONTRACTUAL INFORMATION (PART IV)

The fourth and last part discusses the architectural design for one area of substantive contract law, the pre-contractual phase and mainly information duties arising there. This area has been chosen as the first in chronological

[17] See for this debate, for instance, S. Grundmann, 'Internal Market Conflict of Laws – From Traditional Conflict of Laws to an Integrated Two Level Order', in Fuchs, Muir, Watt and Pattaut (eds.), *Les conflits de lois et le système juridique communautaire* (2004) p. 5.

order, but mainly because information duties are so important in EC Contract Law, and therefore in this phase as well. The approach is to look at this question from the perspective of several national legal orders which all had to transpose a substantial amount of EC Law rules. This would give several examples of how the (quite extensive) 'fragments' in EC Contract Law on the pre-contractual phase can possibly form 'architecture'. Again Romance countries, common law systems and a Germanic and comparative law perspective have been combined.

1. The Perspective of Romance Countries

Roppo, in his contribution mainly on Italian and EC Law, starts from the finding that in the Italian *Codice Civile* (1942) in general contract law there is one rule stating a duty to inform that he knows of – about obstacles to the validity of the contract – and that there are some rules indirectly about a duty to inform – rules on mistake and misrepresentation and on performance in good faith. Moreover there are written information duties with respect to two particular contracts: sales and insurance contracts. This legal basis has been interpreted restrictively by the courts, whereas legal scholarship has mostly developed duties to inform the other party on the basis of the good faith provision contained in article 1337 *Codice Civile* (the courts are reluctant to apply this provision as early as in the negotiation phase). The courts moreover require proof of fraudulent behaviour in any case, i.e. even if they see a duty to inform. Moreover the party harmed does not recover damages where he is negligent and courts assume this to be the case whenever mandatory rules are not known to this party. The core part of Roppo's contribution centres on the question of what kind of information should be omitted. He rejects several suggestions: the one according to which each party would have to disclose (only) material information referring to her own performance (this would go too far, for instance, if the party had to disclose how much her gain is because she has reduced her costs efficiently); and the suggestion that no party should disclose information which was costly to acquire. Roppo is rather inclined to think that what matters most is whether the information is good news to the other party or bad news. And certainly the role of the party (consumer or not) is important.

Roppo then turns to EC Law, where he sees four kinds of information rules (much more consistently than in autonomous Italian Law): rules which do not prescribe the giving of information but make information given (even voluntarily) binding; rules which prescribe that a full picture be given if any information is given; information duties which have the consequence that the information given will be part of the contract; and information duties where the legal consequence is not specified. He then more generally considers the broader picture of information rules and sees – at least to some extent and at least in sector specific rules – that information rules prevail. On the other hand, he criticizes the virtually complete absence of sanctions of specification of legal consequences in EC Law. He even sees a risk of information mannerism, also in national law, i.e. an inconsistent abundance of information rules with no bite (lacking sanctions).

Giménez Costa and Bosch Capdevila, in their invited comment, concentrate on another aspect of the pre-contractual phase, i.e. options. They stress, however, that options are often motivated by information problems (giving the optee the chance to make a more thorough value judgment of the goods, to arrange financing for the transaction or simply to allow for a period of reflection). And they stress that, despite its current use in practice, this option is a phenomenon which has remained largely unregulated (Romance countries typically following the very brief example of article 1589 of the French Code Civil of 1804). The Catalan regulation on pre-contract is one of the most important exceptions. The authors study the phenomenon, however, on a comparative law basis. They discuss theories where the pre-contract is not yet a contract in essence and those where it is in essence identical to the final contract (with the sole exception that a legally binding declaration of intention may still be needed from one of the two sides, this is the case of an option, or from any of the two sides (uni- and bi-lateral pre-contracts)). The authors then discuss the Catalan Law which distinguishes between personal and real options (the latter pertaining to property rights and acting *erga omnes*) and then run through all the requirements of the personal option (capacity, specificity of the object, form, maximum duration, assignment of the option, obligations of the conceder while the option is pending, and exercise of the option). They insist in particular on the moment from which time periods (for instance for avoidance) run. They think that this would be a useful component in any future European regulation of the pre-contractual phase.

2. The Common Law Perspective

Giliker, in her contribution from a common law perspective, first discusses the widespread belief that common law is much more restrictive in assuming information duties. She sees some of the reasons for this in the still more dominant role of freedom of contract, in the concerns English lawyers have with respect to legal security, and in the idea that only the party who has incurred the costs of information retrieval should profit from it (maintaining incentives). The core exceptions seen are those of consumer law – with a strong E.C. Law impact – and overt bad faith, but there are increasingly also others. In two further sections Giliker then discusses, first, the principle and, second, the exceptions and concludes with some consideration on a duty to deal fairly.

The basic rule can be described in the words of court decisions and leading text books: 'Mere silence, however morally wrong, will not support an action of deceit'; 'Ordinarily the failure to disclose a material fact which might affect the mind of a prudent contractor does not give the right to avoid the contract.' This differs considerably from the rule suggested by Roppo on bad news (above). All this is 'really no more than an application of the more general disinclination on the part of the common law to recognize a duty to negotiate in good faith.' The decision in the rather shocking *Sykes v. Taylor-Rose* case of 2000 shows that this is not just old case law. Giliker criticizes such case law because it really puts the burden to address vast catalogues of (potentially!) meaningful questions on the client, thus putting on him the burden to draw up complete contracts.

Giliker then, on the basis of Treitel's treatise, discusses six exceptions (and some even raise the question as to which is the principle and which is the exception). One of the most important are warranties because they impose the burden to disclose whatever is known in order to avoid liability. And these warranties can be implied as well. The most important examples in the law are based on EC Law, sales law and package travel tours, both in good part also mandatory law, but concentrating on consumer protection. Implied warranties can, however, also be found in commercial transactions, the lead case being *Esso Ltd v. Mardon*, where prognostics by an experienced employee on which Mardon had relied were seen as implied warranty, at least in the sense that the prognostics were made with due care. Misrepresentation is the second exception (on the basis of the Misrepresentation Act of 1967), also in the *Esso* case. The core elements – statement of facts – have been extended: While, by requiring a statement, silence is typically excluded as a basis of misrepresentation, both telling only half the truth (and omitting related fact) and not correcting false statements made innocently once their incorrectness has been established, have been seen as (false) statements as well. And the declaration of certain intentions has been seen as a declaration of (internal) facts. In this case, remedies based on contract and on tort run parallel. Besides the Misrepresentation Act, tort can be an independent basis for a duty to disclose only in very extreme cases. And customs and specific laws are a rather rare exception as well. The last exception even is more important. There are quite a few categories of specific contracts where a duty to disclose goes much further: namely insurance contracts and fiduciary relationships (principal agent relationships, agency, company law), and to a limited extent also contracts about sureties and guarantees (some duty to disclose imposed on the creditor).

In her conclusion, Giliker stresses mainly that English Law as described clearly differs from the approach in article 4:107 of the Principles of European Contract Law imposing a more generalized duty to deal fairly and inform and that, while the results between Civil Law and Common Law may not necessarily differ so much anyway, it may nevertheless be advisable for common law to shift from its piecemeal approach to a more coherent theory of disclosure.

3. The Germanic and Comparative Law Perspective

Mankowski, in his contribution on formation and pre-contractual duties to inform, starts out by stating that the law of formation is seen as less important and interesting than the law of performance and breach of contract, probably because it is less regulated and less specific than contract law. Only pre-contractual duties to inform might well fall outside this general trend. The author does in fact deal with these two parts.

First he turns to the formation of contract in general, an area which he still sees mainly as one of national law and where he deals with mistake, duress and, less frequently discussed, the role of third parties in the formation of contracts. Mankowski first discusses at some length why mistake (or 'own error') should give a remedy similar to rescission, namely that of avoidance. He sees the main reason as preventing parties from investing in superoptimal or supra-optimal care in order to avoid mistakes, i.e. the rule should give incentives to invest the optimal level of care. He opts for a solution in which mistakes give rise to a remedy whenever the mistaken party cannot be blamed for gross negligence. The mistaken party carries the onus of proof for this (thus favouring the UNIDROIT rule over that in the PECL). With respect to duress, the author mainly discusses the borderline between creating unproductive hold-up situations and legitimate bargaining tactics, again very much based on economic theory. Finally, third parties in the formation of contracts are seen as a good chance for mediating and reducing information problems, the core problem being ensuring that they are in fact neutral and do not only appear to be (the author is quite critical about the so-called 'house-notary'). The problem is discussed at some length with respect to public standard setters, such as business organizations and associations.

In a second section, Mankowski deals with the pre-contractual duties to inform. Here, European legislation is prominent. Mankowski starts out by identifying information asymmetries as a core ground for market failure and by stating that the key task is nevertheless how much giving of information should be prescribed in these cases (scope of the rule). He then turns to the core reason why information should not be handed over whenever helpful, that is: gathering information comes at a cost and the incentives to amass information, the right to profit from it, should not be taken away too easily. He then asks the question of whether B2C relationships are peculiar in this respect, i.e. whether information duties are particularly justified here, and finds some reasons for maintaining them (there is a major risk of no access to information at all or access only at a prohibitively high cost and a minor risk of exploiting the other party's information). The author ends with the question of whether the other party is worthy of being protected only if he has invested himself (reliance) and with some basics on the problem of 'bounded rationality'.

V. SOME CONCLUDING REMARKS

There are three building blocks for an architecture of European Codes: the structure of the law of obligations or of contracts in important codified systems; the relationship between group specific contract law, namely consumer contract law, and general contract law; and, as a first substantive law step, the structure of the contract law for the pre-contractual phase. Light and shadow have been found in all of them.

Some answers would seem to be of particular importance and rather evident:

- comparative Law, EC Law and European Codification have to be seen as integrated perspectives;
- even the most modern national codes do not seem to reflect many of the very modern problems of contract law, such as standard contracts and bargained for contracts, chains of contracts, information as a universal problem of contract law, a bi-polar system built by spot contracts on the one hand and service and long-term contracts on the other, the integration of (public policy) regulation of contracts and of traditional (liberal) contract law based on the assumption of party autonomy;
- the most important challenge for an optional European Code might be that it embodies a modern model of contract law today and not just a common denominator of what has been in force so far, a model which might serve as a basis for Europe-wide and perhaps even worldwide discussion.

This will need time and more European contract law scholarship. The reflections on an 'Architecture of European Codes and Contract Law' need to be continued.

Part II
The Level of Abstraction: Starting from Contract, Obligation and Juristic Act?

Chapter 2
Structural Elements of the French Civil Code

Pauline Rémy-Corlay

I. INTRODUCTION

Our Code is an old lady, with both wisdom and weaknesses.

One cannot but admire the longevity of Title III of Book III, related to contract. This part, almost unchanged for 200 years, is not merely an historical feature, but is still a living entity. Its longevity can be explained by the way it has been written. As is well known, Title III is not only a fruit of the French Revolution, but comes directly from Domat and Pothier, who themselves were inspired by Justinian Digest and Institutes.

Some articles are known by heart by French students, and one could not bear to see them taken away. I would not dare to translate them: '*Le contrat est une convention par laquelle une ou plusieurs personnes s'obligent envers une ou plusieurs autres, à donner, à faire ou ne pas faire quelque chose*' (article 1101); '*Il n'y a point de consentement valable si le consentement n'a été donné que par erreur, ou s'il a été extorqué par violence ou surpris par dol*' (article 1109); '*Les conventions légalement formées tiennent lieu de loi à ceux qui les ont faites (. . .) Elles doivent être exécutées de bonne foi*' (article 1134) and so on. One can see there the style of the Code: pure, simple, comprehensible. Far from the German Style of the BGB, which is much more precise, but very difficult to understand because of its complexity.

This longevity does not mean that French law did not change for 200 years; changes came from inside (the strong influence of case law, despite article 5 *Code civil* (CC);[1] new codes on contract – insurance, labour law,

[1] '*Il est défendu aux juges de prononcer par voie de disposition générale et réglementaire sur les causes qui leur sont soumises*'.

S. Grundmann, M. Schauer (eds), *The Architecture of European Codes and Contract Law*, 33–55

employment contract, consumer code; broad legislation on many topics related to contract) and from outside (mainly European law: competition law, consumer law, and now the influence of the European Convention on Human Rights[2]). The architecture of the Code does not correspond to French law on contract. But even so, I would say both that there are still lessons to take from our old Code, and that from the beginning there were some deficiencies.

II. THE ARCHITECTURE OF THE CODE – GENERAL STATEMENTS

The general structure of the French Civil Code, even regarding only the law of obligations, is not its best feature and should not be taken as an example. I don't think a single one of my French colleagues today would contradict me: it is not only due to the evolution of law outside the Code and within the Code (although this has a very important impact and should lead to a major reform of the Code – it has been demonstrated many times this year when speaking on the bicentenary of the Civil Code[3] and a French Commission is now working on it). But from its inception, the structure of the Code has been deficient.[4]

The Civil Code contained three books: Persons (and not family law), Property and 'On different means to acquire property' (without mentioning the new and rather odd Book IV on 'Rules applicable to Mayotte'[5]).

Book III, dealing with the 'different means to acquire property', is divided into 20 Titles, among which you find titles on succession (estates), donation and will, contract, torts, quasi-contracts, several specific contracts – matrimonial property regime being dealt as one of those – securities, expropriation and order between creditors, prescription, etc. It is nothing like the well-organized five books of the BGB.

Regarding only the part on contract, one cannot find even this satisfactory. After a preliminary part stating what amounts to contract and giving several definitions, there is a chapter on consent, another on 'Effect', and then one on 'Different kinds of obligations', one on 'Extinction of obligations', and a last one on evidence. There is no part on the content or on

---

2 *Civ. 1re, 21 mars 2000, Bull. I, n° 97, D. 00. 593, n. Atias, RTDCiv. 00. 592, obs. P-Y. Gautier; Civ. 3e, 18 décembre 2002, n° 01-00.519, RDC 2003, 220, obs. A. Marais; Civ. 3e, 12 juin 2003, n° 02-10.778, RDC 2004, 231, obs. J. Rochfeld; Civ. 3e, 19 mars 2003, n° 01-03.730, Bull. civ. III, n° 65, 59, RDC 2004, 457, obs. A. Debet; 618, obs. J. Rochfeld*; on this question, see A. Debet, *L'influence de la Convention européenne des droits de l'homme sur le droit civil* (2002).

3 *V. Le Code civil, Livre du bicentenaire* (2004).

4 See H. Mazeaud, *Travaux de la Commission de réforme du Code civil, 1948–1950* (1959)2 p. 5: '*Il semble impossible de garder le plan du Code civil qui a toujours été critiqué*'.

5 *Ordonnance du 19 décembre 2002 n° 2002-1476*: nothing to do with a proper 'Codification', and a shame for our old Civil Code!

performance of the contract, and neither the part on 'Effect' nor the one on 'Extinction' deal with breach of contract and consequences of the breach as a whole (some parts of those questions being dealt with in chapter 3).

Figure 1: General Overview

French Civil Code, Title 3	On Contracts
Chapter 1 (arts 1101–1107)	Preliminary dispositions (definition of contract stating Freedom of contract; classification of contracts)
Chapter 2 (Essential conditions to validity) (arts 1108–1133)	Section 1 – Consent
	Section 2 – Capacity (arts 1123–1125-1)
	Section 3 – Object and content of the contract (arts 1126–1130)
	Section 4 – Cause (arts 1131–1133)
Chapter 3 Effect of obligations	Section 1 – General dispositions (arts 1134–1135)
	Section 2 – Obligation to give (to transfer property, to deliver the goods) (arts 1136–1141)
	Section 3 – Obligation to do or not to do (arts 1142–1145)
	Section 4 – Damages resulting from non performance of the obligation (arts 1146–1155)
	Section 5 – Interpretation of contract (non binding rules, arts 1156–1164)
	Section 6 – Effect of obligations towards third parties
Chapter 4 Different kind of obligations	
Chapter 5 Extinction of Obligations (arts 1234–1314)	
Chapter 6 Evidence on obligations and on payment (arts 1315–1369)	

III. FORMATION OF CONTRACT

1. Suitable Level of Abstraction

One has to underline however that, even with those deficiencies, the pragmatism of the Code can be praised. The abstraction level is not as high as the one of the BGB: there is no general part and thus no reference to 'juristic act'. This does not mean that this concept does not exist in French Law. If one considers the different text books, one will see that they generally deal with the law of obligation on one hand and specific contracts on the other. And within the law of obligations, you often find a part on 'juristic act', and another one on 'juristic fact'.[6] When, in the mid 20th century, the French tried to reform the Civil Code, this was one of the biggest issues and a new book was prepared on juristic act, which should have been inserted just before the new book on obligation (and not in the Preliminary Book).[7] This abstraction does not seem necessary however:[8] of course, there are some parts of law outside contracts where a juristic act is needed (wills and estates), and there are some juristic acts which don't lead to contract, but – as demonstrated by Grundmann – it seems necessary to have one part dealing with the formation of contract which is not within the Code. The solution held by the PECL seems simple and efficient enough: article 1:107 PECL provides that: 'The Principles apply with appropriate modifications to agreements to modify or end a contract, to unilateral promises and to other statements and conduct indicating intention'.[9] Offer and acceptation are, within the PECL, nevertheless treated as '*empfangsbedürftige Willensklärungen*' (declarations which have to be received) (arg. articles 2202, 2204 and 1:303).

I don't think then that a 'General Part' is necessary: taking contract as a starting point should be more efficient and pragmatic.

2. Lacunae

But the French Code certainly misses a general part on formation of contract.

---

6 Flour, Aubert et Savaux (eds.), Armand Colin. See as well, on the use of the notion of 'juristic act' within the Civil Code, G. Rouhette, '*La doctrine de l'acte juridique: sur quelques matériaux récents*', Droits 1988 n° 7, pp. 29 *et seq.*

7 See *Travaux de la Commission de réforme du Droit privé*, *op. cit.* and Léon Julliot de la Morandière, *Avant – projet de Code civil présenté au Garde des Sceaux par la Commission de réforme du Code civil, première partie, livre préliminaire* (1955), pp. 7 *et seq.*, esp. pp. 27 and 375 *et seq.*

8 V. C. Witz, '*L'influence des codifications nouvelles sur le Code civil de demain*', in: *Le Code civil, Livre du bicentenaire*, *op. cit.*, p. 687, esp. 704.

9 Added art. 2:107 PECL: 'a promise which is intended to be legally binding without acceptance is binding'.

If it deals with consent (see *infra*), there is nothing on the meeting of minds. The model of offer and acceptance given by the BGB is a much better example, even though it does not take into account all the important issues of formation of contracts.

French Case law tried to remedy to this deficiency, but the result is not yet satisfactory[10] and one cannot say with sufficient certainty up until what point a person can withdraw his offer or his acceptance, or when the contract is to be considered as concluded.

Many improvements were made by French law (case law and legislation outside the Code) to take into account the different duties of both parties when entering into a contract (what we call 'Pre-contractual obligations'), especially considering the duty to act in good faith, the *culpa in contrahendo* and the duty to inform. However the regimes of those institutions are not always clearly settled – and that can be partly explained by the way we deal with contract and tort. The so-called '*responsabilité délictuelle*' is so broadly interpreted (article 1382 '*Tout fait quelconque de l'homme qui cause à autrui un dommage oblige celui par la faute duquel il est arrivé à le réparer*'[11]) that it can include nearly everything. We consider that as long as a contract is not concluded, the non performed duty (to inform, to act in good faith, not to break the negotiations unreasonably) is sanctioned by tortuous liability (it is a fault under article 1382) – with the regime applicable to torts (considering prescription and so on). The so called 'pre-contractual obligations' should be treated, however, as a step to enter into the contract and be linked to the formation of contract, and not to tort.

Regarding unfair clauses, we will see that they don't appear within the Civil Code either, as this is dealt with only in the Consumer Code. This can be criticized as well; rules on unfair clauses should certainly be contained in a general part on the formation of contract, even though one can understand that the applicable regime might differ on some points when considering the parties to the contract (professional or not).

The French Civil Code is also missing a part on representation. It is common nowadays to assert that representation is an institution one cannot afford to miss, as it is daily used, not only to contract, but also in company law, incapacity, etc.

Within the Code, the notion of 'representation' does not appear, except when dealing with incapacity – not especially incapacity to contract (articles 1123–1125-1), but general incapacity (articles 388–515, Titles VIII and IX of Book 1, Persons). However, case law and doctrine together drew up a

10 On the remaining problems in French law and the comparative advantages of the PECL, see P. Remy-Corlay '*L'existence du consentement*' in: *Les concepts contractuels français à l'heure des Principes du droit européen des contrats*, Dir. P. Remy-Corlay et D. Fenouillet (2003), esp. pp. 29 *et seq.*

11 Another famous article, beloved by most professors.

Figure 2: Formation of contract

Chapter 2 (Essential conditions to validity) (arts 1108–1133)	Section 1 – Consent – Mistake, fraud and duress (arts 1109–1116) – Avoidance (art. 1117) – Privity of contract (arts 1119–1122) (together with arts 1165 *et seq.*)
	Section 2 – Capacity (arts 1123–1125-1)
	Section 3 – Object and content of the contract (arts 1126–1130) – Licit (art. 1128) – Content (arts 1129–1130) (together with arts 1134 and 1135 *infra*)
	Section 4 – Cause (arts 1131–1133)
Nothing on the meeting of the minds within the Code (see case law)	
Nothing on Representation See T XIII of Book 3 (*Mandat* Agency) (arts 1984–2010)	No distinction within the Code between internal and external relations

concept of representation,[12] even though it is still seen as a consequence only of other institutions.[13] In textbooks, representation is either dealt with in the Part on Formation of Contract,[14] or in the part related to the Privity of Contract.[15] The place of representation within the part related to contract is a question which should be raised. If it is in a part on formation of contract[16] – like in the PECL – it could mean that a general institution called 'representation' is not recognized, the regime of representation might differ depending

[12] See E. Pilon, *Essai d'une théorie générale de la représentation dans les obligations*, Thèse Caen (1897); Ph. Didier, *De la représentation en droit privé* (2000).

[13] *Mandat, gestion d'affaires, personnes morales*, etc.

[14] See Terré, Simler and Lequette, *Les obligations* (2003).

[15] Flour, Savaux et Aubert, *L'acte juridique*, n° 422 ss.; Carbonnier, *Les obligations*, n° 116–117; Malaurie et Aynès, Obligations, n° 664 – in continuity with privity of contract: '*Contrats pour autrui: Représentation, Stipulation pour autrui, Promesse pour autrui*'.

[16] I don't think anyway that it should be treated as a derogation to the privity of contract principle (the so-called '*effet relatif*'): the agent is not bound by the contract since he is not a party to it.

on whether it is a legal representation or a willing representation.[17] According to Pr. Didier, it would be progress, compared to the French Civil Code, as willing representation would be studied for itself, and not related to agency (*contrat de mandat*); but it would not be enough. Representation should be studied in a 'General Part', and not be related to contract only. I think however that a general part is not necessarily needed. We could find the matters related to obligation generally with contract (like the so-called French '*Régime général des obligations*', Chapters IV, V and VI, Title III, Book III). A part on representation, together with '*Gestion d'affaire*' and agency (*Mandat*) could be dealt with in a chapter after formation of contract. If there is a European codification on contract (even if only as an optional instrument), representation will have to be dealt with and the split between internal and external relations – recognized by French Case Law and Doctrine – will have to be established. The question will then be: how far have we to go in the German 'abstraction principle' (*Abstraktionsprinzip*)?

3. Two Questions on the Formation of Contract

a. How are Unfair Contract Terms Treated within the Code?

Unfair contract terms are only treated within the Consumer Code (Cons. C.) as a specific help given to consumers. It is thus considered that between professionals or between consumers, there cannot be unfair terms, parties having equal bargaining power. Contrary to what was stated within the Directive on Unfair terms in Consumer contracts (93/13/EEC) (article 3), a contractual term can be considered as unfair even though it has been individually negotiated. Article L 132-1 Cons. C. doesn't distinguish between negotiated and non negotiated clauses. However, negotiated clauses between professionals and consumers should be few – but it might have been better to use the criteria of negotiated or not negotiated clauses than to use this criterion based on the person.

Between professionals, Cons. C. articles L. 132-1 *et seq*. don't apply.[18] However, this does not mean that professionals have no possibility to avoid some clauses. The Cour de cassation firstly adopted a broad notion of consumers, so that some 'professionals' could use article L. 132-1: a professional could use this legislation if he was in a state of ignorance equivalent to the one of a consumer. Since 1995, under the influence of the Directive, this notion has been superseded; a person is a professional when dealing in his professional activity.

[17] Ph. Didier, thesis *op. cit.* and *L'effet relatif*, in: *Les concepts contractuels français à l'heure des Principes du droit européen des contrats*, esp. pp. 189 *et seq.*

[18] *Ex. Com. 23 novembre 1999, Bull. IV, n° 210.*

Case law then forged other means for professionals to avoid the application of some clauses.[19] For example, when a clause has not been negotiated, it can be considered as annulled if the attention of the party who hasn't written the clause has not been attracted by a special mention.[20] Probably on the basis of article 1135 CC, the Cour de cassation approved a Cour d'appel to deal with clauses 'contrary to the general economy of the contract'.[21] This is actually the broadest means to achieve the same result as when going through the unfair contract terms provisions.

Unfair clauses, not provided within the Code, are generally studied by authors with the study of the 'content' of the contract, object of the contract ('*licéité de l'objet*'; see: Terré, Simler and Lequette;[22] Malaurie and Aynès[23]) or within the formation of the contract (after object and cause –*Carbonnier*,[24] Flour, Aubert and Savaux[25]). I would rather include it in a part on Formation of contract. Within the Directive on Unfair Contract terms, it is provided that a clause cannot be unfair when negotiated. It is then more a question of consent than a question on content – even though consent gives content!

b. What about '*vices du consentement*'?

According to Chapter 2 of Title III, four conditions have to be fulfilled for the validity of a contract: consent, capacity, '*objet*' and cause.

Consent is dealt with in the first section; it states first what is called '*les vices du consentement*' – this is in itself significant: consent is not seen objectively, as a condition for the validity, but subjectively, what amounts to consent – and goes on with the principle of privity of contract.

Three elements can vitiate the consent: *erreur* (mistake), *dol* (fraud) and *violence* (duress, threats).

They were strictly conceived within the Code.

'Mistake' was taken into account only when essential, meaning error on the object of the consent itself; it was then considered that mistakes about essential qualities of the thing were to be taken into account. Mistakes from both parties, from the debtor as well as from the creditor, can lead to the contract being nullified.[26] It is only when the mistake is 'inexcusable' (unfor-

19 On this question, see esp. D. Mazeaud, '*La protection par le droit commun*', in *Les clauses abusives entre professionnels*, 33 s. (1998) Dir. Jamin et Ghestin.

20 See for ex. *Com. 5 fébruary 2002, Cont. Conc. Cons. 2002, n° 88, obs. Leveneur.*

21 Com. 15 February 2000, *Bull. Civ. IV, n° 29.*

22 *Les obligations* (2002).

23 *Obligations* (2004).

24 *Les obligations.*

25 *Les obligations, L'acte juridique* (2004).

26 E.g. a seller can be mistaken about the real quality of the thing he sells. See *Civ. 1re 22 February 1978 – affaire du Poussin.*

givable) that one cannot ask for the nullity of the contract: such is the case for example when the person who made the mistake should have known the real quality of the good, or didn't take the necessary steps to assure this quality.

Recent cases consider however that the mistake provoked by the fraudulent silence of the other party is always 'forgivable'.[27] One has then to wonder when there actually is a fraudulent silence? In this case, it was a professional who was acquiring a hotel from another and who hadn't checked if the good authorization had been given. Maybe it could be explained by the study of the economic risk: it was easier (and less expensive) for the seller to tell the buyer that the authorizations could not be obtained than for the buyer to obtain information.

Such would still be the case if the mistaking party was under the 'psychological dependence' of another one: even an '*erreur grossière*' would lead to nullification of the contract.[28] In this latter case, the mistaken party was a professional as well; the Court doesn't explain why and how he was 'psychological dependent'.

It is thus obvious that French case law, contrary to the Code, is favouring the mistaking party.

This is also the case when there is a '*dol*' (fraud). Traditionally, once again, only the positive fraud was taken into account, when one party had taken measures to obtain the consent of the other in a fraudulent way, or had made a fraudulent misrepresentation. Nowadays, it is well known that a 'fraudulent silence' would be considered as a *dol* as well, giving a right to nullify the contract to the mistaken party, and a right to obtain damages on article 1382 CC (tortuous liability). Fraudulent silence is admitted each time a party has a duty to inform the other on a special point and did not fulfil this duty.

Duress was as well strictly conceived: it could take into account not only physical, but also psychological duress. But economic duress was not taken into account very much. Recent cases however seem to adopt another point of view: when a party took advantage of the ignorance of another party[29] or of the circumstances[30] to obtain unfair advantages or excessive benefits. The Cour de cassation stated that economic duress was to be equivalent to violence (duress) and not to *lésion* (unfair bargain).[31] As such, it is not possible to void an unfair bargain, except in specific cases (incapacity, specific unfairness in some specific contracts.).

The party whose consent has been obtained by duress, mistake or fraud can ask for annulment. He cannot himself notify the cancellation of the

27 *Civ. 3rd, 21 February 2001, Bull. Civ. III n° 20.*
28 *Com.* 29 April 2002, *Bull. Civ. IV, n° 77.*
29 *Civ. 1st, 3 November 1976, Gaz. Pal. 1977.1.67; 29 June 1999, JCP 1999. II. 10187.*
30 *Soc. 8 November 1984, Bull. Civ. V, n° 1984.*
31 *Civ. 1st, 30 May 2000, Bull. Civ. I, n° 169.*

contract: he has to ask to the judge to nullify it, and he could of course refuse to do so. It should not be possible for the judge to adapt the contract – even in the case of economic duress. The contract is either void or withheld. This rigidity has been corrected in some ways: damages can be obtained in the case of fraud or duress and in some cases it was decided to withhold the contract and to reduce the price in case of fraud.[32] Partial nullity is allowed when the object of the mistake is not essential (contrary to what is stated in article 1172 CC); but still this system does not seem satisfactory and the solution held by PECL (articles 4:114–4:117) gives more flexibility – without endangering the interests of either party

Nullity in French law has a retroactive effect so that the contract is considered to have never existed; it would explain, according to French doctrine, why parties have a right to restitution (we have no general rules on restitution, and restitution in contract is only seen as a direct consequence of the nullity or of the resolution of the contract; this is as well an important issue in which French authors should be more interested).[33]

IV. CONTENT, PERFORMANCE AND BREACH OF CONTRACT

1. Structure of the Code

If the general dispositions of Chapter 3 are admirable, by their wording as well as their efficiency, the general structure of the Code on those topics seems even less satisfactory than the one on formation of contracts.

Content and performance are split between Chapter 2 (on essential conditions for the validity of contracts: sections 3 (object) and 4 (cause) and Chapter 3 (on effect of obligations).

---

[32] *Com. 14 mars 1972, D. 1972. 547.*

[33] There are some theses on restitution (ex- M. Malaurie, *Les restitutions en droit civil* (1991) pp. 50–51), but we cannot speak of a French 'law of restitution': when speaking of restitution, we deal with many topics where a good has to be returned to its owner (end of lend, rent, etc.). According to Ph. Remy (*Les restitutions dans un système de quasi-contrats: l'expérience française, à paraître*), the non existence of a system of restitution in French law can be explained because the figure we get from Pothier was a figure of quasi-contract. This explains why we have in the Code, treated only as 'quasi-contracts' – Book II, Title IV (Chapter I) – the *negotiorum gestorum contraria* action (a *quasi-mandat, quasi-agency*) and the *Condictio indebeti* (restitution of a '*quasi-prêt*', quasi-lend). There is nothing on *de in rem verso* action, created only by case law in 1892 (Cass. Req. 15 June 1892, DP 1892.1.596), when the category of quasi-contract was weakened. Since this case, French law has been unable to create a proper law of restitution. This does not mean however that this field of law does not exist. Case law shows that it is still alive and very lively – but it is evolving in a disorderly way.

There is no Chapter on the sanction (or the remedies) of breach of contract.[34] And one has to look at the rules on 'condition' (article 1184) to find that a party can obtain the rescission (resolution) of the contract in case of breach.

Chapter 3 distinguishes between '*obligation de donner*' on one side – which allows in case of breach execution *in natura* – and '*obligation de faire ou de ne pas faire*' on the other – which would give a right only to damages according to article 1142 (see however *infra*). This distinction can be explained by the so-called '*effet réel du contrat*': where there is an obligation to give, the mere consent of the parties is sufficient to transfer property (article 1138). There is no abstraction principle in French law, but a principle according to which once the parties agreed on a sale contract, the buyer, by sole consent, is the owner of the good, even though this good has not been delivered.

On reflection one of the issues for a European Code on contract would be to decide if the French or the German point of view should be taken – neither the CISG nor the PECL chose amongst those two systems. A small part of the French Doctrine now criticizes the transfer of property by mere consent as being unsatisfactory in practice (practically, conventions generally stipulate a transfer of property at the delivery of the goods – or even later, but it is then to guarantee payment).[35] According to Pr J. P. Chazal and S. Vicente, article 1138 of the Civil Code would not establish the principle of the '*effet réel du contrat*', but would only link transfer of the risks to the delivery of the goods. To see here a consecration of the transfer of property on mere consent would be a misinterpretation of the text. The demonstration thereof is very convincing. But nowadays, it is generally considered in French law as obvious that transfer of property does not need delivery of the goods. A European reflection would be a good occasion to come back on this 'obviousness'.

Many other lacunae could be pointed out:

- nothing in the Code on the '*exception d'inexécution*' – right to withhold performance – recognized however by case law;[36]

---

[34] Criticizing: D. Tallon, *L'inexécution du contrat: pour une autre présentation*, *Rev. Trim.dr.civ.* (1994) p. 223.

[35] See Cl. Witz, '*Analyse critique des règles régissant le transfert de propriété en droit français à la lumière du droit allemand*', *Festschrift für Günter Jahr* (1993) p. 533; R. M. Rampelberg, '*La vente est-elle translative de propriété? Variations franco-germaniques sur un thème romain*', *Rev. Hist. Fac. Dr* (1998) p. 49; P. Crocq, *Propriété et garantie* (1995); J. P. Chazal et S. Vicente, '*Le transfert de propriété par l'effet des obligations dans le Code civil*', *RTDCiv.* (2000) p. 477.

[36] As long as they are interdependant obligations (*Soc. 31 mai 1956, Bull. civ. IV, n° 503*) and the non executed obligation is certain (*Soc. 7 juillet 1955, Bull. civ. IV, n° 595*). See on this point Chr. Atias, *Les risques et périls de l'exception d'inexécution*, D. 2003. Chron. 1103; A. Pinna, '*L'exception pour risque d'inexécution*', *RTDCiv.* (2003) p. 31; Roche-Dahan, *L'exception d'inexécution, une forme de résolution unilatérale du contrat synallagmatique*, D. 1994. Chron. 255.

Figure 3: 'Effets du contrat'

Chapter 3 – Effect of obligations	Section 1 – General dispositions (arts 1134–1135) Binding force of the contract, good faith (art. 1134), content of the contract, usage, equity (art. 1135) – unfair contract terms are generally studied here (or with object, *supra*, even though not integrated within the Code.)
	Section 2 – Obligation to give (to transfer property, to deliver the goods) (arts 1136–1141).
	Section 3 – Obligation to do or not to do (arts 1142–1145). This split between obligation to give and obligation to do, can be explained because of the so-called '*effet réel*' of the contract.
	Section 4 – Damages resulting from non performance of the obligation (arts 1146–1155) (Damages – Force majeure – Amount of damages – Penalty clauses).
	Section 4 – Interpretation of contract (non binding rules, arts 1156–1164).
	Section 5 – Effect of obligations towards third parties (privity of contract, together with art. 1121 *supra*).
Chapter 4 – Different kind of obligations	Section 1 – Conditions precedent and subsequent (arts 1168–1184, with resolution of contracts at art. 1184).
	Section 2 – Obligations to execute at a later date (arts 1185–1188) – *obligations à terme*.
	Section 3 – Alternative obligations (arts 1189–1196).
	Section 4 – Multitude of creditors or debtors (arts 1197–1216).

Figure 3 (cont.)

	Section 5 – Divisible and indivisible obligations (arts 1217–1225).
	Section 6 – Obligations with penalty clauses (arts 1126–1233 – together with art. 1152).
Chapter 5 – Extinction of Obligations arts 1234–1314)	Section 1 – Payment (arts 1235–1270)
	Section 2 – Substitution (*novation*) (Assignment of claims are seen in the contract of sale, Title 6, Chapter 8; assignment of debts not received).
	Section 3 – Waiver.
	Section 4 – Set-off.
	Section 5 – Confusion.
	Section 6 – The loss of the thing (arts 1302–1304: see with *force majeure*, art. 1148).
	Section 7 – Action in nullity or in rescission (arts 1304–1314).
Chapter 6 – Evidence on obligations and on payment (arts 1315–1369)	

– nothing on the '*théorie de l'imprévision*' (*Wegfall der Geschäftsgrundlage*), which French private law (case law) did not consider it necessary to establish;[37]
– no general recognition of '*mora creditoris*' – which French law seems to ignore. On this again, a European point of view would be interesting.

[37] Famous case: Canal de Craponne, 6 March 1876, in: Henri Capitant, *Les Grands arrêts de la jurisprudence civile* (François Terré et Yves Lequette, T. 2, 11e éd. 2000) p. 163: '*dans aucun cas il n'appartient aux tribunaux, quelqu'équitable que puisse leur paraître leur décision, de prendre en considération le temps et les circonstances pour modifier la convention des parties et substituer des clauses nouvelles à celles qui ont été librement acceptées par les contractants*'. Even though this position has been maintained, first some special rules allow the taking into account changes of circumstances (ex. art. L. 131-5 Intellectual Property Code); secondly, some cases seem to admit such a position (Com. 3rd November 1992, JCP 1993.II.22164, n. G. Virassamy; 24 November 1998, Bull. civ. IV, n° 277) – but they are not decisive – see N. Molfessis, '*Le principe de proportionnalité et l'exécution du contrat*', in: *Le principe de proportionnalité*, *Petites Affiches* (1998) n° spécial n° 117, 21.

2. Concepts of Performance and of Breach of Contract

a. Concept of Performance has to be Examined in Different Aspects: What has to be Performed? Who has to Perform?

Article 1134 states that 'Agreements legally formed are like statutes for those who have made them (are "legally binding") (. . .) They must be performed in Good Faith.'

aa. What has to be Performed?

What has to be performed is what the parties have decided: within the second half of the 19th century, this was seen as the basis of the 'autonomy of the will'.

However, the doctrine of autonomy of will did not last long – as it was well known that parties were not of equal power. Coming back to what was originally thought (Pothier), it was then considered[38] that it was only the law which was giving effect to the will, so that the will could not be omnipotent, could not be 'unfair'. The binding force of the contract rested on the combination of first the rule of law, then of the power conferred to individual will. It was first considered as meaning that it could not be against '*bona mores*' and 'mandatory rules – *ordre public*' (article 6 CC). But these two notions developed: for the first one, because of sexual liberalism ('*bonne moeurs*' being interpreted mostly as what is considered as 'honest' by common people especially in sexual matters);[39] for the second one, because it took into account not only the political '*ordre public*',[40] but the economical one as well.[41] As this latest notion took more and more room (we can link to it consumers' and employees' protection), individual wills had less.

The 'obligation' to perform in good faith has been strengthened in recent years – so that some professors[42] speak of a 'contractual solidarity'. Parties would not have to act only according to their contract, but according to

[38] Gounod, *Le Principe de l'autonomie de la volonté en droit privé, Contribution à l'étude critique de l'individualisme juridique* (1912).

[39] Might be replaced nowdays by fundamental rights, human rights of the European Convention. See D. Fenouillet, *Mélanges Catala* (2001).

[40] Classical one, interested in the wellbeing of State (organization, especially penal law), family (family structures being generally considered as mandatory, at least when they do not concern patrimonial relationships). Individuals (interference with individuals' integrity or dignity – see art. 16 *et seq.* CC, this latter being stronger since the fundamentalization of human rights).

[41] Protective '*ordre public*', to protect the weakest party in the contract – economically weak; as well as Direction OP (to participate to national economy).

[42] See especially Chr. Jamin, '*Plaidoyer pour le solidarisme contractuel*', *Mélanges Ghestin* (2001) p. 441; D. Mazeaud, '*Loyauté, solidarité, fraternité: la nouvelle devise contractuelle?*', *Mélanges Terré* (1999) p. 603.

good faith, which would integrate not only a duty not to act in bad faith – or to commit no abuse – but to cooperate with one another as well. Good faith would be a general principle leading to 'solidarity' between the parties. Studying case law, one can observe however that, in spite of a general duty of good faith, recognized in the Civil Code, one cannot speak of solidarity. If some spheres of law lead to 'a duty to cooperate' (e.g. duty to inform), this duty can generally be explained by legitimate expectations of both parties or by special relationships between them. Some 'good faith duties' are not explicitly recognized: there is no general recognition of '*mora creditoris*' (even though some cases can be explained having regard to this notion), no recognition of a duty to mitigate damages (it has been explicitly stated by the Cour de cassation in recent cases, concerning however tortuous liability[43]), and no general recognition by civil law[44] of a '*théorie de l'imprévision*' (*Wegfall der Geschäftsgrundlage*).

Even if such duties were recognized, however, they could as well be explained by a concern of economic efficiency as with regard to solidarity. Good faith does not necessarily lead to solidarity.

According to the French Civil Code, the content of the contract must be fixed as well with respect to what we see as the two main conditions of validity of the contract: 'object' and 'cause'.

- The '*objet*' of the contract must be lawful and within commerce; the object of the obligation of each party has to be determined at the time of the contract. This second requirement is in place to assure the true consent of both parties on the content of the contract; it does not mean that the *objet* has to be fixed at the time of the contract, but at least that it can be fixed later depending on objective factors, and not on the will of one of the parties. Regarding the determination of the price, it has been considered that, apart from specific contracts where a special provision within the Civil Code asks for the price to be determined (sale, rent, etc.), one party can fix the price afterwards; however, he should not abuse this right, sanction of such an abuse being either the termination of the contract, or (and) the attribution of damages. The party has no power to propose another price; neither can judges fix the 'good price' themselves.
- The *causa* has firstly to 'exist' and secondly to be 'lawful, licit'. The first meaning of cause was traditionally seen as 'objective': this is the cause of the obligation of one party, generally seen as the object of the obligation of the other party. The second meaning is 'subjective'; this is the 'true cause' of the contract, the reason why both parties decided to contract, their motive. Cause has here two functions: one is to assert that the

[43] Even though the French Doctrine generally took it as a general statement of refusal of the duty to mitigate damages.

[44] Contrary to public law.

obligation of one party has a real counterpart (to protect individuals); the other is a function of social protection. But once again these notions have evolved, especially the first one; subjectivism is sometimes taken into account in the first meaning of the cause, e.g. it has been held that for a loan having as first object the financing of the purchase of a doctor's practice, first *causa* was not only the disposal of money but this disposal within an illicit view[45] (*Civ. 1st*, 1 October 1996, *Bull. Civ. I, n° 235*); it has also been proposed that a contract made for a purpose which could not possibly succeed is without cause. For instance, one party hired from another 200 video cassettes with a view to setting up a video-club in a municipality of 1,315 inhabitants. The renting was seen as impossible as the village was too small for the business to be done; the contract was then voided.[46] This *causa* is also used to limit unfair clauses (see *supra*): it can then be used to equalize the contract, having regard to what are the interests of each party, especially their economic interest in the contract. The cause of the obligation is then seen less as the objective counterpart, what is said in the contract to be owed by the other party (the object of the obligation of this party), than as what is essential for the contract to keep its economy, what the parties should have wished, not what they actually wrote down that they wished.[47]

Those notions are still seen as fundamental in French law, the basis of the structure of a contract. Their different meanings can help to develop this part of law, in which articles haven't been changed since 1804.

However, those different meanings lead as well to great confusion when one has to decide what has to be performed, what the power of each party is, and what the power of judges is. The use of 'cause' to equilize the contract is of course very interesting when one knows that '*lésion*' is not seen as a cause to avoid contracts, that excessive benefit or unfair advantage should not lead to the avoidance of the contract either, nor should a 'change of circumstances' lead to a duty to negotiate. But the vagueness of the criteria is in itself dangerous regarding contractual security and expectation. In this view, specific rules on unfair advantage leading to adaptation of the contract, and not only to its nullity, or on change of circumstances compelling parties to negotiate, would be more efficient.

The other meanings of the cause, cause/counterpart and cause/licit, have long been denounced as useless,[48] as they can be replaced by the requirement of a content fixed at the conclusion of the contract (or to be fixed by

---

45 Buying a civil practice being considered as illicit; however, since then: sale of civil practice is licit if it is still up to the customer to choose their doctor – see *Civ. 1re, 7 nov. 2000, Bull. Civ. I, n° 283.*

46 *Civ. 1re, 3 July 1996, D. 1997.499, Ph. Reigné.*

47 See J. Roshfeld, *Cause et type de contrat* (1999) spéc. n° 166 ss.

48 Planiol, *Traité élémentaire* II (1899), n° 1037.

one party or by a third party), or by the direct recourse to notions such as illegality or immorality.

bb. Who has to Perform?

Another question related to performance is who is to perform. It is of course the party who took the engagement. But to go further, one can wonder if there is good performance when execution is by a third party, and if a failure to perform by this third party would be seen as a breach of the contract from the party who contracted.

- The first question won't be examined further: it is generally thought that, except when there is a special '*intuitus personae*', obligations can be performed by third parties at the demand of the obligee. A third party having interest could even perform the contract instead of the debtor without his consent, except if the latter objects that such a performance would prejudice him.
- A defective performance by a third party should then be seen as a non-performance by the debtor himself (this is also due to the unitary concept of breach of contract – see *infra*). It is however confused nowadays because of the uneasy distinction between contractual and tortuous liability (see *infra*). Seeing damages as what is due by the debtor because of his fault, some think that the debtor should be liable only if he committed a fault in choosing the third party who was to perform the contract. A new concept (in French Law) has been created – which was not useful within the Code, where breach of contract was independent of the idea of fault, so there was no equivalent to § 278 BGB[49] – which is called '*responsabilité contractuelle du fait d'autrui*' (vicarious liability). It comes from its tortuous equivalent (liability of parents for their children, of the teacher for their pupil, of the employer for his employees, article 1384 al. 2 *et seq.*) from which recent case law drew a general liability for damages committed by a person upon whom another person has a permanent control and has in charge the organization of his life.[50] It is then because we now see the 'contractual liability' as a sanction of a fault committed by the contracting party that we need to have recourse to a '*responsabilité du fait d'autrui*', to which we have to find a rational explanation (those explanations differ from one author to another) and rational limits. Those limits are of course difficult to find, because this concept is seen as an exception to a liability based on fault. Such would not be the case if, as the Code provided, damages were due not because of fault but only

[49] I think that § 278 BGB was needed because of the *Verschuldensprinzip*, as there was no fault directly committed by the contracting party. On that see E. Becqué, *De la responsabilité du fait d'autrui en matière contractuelle, contribution à l'étude du droit comparé des obligations*, *RTDCiv*. (1914) pp. 251–320.

[50] AP *29 mars 1991, Blieck, Bull. Civ. n° 1.*

because of breach of contract.[51] One then has to know what 'breach of contract' means in the French system.

b. Concept of Breach of Contract: A Unitary Concept

Originally, the concept of breach of contract (*inexécution contractuelle*) was very simple in French law: there is a breach of a contract whenever a party, without lawful excuse, fails to perform what is due from him under the contract, or performs defectively or partially, or is late in comparison with what is stipulated in the contract.

There was then a 'unitary concept' of breach of contract within the Code: no distinction between the types of obligations, no distinction between the types of breach. It is what comes from the reading of the Code (see articles 1146, 1147, 1184 CC).

If some distinctions are drawn between '*obligation de donner*' (obligation to transfer property/to deliver goods) and '*obligation de faire et de ne pas faire*', it comes only from our concept of transfer of property (see *supra*). It is then necessary to explain how this '*obligation de donner*' can be executed by mere consent, how this type of obligation has to be performed. But this distinction does not lead to a distinction of breach of contract – even though it can be used to explain why in one case there is a right to performance (execution *in natura*) and not in the other; this explanation could come 'naturally', because in one case it is possible to obtain performance by taking the goods, but it is impossible in the other case where performance is impossible without the help of the contracting party.

Nor should a distinction between breaches be drawn because of the doctrinal (and case law) distinction between '*obligation de moyen*' and '*obligation de résultat*': even if it is thought that the regime of those obligations differs, one requiring the fault of the debtor to engage his liability, but not the other (damages being owed except if *force majeure*). This is more a consequence of the content of the obligations itself. The 'obligation of result' means that a party is engaged in obtaining a specific result (for example, when giving a blue car a party would be in breach of his obligation if he gave no car, or a red one, or a defective one). The 'obligation of means' signifies that the debtor is required to use all reasonable means to obtain the result; he is not bound to the result itself (typical is – or was – the obligation of the doctor, not required to cure his patient but to use all reasonable means to cure him). The doctor is not at breach because he didn't cure, but only if he was negligent.

The concept of breach itself is not undermined and should be maintained in a European Code on contract.[52]

---

51 V. Ph. Remy, *La responsabilité contractuelle du droit d'autrui: les incertitudes du droit français, à paraître*.

52 EC Law seems to have adopted such a point of view: see Sales Directive.

3. Sanctions or Remedies?

Three general remedies were provided within the Code: damages (articles 1146 *et seq.*), resolution (rescission with retroactive effects, depending on the type of contracts: *à exécution immédiate ou successive*) or 'enforcement *in natura*' (action to obtain performance) (article 1184).[53]

a. Damages

According to article 1147:

> '*The debtor is liable, where appropriate, to pay damages, either because he has not performed an obligation or because he was late in performing, in all cases in which he cannot prove that the non-performance resulted from a "cause étrangère" (external cause equivalent to "force majeure") for which he was not responsible and even though there was no bad faith on his part.*
>
> *a. 1148: There will be no damages when, as a result of "force majeure" or "cas fortuit", the debtor has been prevented from delivering or doing what he was obliged to deliver or do or has done what was forbidden.*'

These articles are within the part of the Code on contract concerning the 'effects of contractual obligations' (Chapter III of Book III), in a fourth section on 'damages due because of the non performance of the obligation'. Damages are then conceived as the natural sanction of the non-performance.

Today however, damages, due to 'contractual liability' are very often studied in texts within a general study on liability – contractual and non contractual. This topic is covered in J. Ghestin's 'Treatise', with a part on liability written by G. Viney, and was also covered in M. M. Mazeaud and Tunc's Treatises.[54]

The parallelism between those two types of liability led the doctrine to consider that 'contractual liability' needed to fulfil the same conditions as tortuous liability: fault, damage and causation. So Contractual Liability became progressively a fault-based liability.[55]

Since R. Demogue, and especially since M. M. Mazeaud's writings,[56] case law adopted the distinction between '*obligation de résultat*' and '*obligation de moyen*' to consider that in one case it is a fault not to achieve the

[53] Specific sanctions regarding specific contracts are as well established within the Code. But it would need an other analysis.

[54] *Traité pratique et théorique de la responsabilité civile contractuelle et délictuelle*[6], Vol. 1 (1965).

[55] See R. Demogue, *Traité des obligations*, Vol. V (1925), § 1237 *et seq.* where he wrote that contractual liability always presupposes proof of fault, but to prove this fault is either more or less easy, according to the type of obligation, of '*moyens*' or of result.

[56] *Traité pratique et théorique de la responsabilité civile contractuelle et délictuelle.*

result, in the other; one has to demonstrate that the debtor did not use all available means to achieve his obligation. However, this distinction is again more difficult in recent case law, where it is sometimes 'presumed' that a debtor is at fault when he didn't achieved a certain result even if he had only an '*obligation de moyen*'. Generally speaking, one can now consider that French contractual liability system is a fault-based system.[57]

Regarding now what damages are to be given, the basic measure is given by article 1149, which states that '*the damages due to the creditor are, in general, the loss he has suffered and the gain of which he has been deprived, subject to exceptions and modifications below.*'

There is thus a principle of 'full compensation' but it does not go further in the description of damages. The French analysis on this subject – even the doctrinal analysis – is very underdeveloped. For example, there is no distinction between positive (expectation) and negative (reliance) interests.[58] All types of damages (economical, physical, grief, pain, suffering, diminution of sexual prowess, etc.) are recoverable under contractual liability if there is a contract between the parties (whatever was the object of the promise!).

This can explain why French Law needs a non-cumul rule between contractual and tortuous liabilities. Both liabilities are very broadly conceived, both can lead to full compensation for all types of damages. The only limit, in contractual liability, is that only the foreseen damage can be compensated. This could have helped to limit contractual damages to compensate the missed object of the contract; it does not. And, having this concept of types of damages, damages agreed in clauses of the contract (*clauses limitatives de responsabilité*) can seem dangerous, as it could mean that a person suffering physical damage could have only partial damages. So case law considers that those clauses concerning physical damage are ineffective.

One can still observe that there is no general duty to mitigate damages, as damages are now more seen as a sanction (even if not caused by a fault), or as a subjective right of the victim, than as a remedy for the non-performance: the economic value of the contract is not what is important in the modern theory of contractual liability.

b. *Résolution*

Résolution in case of breach of contract is provided by article 1184 CC, in a Chapter dealing with 'Some kinds of obligations' in a section on 'conditional obligations', and not in a section dealing with the different remedies to breach of contract. *Résolution* is seen as a specific kind of 'rescission' with a retro-

---

57 See on this evolution of law and its criticism, Ph. Remy, '*La responsabilité contractuelles: histoire d'un faux concept*', *RTDCiv.* (1997) 323 – with a very strong reaction of the doctrine, either opposing or favourable to this analysis.

58 V. P. Remy-Corlay, '*Exécution et réparation, deux concepts?*' in *RDC* 2005, 13, *colloque Exécution du contrat en nature ou par équivalent*.

active effect, the contract being considered as having never been concluded. The right to restitution would come from this retroactive effect.[59] As '*résolution*' is not adapted to long term contracts, it is considered that those contracts are only rescinded.

Not all breaches of contract can lead to resolution: only 'fundamental non performance', breach of one of the main obligations; it is up to the judge to say if a breach is serious enough to pronounce the resolution of the contract or to award only damages.

A party cannot generally notify a resolution: he can take action against the party in breach, but he himself cannot put an end to the contract. It would be otherwise if parties had agreed a 'resolution clause' within the contract, stating that in case of such or such a breach, either party could terminate it, without asking it to the judge. We consider – which is in my view not always true[60] – that the intervention of the judge is necessary to protect one party from the discretionary power of the other. Even when such a clause is in the contract, the judges might refuse to give effect to the clause if the party using it was not acting in good faith[61] or even in some cases, when the party in breach was acting in good faith.[62]

In some recent cases,[63] a resolution by notification has been recognized as valid when the behaviour of the contracting party was such that it would be unfair to wait for a judicial resolution. One has to remark that it is not the fact that a fundamental obligation has been broken which gives a right to notify a resolution, but the 'behaviour' of the contracting party which is condemned.

c. *Exécution forcée* (Execution *in natura*)

Article 1184 gives a choice between asking for the resolution of the contract and asking for an execution *in natura*.

According to article 1142, this remedy is open only when the non executed obligation is an '*obligation de donner*', or 'not to do'. One could not ask for it in case of an obligation to do. However, in such a case, when a personal action is not necessary, it is possible to ask a third party to execute the obligation and to get the debtor to pay for it. It would be analyzed as an '*exécution forcée*'.[64] It would as well be possible to use what is called

59 As it is when the contract is void – see *supra*.

60 Between professionals, there are generally such clauses so this protection is not given; between a professional and a consumer, it is generally the consumer who wishes the rescission of the contract, and it is easier for him to notify the rescission.

61 *Civ. 3e, 6 juin 1984, Bull. Civ. II, n° 111.*

62 *Civ. 3e, 13 avril 1988, D. 1989. 334, n. Aubert*; – see however *Civ. 3e, 10 mars 1993, D. 1993. 357, n. Bihr.*

63 *Civ. 1re, 13 octobre 1998, Bull. civ. I, n° 300; Civ. 1re, 20 février 2001, Bull. Civ. I, n° 40.*

64 On this problem see *RDC* 2005 n° 1, '*Exécution du contrat en nature ou par équivalent*', *Dir. D. Mazeaud et Th. Revet.*

'*l'astreinte*', which is to force the debtor to pay the creditor a certain amount of money for each day (or each week) of non execution. *Astreinte* must not be considered as damages: the creditor can claim some damages for the late execution; this is a 'private penalty' given to the creditor to push the debtor to do what he has to do.

Execution forcée is thus considered as a third remedy, alongside rescission and damages. Conditions to it are only a '*mise en demeure*' (notice asking for the execution – even if the debtor is already late to execute) and the execution must still be possible.

d. Combination of those Sanctions

One has of course to choose between execution and rescission. But damages can be given in both situations – to compensate for the delay or for the loss because of the termination of the contract.

But the choice between damages and execution rests upon the creditor: one traditionally considers that forced execution is the prime remedy.[65] It is so, according to French Doctrine, because of the so-called '*force obligatoire*' of the contract.[66] Awarding damages is not satisfactory so the creditor should have the choice to ask for the execution of the contract, except when impossible. Whenever possible, the judge should not refuse to order the execution of the contract, whatever the consequences are for the debtor.

On this point again, a reflection is necessary and the German example (§ 275 BGB) could help to find some 'proportional' remedies.

V. CONCLUSION

The French Civil Code can be seen as a model to set up a European (optional) Code, as it draws rules on contract generally, without any general part related to other fields of law. The way it treats what we call '*le régime général des obligations*' (assignment, multitude of creditors, debtors, etc.), within the contract, whatever the source of the obligation, should be maintained.[67] The unitary concept of breach of contract – which since 2002 we can find in the German BGB – should as well be adopted.

But our Code is old and many parts of French law on contract cannot be found within it; one would be grossly mistaken if he applied the Code as it is written. Some changes are necessary; case law is not sufficient in a civil

---

65 See '*Exécution du contrat en nature ou par équivalent*', *Dir. D. Mazeaud et Th. Revet, RDC 2005 n° 1*.

66 See F. Bellivier & R. Sefton-Green, '*Force obligatoire et exécution en nature du contrat en droit français et anglais: bonnes et mauvaises surprises du comparatisme*', in: *Mélanges Ghestin* (2001) pp. 91 *et seq*.

67 v. Ph. Remy, Réviser le livre III du Titre III du Code civil, *RDC* 2004, 1169.

law system (because of uncertainty and difficulties in reading it). A French Commission is now working on a reconsideration of this part of the Civil Code. Let's see the solutions it has in store – and hope it will be European enough!

Chapter 3

Structural Elements in the Contract Law Parts of the German Civil Code

Stefan Grundmann

This paper deals with the 'architecture' of the contract law parts of the German Civil Code, the *Bürgerliches Gesetzbuch* (BGB), i.e. the first and second books of the BGB. Like the other papers in this section, it does so by explaining how some core regulatory questions are arranged in the Code, namely: mistake and misrepresentation, and nullity for violation of the law or *bona mores*; standard contract terms; and the regime of remedies for breach of contract, namely rescission and damages (see below IV). To begin, it may be helpful to explain the scope of this paper, introducing this part with some words on the style of the German Civil Code (see below I) and to present the overall scheme of the 'General Part' of the BGB (first book) which, in its contract related sections, deals with the formation of contracts (see below II), and the overall scheme of the 'Part on Obligations' (second book) which deals primarily with contracts and here primarily with content, performance and breach of contract, including remedies (see below III). The latter two sections, like the one dedicated to the examples, will contain some elements of evaluation. An overall evaluation can be found in the conclusion (see below V).

S. Grundmann, M. Schauer (eds), *The Architecture of European Codes and Contract Law*, 57–81

I. SOME WORDS ON THE 'STYLE' OF THE GERMAN CIVIL CODE AND ON WHY ARCHITECTURE MAY BE OF IMPORTANCE

1. The *Bürgerliches Gesetzbuch*: One Century of Preparation

When the *Bürgerliches Gesetzbuch* entered into force in 1900, it was one of the last important Codes to be implemented on the continent; virtually all other countries already had one.[1] It was probably the code where formal liberal thinking most dominated over elements of social engineering,[2] and it was one which was considered to be – above all – technically perfect or at least outstandingly good. The 'architecture' was praised, not only by German authors but internationally.[3]

Indeed, it was a Code which was based on one century of continuous development of (private law) legal science. Initially it was the influence of the brilliant personality of Friedrich Carl V. Savigny, professor at Humboldt University and the great opponent Anton Friedrich Justus Thibaut, professor at Heidelberg University, that prevented the elaboration of a German Code in the first half of the 19th century.[4] Instead, V. Savigny had formulated the idea that concepts are superior to statutes and, as they are a question of (eternal) truth rather than of decision making, they had to be detected rather than formulated at will.[5] The famous *Begriffsjurisprudenz* in the pandectist school, (i.e. thinking in and deducing legal results from concepts) was the heritage of this core idea.[6] This led to an extremely sophisticated

---

1 Later than the French Code Civil of 1807, the Austrian *Allgemeines Bürgerliches Geesetzbuch* of 1811 (in parts of the Empire, Galicia, already enacted in 1798), the Italian *Codice Civile* of 1867, the Swiss *Zivilgesetzbuch* of 1907. It was followed mainly by the (new) Italian *Codice Civile* of 1942 and the Dutch *Burgerlijk Wetboek* of 1992, both very much of another time already. See for all this survey in: Schlosser, *Grundzüge der Neueren Privatrechtsgeschichte* (9th ed. 2001) pp. 125 *et seq.* and 208 *et seq.*

2 Markesinis, Lorenz, Dannemann, *The German Law of Obligations*, Vol. 1 (1997) p. 13; Wassermann (ed.), *Kommentar zum Bürgerlichen Gesetzbuch (Alternativkommentar)* Vol. 1 (1987), Introduction, para. 53 (p. 23); Wieacker, *Privatrechtsgeschichte der Neuzeit* (1967) p. 479.

3 Maitland, 'The Making of the German Civil Code', in: Fisher (ed.), *The Collected Papers of Frederic William Maitland*, Vol. 3 (1911) p. 484.

4 Robbers, *An Introduction to German Law* (2003) p. 202; Wieacker *supra* n. 2 at 396; Schmoeckel, Rückert, Zimmermann (eds.), *Historisch-kritischer Kommentar zum BGB*, Vol. 1 (2003), before § 1, para. 8 (p. 7).

5 Ebke, Finkin (eds.), *Introduction to German Law* (1996) p. 5; Robbers, *supra* n. 4 at 202; Helmut Coing, in: *J. von Staudingers Kommentar zum Bürgerlichen Gesetzbuch* Vol. 1 (13th Ed., 1995) Introduction, para. 53 (p. 38); Schmoeckel, Rückert, Zimmermann, *supra* n. 4 at 6; Wieacker, *supra* n. 2 at 430.

6 Ebke, Finkin, *supra* n. 5 at 5; Robbers, *supra* n. 4 at 203; Coing, in: *J. von Staudingers Kommentar zum Bürgerlichen Gesetzbuch* Vol. 1 (13th Ed., 1995) Introduction, para. 53 (p. 38); Schmoeckel, Rückert, Zimmermann, *supra* n. 4, before § 1, para. 6 (p. 6).

German legal science in the 19th century, which most authors at that time considered to be the most developed in Europe.[7]

At the end of the century, even the most loyal followers, namely the outstanding pandectist Bernhard Windscheid, again from Heidelberg University, and also the leading (legal) historian, Theodor Mommsen, again from Humboldt University, now advocated a German Civil Code and Windscheid was very influential in its elaboration.[8] Concepts had indeed been clarified; one just has to consider that the German Civil Code, indeed contrary to what is the case in the Romance Codes and also the Austrian ABGB, is divided into five books which represent what we nowadays see as legal subjects: family law; wills and estates; property law; contracts; and torts (the law of obligations).[9] And it brings this core part of private law into an order which is more adapted to modern times, the day to day transactions coming first (and here the more dynamic contracts, then torts, still before property law), status last (family law and wills and estates), thus clearly highlighting the transition from 'status' to 'contract'.[10] However, not just – and not even primarily – the overall order was praised. Many very concise distinctions in particular questions stem from this time as well, for instance the distinction between power of representation in the third party relationship and the internal relationship, typically an agency relationship.[11] For our subject matter though, it is curious that probably the area where the split into modern subjects was least clear and successful in the German Civil Code is precisely contract law: There is no book on contract law, but one on obligations (including also torts and restitution), and large areas of contract law can be found in the first book, the famous 'General Part' of the BGB. Thus, probably the tendency to abstraction, which led to new and meaningful

---

7 Ebke, Finkin, *supra* n. 5 at 5; Schmoeckel, Rückert, Zimmermann, *supra* n. 4, before § 1, para. 6 (p. 6).

8 Markesinis, Lorenz, Dannemann, *supra* n. 2 at 400; Ebke, Finkin, *supra* n. 5 at 6; Wieacker, *supra* n. 2 at 417 *et seq.*, 469, 473 *et seq.*; Schmoeckel, Rückert, Zimmermann, *supra* n. 4, before § 1, para. 9 (p. 7).

9 On this see already Grundmann, '*Die Aufgabe einer nationalen Kodifikation vor dem Hintergrund der Europäisierung des Privatrechts*', in: Fischer-Czermak, Hopf, Schauer (eds.), *Das ABGB auf dem Weg ins 3. Jahrtausend* (2003) pp. 19, 22–25.

10 See Maine, *Ancient law: it's connection with the early history of society and it's relation to modern ideas* (new edition 1930) p. 182; see also Böhm, '*Privatrechtsgesellschaft und Marktwirtschaft*', *Jahrbuch für die Ordnung und Wirtschaft der Gesellschaft* (ORDO) 17 (1966) pp. 75–151.

11 The 'German' origin of this distinction was sensed still in modern times in Europe when it gained 'European' dimension with its introduction into art. 9 of the first Company Directive. See for this, for instance, Edwards, *EC Company Law* (1999), 35 *et seq.*; Einmahl, '*Die erste gesellschaftsrechtliche Richtlinie des Rates der Europäischen Gemeinschaften und ihre Bedeutung für das deutsche Aktienrecht*', *Die Aktiengesellschaft* (AG) (1969) pp. 167, 169; Grundmann, *European Company Law* (2005), paras 248–250; Schmid, '*Die gemeinschaftsrechtliche Überlagerung der Tatbestände des Mißbrauchs der Vertretungsmacht und des Insichgeschäfts*', *Die Aktiengesellschaft* (AG) (1998) pp. 127, 130.

distinctions and as well to a clear order of subject matters, was also the reason for a contract law where these qualities are at least not omnipresent.

2. Why Does the Architecture of National Codes Matter?

If two major advantages of codification can be seen in the fact that systematic relationships are made explicit and that (when the order is convincing) rules can rather easily be found, commented on and problems thus discussed by reference to them,[12] these two advantages certainly are of even greater importance on a European level. Architecture matters because an understanding across boundaries of national contract law traditions is facilitated and is needed even more. And it matters, because there are so many new phenomena[13] that the relationship between them is again an issue, often not completely solved in traditional codes, because they did not deal with these phenomena. Speaking about architecture is therefore after all speaking about the inherent structure of contract law as we see it today. Establishing new architecture – for instance on the European level or in young national Codes – is always a new design of what are the core issues in the contract law of today.

In all this, the architecture of national codes is a vast field of experimentation, a large stock from which to draw one's inspiration. Europe gives us the chance to learn more from each other, but also to establish a new design which, because of its coverage, will be influential far beyond the boundaries of Europe.

In this paper and conference, this refers to contract law only, rather than to the whole of private or civil law. It will, however, be argued, that this restriction is not only due to the coverage of SECOLA and this conference,

---

12 For a discussion of advantages of codification see, for instance, Lurger, *Grundfragen der Vereinheitlichung des Vertragsrechts in der Europäischen Union* (2002), 36 *et seq.*; Schreckenburger, 'Die Gesetzgebung der Aufklärung und die Europäische Kodifikationsidee', in: Merten, Schreckenburger, *Kodifikation gestern und heute* (1995), 89 *et seq.*; Schmidt, *Die Zukunft der Kodifikationsidee* (1995); Münch, 'Strukturprobleme der Kodifikation', in: Behrends, Sellert (eds.), *Der Kodifikationsgedanke und das Modell des Bürgerlichen Gesetzbuches (BGB)* (2000), 147–173; Canaris, *Systemdenken und Systembegriff in der Jurisprudenz entwickelt am Beispiel des deutschen Privatrechts* (1969); Zimmermann, 'Codification: history and present significance of an idea', *European Review of Private Law*, Vol. 3 (1995), 95–120.

13 See for some examples Grundmann, in: Bianca, Grundmann (eds.), *EU Sales Directive – Commentary* (2002), Introduction, para. 7 *et seq.*, 19 *et seq.*; *id.*, 'The Optional European Code on the Basis of the Acquis Communautaire – Starting Point and Trends', 10 *European Law Review* 698 (2004) pp. 705–708 (information media and tools, chains and networks of contracts as normal phenotype, standard contract terms as phenomenon, long-term and services contracts which are typically more complex and nowadays more important, etc.).

but is needed for intrinsic reasons. The questions about the architecture of codes should indeed be – at least on the European level – narrowed down; what should be discussed is the architecture of contract law. There is one practical argument for this: It is very likely that a European Contract Code will come soon, whereas it seems very unlikely that a European Civil Code will be a reality in the shorter term. And the advantages of unification in other areas, such as family, succession or even parts of property law, are far less clear than in contract law. There is also one intrinsic argument for such a limitation: contract law as such covers so many aspects – ranging from the traditional default rules to what is called the (public order) regulation of contract, ranging from privity to chains of contracts, ranging from on the spot contracts to long-term relational contracts – that an order for this is difficult enough without burdening it with other areas of the law which after all do not have too much in common with it. Nobody nowadays has the idea to combine a potential company law code with other areas of the law, and 'market' (i.e. contract law) as the second large organizational form for the market economy is certainly no less complex than the 'firm'.[14]

II. GENERAL PART OF THE BGB (FIRST BOOK) ON FORMATION OF THE CONTRACT AND PRECONTRACTUAL PHASE

1. Contents (Sections and Titles)

The 'General Part' of the BGB contains first two sections which are relevant mainly for other books or parts of private law and not contracts: a section on persons, also legal persons,[15] and then one on movables and land. Section 3, however, is then devoted to the juristic act (*Rechtsgeschäft*) and thereby also to contracts. Sections 4 and 5 are much smaller and deal with prescription, which is certainly very important again for contract law, and the computation of terms and time limits.

Section 3 is divided under six titles: 'Legal Capacity'; 'Legally Binding Declaration of Intentions' (i.e. offer and acceptance, each one to be considered

[14] For this dichotomy (universally accepted today in economics) and the fundamental importance of both models of organization see, path breaking, Coase, 'The Theory of the Firm', 4 *Economica* 386 (1937); today, for instance Easterbrook, Fischel, *The Economic Structure of Corporate Law*^{2} (1996) 8 *et seq.*; Eidenmüller, '*Kapitalgesellschaftsrechts im Spiegel der ökonomischen Theorie*', *Juristen-Zeitung* (JZ) (2001) pp. 1041, 1042; Hart, *Firms, Contracts, and Financial Structure* (1997) pp. 6–8, 15–55; very influential as well Williamson, *The Economic Institutions of Capitalism* (1985) pp. 29–32, 56–66 *et passim*; and for a short description Grundmann, *supra* n. 11, para. 80 *et seq.*

[15] What is quite important for contrat law though, is the definition of consumers and professionals contained in §§ 13 and 14 BGB.

Figure 1: German Civil Code, First Book

German Civil Code, First Book (General Part, Section 3)[16]	Juristic Act, namely: Formation of Contracts
– Title 1 (§§ 104–115)	Legal Capacity
– Title 2 (§§ 116–144)	Legally Binding Declaration of Intention (e.g. Offer and Acceptance) – Mistake and Misrepresentation (§§ 116–124, and below §§ 142 *et seq.*) – Requirements of Form (§§ 125–129) – Relevant Moment (when the declaration of intention becomes binding) and Interpretation (§§ 130–133) – Exceptions from Validity (Nullity) in Case of Violation of the Law or *Bona Mores* (§§ 134–138) – Partial Nullity, Validation, Avoidance (§§ 139–144, all Specifying and Modifying §§ 116–138)
– Title 3 (§§ 145–157)	Meeting of the Minds, Consent, Concerning the Questions – Binding Force of an Offer (§ 145) – When Acceptance is Possible (§§ 146–153) – How to Deal With a Potential Divergence (§§ 154 *et seq.*) – Meeting of the Minds in Case of Auctions (§ 156) – Interpretation (§ 157, see already § 133)
– Title 4 (§§ 158–163)	Conditions Precedent and Subsequent
– Title 5 (§§ 164–181)	Representation, namely – Power of Representation (§§ 164–178, 180 *et seq.*) – Transparency of Acting in Another Person's Name (§ 164) – Liability for Missing Power of Representation (§ 179)
– Title 6 (§§ 182–185)	Validation by Person Concerned

16 Sections 1 and 2 (§§ 1–103) on Legal Persons and on Movables and Land ('Goods'), sections 4 and 5 (§§ 186–240) – already more related to contract law – on prescription and computation of terms and time limits.

individually, but subject to the very same rules); 'Consent'; 'Conditions Precedent and Subsequent'; 'Representation'; and 'Validation by the Person Concerned'. Whenever there are problems in these respects, Austrians so beautifully speak of '*Wurzelmängel*' – defects of the roots (of the contractual obligation) as opposed to those in the course of performance. This means that the 'General Part' of the BGB (in section 3) is mainly about the formation of the contract and defects in this respect.

2. Three Questions about a Suitable Level of Abstraction

The 'General Part' of the German Civil Code is also the *sedes materiae* of the dogmatics of juristic act (*Rechtsgeschäftslehre*), which forms a famous triad with contract and obligation and as such has even found its way into the title of the first section of this conference. It did so as *pars pro toto*. These three are just one example of the question as to which level of abstraction is suitable. In this section, of the triad mainly juristic act and contract come into play. The juristic act is characterized by the legally binding declaration of intention which changes the law. It may consist of one declaration only, for instance in the case of avoidance. In others, mainly in the case of a contract, two declarations are necessary for the juristic act as only the two lead to a change in the legal relationship. A first question would then be whether taking the distinction between juristic act and contract as a starting point is really helpful for codification. This coincides very much with the question of whether a 'General Part' is helpful. A second question is whether there should be several parallel sets of contract law rules. In one aspect, consumer contract law, this question is treated separately in this conference, but this is a more general question. And the third question which occurs when considering the scheme of the German Civil Code (and others) is whether generalizing for all contracts is meaningful.

a. General Part?

The invention of the juristic act as a category was paradigmatic for German legal scholarship of the 19th century and very influential. It is paradigmatic as well for the formation of a separate 'General Part' (first book). The idea is that this category does not necessarily involve two parties declaring their intentions, i.e. legal consequences can also flow from only one such declaration. This is already so in contracts, for instance where only one party, e.g. the party defrauded, has the right to avoid the contract. In other fields of law, this is much more than an exception (as in contracts); there it constitutes the typical case. Good examples are wills and estates. The idea in the BGB is that all such declarations of intention should, in principle, be subject to one set of rules. Even though for contracts, for sure, it would have been more pragmatic to start from a set of two matching declarations and then specify that in certain instances, fixed by law or agreement, one side has a unilateral right to change the legal relationship. Even the German legislation recognizes this, when later on it specifies that the source of an obligation (or change of obligation) is either the meeting of minds (without any other prerequisites) or a unilateral declaration of intention whenever (exceptionally) the law supports such a possibility (see § 311 paragraph 1 BGB).

If concepts (‘*Begriffe*’) are not sacrosanct, the core question when evaluating the scheme must be whether there is really so much in common between declarations of intention in contracts, family law and wills as to justify a common ‘General Part’, i.e. whether the gains from treating all phenomena jointly are high enough to compensate for the disadvantage of the fact that contract formation can perhaps no longer be treated in one set of rules because not all of them are ‘general’ to the whole of private law. If one looks through the rules, the rules on capacity seem to be quite similar in all areas of private law, but these are rules which could easily be linked to the law of persons as well (being then general anyway). The same is no longer true for mistake and misrepresentation which are largely immaterial in family law (no simple avoidance) and pose different and specific problems in the case of wills (a new will is always possible, even without mistake, but how to handle the case in which the decedent can no longer decide on whether he rather wants to void the will or stick with it?). Requirements of form are very different in family law and wills and estates, and finally, representation is largely excluded there. Summarizing this short round-up, it has to be said that contracts, family law and wills and estates have little in common as to the declaration of intention. There are certainly some similarities between contract law and property law as to declarations of intention. But where they run parallel, it is mainly the (German) principle of splitting both transactions (‘*Abstraktionsprinzip*’)[17] which creates the need to consider two transactions at all. The common denominator thus does not seem very large. This brings us to the second question: what are the disadvantages of not having a common body of the law for the questions of formation of contracts (see below b)?

The first sub-result, however, might already teach us some lessons for a future ‘European Code’. If the common parts are rather modest even in the German Civil Code, which most stresses them, it may well be advisable to opt for a Contract Law Code only on the European level. This is so because (contract) law is so much more complex than: (1) on a national level only; and (2) centuries or even only decades ago. If an Optional Code is really what Europe is striving for, there is moreover not only complexity in the host of sources of inspiration of a European Code, but also in the interplay between different levels. And (contract) law is infinitely more complex today:

---

17 For its contents see, for instance, Markesinis, Lorenz, Dannemann, *supra* n. 2 at 20–21; Ebke, Finkin, *supra* n. 6 at 173; Robbers, *supra* n. 4 at 215 *et seq.*

No longer only the dimensions of party relationships, but also of market order are increasingly important; not only the set of default rules, but regulation, and there are a host of problems which did not exist some 20, 50 or 100 years ago.[18] This supports the integration of these (contract law) aspects rather than building a grand, all embracing Code with a General (and necessarily formal) Part.

b. Several Sets of Rules on Formation of Contracts?

A second question is whether it is positive or negative to deal with questions of formation of contracts at various places in the Code or in the legal system. This question has at least two aspects.

There is, first, the question of whether questions of formation of contracts should be dealt with in various Codes, the Civil Code, a Commercial Code, possibly also a Consumer Code. In Germany for instance, the requirement that the declaration of a surety be in writing – this is the general rule for the formation of a surety contract under § 766 BGB – does not apply to professionals and the rules are to be found in the Commercial Code (§ 350). There is a separate rule on interpretation there as well as on the question of whether a service is to be presumed to be granted for free (§§ 346 and 354 Commercial Code). There were several bits of consumer legislation up to 2001 as well, but no comprehensive Consumer Code in Germany. These bits were then integrated into the German Civil Code as of 2002 (excluding, however, commercial law). There are much stronger reasons (in my view) for such an integration – of the law of consumer contracts and also of commercial contracts – and this is for two main reasons:[19] Market economy is about professional relationships (mainly what Adam Smith called specialization) and about the exchange with those who are not part of the specialization (the retail marketing, i.e. what Adam Smith called the exchange). These are the

---

18 See above *supra* n. 13.

19 Grundmann, '*Generalreferat – Internationalisierung und Reform des deutschen Kaufrechts*', in: Grundmann, Medicus, Rolland (eds.), *Europäisches Kaufgewährleistungsrecht – Reform und Internationalisierung des deutschen Schuldrechts* (2000) pp. 281, 282–288; for consumer law: *id.*, 'Consumer Law, Commercial Law, Private Law – How can the Sales Directive and the Sales Convention be so similar?' (2003) 14 EBLR 237 (*Archiv für civilistische Praxis* 202 (2002) pp. 40, 57–70); similar (for different reasons), for instance, Drexl, '*Verbraucherrecht, Allgemeines Privatrecht, Handelsrecht*', in: Schlechtriem (ed.), *Wandlungen des Schuldrechts* (2002) pp. 97, 105; Hondius, 'Consumer Law and Private Law – the case for integration', in: Heusel (ed.), *Neues Europäisches Vertragsrecht und Verbraucherschutz – Regelungskonzepte der Europäischen Union und ihre Auswirkungen auf die nationalen Zivilrechtsordnungen (New European Contract Law and Consumer Protection – the concepts involved in Community regulations and their consequences for domestic civil law – Le nouveau droit des contrats et la protection des consommateurs – concepts de la réglementation communautaire et leurs conséquences pour le droit civil national)* (1999) p. 19.

two pillars of a market economy, as has been seen since Smith's times. And if all contract law rules are integrated into one set of rules, this forces everybody to always think about the relationship between the rules for different types of persons, i.e. what really are the reasons for treating one differently from the other. In other words, differentiations are always made much more transparent and evident to everybody and are thus put to the test of constant scrutiny by the whole legal community. The most important concern for integration is, however, one of substance: In most aspects, the laws of consumer contracts do not deviate enough from each other and indeed almost only with respect to information duties. In fact, for the classical type of contracts, sales contracts, the UN Convention on the International Sale of Goods (for commercial sales) and the EC Sales Directive (for consumer sales) hardly deviate from each other at all. In this conference, however, the question of whether to integrate consumer law or not is one covered in another section. Therefore, what is more important in this first section of the conference is how consumer law is integrated (if it is integrated). This question is related to the second aspect of this Chapter.

The question as to whether there should or should not be several sets of rules on formation of contracts is not only raised when there are several Codes, but also within one Code, in Germany between the 'General Part' (first book) and the 'Part on Obligations' (second book). Again, if the system is to be made transparent, if rules regulating similar phenomena are to be closely related, a split of the body of law into two different books in the Code has to be justified. One example in this respect is certainly standard contract terms, taken up in more detail below in section IV, and this is a body of the law which indeed has been integrated into the second book in 2002, far away from the regulation of the parallel problems for an individually bargained for contract. This question will indeed be raised for standard contract terms, although it certainly is a more general one, important also in other instances. Even as such, however, it can better be discussed when the second part of the comparison has already been introduced as well, i.e. when discussing the second book and its contents. It will then be argued that the high level of abstraction in the 'General Part' (more precisely the fact the formation of contract does not seem to be regulated there, but instead the creation of juristic acts) produced negative effects and misdirected the German legislature to put other questions of formation of contract into the second book, even though closely related to those in the General Part (for the 'juristic act'), rather far away from each other.

c. Rules on Formation of Contracts Generally?

The third question is whether a general contract law is needed at all or whether it would not be preferable to have rules for specific types of contracts only. For the formation of contracts, this question is easy to answer. It may well be true that the General Part of the BGB does not deal with all the important issues of formation of contracts. The model of offer and acceptance which is paramount here may, for instance, not work smoothly in the case of contracts intensively negotiated, where there is not really an offer and then acceptance, but continuous negotiating, and potentially some binding force already in the course of the negotiations. This may be so even more often in the case of complex contracts, for instance also in long-term contracts, but it is nevertheless a general question, not specific only to one or a few types of contracts. Even the typical on the spot contract, the sales contract, follows partly the model of offer and acceptance (sale of a journal), partly that of negotiation (sale of a firm). Likewise, specific problems such as a potential duty to renegotiate may be more typical for some contracts (for instance those of longer duration) than for others, but are general nevertheless. In fact, the formation of contracts is typically not different from one type of contract to another. Types of contracts are ordered (so far) according to diverging characteristic duties (transfer of goods, lease of goods, services, and certainly duties to pay, also as abstract duties). Therefore, this third question can be posed, if at all, for the phase of performance only. Differentiating according to different types of contracts is meaningful mainly for the phase of performance and, even then, the question is whether general rules cannot be found, perhaps even a considerable number. The creation of a general part is therefore indicated at least for questions of formation of contracts.

3. Lacunae in the 'General Part' (with Respect to Formation of Contracts)

The General Part, in itself, does contain a rather convincing order: ranging from capacity of the parties to their individual declarations of intention and consent (agreement by parties capable of such agreements), then to exceptions from validity, then public order intervention entering the scene, which is needed for the protection of one party or third parties and finally dealing with more specific situations such as conditions precedent and subsequent and representation.

In this scheme, however, three lacunae seem to be of particular importance:

(1) Modern contract law, as far as formation of contract is concerned (including the pre-contractual phase), has developed important duties for this phase, namely information rules. Questions concern the binding force of information given, and while information may be different in different specific contracts (and therefore related to some extent to specific contracts, for instance specific for long-term contracts), there are certainly general rules on the duty to inform the other party and on the binding force of any material information (if) given.

(2) Standard contract terms are today the most common phenotype of contract making and unfair contract terms law concerns formation of contract, with the validity exceptions.[20] In this respect, it could not even be argued that the rules on this phenomenon have not been included into the 'General Part' of the German BGB because they are not general (they apply, for instance, also to property law, e.g. retention of title). The failure to properly integrate the law of standard contract terms shows rather that contract law in itself is already so complex that adding complexity by drafting general rules for all areas of the law is suboptimal. It will be argued that rules on standard contract terms should today – whenever possible – be placed in the context of the rule on the traditional individual agreement from which they diverge.

(3) Possibly also the right of revocation, which is granted mainly in the case of atypical marketing techniques, should be regulated in the part on formation of contracts. In all cases, it has to do with a specific type of formation (marketing technique) and – functionally speaking – the right of revocation allows for the normal information which would have been possible had this specific marketing technique not been used.[21] The revocation right is thus closely linked to (precontractual) information rules or regimes.

III. THE LAW OF OBLIGATIONS IN THE BGB (SECOND BOOK) – CONTENT, PERFORMANCE AND BREACH OF CONTRACT

1. Contents (Sections and Titles)

The second Book of the BGB contains eight sections, the eighth being devoted to specific contracts (almost all titles from 1–25), but as well to restitution and torts (titles 26 and 27). The recent modernization has rather stressed the general part, doing away with the most important regimes of breach of

[20] The EC Council Directive 93/13/EEC of 5 April 1993 on unfair terms in consumer contracts, OJ L 95/29, 1993, is mainly about validity exceptions; German Law (§§ 305–305c BGB) contains more rules also about the integration of standard terms into the contract, i.e. a problem of declaration of will and meeting of the minds.

[21] Grundmann, 'Information, Party Autonomy and Economic Agents in European Contract Law', (2002) 39 CMLR pp. 269, 276; Riesenhuber, *System und Prinzipien des Europäischen Vertragsrechts* (2003) p. 326; characterizing the revocation rights as a category distinct from information rules, for instance, Schirmbacher, *Verbrauchervertriebsrecht – Die Vereinheitlichung der Vorschriften über Haustürgeschäfte, Fernabsatzverträge und Verträge im elektronischen Geschäftsverkehr* (to apperar in the near future), Lorenz, *Der Schutz vor dem unerwünschten Vertrag* (1997), 123 *et seq.*; Fuchs, '*Zur Disponibilität gesetzlicher Widerspruchsrechte im Privatrecht*', *Archiv für civilistische Praxis* (AcP) 196 (1996) pp. 313–394, 338 *et seq.*

contract specific to one type only (mainly sales law). Sections 1–7 fall again into two parts; sections 5–7 dealing with rather particular questions going beyond one simple contract, i.e. assignment of claims, assignment of debts and multitude of creditors and debtors. Sections 1–4 deal with obligations, standard contract terms, contracts and extinction of obligations (via proper performance). Thus, in this section, the second part of the triad, contract and obligation, come into play. The contents of the different titles in these four sections on which the following discussion focuses are as follows:

Figure 2: Second Book, sections 2–7

German Civil Code, Second Book, sections 1–7 (General Part of the Part on Obligations)[22]	Content, Performance, and Breach of Contracts, but in Part also Formation
– Section 1: Obligations (§§ 241–304)	Title 1: Many subjects, namely: – Possible Duties Deriving from Obligations (§ 241) – Duty to Act in Good Faith (§ 242) – What, where, when (§§ 243–245, 262–271) – Some Rules on Interests (§§ 246–248) – Damages, Amount of (§§ 249–255) – Compensation for Expenses and Others (§§ 256–261) – Extinction of the Obligation Because of Impossibility (§ 275) – Standard of Liability, also for Third Parties (§§ 276–279) – Damages, Prerequisites and Option to Choose Surrogates (§§ 280–283, 284 *et seq.*) – Default (of the Debtor) (§§ 286–292) Title 2: Creditor's Default of Acceptance (§§ 293–304)
– Section 2: Standard Contract Terms (§§ 305–309) (*Introduced into the Code in 2002*)	Namely: – Rules on Integration of Standard Terms Into the Contract (§§ 305–305c, 'Formation of the Standard Term Contract')

[22] Section 8 then on specific 'obligations', mainly specific contracts (almost all titles in 1–25), but also restitution (26th title) and torts (27th title).

Figure 2: (cont.)

	– Rules on Nullity of Standard Terms (§§ 307–309, 'Exceptions to Validity') – Partial Nullity or Non-Integration of Standard Terms into the Contract (§ 306)
– Section 3: Contracts (§§ 306–361) (*Partly Introduced into the Code in 2002*)	Title 1: Formation, Content and Termination of Contracts, Namely: – Sources of Contractual Obligations, including *culpa in contrahendo*, and More Requirements of Form (§§ 311–311c) – Rules for Specific Marketing Techniques, mainly with a Right of Revocation (Doorstep and Distance Selling, E-Commerce) (*Introduced into the Code in 2002*) (§§ 312–312f) – Adaptation of Contracts and Termination of Long-Term Contracts) (*Introduced into the Code in 2002*) (§§ 313 *et seq.*) – Unilateral Fixing and Changing of Contract Conditions (§§ 315–319) Title 2: Contracts Creating Mutual Obligations (§§ 320–327), Namely – Duty to Perform, Rescission and Damages (the Latter, however, in Good Part already in section 1) Title 3: Promises to Third Parties (§§ 328–335) Title 4: Penalties (§§ 336–345) Title 5: Rescission and Revocation (Execution, Consequences) (§§ 346–354, §§ 355–361) For the Right to Rescind or Revoke a Contract see, however, Already Titles 1 and 2

Figure 2: (cont.)

– Section 4: Extinction of Obligations (§§ 362–397)	Namely: – Performance (title 1) – and Substitutes (title 2) – Set-Off as one Particular Substitute (title 3) – Waiver (title 4) But Not: – Because of Breach of Contract, see above
– Sections 5–7: Assignment of Claims etc., Multitude of Creditors or Debtors (§§ 398–432)	Namely: – Assignment of Claims (section 5) – Assignment of Debts (section 6) – Multitude of Creditors or Debtors (section 7) But Not: – Assignment of the Contract as such – Chains and Networks of Contracts

2. Three Questions about a Suitable Level of Abstraction

a. 'General Part' (now within the Second Book)?

The second book of the BGB contains again a 'General Part' (sections 1–7; mainly section 1), followed by a part on specific contracts and other obligations (restitution, torts) (all this in section 8). The main question with respect to this general part is whether the advantages of regulating torts and contracts in the same set of rules are worthwhile.

Restitution can largely be excluded from this inquiry, as restitution is either contract related (the so-called '*Leistungskondiktion*') or has to do with the protection of rights attributed exclusively to one person (torts, property law, so-called '*Eingriffskondiktion*'). In its contract law related branch, however, the difference between restitution and – the contract law regime of – rescission (with restitution as a consequence) has been criticized by most authors (and the courts)[23] and has in fact largely been done away by one old

[23] See for criticism (often indirect): Reuter, Martinek, *Ungerechtfertigte Bereicherung* (1983) pp. 595 *et seq.*; Medicus, *Bürgerliches Recht* (18th Ed., 1999) pp. 168 *et seq.*; Flessner, '*Haftung und Gefahrbelastung des getäuschten Käufers*', *Neue Juristische Wochenschrift* (NJW) (1972) pp. 1777–1783, 1780 *et seq.*; Weitnauer, '*Der arglistig getäuschte Käufer*', *Neue Juristisch Wochenschrift* (NJW) (1970) pp. 637–640, 639; Huber, '*Der Unfall des*

development in the law of restitution, the so-called *Saldotheorie*,[24] and by one fundamental reform in the law of rescission in 2002.[25]

If then the question is whether torts and contracts need a common regime (in a law on obligations), one must again compare the advantages of having a common core of rules and the disadvantages of splitting up contract law. The rules which are really common are not so numerous. One can refer mainly to those on the amount of damages (§§ 249–254 BGB), much less so to the rules on interests (§§ 246–248, 286–290 BGB), because interests are often agreed on in contract law and only there.

On the other hand, contract law related rules which should be closely linked are to be found in quite different places, the main distinction made within the law of obligations in the Code (section 1 of the second book) being a very formal one for today's standards. This, however, is already part of the second question:

b. Several Sets of Rules on Content, Performance and Breach of Contracts?

The second question is again – but now for content, performance and breach of contract – whether several sets of rules are needed. With respect to the differentiation between general contract law, consumer contract law and commercial contract law, the same arguments apply as for the formation of contract. With respect to the arrangement within the BGB, the second aspect, the question is slightly different from the parallel question of problems of formation. It is no longer the question whether to integrate parts on forma-

betrogenen Gebrauchtwagenkäufers', *Juristische Schulung* (JuS), pp. 439–445, 443; Blomeyer, '*Fortschritte der modernen Schuldrechtsdogmatik*', *Archiv für die civilistische Praxis* (AcP) 154 (1955) pp. 527–544, 537; Markesinis, Lorenz, Dannemann, *supra* n. 2, 643 *et seq.*; Leser, *Von der Saldotheorie zum faktischen Synallagma* (1956) pp. 22 *et seq.*, 55 *et seq.*; Judgment of 8 January 1970, *Bundesgerichtshof* (hereinafter: BGH), *Entscheidungen des Bundesgerichtshofs* (hereinafter: BGHZ) Vol. 53, pp. 144–149; Judgement of 14 October 1971 and also BGH, BGHZ Vol. 57, pp. 137–153, 146 *et seq.*; Judgment of 26 October 1978, BGH, BGHZ Vol. 72, pp. 252–257. For a description of the two regimes in English see Robbers, *supra* n. 4 at 252 *et seq.*, Markesinis, Lorenz, Dannemann, *supra* n. 2 at 641 *et seq.* and 710 *et seq.*

24 The main idea is that in synallagmatic contracts one party that can no longer restitute the benefit received cannot invoke this impossibility if he wants to claim back the benefit which the other party received from the contract: see Robbers, *supra* n. 4 at 256–257; Markesinis, Lorenz, Dannemann, *supra* n. 2, pp. 764–766; Medicus, *Bürgerliches Recht* (20th ed. 2004) pp. 163 *et seq.*

25 Until 2001, in principle, the party which could not restitute in kind the benefit received could not rescind. This is no longer the case today, this party may just have to pay damages (in case he was responsible for the loss of this benefit): see § 346 para. 4 BGB; and on this Dauner-Lieb, Heidel, Lepa, Ring, *Das neue Schuldrecht* (2002) p. 161; on the former situation: Ebke, Finkin, *supra* n. 5 at p. 185.

tion in the second book whereas, initially, these questions had been treated within the theory of the juristic act in the General Part (first book) of the BGB. The question is now rather whether distinctions within the second book, and mainly sections 1 and 3, are meaningful (section 2 being about formation anyway, section 4 being quite clearly distinct in that it deals with the extinction of obligations as a consequence of proper performance, and sections 5–7 being about particular problems anyhow, see above 1).

If one takes sections 1 and 3 together (which is already difficult enough, because the order does not indicate this), one can state that this is the German law on content and breach of contract, section 4 then being about (proper) performance. In these two sections, however, even if seen as one block, it can easily be realized that the distinctions are quite formal. In section 1, the code distinguishes between duties owed to the other party and obligations the violation of which only leads to a loss of legal positions without giving the other party a right to claim performance (obligations only to oneself). And therefore, for instance, delay on the part of the creditor and delay on the part of the debtor are treated in different sections, but delay on the part of the debtor then in conjunction with such diverse questions as the amount of damages, interests, good faith and the source of obligations. More important still, core alternatives and parallel treatment cannot be easily recognized. The core example is that of rescission and damages, this example is taken up separately. These splits which obscure important links are due to the fact that within the section dedicated to contracts (section 3), the distinction is again very formal: First remedies are dealt with, which have their importance also in a contract which obliges only one partner (in section 1) and then remedies which are meaningful only in the 'normal' case where the contract gives rise to duties of both partners (in section 3, title 2). Therefore section 3, dedicated to contracts, remains without a rule on contractual claims for damages! These rules are to be found in section 1. Also the remedy of rescission is split up, the grounds for rescission being first, mainly in §§ 323–325 BGB, the consequences much later, in §§ 346 *et seq*. BGB. The sequence in section 3 (title 1: formation, content and termination; title 2: obligations flowing from contracts with obligations for both parties; title 3: third party promises; title 4: penalties; title 5: consequences of rescission) is no longer self-evident and highly convincing. It would take too long to explain the historical roots for this order. Moreover, also with respect to this body of law, the spirit of this arrangement did not seem accessible to the reforming legislature in 2002;[26] it did not seem possible to give it an appropriate form for our times.

[26] With the exception of tenant law, the law of obligations had remained largely unchanged during the 20th century.

c. Rules on Content, Performance and Breach of Contracts Generally?

The last question is again that of whether general rules on content, performance and breach of contracts should be developed at all or whether these questions are not better regulated for specific contracts only. As the core criterion for distinguishing specific contracts is the characteristic duty, it might well be that breach of this duty is a phenomenon which diverges so much from one type of contract to the other that developing general rules rather obscures the policy considerations which really matter. The recent reform of the German Civil Code – largely owing to the transposition of the Sales Directive – seems, however, to show that it is the contrary which is true and that a systemization of remedies is possible even to a larger extent than has been the case traditionally. It seems evident that a broad split has to be made between on the spot contracts and long-term contracts (with additional grounds for resiliation, at least *ex nunc*), and that content is certainly different to a large extent from one specific type of contract to another, i.e. that general rules with respect to content are much more marginal than general rules for the formation of contract and also than general rules for the breach of contract. And it is certainly true that while general contract law for content, performance and breach of contract is possible (and even desirable), an inductive approach is preferable as a method: starting from specific contracts and the policy considerations there and only then, in a second step, generalizing. And the question of what is specific and what is general may well be answered in different ways in different legal systems and this is worth discussing – from a comparative law perspective and very much so in the course of the development of a European Code. Again, rescission and damages are a good example for this (see below IV). Summarizing, one can say that the order of the rules on content, performance and breach of contracts in the second book is much less convincing than that of the rules on formation in the first book (if one does not consider the lacunae pointed out for the first book).

3. Lacunae in the Part on Obligations (with Respect to Content, Performance and Breach of Contracts)

The question of lacunae has to be approached in a different way for content, performance and breach of contracts than for the formation of contracts. With respect to the formation of contracts, quite some lacunae had been isolated, mainly because these problems have not been regulated in the General Part, but elsewhere (now, i.e. after the integration of the consumer law legislation, mainly in the second book). With respect to content, performance and breach of contracts, the situation is different. These rules are gathered in one book, not scattered over two books. Therefore the question of distribution of the rules within this book is more important. There is only one substantial set of rules outside the second book of the BGB for these problems, and this is the regulation in the fourth book of the Commercial Code. The rules there, however, either deal with specific contracts (commercial sales, sales on commission) or contain only rather limited deviations from the rules contained in the second book of the BGB for specific situations. Therefore, one cannot really speak of lacunae but rather of a regime which makes finding the relevant rules a bit difficult.

On the other hand, with respect to content, performance and breach of contracts, there are at least two areas where not only the second book of the BGB seems too sparse, but German private law as a whole, i.e. where the lacunae are not just a matter of the system within the BGB but one of the private law in general. There are virtually no rules for chains and networks of contracts in German law at all, an area where sections 5–7 of the second book could be supplemented.[27] And the paradigm of a long-term contract and in part also a service contract is developed much less in German law (as in most national laws) than the typical on the spot contract. This is problematic in the era of a services society and where the hybrids between firm and contract are becoming increasingly important, the so-called 'relations', often heavily characterized by symbiotic elements.[28]

IV. SOME CORE EXAMPLES

At this stage, it may be helpful to summarize some of the most important examples given, adding perhaps a few more.

1. Mistake, Misrepresentation, and Nullity for Violation of the Law or *Bona Mores*

It may well be that the German law on mistake can be criticized in its content, mainly because avoidance is allowed even if the party mistaken could have avoided this mistake (negligence) and the other party did not

[27] On these questions under German law see mainly Möschel, 'Dogmatische Strukturen des bargeldlosen Zahlungsverkehrs', *Archiv für civilistische Praxis* (AcP) 186 (1986) 187; Rohe, *Netzverträge – Rechtsprobleme komplexer Vertragsverbindungen* (1998).

[28] On relational contracts see Macauley, 'Non-contractual Relations in Business: A Prliminary Study', *American Sociological Review*, Vol. 28 (1963) pp. 55–67; Macneil, 'The Many Futures of Contracts', *Southern California Law Review*, Vol. 47 (1974) pp. 691–816; Oechsler, '*Wille und Vertrauen im privaten Austauschvertrag – Die Rezeption der Theorie des Relational Contract im deutschen Vertragsrecht in rechtsvergleichender Kritik*', *Rabels Zeitschrift für ausländisches und internationales Privatrecht* (RabelsZ), Vol. 60 (1996) pp. 91–124.

influence the mistake.[29] It may well be that the exceptions from validity, as provided for in the original Code, did not catch enough cases, i.e. that the model was too liberal and not protective enough.[30] As for the architecture, however, the arrangement seems laudable. Indeed this seems to be a well ordered arrangement for the questions of formation of contract: legal capacity; other questions for each individual declaration of intention (offer and acceptance), namely mistake, misrepresentation, requirements of form (sometimes not encompassing the contract as a whole, but only the declaration of the partner to be protected), then exceptions to validity and consent; and afterwards conditions precedent and subsequent, representation and finally validation by the person concerned. If the order of consent and exceptions to validity was inverted, the order would be: first the rules on the agreement as such, and in this context first the questions which can be raised for each declaration individually, then the questions of the interplay between them and of the consent; secondly the limits set by public regulation to such agreements, namely for violation of the law and *bona mores*; and thirdly some particular situations which need a bit more extensive regulation, namely conditions, representation and validation by the consent of the party concerned if this party did not participate in the formation. To isolate the step third-mentioned is at least a sensible option, because including all these features in a two-tier order (agreement and public order limits) might create an overload in the first part and make it less transparent.

For this order, however, one does not need the distinction of contract and juristic act. A regime would be more transparent if contract was regulated and then the few rules which apply also outside contract law were mentioned and made applicable by analogy in other areas of the law. The theory of juristic act does not make this last step superfluous either, at least not in all cases, i.e. it does not save dogmatic energy, and thus does not offer considerable advantages over an approach where contract is the core element from which to start.

The problem with this order under German Law is that further developments in the 20th century were no longer integrated into it, i.e. into the first book, and that therefore, the regime on formation of the contract is no longer systematic. What is missing in the General Part (on formation of contract) has been mentioned above: it is the relevant rules on particular marketing techniques, it is the duties, mainly information rules, in the phase of formation of the contract (in part pre-contractual), also the rules on *culpa in contrahendo*, and it is the relevant rules on standard contract terms. All

---

29 At least this regime is considered to focus insufficiently on what the other party could understand: Bydlinski, *Privatautonomie und objektive Grundlage des verpflichtenden Rechtsgeschäftes* (1967) pp. 176–179; considering the regime too broad: Kramer in: *Münchner Kommentar zum Bürgerlichen Gesetzbuch* Vol. 1 (3rd Ed., 1993), § 119, para. 7 *et seq.* (pp. 910–912), see also n. 16.

30 See only n. 2.

this has been integrated only formally (now in the second book and mostly only in 2002), not linking the rules to the parallel phenomena regulated in the General Part – section 3 on the so-called juristic act which, however, in the original scheme of the BGB, can also be conceived as the section on formation of contract.

2. Standard Contract Terms

Standard Contract Terms, as is still the case in other countries today,[31] were regulated in Germany outside the Civil Code in a particular law.[32] This law was well accepted, created an enormous body of case law[33] and was highly influential for the European Directive.[34] It may be questionable whether the protection of professional clients also produced good results.[35] As to the order in the law, however, the main problems seemed to have been individualized and then regulated in an easily accessible order: (1) definition of which phenomena are to be considered as standard contract terms (§ 1 AGBG); (2) rules on their integration into the contract (§§ 2–7 AGBG, with rules on

---

31 This is still the case, for instance, in France, whereas Italy (where standard contract terms were regulated as early as 1942) integrated its rules from the outset into its *Codice Civile*. Austria regulated standard contract terms within the *Konsumentenschutzgesetz*, the law concerning consumer protection, while the Netherlands integrated those regulations into their new civil code (*Nieuw Burgerlijk Wetboek*) from 1992; see Ulmer, Brandner, Hensen, Schmidt, *AGB-Gesetz* (9th ed., 2001), 'Introduction', para. 86 *et seq.* (pp. 99–120); Bennemann, *Fiktionen und Beweislastregeln in Allgemeinen Geschäftsbedingungen* (1987), pp. 26–149.

32 *Gesetz zur Regelung des Rechts der Allgemeinen Geschäftsbedingungen* (AGB-Gesetz) of 9 December 1976, BGBl. (German Offical Journal) 1976 I, p. 3317; last important amendment art. 1 of *Gesetz zur Änderung des AGB-Gesetzes und der Insolvenzordnung* of 19 July 1996, BGBl. 1996 I, p. 1013.

33 See only the two leading – and very extensive – commentaries by: Ulmer, Brandner, Hensen, Schmidt, *AGB-Gesetz – Kommentar zum Gesetz zur Regelung des Rechts der Allgemeinen Geschäftsbedingungen*, 9th ed. (2001); Wolf, Horn, Lindacher, *AGB-Gesetz – Gesetz zur Regelung des Rechts der Allgemeinen Geschäftsbedingungen* (4th ed. 1999).

34 Besides, perhaps, the English Unfair Contract Terms Act of 26 September 1977 and the French Law 78–23 of 10 January 1978, see, for instance, Ulmer, *in:* Ulmer, Brandner, Hensen, Schmidt, Introduction para. 89, 91 (pp. 102, 106).

35 In theory, professional clients are certainly subject to a problem of structural information asymmetry as well (also in professional relationships the party proposing the terms typically uses them thousands of times, certainly much more often, and therefore can invest much more into them and nevertheless write off his costs): Habersack, *Vertragsfreiheit und Drittinteressen – eine Untersuchung zu den Schranken der Privatautonomie unter besonderer Berücksichtigung der Fälle typischerweise gestörter Vertragsparität*, (1992) pp. 106–109; Lieb, '*Sonderprivatrecht für Ungleichgewichtslagen? Überlegungen zum Anwendungsbereich der sogenannten Inhaltskontrolle privatrechtlicher Verträge*', *Archiv für civilistische Praxis* (AcP) 178 (1978) pp. 196, 200 *et seq.*; Schäfer, Ott, *Lehrbuch der ökonomischen Analyse des Zivilrechts*, (3rd ed. 2000) pp. 478–480. In practice, however, legal security, so important in professional contract relationships in particular, seemed seriously entrenched.

interpretation and also one rule on the consequences of non-integration or nullity, § 6 AGBG); and (3) finally rules on the (public order) control of the terms, starting out with an exception of what should not be controlled (price etc., § 8 AGBG) and with a general standard (§ 9 AGBG, standard terms presumed to be abusive when considerably diverging from the default rules in the law) and continuing with a list of particular terms presumed to be abusive (§ 10 AGBG) or declared to be abusive in any case (§ 11 AGBG).

In 2002, these rules were integrated into the Civil Code. This has been criticized because the body of law was seen not to fit into a Civil Code and because there was the fear that it would change the character of it.[36] Others, on the contrary, advocated such integration vigorously, and in my view the best reason for doing so is that without a regulation of the standard terms, nowadays the practice of contract making is not regulated in the contract law parts of the Code. The core argument for integration would then be that it is important for each individual question to be more transparent where there are differences between individual contract drafting and drafting via standard contract terms.

The integration, however, remained a purely formal one, §§ 305–309 BGB largely reproducing the law on standard contract terms of 1974 (with amendments), not changing the order and not attributing the different parts to the parallel sections in the Civil Code, but keeping the standard contract terms regulation in one block. For questions of integration of standard contract terms into the contract, a place in the General Part could easily have been found. For questions of public order control, this would have been possible only in part (near §§ 134–138 BGB, dealing with the public order control in general). With respect to public order control, however, quite a few rules in the law on standard contract terms are related to specific contracts or to specific questions of breach of contract and performance and thus would have to be split up. The core question is therefore whether such a splitting up of the subject matter would have been preferable. The criterion should be whether the law on standard contract terms is, like for instance representation, one body of the law which at times applies but deals with one particular deviation from the normal type of contract making, i.e. is one particular technique of formation, or whether the law on standard contract terms is one of the now typical ('basic') forms of contract making which changes rules at various places in the system (agreement, validity, performance). In fact the latter seems to be the case. Creating the model of a really integrated law on standard contract terms would have been a thrilling en-

36 Mainly Ulmer, see discussion report in: Ernst, Zimmermann (eds.), *Zivilrechtswissenschaft und Schuldrechtsreform*, (2001) pp. 549–551; in a similar sense already before Hommelhoff, Wiedenmann, '*Allgemeine Geschäftsbedingungen gegenüber Kaufleuten und unausgehandelte Klauseln in Verbraucherverträgen*', *Zeitschrift für Wirtschaftsrecht* (ZIP) (1993) pp. 562, 564–572.

deavour, important because standard terms are nowadays possibly even the normal type of contract making.

3. Rescission and Damages

It has been pointed out that rescission and contract based damages are regulated quite separately from each other in the second book (section 1 (damages) and section 3 (rescission), again different titles). Indeed, dogma in Germany still today stresses that rescission and damages, while being the two core alternative remedies for the breach of contract, are quite diverse and that this can be seen by the mere fact that the one presupposes negligence while rescission is granted also in case of non performance or late or defective performance irrespective of negligence.[37]

This obscures the distinctions that really matter for the legal community. There are two types of contract law based damages now under German law (§ 280, §§ 281–283 BGB), the one running parallel to performance and just bridging the gap to complete and timely performance, the other substituting performance. As to the practical consequences, the two types of damages are typically less closely related to one another than damages substituting performance on the one hand and rescission on the other. This is so because in both cases, the party in breach of contract (mostly, when these questions matter, the debtor of the characteristic duty) may no longer perform. This has the consequence for him that he gets back the service or the good delivered, but now as a used good or as a service (for instance a defective expert opinion) which he cannot use for anybody else. He loses not only the gain from the deal but also to a large extent the value of the good or service delivered. This is not so in the case of damages only supplementing performance, but this is so also in case of rescission. Therefore rescission may well be much more burdensome to him than damages which only supplement, but do not substitute his duty to perform. And if one considers the requirements for damages supplementing performance, for damages substituting performance and for rescission, the requirements for the latter two are indeed more stringent typically: The creditor has to give the debtor a second chance (the German '*Nachfrist*'), whereas the 'hard' requirement of negligence (for all claims for damages, but not for rescission) is in fact a very soft one typically, especially because there is a presumption of negligence anyhow (§ 280, paragraph 1 (2) BGB).

Summarizing, one has to say that in substance the regime on damages and also very much on rescission was considerably improved in the reform of 2002, but that in architecture, the links which really matter are still not

[37] See, for instance, Canaris, '*Die Reform des Rechts der Leistungsstörungen*', *Juristen-Zeitung* (2001) pp. 499, 514.

transparent; dogma still partly stresses characteristics which rather obscure these links.

4. Other Important Distinctions with Respect to Breach of Contract

One last distinction with respect to breach of contract can only be mentioned, not explained, in this short survey. During the reform of German contract law, there had first been a draft where breach of contract was seen largely as a unitary concept – like in the UN Convention on the International Sale of Goods (CISG), very much taking the perspective of the normal client who takes any deviation from the plan of the contract performance as a basis for claiming damages or rescission. This model, however, deviated very much from the Germanic model of differentiating different types of breach (formerly with respect to its relevance, to its influence on the validity of the contract, etc.).[38] In the adopted version, there has been a step halfway back to these models of differentiation, the main legitimation being that a uniform concept of breach was just too diffuse, the patterns not appearing clearly enough.[39] It has, however, to be stressed (without explaining this here) that the differentiations which can be found nowadays are quite different in kind from those which could be found formerly: The new regime has differentiations, yes, but they no longer create diverging legal consequences or only in very exceptional cases. In other words, these differentiations only seem to be of importance (for the legal consequences). Thus, while German law seems to adhere to a model of a differentiated system of different kinds of breach of contract even today, in fact, for instance in terms of legal consequences, it is now very much a unitary system.[40] And in fact, developing different fact patterns under these circumstances seems rather problematic.

---

[38] For the multitude of differentiations which were formerly of importance, see for instance Markenisis, Lorenz, Dannemann, *supra* n. 2, pp. 398–434; Medicus, *Bürgerliches Recht*, 18th ed. (1999) pp. 175 *et seq.*; Emmerich, in: *Münchner Kommentar zum Bürgerlichen Gesetzbuch*, Vol. 2, 3rd ed. (1994), before § 275, para. 8 *et seq.* (Vol. 2, pp. 667 *et seq.*).

[39] Canaris, '*Die Reform des Rechts der Leistungsstörungen*', *Juristen-Zeitung* (JZ) (2001) p. 499; Huber, '*Das geplante Recht der Leistungsstörungen*', in: Ernst, Zimmermann (eds.), *Zivilrechtswissenschaft und Schuldrechtsreform* (2001) pp. 31, 48 *et seq.*, 142 *et seq.*; Ernst, '*Kernfragen der Schuldrechtsreform*', *Juristenzeitung* (JZ) (1994) pp. 801–809, 805 *et seq.*; Brüggemeier in: *Verhandlungen des sechzigsten Deutschen Juristentags* (1994) Vol. II/1, K 46-K 97, K 59 *et seq.*; Wilhelm, Deeg, '*Nachträgliche Unmöglichkeit und nachträgliches Unvermögen*', *Juristenzeitung* (JZ) (2001) pp. 223–233, 230 *et seq.*; Canaris, '*Zur Bedeutung der Kategorie der "Unmöglichkeit" für das Recht der Leistungsstörungen*', in: Schulze, Schulte-Nölke (eds.), *Die Schuldrechtsreform vor dem Hintergrund des Gemeinschaftsrechts* (2001) pp. 43–66, 44 *et seq.*

[40] Grundmann, '*Der Schadensersatzanspruch aus Vertrag – System und Perspektiven*', *Archiv für civilistische Praxis* (AcP) 204 (2004) pp. 569–605.

V. CONCLUSIONS

The German Civil Code has added a lot to distinguishing concepts and – perhaps even more importantly – to areas of the law within a Codification. On the other hand, the famous 'General Part' of the BGB may well be a strong argument for not integrating many fields of law into one European Code, but rather have one strong (Optional) European Contract Law Code. It is more important to have the contract law rules on the same problems integrated into one legal instrument than to have a theory of (rather weak) common denominators with other areas of the law. Let legal science do this last job! The much more evident order, an order more easily understandable to all Europeans, would probably be that of the 'life' of contract (formation, with validity; content; performance and breach, with termination), supplemented then by problems which go beyond one simple contract (assignment, multitude of creditors and debtors, chains of contracts).

The German Civil Code has, however, the advantage of being recently remodelled and of containing now a rather broad contract law, including consumer contracts, new marketing techniques, standard terms regulation, etc. It can thus serve as one model for the discussion, as a source whose materials would all have to be taken into consideration for an alternative, more approachable order.

The broad categories could then be:

(1) Formation of contracts (with) declarations of intention and consent (agreement):
  (a) validity exceptions (public order intervention for the protection of one party or of third parties); and
  (b) Duties in the phase of formation (namely information rules).
(2) (General rules on) contents of contracts.
(3) (Proper) Performance and as a consequence extinction of the primary claims flowing from the contract.
(4) Breach of contract (with remedies, in German literature the so-called secondary claims).
(5) Sections on the problems mentioned above, going beyond one simple contract ('contracts and third parties').

Here, new problems, not really regulated in the German Civil Code, seem quite important, for instance general rules on chains and networks of contracts. In my view, the German example also shows that developing a 'General Part' of contract law (as opposed to a 'General Part' of all private law) may well have its advantages – although it probably has to be the synthesis of a regulation of specific contracts, and not the starting point. But wasn't this the development in the contract law of the Community anyway?

Chapter 4
Structural Elements of the Austrian Civil Code

Martin Schauer

I. INTRODUCTION

The topic of this conference is 'The Architecture of European Codes and Contract Law' which is concerned with the question of what can be learned from national codifications that will help when creating a future European Contract Law.

The first part of the conference analyses the question of, 'The level of abstraction: Starting from contract, obligation and juristic act?' or, to express it in simpler terms: What approach should the legislator take? At first glance, the question seems to be of a rather 'technical' nature and of little theoretical interest. However, when examining the question more deeply, the issue is more profound: the system governing any contract law, or – more generally – any civil law, codification will determine whether such codification is all-encompassing and complete or whether it leaves gaps, and whether or not the applicable rules are easy to access and transparent. The system governing a codification can either help reveal, or it can create inconsistencies.

This paper will deal with the Austrian civil law codification and its possible contribution to a European codification. I will first describe the creation and development of the Austrian Civil Code (ABGB), a few of its main characteristic features, and also its need for reform (section II). In section III, I will analyze the system that governs the Austrian Civil Code, focusing on contract law as the overall topic of this conference, and show how general and specific contract law provisions are organized and systematically connected. There will be a more detailed analysis of the conclusion of

S. Grundmann, M. Schauer (eds), *The Architecture of European Codes and Contract Law*, 83–103

contracts (section IV), the scope of contractual obligations, and breach of contract (section V). Conclusive remarks (section VI) and a summary of the main points (section VII) will conclude this paper.

II. DEVELOPMENT, CHARACTERISTIC FEATURES, AND NEED FOR REFORM OF THE AUSTRIAN CIVIL CODE (ABGB)

The ABGB is one of the older codifications in Europe. It was created as part of the first 'wave' of major codifications at the turn of the 19th century and is thus on the same level as the Prussian General National Code (das *Preußische Allgemeine Landrecht*) and the Code Civil.[1] Nevertheless, in certain aspects the ABGB also shows significant differences from these codes as well as from the German Civil Code (BGB) which is almost 100 years younger.[2] The following three features are characteristic of the ABGB:

(a) The ABGB is strongly influenced by natural law,[3] for which the famous § 16 of the ABGB may serve as an example: every man 'has inherent self-evident rights' (*jeder Mensch hat 'angeborene, schon durch die Vernunft einleuchtende Rechte'*). This wording, pursuant to which every man already 'has' such rights, shows that the law is not intended to create these rights but instead assumes that these rights already exist, thus making § 16 ABGB appear to be a description of a pre-existing legal situation, created by natural law.

---

1 See Wieacker, Aufstieg, '*Fall und Krisis der Kodifikationsidee*', *Festschrift for Boehmer* (1954) pp. 34 (39 *et seq.*); on the influence of the ALR on the creation of the ABGB see Brauneder, '*Das ALR und die österreichische Privatrechtsentwicklung*', in: Dölemeyer/Mohnhaupt (eds.), *200 Jahre Allgemeines Landrecht für die preußischen Staaten* (1995) pp. 415 *et seq.*; see the statements concerning the close relationship between ABGB and Code Civil by Mayer-Maly, '*Die Auswirkungen des Allgemeinen Teils des deutschen BGB auf das österreichische Privatrecht, insbesondere auf die höchstrichterliche Rechtsprechung*', in: *100 Jahre BGB – 100 Jahre Staudinger, Staudinger Sonderband*, (1999) 41, and Kramer, '*Der Einfluß des BGB auf das schweizerische und österreichische Privatrecht*', *AcP* 200 (2000) pp. 365 (366).

2 On certain differences between ALR, BGB, and Code Civil on the one hand and the ABGB on the other hand, see the article – even though not totally free of Austrian patriotism – by Gschnitzer, '*Österreichische Eigenart im ABGB*', *ÖJZ* (1954) pp. 465 *et seq.*; on certain differences between ABGB and BGB also see the brief overview by Mayer-Maly, '*Renaissance der laesio enormis*', *Festschrift for Larenz zum 80. Geburtstag* (1983) p. 395 (402); Mayer-Maly (n. 1) p. 41.

3 Extensively Wellspacher, '*Das Naturrecht und das ABGB*', *Festschrift Jahrhundertfeier ABGB* Vol. II (1911) p. 175; with a special focus on contract law Wesener, '*Naturrechtliche und römisch-gemeinrechtliche Elemente im Vertragsrecht des ABGB*', *ZNR* (1984) p. 113; most recently also see Kramer, '*Der Beitrag des Zivilrechts zur Europäischen Rechtskultur – aus der Optik des österreichischen und schweizerischen Privatrechts*', *Jahrbuch des öffentlichen Rechts der Gegenwart*, Neue Folge Vol. 52 (2004) pp. 121 (122 *et seq.*).

(b) Another characteristic of the ABGB is its relative brevity. Consisting of 1502 articles in its original version, the Code is not only much shorter than the extremely casuistic Prussian General National Code (*das Preußische Allgemeine Landrecht*), but also shorter than the Code Civil. This was possible because the drafters of the law consciously focused on the creation of basic rules and principles and took the risk of leaving gaps.[4] This concept is reflected in § 7 ABGB (which is another provision influenced by natural law)[5] which instructs the judge in how to deal with gaps in the law. The judge must develop rules, primarily considering similar provisions in the same law, then provisions in related laws, and finally the natural principles of law (*natürliche Rechtsgrundsätze*). Today, these rules on the analogous application of laws as set forth in § 7 ABGB seem to be a matter of course; from a historical perspective, however, § 7 ABGB is rightfully deemed one of the special achievements of the ABGB.[6]

(c) A third characteristic of the ABGB is its language, which is often praised as being 'colloquial'.[7] This seems to be a bit exaggerated; however, it is true that the language style of the ABGB is in clear contrast to the German Civil Code (BGB): the ABGB was written to be descriptive and tangible rather than abstract and technical. Sometimes one can even find provisions in the ABGB that have no imperative quality but instead resemble statements from a study book.[8]

Despite all its positive features, the ABGB does have its weak points, which is almost unavoidable for a law that has been in force for almost 200 years. There are a number of reasons for this. One reason lies within the legislative methods: by passing an increasing number of special acts, many matters of law have been 'outsourced' from the ABGB. Another reason lies within the

---

4 See Bernd Mertens, *Gesetzgebungskunst im Zeitalter der Kodifikationen* (2004) pp. 329 *et seq.*, 340 *et seq.*

5 See Wellspacher, *Festschrift Jahrhundertfeier ABGB* Vol. II, pp. 175 (184 *et seq.*); Wesener, *ZNR* (1984) pp. 113 (116 *et seq.*); Kramer, *Jahrbuch des öffentlichen Rechts der Gegenwart*, Neue Folge Vol. 52, pp. 121 (123).

6 Gschnitzer, '*Geschichte des europäischen Zivilrechts im 19. und 20. Jahrhundert, entwickelt am Beispiel des österreichischen ABGB*', *JBl* (1960) p. 213 considers this a manifestation of the ingenuity of the law; on the history of its creation see Schambeck, '*Die natürlichen Rechtsgrundsätze des § 7 ABGB, Internationale Festschrift for Verosta 1980*', pp. 479 (480 *et seq.*); also see the Einleitung § 49 ALR, which also already contained a rule on gap filling (see Schulze, '*Allgemeine Rechtsgrundsätze und europäisches Privatrecht*', *ZEuP* (1993) pp. 442, 450; Kramer, '*Funktionen allgemeiner Rechtsgrundsätze – Versuch einer Strukturierung*', *Festschrift for Bydlinski* (2002) pp. 197, 206).

7 Gschnitzer, *ÖJZ* (1954) pp. 465, 468; also see Wellspacher, *Festschrift Jahrhundertfeier ABGB* Vol. II, pp. 175, 182; on the general comprehensibility and popularity of the German language codifications in the 18th and early 19th centuries in detail (including references to the ABGB) B. Mertens (n. 4), 380 *et seq.*

8 Also see *B. Mertens, Gesetzgebungskunst* 319 f.

ABGB itself: a substantial number of its provisions have become outdated and are de facto dead law. At the same time, the ABGB does not always meet modern demands, which is why the courts are increasingly forced to further develop the law. Therefore, the text of the law only partly reflects legal reality. All these factors contribute to the ABGB no longer being fully able to take 'overall responsibility'[9] as a codification for the civil law system. As a consequence, its future is not clear. While some consider a new codification an option,[10] others are cautious and do not see a need for action.[11] What surprises me is that the slowly materializing plans for a civil law codification on a European level seem to weaken rather than strengthen the reform efforts in Austria. In Germany the situation is different. There, one of the arguments used in favour of a modernization of the Law of Obligations (*Schuldrecht*) in 2002[12] was that a more current codification would allow Germany to more strongly influence European legal development.[13] In Austria, however – at least partly – a 'wait and see' attitude seems to prevail; an argument frequently used is: Why reform the Law of Obligations or even risk a new codification, given that there might be a European codification within a foreseeable period?[14]

III. THE SYSTEM GOVERNING THE ABGB

1. Overview

The ABGB is governed by the Roman law 'institutions system'; this puts it in close proximity to the Code Civil,[15] but without the two codifications being organized the same way. The institutions system is divided into three basic areas: *personae* (law of persons), *res* (law of property), and *actiones* (actions). The ABGB generally follows this system without, however, completely

9 Graf, ABGB forever?, in: Fischer-Czermak, Hopf and Schauer (eds.), *Das ABGB auf dem Weg in das 3. Jahrtausend* (2003) p. 1 (4).

10 Eg Graf (n. 9) p. 1 (16).

11 This was most recently stated – in relation to the Law of Obligations – by Welser, '*Braucht Österreich ein neues Schuldrecht?*', *Festschrift for Michalek* (2005) pp. 391 *et seq.*

12 On general aspects, Grundmann, Germany and the *Schuldrechtsmodernisierung*, *ERCL 1* (2005) p. 129.

13 See for example Weis, *Einführung in den Diskussionsentwurf*, in: Ernst and Zimmermann (eds.), *Zivilrechtswissenschaft und Schuldrechtsreform* (2001) pp. 25, 28 *et seq.*

14 Most recently – concerning the Law of Obligations – Welser, *Festschrift for Michalek* (2005) pp. 391 (399).

15 See Ranieri, *Europäisches Obligationenrecht* (2003) pp. 15 *et seq.*; on the relevance of the institutions system for the Code Civil also see Ferid and Sonnenberger, *Das Französische Zivilrecht* (1994), Vol. I/1, A 313. On the different organization of the ALR see Dernburg, *Lehrbuch des Preußischen Privatrechts und der Privatrechtsnormen des Reichs*, Vol. I, (1879) pp. 13 *et seq.*; Eccius, *Preußisches Privatrecht*, Vol. I (1896) pp. 23 *et seq.*

adhering to it.[16] It starts with a brief introduction dealing with the validity and interpretation of laws, followed by the First Section 'On the Law of Persons' dealing with the law of persons and family law. The Second Section 'On the Law of Property' deals with – speaking in pandectist terms – property law, inheritance law, and the Law of Obligations. The Third Section is on 'Joint Provisions on the Law of Persons and the Law of Property'.

Figure 1: A simplified overview of the organization of the ABGB

Introduction (§§ 1–16) First Section: On the Law of Persons (§§ 15–283)	– Sources of law and application – Law of persons – Certain parts of family law
Second Section: On the Law of Property (§§ 285–1341) – On things and their legal categorization (§§ 285–308) – First Subsection: On *in rem* rights (§§ 309–858) – Second Subsection: On personal rights in property (§§ 859–1341)	– Legal categories of things – Law of in rem rights – Inheritance law – Law of Obligations (contracts, torts)
Third Section: Joint Provisions on the Law of Persons and the Law of Property (§§ 1342–1502)	– 'Securing' of rights and obligations (e.g. surety agreements) – Modification of rights and obligations (e.g. assignment, substitution) – Termination of rights and obligations – Statute of limitations, adverse possession (*Ersitzung*)

As one can see from the number of provisions contained in each section, the vast majority of legal provisions deal with 'Property Law', located in the Second Section, with contract law being subsumed under the very widely understood term 'property law'.

[16] Tabular comparison between the institutions system and the organization of the ABGB, see Kreller, *Römische Rechtsgeschichte* (1948) p. 86.

2. The Contract as a 'Starting Point'

a. The Contract in the ABGB

The above overview shows that the ABGB does not contain a 'Section Dealing with General Issues' (*Allgemeiner Teil*). This is not surprising, considering the fact that the Roman law institutions system did not contain such a section. The concept of a Section Dealing with General Issues is the result of the legal developments in the 18th and early 19th centuries,[17] which apparently came too late to influence the ABGB.[18]

This brings us to the question of how the ABGB deals with those issues on legal transactions (*Rechtsgeschäfte*) that are typically dealt with in a section dealing with general issues. The answer is simple: the provisions are not 'anchored' to an abstract legal transaction (*Rechtsgeschäft*) as such, but instead to the contract. For a better understanding, let us take a closer look at the Second Subsection (*Zweite Abteilung*) of the Second Section (*Zweiter Teil*) of the ABGB 'On personal rights in property': It starts with the 17th chapter (*Hauptstück*) 'On contracts and legal transactions in general',[19] which contains provisions on the conclusion of contracts, defects in concluding contracts (in Austria also called 'root defects'[20]) – e.g. mistake, fraud, duress, violation of law or public policy – and on the formal requirements for contracts. This Chapter further contains provisions on the interpretation of contracts and on the scope of obligations thereunder (i.e. on when, where, and how a contract is to be performed). Also, this Chapter deals with various types of breach of contract that in legal theory are summarily called 'breach of contract' (*Leistungsstörung*). It shows that numerous provisions are concentrated in this Chapter that would, in the pandectist system, be contained either in the 'Section Dealing with General Issues' (*Allgemeiner Teil*) or in the 'Law of Obligations' (*Schuldrecht*).

The following Chapters (*Hauptstücke* 18–29) contain special provisions on specific types of contracts, such as purchase, gift, lease, and service contracts. It is noteworthy that contracts with a family law character, i.e. the so-called 'pre or postnuptial contracts' (*Ehepakte*) are also regulated here. The 30th Chapter, dealing with damages law, concludes the Second Section.

The following chart gives a partial overview of the organization of the Second Subsection (*Zweite Abteilung*) of the Second Section (*Zweiter Teil*) of the ABGB.

---

17 See Schmoeckel, in: Schmoeckel, Rückert and Zimmermann (eds.), *Historisch-kritischer Kommentar zum BGB* Vol. I (2003) vor § 1, *Der Allgemeine Teil in der Ordnung des BGB* (Rz 14 ff *zur Entwicklung des Allgemeinen Teils*).

18 On the influence on legislation of the development by legal theory of a section dealing with general issues, see B. Mertens (n. 4) pp. 446 *et seq*.

19 On the intellectual and philosophical basis for this Chapter, particularly on Zeiller's influence on its creation, see the extensive analysis at Wesener, Zeillers Lehre '*von Verträgen überhaupt*', in: Selb and Hofmeister (eds.), *Forschungsband Franz von Zeiller* (1980) p. 248.

20 Also see the reference in Grundmann's paper, II. 1.

Figure 2: Overview of Second Subsection

Second Subsection: On personal rights in property (§§ 859–937)	
– 17th Chapter: On contracts and legal transactions in general (§§ 859–937)	e.g.: – Conclusion of contracts – Mistake, fraud, duress – Violation of law or public policy – Formal requirements for contracts – Scope of obligations – Obligor's delay – Breach of contract
– 18th–29th Chapters: Special provisions on specific types of contracts	e.g.: – Purchase contract – Gift contract – Lease contract (*Miete, Pacht*) – Service contract – also: pre or postnuptial contracts (*Ehepakte*)
– 30th Chapter:	Damages law

The fact that the ABGB focuses on contracts as the basis for provisions on legal transactions might give rise to the question of what rules are to apply in case of unilateral legal transactions (*einseitige Rechtsgeschäfte*). The answer is not particularly difficult, given that the existing gaps can usually be closed by way of analogy. Let me give the following example: the acceptance (of an offer) that leads to the creation of a contract is considered to be timely if the recipient of such acceptance has received it within the acceptance period (§ 862a ABGB). This rule lays down the receipt principle (*Zugangsprinzip*) that is characteristic of Austrian as well as German contract law. Despite the fact that the above-quoted provision, for its immediate scope of application, only refers to the acceptance (of an offer) that leads to a contract being concluded, it is absolutely undisputed that it also applies to all other declarations that need to be received by the recipient in order to become effective (*empfangsbedürftige Erklärungen*).[21]

I already mentioned that important parts of what would typically belong to a Section Dealing with General Issues as such or a Section Dealing with General Issues of the Law of Obligations are contained in the 17th Chapter. This, however, does not mean that everything, or at least a large part, of

[21] See F. Bydlinski, *Juristische Methodenlehre und Rechtsbegriff* (1991) pp. 477 *et seq.*

what we today consider belongs in the Section Dealing with General Issues or a Section Dealing with General Issues of the Law of Obligations is actually contained in the 17th Chapter. On the contrary: we find provisions spread over the ABGB that would belong together in the pandectist system. For example, the provisions on the personal capacity (*Geschäftsfähigkeit*) of a person are – appropriately – located in the First Section on the Law of Persons (§ 151 *et seq.* ABGB). A directly related provision can be found – out of context for that matter – as part of the provisions on the conclusion of contracts (§ 865 ABGB).

b. The 'Trialism' of Austrian Contract Law

Austrian contract law is characterized by another feature: it is not entirely contained in the ABGB. There are two additional sources of law that are important, though their applicability is limited to certain types of persons and entities. On the one hand, there is the Commercial Code (*Handelsgesetzbuch* (HGB)), which in its fourth Book contains specific provisions on contracts that partly concern issues typically regulated in a Section Dealing with General Issues, and partly concern issues typically regulated in the Law of Obligations. The HGB applies to merchants (*Kaufleute*); however, the contract-related provisions usually also apply to any person dealing with a merchant, even if such a person is not a merchant. As far as the HGB is concerned, Austrian and German law are almost completely identical because the German HGB also applies in Austria.

On the other hand, there is the Consumer Protection Act (*Konsumentenschutzgesetz* (KSchG)), which contains specific protective provisions on contracts between businesses and consumers. Just like the HGB, the Consumer Protection Act also contains provisions typically belonging to a section dealing with general issues as such or to the 'Law of Obligations'. This spreading of provisions that concern the same area of law over three legal acts is often called the 'trialism of contract law'.[22]

This system cannot be recommended as a model for a European codification. The fact that both the commercial and the consumer protection provisions are only specific manifestations of *one* business contract law, serves as a strong argument against them being kept separate.[23] And placing them

[22] Kramer, '*Handelsgeschäfte – eine rechtsvergleichende Skizze zur rechtsgeschäftlichen Sonderbehandlung unternehmerischer Kontrahenten*', *Festschrift for Ostheim* (1990) pp. 299 (306); Schauer, '*Integration des Handels- und Unternehmensrechts in das ABGB?*', in: Fischer-Czermak, Hopf and Schauer (eds.), *Das ABGB auf dem Weg in das 3. Jahrtausend* (2003) pp. 137 (151).

[23] Extensively: Grundmann, '*Generalreferat: Internationalisierung und Reform des deutschen Kaufrechts*', in: Grundmann, Medicus and Rolland (eds.), *Europäisches Kaufgewährleistungsrecht* (2000) pp. 281, 284 *et seq.*; Grundmann, Verbraucherrecht, Unternehmensrecht, '*Privatrecht – warum sind sich UN-Kaufrecht und EU-Kaufrechts-Richtlinie so ähnlich?*', *AcP* 202 (2002) pp. 40, 68 *et seq.*; for Austrian law also Schauer (n. 22) pp. 137, 151 *et seq.*

both together in a general codification would be justified and would clearly be beneficial: first, this would show that one or the other provision that today is considered a special provision might be generalized and could take its place in a general codification. Secondly, the legislator would have to focus on, and justify, deviations from the general rules, and remaining inconsistencies would become more apparent. Thirdly, the law would become more transparent for those who have to apply it. It is therefore not surprising that, in the European codifications of the current generation, the 'monistic codification' model that includes the special rules for consumer transactions and commercial transaction is gaining influence.[24]

3. The Influence of German Law on the Development of Austrian Law

The above brief overview of the structure of the ABGB would be incomplete if we did not consider the substantial influence of the (pandectist) historical school of law on the development of Austrian law. This influence has had its effects on two levels: (1) on legislation; and (2) on legal theory.

In the second half of the 19th century, the need for reform of the ABGB became apparent. The problem intensified when Germany, after the BGB entering into force in 1900, had a much more modern codification, which benefited from the rich fruit of legal science in the 19th century. In Austria, the future of the ABGB became a subject of discussion. As a result, three partial amendments (*Teilnovellen*) were passed[25] that entered into force in 1914 through 1916 and whose contents were partly inspired by the *BGB*.[26] It is noteworthy that the title of the 17th Chapter was changed: The original title 'On contracts in general' was replaced by the wider title 'On contracts and legal transactions in general'.[27] This makes the influence of German legal theory visible.[28] The organization of the law, however, remained unchanged,[29] just like the fact that the provisions contained in this Chapter deal mainly with contracts.

In addition, legal scholars required a more extensive orientation towards German law. *Moriz von Wellspacher*, one of the most renowned Austrian civil law scholars at the turn of the 20th century, on the occasion of giving

---

[24] See Schauer (n. 22), pp. 137, 149 *et seq.*

[25] On the creation and development: Dölemeyer, *Die drei Teilnovellen zum ABGB* (1914–1916), in: Coing (ed.), *Handbuch der Quellen und Literatur der neueren europäischen Privatrechtsgeschichte*, Vol. III/2 (1982) pp. 1782 *et seq.*

[26] See Kramer, *AcP* 200 (2000) pp. 365, 386 *et seq.*; Dölemeyer (n. 25), pp. 1782, 1787 *et seq.*

[27] See for instance Schlesinger in: Klang (ed.), *Kommentar zum Allgemeinen Bürgerlichen Gesetzbuch*, Vol. II/2 (1934) p. 7.

[28] Kramer, *AcP* 200 (2000) pp. 365 (386); Ranieri (n. 15) p. 17, ignoring the change of the title, does not take this into consideration.

[29] Correct in this respect: Ranieri (n. 15) p. 17.

his inaugural lecture at the university in 1907, complained about the – in his opinion – unsatisfactory state of Austrian legal theory, his statements culminating in these words: 'The only possible way that I see is to again follow German legal theory and to follow it to the new grounds where it now stands, to the grounds of the German BGB. The German theory of civil law has to take the place in Austrian civil law that has so far been taken by the *ius commune* of the historical school of law . . . ; we need to attempt to relate Austrian law to German theory to the extent at all possible, and to quasi adjust our Civil Code to German law.'[30]

Conformity – if not with the laws themselves, then at least with the legal theory – with German law (that was considered more modern) was the programmatic demand of the time. Its effects – a number of non-beneficial developments meanwhile having been corrected – are still visible today in many areas of Austrian civil law.[31] The influence of German pandectism becomes most obvious with the fact that all overall descriptions of Austrian civil law, including the study books, follow the pandectist system rather than the institutions system. One cannot overestimate this fact: the law is organized following the institutions system, but we think (legally) within the categories of the pandectist system. In legal theory, we therefore acknowledge a 'Section Dealing with General Issues' that does not even exist in the law. Thinking in pandectist categories has become so matter-of-fact that in everyday legal practice, for example, the analogous application to unilateral legal transactions (*einseitige Rechtsgeschäfte*) of the provisions on the conclusion of contracts is no longer considered an issue.

IV. CONCLUSION OF CONTRACTS

1. General

As already mentioned, the provisions on the conclusion of contracts are located in the 17th Chapter, where one will find the rules on offer and acceptance, validity periods of offers, and the requirement for offer and acceptance to be received in order to become effective.[32] The 17th Chapter further contains provisions on the interpretation of contracts, on mistake, fraud, and duress, on contracts that violate the law or public policy, on the formal requirements for contracts, and on conditions. These rules fundamentally apply to all contracts, including contracts concluded in the areas of family law or inheritance law. Nevertheless, since family law and inheritance law contain so many special provisions on contracts, the applicability of the 17th Chapter in many aspects is limited to the Law of Obligations and

[30] v. Wellspacher, *Die Zukunft der österreichischen Privatrechtswissenschaft* (1907) pp. 11 *et seq.*
[31] Also see Kramer, *AcP* 200 (2000) pp. 389 *et seq.*
[32] On the influence of the BGB: Kramer, *AcP* 200 (2000) pp. 386 *et seq.*

Property Law. Unilateral legal transactions (*einseitige Rechtsgeschäfte*) are subject to these rules by way of analogy to the greatest extent possible. In general, this organization has proven to be functional. A Section Dealing with General Issues as it is contained in the BGB has so far not been really missed.

2. Deficits and Gaps

Nevertheless, I would like to draw the reader's attention to certain deficits and gaps:

First, as with many other legal systems, the ABGB does not contain a general provision on obligations in the pre-contractual phase, in particular on duties to furnish information. However, this issue was not totally unknown to the authors of the ABGB. Therefore, the original version of the ABGB, almost 200 years ago, already contained a number of pro-visions which allowed – even though limited to specific pre-contractual situations – the inference of an obligation to provide pre-contractual information (in particular, § 866,[33] § 874, § 878 ABGB).[34] Legal theory in later years was able to develop a general principle from these special rules, which principle laid the foundation for what we know today as *culpa in contrahendo*.[35] Specific information obligations with a view to protecting consumers usually have their roots in European law and are not contained in the ABGB, but rather in the Consumer Protection Act and other ancillary laws.

The growing understanding of the importance of pre-contractual obligations, specifically the obligation to furnish pre-contractual information, should be acknowledged by the European legislator by stipulating it in a general provision. The German BGB appropriately took this step upon the occasion of modernizing the Law of Obligations (§ 311 (2) BGB). It is yet another issue whether the numerous detailed obligations to furnish information as provided in consumer protection law should be integrated in the codification of a European Contract Law. I would recommend against it. A codification limited to principles is the wrong place to put them.[36] To the extent that obligations to furnish information concern specific types of contracts, they might be provided for together with the other specific rules on such contracts.

33 This provision was repealed by BGBl I 2000/135.

34 See, however, ALR I 5 § 284, which already contained a general provision for pre-contractual obligations.

35 For Austrian law, fundamentally Frotz, '*Die rechtsdogmatische Einordnung der culpa in contrahendo*', *Gedenkschrift for Gschnitzer* (1969) p. 163 and first of all Welser, *Vertretung ohne Vollmacht* (1970); Welser, '*Das Verschulden beim Vertragsschluß im österreichischen bürgerlichen Recht*', *ÖJZ* (1973) p. 281.

36 Also see the delegation to administrative regulations in art. 238 ff of the German EGBGB.

Secondly, an important instrument of consumer protection is the right to terminate the contract (*vom Vertrag zurücktreten*). As an analysis of Austrian law performed in 2001 shows, there are at least 29 different rights of termination with a consumer protection orientation;[37] meanwhile, the number has grown even more. However, these rights are not located in the ABGB, but instead in the Consumer Protection Act and in numerous other ancillary laws. These provisions are characterized by a barely surmountable level of non-homogeneity, both in respect of the prerequisites for termination and the legal consequences of termination. The reason for this rather unsatisfactory situation lies less with Austrian law than with European community law, because most of these rights of termination are based on European consumer protection directives passed as Austrian laws. Therefore, a European codification could, and should, aim at simplifying and systematizing consumer protection motivated termination rights. The commission notification on European Contract Law gives hope that the commission is aware of this issue.[38] If a European Contract Law actually materializes, the provisions on the conclusion and termination of contracts should be concentrated in one section.

Thirdly, the 17th Chapter does not contain any provisions on agency (*Stellvertretung*). In the 22nd Chapter of the ABGB, there are joint provisions, entitled 'Power of Attorney Agreement', on powers of attorney and on agreements by which one party to the agreement undertakes to enter into a legal transaction on behalf of the other party to the agreement (*Auftragsvertrag*).[39] Today, however, following German legal theory (Section II.C.2 above), legal scholars and courts strictly distinguish between the two instruments and acknowledge the 'abstract nature' of the power of attorney.[40]

When a European codification is drafted, I certainly recommend including an agency section, whose scope should depend on the scope of the codification itself. If a European Civil Code were created, it would be advisable – to the extent this can be done by general rules – to include provisions on all types of agencies, including, but not limited to, agency by operation of law (*gesetzliche Vertretung*) for persons without legal capacity (*geschäftsunfähig*) and agency by appointment to an office (*organschaftliche Vertretung*). If the codification were limited to a European Contract Law, it would be sufficient to include a provision on powers of attorney (*Vollmacht*). In this context, the introduction of standardized powers of attorney to be issued by businesses

37 Overview in Kalss and Lurger, *Rücktrittrechte* (2001) p. 9; critical also Welser, *Festschrift for Michalek* (2005) pp. 391, 394.

38 See the Communication from the Commission to the European Parliament and the Council – European Contract Law and the revision of the *acquis*, 11 October, 2004, COM(2004) 651 final, p. 4.

39 See Ranieri, (n. 15), pp. 216 *et seq*.

40 Koziol and Welser, *Bürgerliches Recht*, Vol. I (2002) p. 183.

might be con-sidered, such as for example the general commercial power of attorney (*Prokura*) that exists under German and Austrian commercial law.

3. General Terms and Conditions

A particular problem in connection with the conclusion of a contract is how to regulate general terms and conditions ('General Terms', AGB). Under Austrian law, the relevant provisions are spread through a number of laws: the ABGB contains two general provisions concerning validity and contents of General Terms (§ 864a, § 879 (3) ABGB). Since they are located in the ABGB, these provisions apply to all General Terms, including those that are agreed upon between businesses.[41] Other provisions can be found in the Consumer Protection Act. These include, for example, an extensive list of prohibited terms in contracts, which is partly based on the Annex to the Council Directive 93/13/EEC of 5 April 1993 on unfair terms in consumer contracts ('Unfair Terms Directive') and the implementation of the transparency requirement pursuant to article 5 of the Unfair Terms Directive. Since these provisions are located in the Consumer Protection Act, they are applicable only to contracts between businesses and consumers, which complies with the Directive. However, within the Austrian legal system, this legislative distinction does not seem justified. Therefore, the question has already been raised as to whether the transparency requirement should apply analogously to general terms between businesses.[42]

Regulating General Terms has two main aspects: their valid inclusion (*Einbeziehung*) in a contract (inclusion regulation); and the legality of their contents (contents regulation), with inclusion regulation concerning the inclusion of General Terms as a complete set of rules as well as the inclusion of individual terms. It is apparent that all of the above questions have to do with the general issues concerning the conclusion of contracts. As to inclusion, we are dealing with the problem of what has been validly agreed at all. As to contents, we are dealing with the question of whether what is agreed is in line with the values of our legal system. As one can see, these are general issues rather than specific issues occurring in connection with specific types of contracts. These issues are clear arguments in favour of providing special rules on General Terms together with the general rules on the conclusion and validity of contracts. This is certainly true for general rules on the inclusion and contents of General Terms. The same is probably true for the lists of prohibited terms, the vast majority of which apply to all types of consumer

---

[41] Unclear Ranieri (n. 15) pp. 176 *et seq*., pursuant to whose statements even § 864a ABGB seems to only relate to contracts between businesses and consumers (correct, however, 197).

[42] See extensively – supporting the analogy – Leitner, *Das Transparenzgebot* (2005) pp. 129 *et seq*.

contracts rather than just specific types of contracts.[43] This concept would still allow distinctions as to whether certain regulations should apply only to contracts between businesses and consumers, or to contracts between businesses also.

V. OBLIGATION AND BREACH OF CONTRACT

1. Obligations

The ABGB contains general rules on the scope of obligations. As mentioned above, these are largely located in the 17th Chapter. There we find provisions on when and where the obligor has to perform (§§ 902 *et seq.* ABGB). If an obligation may be performed in more than one way (alternative obligation (*Wahlschuld*)), there is a rule as to who is entitled to choose the way it is performed (§§ 906 *et seq.* ABGB). We further find provisions on down payments (*Angelder*) and termination fees (*Reugelder*) (§§ 908 *et seq.* ABGB) and on multiple obligees or obligors (§§ 888 *et seq.* ABGB). However, these provisions are incomplete and must be completed by analogous application of specific rules. Let me illustrate this with the following two examples: An express provision to the effect that one party to a contract is obligated to perform only if the other party is also prepared to perform (performance for performance) (*Erfüllung Zug um Zug*; §§ 1052, 1062 ABGB) only exists in connection with a barter agreement (*Tausch*) and a purchase contract. Nevertheless, Austrian law acknowledges that this rule is a general principle applicable to all bilateral contracts (*entgeltliche Verträge*).[44] The second example: As already mentioned, the Fourth Book of the Commercial Code contains special provisions on contracts; a number of these, which are not tailored to merchants, are analogously applied in civil law. This is true, for example, for § 360 HGB,[45] pursuant to which obligations to supply unascertained goods (*Gattungsschulden*) may be performed by delivering goods of medium type and quality unless otherwise agreed.

2. Breach of Contract

a. Types and Architecture

Breach of contract law deals with the non-conforming performance of a contract. The relevant Austrian set of rules is characterized by a complex interplay of generalizing and distinguishing features. Let me briefly explain this:

43 Like §§ 308, 309 of the German BGB after modernization of the Law of Obligations.
44 See Aicher in: Rummel (ed.), *Kommentar zum Allgemeinen bürgerlichen Gesetzbuch*, Vol. 1 (2000) § 1052 Rz 1, 4; Koziol and Welser, *Bürgerliches Recht*, Vol. II (2001) p. 38.
45 Koziol and Welser (n. 44) p. 26.

(i) Breach of contract law is general in that the majority of its rules apply to all types of bilateral contracts (*entgeltliche Verträge*). The ABGB therefore does not differentiate between breaches of contract depending on the type of contract being breached, even though there are a few specific rules on individual types of contracts.

(ii) Breach of contract law does differentiate in that it is not based on the concept of one uniform breach of contract scenario. Instead, we distinguish between several types of breach of contract that lead to different legal consequences. This sometimes raises complicated issues in deciding which rules are applicable. In addition, certain breach of contract categories are insufficiently regulated. This is true, for example, for the obligee's delay (*Gläubigerverzug*), in respect of which § 1419 ABGB only provides that the obligee shall bear the 'detrimental consequences'.[46] The law does not explain what this means, leaving it to legal scholars and the courts to determine the consequences of an obligee's delay.[47]

Austrian law distinguishes among the following types of breach of contract: If the obligor does not perform although performance is still possible, this is called a 'delay' (*Verzug*). As for the legal consequences of a delay, we need to determine whether or not such delay is the obligor's fault. If the contract cannot be performed for reasons within the obligee's sphere of responsibility, this is called an 'obligee's delay' (*Gläubigerverzug*). If performance of the contract is prevented by insurmountable obstacles, this is called 'impossibility' (*Unmöglichkeit*). Here, one needs to determine whether performance was already impossible at the time the contract was concluded (initial impossibility) or whether it became impossible thereafter (subsequent impossibility). Initial impossibility, however, is not considered a case of breach of contract; instead, it prevents the valid conclusion of the contract. However, legal scholars and courts have severely restricted the applicability of the relevant provision (§ 878 ABGB) so that in most cases of initial impossibility one actually has to assume that the contract is nevertheless valid. If the obligee's performance was non-conforming, this is a case of breach of warranty (*Gewährleistung*). The legal consequences depend on the type of non-conformity. The relevant legal provisions are based on a generalizing transformation of the Council Directive on the Sale of Consumer Goods and Associated Guarantees.

Further, Austrian law contains the *laesio enormis*,[48] a legal instrument rooted in the late Roman period, offering one party the possibility of terminating a contract if the value of the other party's performance is

46 In addition, the obligor can deposit the goods with the court (§ 1425 ABGB).

47 See for example Koziol and Welser (n. 44) pp. 57 *et seq.*

48 The *laesio enormis* probably goes back to Diokletian; see Kaser, *Das Römische Privatrecht*, Vol. II (1975) pp. 389 *et seq.*; Pennitz, '*Zur Anfechtung wegen laesio enormis im römischen Recht, Festschrift for Mayer-Maly*' (2002) pp. 575, 576 *et seq.*

less than 50 per cent of the value of the first party's performance. However, there is a dispute whether the *laesio enormis* is really a breach of contract issue or rather a type of mistake.[49]

(iii) The above-described distinctions between the various types of breach of contract are reflected in the relevant legal provisions, which are widely distributed throughout the ABGB. While the majority of provisions are located in the 17th Chapter, several provisions have been put into a totally different systematic context. For example, the rules on payment default interest are located in the Chapter on Damages Law, and the provisions on obligee's delay and on subsequent impossibility not the obligor's fault can be found under 'The Ending of Rights and Obligations' (*Aufhebung der Rechte und Verbindlichkeiten*).

The following is a rough overview of the organization of Austrian breach of contract law:

Figure 3: Overview of the organization of Austrian breach of contract law

Obligor's delay	– not due to fault	2nd Section, 17th Chapter – §§ 918, 919
	– due to fault	2nd Section, 17th Chapter – §§ 918, 919, 921
	– default interest	2nd Section, 30th Chapter – § 1333
Obligee's delay		3rd Section, 3th Chapter – § 1419
Impossibility	– initial (root defect)	2nd Section, 17th Chapter – § 878
	– subsequent, not due to fault	3rd Section, 3rd Chapter – § 1447
	– subsequent, due to fault	2nd Section, 17th Chapter – §§ 920, 921
Breach of warranty		2nd Section, 17th Chapter – §§ 922–933b
Laesio enormis		2nd Section, 17th Chapter – §§ 934, 935

[49] Expressly arguing that it is a specific type of mistake P. Bydlinski, '*Die Stellung der laesio enormis im Vertragsrecht*', *JBl* (1983) pp. 410 *et seq.*; see also Koziol and Welser (n. 44) p. 93, pursuant to which it is not a breach of contract 'within the actual meaning of the term'.

What conclusions can we draw from this for a European Civil Code? General breach of contract rules having prevalence over contract-specific provisions certainly has proven to be a successful model. The purchase contract, the service contract, and other bilateral contracts have enough in common to be subject to a joint breach of contract law. Austrian legislation recently even intensified the generalization of breach of contract law. Upon the occasion of amending the breach of warranty regime,[50] when implementing the Council Directive on the Sale of Consumer Goods and Associated Guarantees, a special provision for service contracts was removed[51] without this leading to any problems. There is of course always the possibility that provisions need to be passed that are specific to certain contracts; however, this does not preclude the general model being appropriate and being recommended for a European codification.

It has become apparent that Austrian law, with its differentiating approach, does not follow the more modern system which has only one uniform type of breach of contract,[52] as is the case mainly for the CISG, the Principles of European Contract Law, the Unidroit-Principles, and – since the modernization of the Law of Obligations – largely for German law.[53] In this respect, basing a European codification on Austrian law does not seem advisable, given the fact that the uniform model has clear advantages over the differentiating system. First, the uniform model is systematically simpler and clearer. It avoids certain problems in deciding which provisions apply. For example, the difficult distinction between an obligor delivering goods other than the ones agreed upon (*aliud*), and delivering non-conforming goods, is obsolete in the CISG.[54] At the same time, one should not overlook the fact that even the uniform model requires certain differentiations because it provides different remedies. Second, the uniform model is more suited than the differentiating system to developing a coherent system free from inconsistencies.

b. Termination and Damages

A breach of contract may result in the obligee suffering damage. If the obligee terminates the contract as a result of the obligor's breach, the question arises of what the relationship is between the termination of the contract

[50] BGBl I 2001/48.

[51] See Welser/B. Jud, *Die neue Gewährleistung* (2001) Vorbem Rz 18, § 1167 ABGB Rz 1.

[52] On comparative law, Zweigert and Kötz, *Einführung in die Rechtsvergleichung* (1996) pp. 485 *et seq.*, 501 *et seq.*; also see Ranieri (n. 15) 271 *et seq.*

[53] More details in Grundmann, *ERCL* 1 (2005) pp. 129, 133 *et seq.*

[54] Schwenzer in: Schlechtriem and Schwenzer (eds.), *Kommentar zum Einheitlichen UN-Kaufrecht – CISG* (2004), art. 35 Rz 9; also see Magnus in: J. von Staudinger's, *Kommentar zum Bürgerlichen Gesetzbuch mit Einführungsgesetz und Nebengesetzen – Wiener UN-Kaufrecht* (CISG) (2005) art. 35 Rz 9.

and damages. We need to examine two issues: First, does the obligee have to give the obligor a second chance to fulfil the contract before the obligee is entitled to terminate the contract? Despite the breach of contract law following the differentiating model, we can say – slightly simplifying – that the obligee must always grant the obligor a grace period (provided that performance is still possible and reasonably acceptable) before the obligee may terminate the contract. Secondly, is the obligee entitled to damages despite having terminated the contract? Under Austrian law, the termination of the contract leaves the right to damages unaffected (§ 921 ABGB, also see § 933a ABGB). In this respect, Austrian law, which already introduced this rule with the Third Partial Amendment in 1916, proves to be more modern than German law[55] which only decided to adopt this rule as part of the modernization of the Law of Obligations in 2002. The damages claim is aimed at monetarily putting the obligee into the same position as if the contract had been properly fulfilled ('interest in fulfillment' (*Erfüllungsinteresse*)). There is one exception to this: if performance was already impossible at the time the contract was concluded, the obligee is only entitled to compensation for the damage incurred as a consequence of the obligee's reliance on the validity of the contract ('reliance damage' (*Vertrauensschaden*)).[56] This is due to the fact that under Austrian law an obligor's promise to perform is usually not considered a guarantee for the performance for which the obligor would be liable under any circumstances.

3. Deficits and Gaps

Grundmann, in his paper (III.3), complains that German law has two deficiencies in that it does not sufficiently consider the specific characteristics of long-term legal relationships and of network contracts. Austrian law also lacks special provisions for these types of legal relationships and contracts. The German legislator resolved this issue as part of the modernization of the Law of Obligations by introducing the new § 314 BGB that permits any party to a long-term contract to terminate the contract for cause. In Austria,

[55] Welser, *Festschrift for Michalek* (2005) pp. 391 (397) recently pointed this out again; also see Welser, '*Reform des österreichischen Leistungsstörungsrechts*', in Fischer-Czermak, Hopf and Schauer (eds.), *Das ABGB auf dem Weg in das 3. Jahrtausend* (2003) pp. 63, 76 *et seq.*

[56] Koziol and Welser (n. 40) p. 157; Lukas, '*Zur Haftung beim anfänglich unbehebbaren Mangel*', *JBl* (1992) pp. 11, 27 *et seq.*; Welser and B. Jud, *Die neue Gewährleistung* (2001) § 933a Rz 12; OGH (Austrian Supreme Court) RdW (1998) p. 189; EvBl 2003/128; of a different opinion primarily Reischauer in: Rummel (ed.), *Kommentar zum Allgemeinen bürgerlichen Gesetzbuch*, Vol. 1 (2000) § 920 Rz 18a, who, however, also presumes that § 1298 ABGB is applicable; of the same opinion B. Jud, *Schadenersatz wegen mangelhafter Leistung* (2003) pp. 117 *et seq.*; W. Faber, *Handbuch zum neuen Gewährleistungsrecht* (2001) pp. 182 *et seq.*

in order to reach this result one needed to develop, by way of analogy, a general principle out of a number of special provisions related to individual types of contracts.[57] A general rule would definitely be advisable for a European codification.

As for network contracts, special rules are lacking in Austrian law as well as in most other legal systems. However, this is due less to the fault of the Austrian legislator than due to the fact that special rules for network contracts[58] have not yet developed far enough to allow their codification.

Contract Law is often understood as the law concerning market related exchange transactions. This is mostly correct. However, one should not overlook the fact that non-market related contracts also exist, mainly meaning contracts without consideration (*unentgeltliche Rechtsgeschäfte*), such as the gift contract (*Schenkungsvertrag*). Contracts without consideration are partly subject to different rules, e.g. concerning interpretation and breach of contract. The ABGB does not contain a section with general rules for contracts without consideration. However, it certainly takes them into consideration by, for instance, providing a special rule on interpretation (§ 915 ABGB); by limiting the breach of contract rules to bilateral contracts, which *e contrario* do not apply to contracts without consideration (§§ 918 *et seq*. ABGB); and by dedicating a special chapter to gift contracts (Second Section, 18th Chapter). When preparing a European Contract Law, the theory on contracts without consideration could be explored more profoundly and possibly these contracts could be granted more attention in the general provisions on contracts.

VI. CONCLUDING REMARKS

Let us return to the original question: What contributions can national law, can Austrian civil law, make towards the architecture of a European Contract Law? Our deliberations on Austrian law shall end with two conclusive remarks: one probably obvious and almost trivial; the other perhaps slightly provocative.

First, the architecture of a European codification will primarily depend on the scope of such a codification. Grundmann, in his paper (I.2), pointed out that it makes a fundamental difference whether the codification encompasses the entire civil law or only the law of contracts. He is probably correct in assuming that a European Contract Law is substantially more probable than of an overall civil law codification. Should an all-encompassing European

[57] Rummel in: Rummel (ed.), *Kommentar zum Allgemeinen bürgerlichen Gesetzbuch*, Vol. 1 (2000) § 859 Rz 27; Koziol and Welser (n. 40) p. 8.

[58] See for instance Rohe, *Netzverträge* (1998); Kulms, *Schuldrechtliche Organisationsverträge in der Unternehmenskooperation* (2000); Teubner, '*Das Recht hybrider Netzwerke*', *ZHR* 165 (2001) p. 550.

Civil Code nevertheless be achieved, I believe that a highly developed pandectist system should be the system of choice. It is the furthest developed model, allowing different levels of abstraction, and offers the chance of creating a complete codification largely free from inconsistencies. For these reasons the BGB, as one of the younger codifications in Europe, is influential.[59]

In a European Contract Law, a Section Dealing with General Issues would not be necessary. The contract would then be the systematic basis for the codification. The ABGB proves that this is a functional model.

Secondly, however, it seems questionable what role national codifications can play at all in the creation of a European uniform law. It is an indisputable fact that fundamental preparatory work for a European Contract Law has already been done. Let me just mention the CISG and the programs for uniformity developed by legal scholars, such as the Principles of European Contract Law, the Unidroit Principles, and others.[60] All of these take into consideration the contents and practice of national laws and thus are sets of rules immediately drawn from a comparison of various legal systems. They certainly are not qualified to directly, and without being revised, serve as a basis for a supranational uniformity of law. This is evident from the fact that they are entitled 'Principles', despite the fact that their contents are partly compact enough to make them cross the border to being rules.[61] Even though their contents require concretization, they are definitely systematically organized. And the answer they offer to the question of the optimum level of abstraction is in my opinion certainly plausible: they are connected with the conclusion of contracts. This actually shifts the question a bit: the primary issue is not so much the level of abstraction as the question of what elements of a section dealing with general issues should be contained in a European Contract Law. In other words: where should the border be set between national codes and a European Contract Law? The CISG and the Principles of European Contract Law give different answers: While the CISG is rather restrictive, excluding from its scope questions concerning the validity of contracts or agency questions; these questions are included in the Principles of European Contract Law. In my opinion, the second solution is the preferable one. It is justified not only by the fact, already emphasized by Grundmann, that there are considerable differences between the various legal transactions in the areas of contract law, family law, and inheritance law, but also by the goal of unifying the law as such in order to provide the market participants with a uniform and transparent framework.

---

59 See Ranieri (n. 15) pp. 18 *et seq.*

60 Detailed: Riedl, *Vereinheitlichung des Privatrechts in Europa* (2004); Wurmnest, *Common Core, Grundregeln, Kodifikationsentwürfe, Acquis-Grundsätze – Ansätze internationaler Wissenschaftlergruppen zur Privatrechtsvereinheitlichung in Europa*, ZEuP (2003) p. 714; also see Ranieri (n. 15) pp. 30 *et seq.*

61 See Kramer (n. 6) pp. 201 *et seq.*, 213.

VII. SUMMARY OF THE MAIN POINTS

(1) (a) If a European Civil Code is created, its orientation in accordance with the pandectist system with a Section Dealing with General Issues (Section VI.1) will be the best solution, the legal transaction being the starting point.

(b) If the codification is limited to a European Contract Law, which seems to be the more probable case, a Section Dealing with General Issues should not be included. The starting point should then be the contract. The Austrian ABGB shows that this is a functional model. The CISG, the Principles of European Contract Law, and the Unidroit Principles follow this model (Sections IV.1, VI.2).

(2) A contract law codification should integrate provisions specific to businesses and consumer protection. The 'trialism' of Austrian contract law – i.e. the distribution of these special provisions throughout the Commercial Code and the Consumer Protection Act – is not an example to be followed (Section III.2.b).

(3) A European Contract Law should, at least in a general provision, cover the issue of pre-contractual obligations, specifically duties to furnish information. It should also regulate consumers' rights to terminate contracts, provided that it succeeds in simplifying and systematizing the existing rights of termination. Finally, it should contain provisions on agency (Section IV.2).

(4) The inclusion in contracts and the contents of general terms and conditions should be regulated in a European Contract Law.

(5) As under Austrian law, breach of contract should be regulated as generally as possible and with respect to the individual types of contracts. Different from under Austrian law, but in line with the CISG and the Principles of European Contract Law, there should be one uniform definition of breach of contract, rather than a number of different types of breach of contract (Section V.2.a).

(6) Long-term legal relationships should be given special attention. The rules on network contracts have not yet been developed far enough to allow their codification (Section V.3.a).

(7) Finally, the creation of special rules for non-market related contracts, i.e. contracts without consideration, should be considered (Section V.3.b).

SUMMARY OF THE MAIN POINTS

Chapter 5

The Dutch Civil Code and its Precedents (1990–1992)

Bea Verschraegen

I. INTRODUCTION

In 1813, when Dutch independence was restored and the new Constitution demanded a new Civil Code, immediate attempts were made to draft such a Code. The Code of 1838 more or less reflected the *Code Napoléon*.[1] But only approximately; there were indeed important differences, such as the requirement of delivery for the transfer of ownership which made it necessary to draw a clear distinction between the law of property and the law of obligations. These branches of law were codified in Books 2 and 3. The Second Book also embraced the law of succession, Book 4 dealt with the law of evidence and the law of prescription. A further distinction from the *Code Napoléon* was a title dealing with general provisions on the law of obligations. Parts of the Code of 1838 were in force until quite recently and some parts still are. But the Code has far from remained unchanged for 160 years; rather substantial changes were made with regard to a number of socially and economically important issues, for instance, lease and hire, labour law, company law, etc. However, the law of property and the law of obligations remained unchanged. The needs of society changed, though, and therefore many gaps in the Code were filled by case law. The result was that private

[1] See for an introduction Schrage, *Das System des neuen niederländischen Zivilgesetzbuches*, JBl (1994), pp. 501 *et seq.*; Hartkamp, Tillema and ter Heide, Netherlands, in Blanpain and Herbots (eds.), *Contracts, International Encyclopaedia of Laws*, Suppl. 34 (2003), pp. 38 *et seq.*

S. Grundmann, M. Schauer (eds), *The Architecture of European Codes and Contract Law*, 105–115

law was embodied in the Code 1838, in special statutes and in case law. This situation was generally regarded as unsatisfactory. It was not until 1947 that professor Meijers of the University of Leiden was asked to draft a new Civil Code.[2] The extant Civil Code of 1838 and the Commercial Code of the same year were to be replaced by one single Code. This new Code[3] was to entail civil law, commercial law, consumer protection law, the bits and pieces enacted in special statutes and last but not least the whole of case law. It was highly controversial whether the new Code was to deal with specific contracts; some specific contracts were, in due time, included.[4]

II. STYLE AND STRUCTURE OF THE DCC[5]

Basically, the Dutch Civil Code seems to be more detailed than the French CC, but it is less conceptual than the German BGB. Understanding the Dutch Civil Code is not an easy undertaking, as I will try to show you with some examples. The Code should certainly not be read merely on the basis of the text such as it entered into force, but in connection with the case law and the explanatory commentaries.

Meijer envisaged nine books preceded by a preliminary title:

(1) Law of persons and family law (including matrimonial property law).
(2) Legal persons (general part, associations, corporations with limited liability, foundations).
(3) Patrimonial law in general, applicable to the subsequent books.
(4) Law of succession.
(5) Property and real rights (rights in rem).
(6) General part of the law of obligations.
(7) Special contracts.
(8) Law of transport.
(9) Intellectual property.

The Preliminary Title and Books 1 to 4 together with the Explanatory Commentary were published in 1954. When Meijers passed away, Drion, de Jong and Eggens, later on replaced by de Groot, continued the work. The draft of Book 5 was published in 1955, the draft of Book 6 in 1961, they were introduced in 1956 and 1964 respectively. Book 1 (enacted in 1959) and Book 2

---

2 Dazu Meijers, *La réforme du Code Civil néerlandais*, *Verzamelde Privaatrechtelijke Opstellen* (VPO) I (1954) pp. 150 *et seq.*; Snijders, *Vers un nouveau Code Civil néerlandais. Etat des Traveaux*, *Revue de Droit International et de Droit Comparé* 56 (1979) p. 223.

3 See, for instance, Hondius, *Das neue niederländische Zivilgesetzbuch*, *AcP* 191 (1991) pp. 378 *et seq.*

4 Hondius, in Chorus, Gerver, Hondius and Koekkoek (eds.), *Introduction to Dutch Law* (3rd edn., 1999), pp. 225 *et seq.*

5 Details in Schrage, *System*, JBl 1994, pp. 504 *et seq.*

(enacted in 1960) entered into force in 1970 and 1976 respectively. Books 3, 5 and 6 were enacted from 1979 to 1980, but entered into force much later.

What sounds simple was in fact extremely difficult: A special Act dealt with transitional law and the adaptation of other Codes and Statutes. A new Code on Civil Procedure was elaborated, an Act on public registers for registered immoveable property and four Titles of Book 7 on Special contracts, including the contract of sales, were enacted. The new rules came into force in 1992. Time pressure as well as structural reasons explains why only some types of special contracts were enacted: namely those contracts which could not be separated from the General Part. Book 4 on the law of succession, enacted in 1969, entered into force in 2003. Some parts of Book 7 (special contracts) were re-codified, mainly the sale of goods, supply of services, deposit, employment, suretyship and settlement, or codified for the first time, such as package travel contracts. Other parts must still be re-codified. Book 8 on the law of transport came into force in 1991 and entails general provisions, maritime law, inland navigation law and road transport law, but some chapters are still missing. Book 9 is on intellectual property and an envisaged Book 10 is on Private International Law. Book 7A includes the special contracts of the old Code.

The Preliminary Title of the Code was deleted. It envisaged two topics. First of all, provisions dealing with sources of law and their hierarchy: statutory law, customary law and equity. It provided that non-mandatory rules could be set aside by customary law and equity. The second topic dealt with subjective rights, especially the doctrine of abuse of rights. These provisions are now in the first Title of Book 3.

Typical features of the Dutch Code are: the legislator proceeds from general notions or concepts to specific issues. It is therefore impossible to deal with, say, a sales contract of Book 7 without consulting Book 3 on Patrimonial law in general and Book 6 on the General Part of the Law on Obligations. By thus classifying concepts, a rather high degree of abstraction is reached (especially in Book 3). Indeed, the necessity of a real General Part was intensively discussed. Meijers studied of course the General Part of the German BGB and he also knew why Huber's Swiss Civil Code deliberately avoided a General Part. Huber had said that general statements on persons belonged to provisions on persons, statements on goods to property law, etc. In other words, a general classification seemed useless outside the context in which the issue itself is dealt with.

So Meijers chose a compromise. He was in favour of a general part that should be limited to patrimonial law and should deal with definitions and the concept of juridical acts. The consequence was that the basic distinction between the law of persons and the family on the one hand and patrimonial law on the other – a distinction we know from Roman law – was laid down in the Code.

The technique of moving on from general provisions to more specific ones – 'priority principle' – and of a structured architecture, is somewhat opposed to another technique, also well known in the Dutch Code, namely the 'switch-over technique' (*Schaltbestimmung*).[6] Here the legislator puts a key provision in the most important context of the issue in question and then states that it can be applied by analogy to other legal issues. Both techniques have their advantages and disadvantages: the advantages are structure and classification as well as efficiency from the point of view of the legislator; the disadvantages are reduction of practicability and more difficult access for the user of the Code.

III. BOOKS 3 AND 6: PATRIMONIAL LAW AND GENERAL LAW OF OBLIGATIONS

For the purpose of this conference, the Books 3 and 6 seem to deserve special attention. Let me start with Book 3 on Patrimonial law ('*Allgemeines Vermögensrecht*') in general. The high degree of abstraction is typical for this Book.[7]

Book 3 has 11 Titles: Title 1 – General Provisions; Title 2 – Juridical Acts; Title 3 – Agency; Title 4 – Acquisition of things; Title 5 – Owner-possession and possession; Title 6 – Administration; Title 7 – Community; Title 8 – Usufruct; Title 9 – Lien; Title 10 – Right to satisfaction out of goods; and Title 11 – Claims.

The first Title deals with obligations in general. This 'general part' is, though, not a general part in the sense of the German BGB. Rather, certain concepts are defined, such as 'things', which are goods and rights, or general property law, for instance on acquisition and loss of goods, on possession, usufruct, lien, etc., further on movables and immovables, on patrimonial rights, good faith, and the prohibition of legal abuse and the priority of public law over private law.

These provisions are applicable by analogy also in contexts other than patrimonial law (3:15).[8] A number of further provisions order the application of provisions by analogy (3:59, 3:78 f; 3:326). This is interesting for different reasons. First, the legislator explicitly urges for application per analogiam, and, secondly, what can be called the foundation of such an analogy would, from a systematic point of view, fit within a genuine General Part, which is missing. Title 1, including provisions on performance of

6 Details in Schrage, *System*, JBl 1994, pp. 507 *et seq.*

7 Statutory law, case law and scholars have influenced one another, see Hartkamp, *Interplay Between Judges, Legislators and Academics*. The case of the New Civil Code of The Netherlands, in, Markesinis (ed.), *Law Making, Law finding, and Law Shaping. The Diverse Influences* (1997) pp. 91 *et seq.*

8 Such as public contracts, i.e. contracts with public law character, between administrative bodies and private parties, Hoge Raad, 10.4.1987, *NJ* (1988), p. 148.

obligations, deals with the effects of non-performance and the legal obligation to repair damages. These provisions are also applicable to the obligations resulting from contracts.

The second Title of Book 3 deals with the doctrine of juridical acts. It deals with their formation, discrepancies between real and declared intention, nullity for lack of form or illegality, severability of null juridical acts and their transformation by operation of the law into valid substitutes, voidability for reasons of threat (duress), fraud, abuse of circumstances (undue influence) and *fraus creditorum*. It also deals with the technique and effects of annulment, *confirmatio* and *ratihabitio*. In case of doubt, the provisions apply only to contracts but not to all juridical acts. However, some provisions provide for application by analogy to juridical acts.

Among the different kinds of contracts (contracts in the field of family law, contracts in the field of property in the sense of real rights, contracts in the field of procedural law, public law and finally obligatory contracts) I would like to briefly turn to property contracts, which are aimed at the establishment or transfer of a right or a thing and which are closely related to obligatory contracts. As in some other legal systems, mere consensus for the actual transfer of ownership does not suffice; a material act of transfer is necessary. The provisions of the second Title of Book 3 on juridical acts are applicable to such contracts and the provisions of Book 6 Title 5 can be applied by analogy (6:216).

Book 3, more specifically Titles 2 and 5, in which application by analogy is stated, are also of relevance in the field of procedural contracts. Say, for instance, contracts by which parties deviate from the legal rules on evidence, which is possible as long as mandatory rules are not infringed upon.

Book 6 deals with the General Part of the Law of Obligations and entails 5 Titles: Title 1 – obligations in general; Title 2 – transfer of claims and debts and waiver of claims; Title 3 – torts; Title 4 – obligations that lie outside contract and tort (management of another person's affairs, undue payments and unjust enrichment); and Title 5 – General provisions on contracts.

However, the obligatory contracts are the key type of contracts. Special provisions are embodied in Title 5 of Book 6. According to the law (6:213 paragraph 1) an obligatory contract is a multilateral juridical act whereby one or more parties assumes an obligation towards one or more other parties. The Code then – moving from general to more specific issues – draws further distinctions: named or unnamed contracts, mixed contracts, consensual, real and formal contracts, bilateral and unilateral contracts. With regard to bilateral contracts (reciprocal or synallagmatic contracts) the Code contains special provisions in Title 5 of Book 6. Basically, only in bilateral contracts can non-performance give rise to the *exceptio non adimpleti contractus* and to the rescission of the contract. Bilateral contracts are, for instance, sale, rent, labour contracts and insurance; unilateral contract are, for instance, gift and suretyship. Most of the provisions of Title 5, which only envisage obligatory contracts, are applicable by way of analogy to other multilateral juridical acts in the field of patrimonial law, if such analogy is not incompatible with the relevant provisions, taking into account the nature of the juridical act (6:216). The court can apply the provisions of Title 5 to other juridical acts if it seems appropriate under the given circumstances.

Nullity and annulment[9] are regulated in Book 3 dealing with patrimonial law in general. The reasons for nullity or annulment are lack of capacity, legal prohibitions, violation of good morals or public order, defects of consent and *fraus creditorum*. Mistake, however, is regulated in Book 6, the general part of the law of obligations. Nullity basically has an effect *ex tunc* and what was given can be claimed back. In case of partial nullity the rest of the contract remains valid, unless it is inextricably related to the null part of the contract (3:41). A contract which is null can be saved by conversion into a valid contract if its conditions are met (3:42).

Defect of consent only leads to voidable contracts (mistake, duress, fraud and undue influence, 3:44).[10] These rules apply to all juridical acts. Rules on mistake (6:228) can be applied by analogy to the juridical acts. Mistake can be caused by misrepresentation, or reinforced by the breach of a duty to disclose information and mistake on both sides.[11]

With regard to mistake the general rules of Book 3 (3:49) apply. Retroactive effect is not mandatory; the judge can deviate from this effect. Also the other party can suggest a solution in order to compensate the damages (6:230 I).

Leaving aside other types of contracts, I now turn to some key examples of the law of obligations.

IV. SELECTED ISSUES

1. First Example: Contract and Tort

The law of contract and the law of unlawful acts are treated under the heading of the law of obligations, together with some obligations from other sources, such as management of the affairs of another, undue payment and unjustified enrichment.[12]

---

9 See, for instance, Hartkamp, Tillema and ter Heide, Netherlands, in Blanpain and Herbots (eds.), *Contracts*, Suppl. 34, pp. 90 *et seq*.

10 See, for example, Hartkamp, Tillema and ter Heide, 'Netherlands', in Blanpain and Herbots (eds.), *Contracts*, Suppl. 34, pp. 81 *et seq*.

11 See Zimmermann, *The Law of Obligations* (1996) pp. 583 *et seq*. for an historical analysis.

12 Details in Hartkamp, Tillema and ter Heide, 'Netherlands', in Blanpain and Herbots (eds.), *Contracts*, Suppl. 34, pp. 44 *et seq*.

There seems to be no fundamental difference between an unlawful act and a failure in the performance of a contractual obligation. Merely practical reasons, so it seems, had led to the introduction of special provisions on the legal effects of a failure in the performance of an obligation (6:74 *et seq.*). These provisions then prevail over the provisions on unlawful acts (6:162 *et seq.*) when there is a failure in the performance of an obligation. In cases where the failure in performance of an obligation is covered by the special provisions and at the same time by the provisions on torts, the consequences are the same (under 6:95 *et seq.*), which leads to the conclusion that it does not seem that relevant whether the claim is based on torts or on failure in the performance of an obligation. For instance a person is asked to repair something and he/she causes damage to goods: damaging the property of somebody else without that person's consent is a tort irrespective of the contract by virtue of which the debtor took power of the goods. But, at the end of the day, the distinction between torts and failure in performance of an obligation is important in cases in which, for example, the law distinguishes contractual liability from non-contractual liability, or provides for different periods of prescription.

2. Second Example: Quasi-Contracts

Contrary to the *Code Napoléon*, the old Code did not distinguish between the sources of obligations, more precisely between contracts, quasi-contracts, torts, etc. It merely stated that all obligations resulted from contracts or from the law.[13] Contracts resulting from the law were contracts resulting from law only or from acts of people, and these acts could be lawful or unlawful. So, in fact, quasi-contracts were a part of lawful acts. Book 6:1 of the new Code states, by contrast, that obligations can only arise from law. Case law helps to understand what is meant by this. In cases which are not expressly provided for in the law, the Supreme Court ruled in 1959 before Book 6 entered into force,[14] that the solution should be adopted which fits into the statutory system and is in conformity with rules already laid down for similar situations. Indeed Book 6:1 is to be understood in this sense. The Code deals with unlawful acts, contracts and three other sources of obligations, namely the management of the affairs of another person (*negotiorum gestio*), undue payment (*solutio indebiti*) and unjustified enrichment.[15]

---

[13] In extenso Hartkamp, Tillema and ter Heide, 'Netherlands', in Blanpain and Herbots (eds.), *Contracts*, Suppl. 34, p. 45.

[14] Hoge Raad, 30 January 1959, *NJ* (1959) p. 548.

[15] Hartkamp, Tillema and ter Heide, 'Netherlands', in Blanpain and Herbots (eds.), *Contracts*, Suppl. 34, 45.

3. Third Example: Good Faith (Reasonableness and Fairness)[16]

The concept of good faith is characteristic for the law of obligations and contracts. According to the law (6:2, pararaph 1) both parties to an obligation should behave in their relationship according to reasonableness and fairness. A rule binding upon them by virtue of the law, custom or a juridical act does not apply if this were unacceptable according to the standards of reasonableness and fairness (6:2, paragraph 2).

The concept of good faith has three functions:

- All contracts must be interpreted according to good faith.
- Acting in good faith refers to the observance of reasonable commercial standards of fair dealing, i.e. acting in accordance with reasonableness and fairness, and also, that the party concerned did not know the relevant state of affairs and also ought not to have known it (3:11).
- Good faith has also a restrictive function. The law (6:248, paragraph 2, applying good faith to contracts) demonstrates this function: a rule, which would normally bind the parties as a result of a contract, does not apply to the extent that, in the given circumstances, this would be unacceptable according to the criteria of reasonableness and fairness.

So even express terms of a contract can be set aside if their performance was grossly unjust. The concept turns up in other contexts as well: For example, in unforeseen circumstances, the law (6:258) provides for a possibility of modification or rescission of the contract when reasonableness and fairness so require. The two provisions can be applied in a cumulative way, but rescission or modification of the contract cannot be reached based on the first provision.

As was mentioned before, the two provisions dealing with good faith in Book 6 apply to contracts, but also to other multilateral patrimonial juridical acts (6:216). Article 2 of Book 6 applies to all obligations.

4. Fourth Example: Express and Implied Terms

A contract not only has the legal effects agreed upon by the parties, but also those, which according to the nature of the contract, result from the law, usage or the requirements of reasonableness and fairness (6:248, paragraph 32).

Starting point is the agreement – express or implied of the parties.[17] The law, usage and requirement of reasonableness and fairness are supplementary sources of obligations. With regard to general terms and conditions, the

---

[16] Details in Hartkamp, Tillema and ter Heide, 'Netherlands', in Blanpain and Herbots (eds.), *Contracts*, Suppl. 34, pp. 49 *et seq.*, 96.

[17] See Hartkamp, Tillema and Heide, 'Netherlands', in Blanpain and Herbots (eds.), *Contracts*, Suppl. 34, pp. 96 *et seq.*

new Code contains a provision (6:231:3) which was inspired by the German BGB: these are written stipulations which have been drafted to be included into a number of contracts, with the exception of stipulations involving the characteristic obligation itself.

In the interests of legal certainty the applicability of a set of general terms and conditions is easily attained. It is sufficient that a party has accepted, in writing or in another way, the applicability of general terms and conditions; whether this is the case must be answered according to Book 3:33 and 3:35. Usually, it suffices that the conditions are printed on an offer or acceptance, sent to the other party and not followed by a protest by the other party. The law (6:225, paragraph 3) states that in case of a 'battle of general terms' the second reference in general conditions is without effect, unless it explicitly rejects the applicability of the general conditions of the first reference. The user of the conditions must give a copy of the general terms and conditions to the other party before or at the time of entering into the contract. The Supreme Court ruled that this provision must be read in a reasonable way, conforming to practice.[18] If the user did not even give the other party a copy of his general terms and conditions at the time of conclusion of the contract he is deemed to have given the other party a reasonable opportunity (6:234) assuming the other party was aware of the term, because, for instance, he had contracted with the user under the same standard terms.[19]

Unreasonably onerous stipulations can be challenged before the court and may be annulled. The Code contains lists of such onerous terms (6:233a) and a 'black list' (6:236). There is, further, a 'grey list', according to which stipulations are presumed to be onerous (6:237); this presumption can be rebutted. A stipulation which is neither on the black nor on the grey list may still be an onerous one (6:233a), if it is unreasonably onerous to the other party, taking into consideration the nature and the further content of the contract, the manner in which the terms and conditions were established, the mutually apparent interests of the parties and the other circumstances of the case. Both consumers and legal persons acting in the course of a business are protected by this provision.

5. Fifth Example: Performance and Breach

Performance means fulfilment of the contents of an obligation (6:1:27–51).[20] Basically, there is no such thing as an independent obligation to make the

---

[18] HoGe Raad, 1 October 1999, NJ (2000) p. 207.

[19] Hartkamp, Tillema and ter Heide, 'Netherlands', in Blanpain and Herbots (eds.), *Contracts*, Suppl. 34, p. 97.

[20] See Hartkamp, in Chorus, Gerver, Hondius and Koekkoek (eds.), *Introduction to Dutch Law*, pp. 128 *et seq.*; Hartkamp, Tillema and ter Heide, 'Netherlands', in Blanpain and Herbots (eds.), *Contracts*, Suppl. 34, pp. 119 *et seq.*

necessary preparations for the performance. It is only after the breach of contract (late or inadequate performance) that the creditor has a remedy.

The effects of failure in the performance are regulated in the Code (6:1:9; 6:5:5, synallagmatic contracts). When a debtor does not fulfil his obligation on time, in a proper way or when he does not fulfil his obligation at all, he fails in the performance of his obligation. The term has a broad and neutral meaning. It envisages all cases in which the debtor falls short of what the obligation requires and comprises both the case that the failure can be attributed to the debtor as well as the case that it cannot be attributed to him. In the former case or when performance is permanently impossible, there is a failure of performance as such. In all other cases, there is only failure in performance when the debtor is in default.

Different remedies are provided for when the debtor does not fulfil his obligations:[21] (1) performance; (2) performance and compensation for late performance; (3) damages instead of performance; and, in addition, in case of synallagmatic contracts, (4) rescission of the contract; (5) rescission and damages.

Basically, the creditor owes specific performance (3:296; 6:1:27–51). As long as specific performance is possible the creditor is not obliged to accept a substitute. Instead of performance the creditor may choose one of the remedies mentioned previously. In case of synallagmatic contracts the creditor may opt for damages and rescission, in which case different modes of non-performance must be distinguished. The law distinguishes between attributable and non-attributable performance. The first case is considered as non-performance and damages are due, in the second case no damages are due (6:74). Subsequently, permanent and temporary impossibility to perform are distinguished. The first case leads to damages *ipso iure*; in the second case the debtor will be held responsible only if he is in default (6:81). Default results in defective performance or in non-performance. Damages may be claimed for late performance. The creditor can issue a claim to perform with or without compensation for late performance, and he has the right to renounce his right to performance claiming damages instead and opting for rescission of the contract.

Rescission (6:265–277) is directed at bilateral contracts, but applies also to comparable bilateral relationships (6:261, paragraph 2) and multilateral contracts (6:279). Rescission is possible not only in case of fundamental breach of the contract but also when the debtor is in default. Damages are due only if non-performance is attributable to the debtor. Unlike French law rescission does not require a lawsuit.

---

21 Hartkamp, Tillema and ter Heide, Netherlands, in Blanpain and Herbots (eds.), *Contracts*, Suppl. 34, pp. 139 *et seq.*

V. CONCLUDING REMARKS

The Dutch Civil Code can be compared with the '*sagrada familia*'. The architecture is highly interesting and sophisticated, but is an unfinished work of art. It is also an architecture which demands specialist knowledge and much experience. From an intellectual point of view the Dutch Civil Code, with its principle to move from general to more specific issues and its 'switch-over' principle, demonstrates the decades of work invested in its elaboration. Any project of a European Code on Contract should focus on its applicability to different states with different traditions. There is, in other words, a long way to go.

Chapter 6
Models in Central-Eastern European Codes

Lajos Vékás

I. INTRODUCTION

The former socialist states of Central and Eastern Europe and their economies returned to a market economy after 1990. This process was accompanied by a demand for solving several projects in the private law legislature as well; the accomplishment of only one of these projects being a substantial task, let alone several of them.[1]

The first task was the privatisation of state-owned property, in historically unprecedented and substantial magnitudes and in record time. In these countries, 70–90 per cent of property was state-owned before the collapse of the old regime, and this structure had to be dismantled in just over a decade. It is not difficult to imagine the problems raised by such a significant change of privatisation and the social tensions associated with it. We need not go very far back in time to remember the continuous societal conflicts experienced under the Thatcher-era in Britain, when the government sought to privatise only a minimal percentage of state-owned property. Furthermore, in Central Europe, privatisation had to be carried out in countries

[1] See Frankowski and Stephan (eds.), *Legal Reform in Post-Communist Europe* (1995); Gärtner, *Die Neugestaltung der Wirtschaftsverfassungen in Ost-Mitteleuropa* (1996); Hobér, *Transforming East European Law* (1997); Mádl, *Investitionsschutz und Transformation in Mittel- und Osteuropa* (2001).

S. Grundmann, M. Schauer (eds), *The Architecture of European Codes and Contract Law*, 117–128

poor in capital, which inevitably led to a disproportionately great loss in wealth.[2]

Privatisation and the establishment of a regime for regulating private property was necessary, but by no means the only condition for the creation of a functioning market economy. The whole legal infrastructure also had to be created: the law of securities,[3] commercial companies, competition and cartel law, banking law and so on.

In the course of accomplishing these tasks, which we have roughly sketched above, in rapidly changing circumstances, it was not easy to think about codification, which at the same time, however, would have signalled the stabilisation of the situation. Some Central European countries did link the reforms with the creation of new codes, and in other states in the region work is currently being undertaken to realise codification proposals.

Codification of private law in these states has a great tradition. All the legal systems of the region have a markedly continental character: their development before the Second World War was earmarked by the great European codification movements.[4] Hungary was the only country that 'survived' with case law made customary law until 1960, but there were in fact

---

2 See Šarčević, *Privatization in Central and Eastern Europe* (1992); Dallagao, Ajani and Grancelli, *Privatization and Enterpreneurship in Post-Socialist Countries* (1992); Borić and Posch, *Privatisierung in Ungarn, Kroatien und Slowenien im Rechtsvergleich* (1993); Roggemann and Kuss, *Unternehmensumwandlung und Privatisierung in Osteuropa* (1993); Frydman and Rapaczinsky, *Privatization in Eastern Europe, Is the State Withering Away?* (1994); Smit and Pechota (eds.), *Privatization in Eastern Europe, Legal, Economic, and Social Aspects* (1994); Borić, *Eigentum und Privatisierung in Kroatien und Ungarn* (1996); Herwig and Roggemann, Eigentum *in Osteuropa* (1996); Sárközy, *Rendszerváltozás és a privatizáció joga (Systemchange and Privatisation)* (1997); Sárközy, 'Die Modelle der Privatisierung in den ehemaligen sozialistischen Ländern', in Basedow, Hopt and Kötz (eds.), *Festschrift Drobnig* (1998), pp. 661–675; Hink, *Vergleich der Gesetze zur Privatisierung der staatlichen Unternehmen in der ehemaligen DDR, Polen, Ungarn und der Tschechischen Republik* (1995); Lowitzsch, *Privatisierung und Beteiligung* (2002); Roggemann and Lowitzsch, *Privatisierungsinstitutionen in Mittel- und Osteuropa* (2002); Popowska, *Der Wandel der rechtlichen Rahmenbedingungen für das Eigentum in Polen in den Jahren* (1989–2003), *Jahrbuch für Ostrecht* 45 (2004), 1. Halbband, pp. 11–27.

3 See Horn and Pleyer (eds.), *Handelsrecht und Recht der Kreditsicherheiten in Osteuropa* (1997); Drobnig, Hopt, Kötz and Mestmäcker (eds.), *Systemtransformation in Mittel- und Osteuropa und ihre Folgen für Banken, Börsen, Kreditsicherheiten* (1998); Drobnig, Roth and Trunk (eds.), *Mobiliarsicherheiten in Osteuropa* (2002).

4 See Ginsburgs, Barry and Simons (eds.), *The Revival of Private Law in Central and Eastern Europe* (1996); Horn (ed.), *Die Neugestaltung des Privatrechts in Mittelosteuropa und Osteuropa (Polen, Russland, Tschechien, Ungarn)* (2002); Vékás, *Integration des östlichen Mitteleuropa im Wege rechtsvergleichender Zivilrechtserneuerung*, *ZEuP* (2004), pp. 454–476; Stalev, *Transformation der Rechts- und Wirtschaftsordnung Bulgariens*, *ZEuP* 1996, pp. 444–451; Harmathy, *Zivilgesetzgebung in mittel- und osteuropäischen Staaten*, *ZeuP* 1998, pp. 553–563; Poczubut, *Zur Reform des polnischen Zivilrechts*, *ZEuP* (1999), pp. 75–90; Vékás, *Über die Neugestaltung des ungarischen Zivilrechts*, in Basedow, Hopt and Kötz (eds.), *Festschrift Drobnig* (1998), pp. 713–724; Vékás, *Privatrechtsreform in einem Transformationsland*, in Basedow, Drobnig, Ellger, Hopt, Kötz, Kulms and Mestmäcker (eds.), *Aufbruch nach Europa, 75 Jahre Max-Planck-Institut für Privatrecht* (2001) pp. 1049–1064.

very sophisticated codification proposals between 1900 and 1928. These proposals demonstrate a high level of originality, but they also show the influence of the Austrian ABGB, the German BGB or the Swiss ZGB. In some areas the influence of the French *Code Civil* is also noticeable, albeit not to such a great extent as in the Romanian codification, where the French Code is deemed to be the dominant source of inspiration. In the socialist era, the appropriate codification of private law was completed in all or at least some areas of law in every country in the region, following the socio-economic structure of the time. Separate laws governed family law. Where there was no comprehensive code, partial areas were regulated, for example the law of contracts and torts in Yugoslavia. The comprehensive reform of these codes became a part of the agenda after the changes in the 1990s.

This paper seeks to summarize the conclusions drawn from the Central and Eastern European private law codification movements. The author is first and foremost familiar with his own legal system, Hungarian private law; his thoughts are therefore channelled from that starting point.[5] The paper does, however, cover the development of other private law regimes in the region as well.

The codification movements of the countries in the region have so far developed along mostly different lines. In the still united Czechoslovakia, a new commercial code was made in 1991[6] to replace the 'economic' code of 1964, which was created in socialist spirit. In both the Czech Republic and Slovakia, continuous work is being undertaken to reform the 1964 private law code as well. In Slovenia,[7] the codification process goes from book to book: the book on the law of contracts was finished in 2001, and the book on rights *in rem* was finished in 2002. Poland and Hungary seem to be following a similar route. Both states gave up on creating a commercial code, and gave up their old commercial codes at the same time.[8] The creation of a

5 To the Hungarian private law see Harmathy (ed.), *Introduction to Hungarian Law* (1998).

6 Law No. 513/1991, with the important modification of Law No. 370/2000. To a new civil code see Jiři Zemánek, *Der Vorentwurf des neuen tschechischen ZGB im Blickwinkel des europäischen Verbraucherschutzrechts*, in Basedow, Drobnig, Ellger, Hopt, Kötz, Kulms and Mestmäcker (eds.), *Aufbruch*, pp. 1089–1096; *Verny*, '*Die Entwicklung des Zivilrechts in der Tschechischen Republik*', in Horn (ed.), *Neugestaltung*, pp. 89–110.

7 In Slovenia are two new books of the Civil code promulgated till now, the Law of Obligations in 2001 (U. l. Nr. 83 from 25 October 2001, Pos. 4287) and the Law of Property in 2002 (U. l. Nr. 87 from 17 October 2002, Pos. 4360). See Trstenjak, '*Das neue slowenische Obligationenrecht*', *WGO Monatshefte für Osteuropäisches Recht* 44 (2002), pp. 90–110; Tratnik, '*Das neue slowenische Sachenrecht*', *WGO Monatshefte für Osteuropäisches Recht* 45 (2003), pp. 94–108; Trstenjak, '*Zivilrecht in Slowenien*', *ZEuP* (2000), pp. 77–90.

8 To the developments in Poland see Kordasiewicz, in: *International Encyclopaedia of Comparative Law, Volume I*, National Reports, Poland, (2000), p. 157; Kordasiewicz, *Änderungen im polnischen Zivil- und Handelsrecht*, in Horn (ed.), *Neugestaltung*, pp. 55–83; Poczubut, *Zur Reform des polnischen Zivilrechts*, *ZEuP* (1999), pp. 75–90. To the developments in Hungary see Lajos Vékás, *Über die Neugestaltung des ungarischen Zivilrechts*, in Basedow, Hopt and Kötz (eds.), *Festschrift für Drobnig*, pp. 713–724; Vékás, *Privatrechtsreform in einem Transformationsland*, in Basedow, Drobnig, Ellger, Hopt, Kötz, Kulms and Mestmäcker (eds.), *Aufbruch*, pp. 1049–1064.

comprehensive law on commercial companies[9] did, however, precede the ongoing creation of the civil code in both countries. We also note that intensive codification work is also being undertaken, (in the neighbouring countries), for example in Bulgaria,[10] where a new commercial code was created. As regards the Baltic States, Estonia and Lithuania have created a civil code recently.[11]

II. SOME THEORETICAL CONCLUSIONS OF THE PRIVATE LAW CODIFICATIONS

Despite the fact that the countries of Central Europe entered the third millennium with a significant social backlog, and this has obviously had an impact on the state of development of the legal system as well, the theoretical questions about private law codifications do not differ from the codification problems faced by the 'old' member states of the European Union:

- There is a need to define the relationship between the development of private law in a national context and the creation of a common European civil law.
- The new, comprehensive codes in Central Europe (also) face the question about monist or dualist codification of civil law. It needs to be decided whether the new code being created will be applicable to the assets of private persons and commercial entities' (monist interpretation) or whether the latter will be included in a separate commercial code (dualist interpretation).
- The law on consumer protection, especially by the implementation of EU law, needs to be created in Central European countries as well. This raises a number of questions of methodology for national codes.

1. First of all, it is impossible to ignore the following question: taking into account the foreseeable prospects of harmonization of law in Europe, does it

---

9 In Poland, Law from 15 September 2000 (Dz. U. Nr. 94., 1037), in force since 1 January 2001; I Hungary, present version: Law Nr. IV/2006, in force since 1 July 2006.

10 See Stoyan Stalev, *Transformation der Rechts- und Wirtschaftsordnung Bulgariens, ZEuP* 1996, pp. 444–451.

11 In Estonia, Law of Property, from 9 June 1993; Law of a General Part of the Civil code, from 28 June 1994; Law of Obligations, from 26 September 2001. See Mikk, '*Zur Reform des Zivilrechts in Estland*', *Jahrbuch für Ostrecht* 42 (2001), pp. 31–52. In Latvia (with modifications from the 1990s) is the Civil code from 28 January 1937 in force again. In Lithuania in 2000 a new Civil code promulgated. See Mikelenas, '*Unification and Harmonisation of Law and the Turn of Millennium*', the Lithuanian Experience, *Uniform Law Review/Revue de Droit Uniforme* V (2000), pp. 243–261. These laws see Brunner, Schmid and Westen, *Wirtschaftsrecht der osteuropäischen Staaten (WOS, Loseblattsammlung)*, Vol. IV/1 (Estonia), Vol. IV/2 (Latvia and Lithuania). See also in Chapter II/2.

make sense at all to start creating a code based on national lines? We must ask this question in spite of the fact that such an extreme suggestion has not yet been made in any legislature that we know of.

The Dutch example is not necessarily conclusive. The achievements in the decade-long codification process have gradually become law, and most of the books of the Dutch civil code were complete and entered into force by 1992. EU legislation on private law matters, however, only became noteworthy in the mid-1990s, and that is when the achievements of the codification movements came to light: namely the UNIDROIT Principles[12] and the European Principles[13] as well. We may observe that the movements to unify European private law are taking place at the same time that Central and Eastern European countries begin to create their new national codes.

While it is impossible to comprehensively evaluate the European harmonization efforts in this paper, we must observe that in the foreseeable future the development of private law will still take place primarily but not exclusively within national bounds. This observation is valid despite the fact that the foreseeable perspectives and main characteristics of harmonization are becoming clearer every day.[14]

Law-making in the European Union as regards private law in particular is becoming more voluminous every year. Regulations and Directives take away more and more of autonomy from the Member States powers of national legislation. Moreover, EU legislation, with its fragmentary, sometimes even random selection of legislative topics – as it is repeatedly pointed out – is exactly the reverse of the method of systematic thought; therefore it goes against codification itself. It is not surprising that European harmonization efforts carried out by way of Directives are often the subject of intense criticism. The criticisms are mainly directed at the fragmented, 'pointillist' style, theoretical obscurity of EU legislation, and the inapplicability of the method for the creation of a systematic structure, but it is also often criticised for its costly implementation.[15] We should not be surprised if in future

12 The modified version, 2004.

13 *Principles of European Contract Law* (PECL) Parts I and II, edited by Lando and Beale; Part III, edited by Lando, Clive, Prüm and Zimmermann (2000, 2003).

14 See Christian von Bar about the work of the Study Group on European Civil Code, in *Festschrift Heinrich* (2000), pp. 1–11.

15 See among others Kötz, *Rechtsvergleichung – Nutzen, Kosten, Methoden, Ziele*, *RabelsZ* 50 (1986) pp. 1–18; Hommelhoff, *Zivilrecht unter dem Einfluß europäischer Rechtsangleichung*, *AcP* 1992, pp. 71–107; Steindorff, *Urteilsanmerkung zu EuGH* v. 2.8.1993 – Rs. C-259, 331 und 332/91 Allué II, *Juristenzeitung (JZ)* (1994), pp. 95–98; Blaurock, *Europäisches Privatrecht*, *JZ* 1994, pp. 270–276; Rittner, *Das Gemeinschaftsprivatrecht und die europäische Integration*, JZ 1995, pp. 849–858; Basedow, *Anforderungen an eine europäische Zivilrechtsdogmatik*, in Zimmermann, Knütel and Meincke (eds.), *Rechtsgeschichte und Privatrechtsdogmatik* (2000), pp. 79–100; Leible, *Mitteilung der Kommission zum Europäischen Vertragsrecht – Startschuß für ein Europäischen Vertragsgesetzbuch?*, *Europäisches Wirtschafts- & Steuerrecht (EWS)* 2001, pp. 471–481.

decades academic literature will refer to this phenomenon as something in such an immature state of development to be called a 'children's illness'. We, the contemporaries of Directive-made-harmonization, however, are aware of the method's advantages as well: its flexibility, which makes implementation of the common European law into separate national legal systems possible. At the same time it is not an exaggeration to state that a common European private law will never come into existence through Directives alone.

Because of the weaknesses of the approach of harmonization through Directives, we are witnessing increasing academic activity in the direction of creating a common European private law. The working groups[16] are operating with huge ambition coupled with considerable intellectual capacity on the harmonization of contract law in particular, but there are ideas at an advanced stage on the harmonization of tort law, securities and other institutions as well.

While appreciating the quality of professional work being done and the importance of these developments as the theoretical preparation for a common European private law, we must not ignore one fundamental question. How timely and realistic is the total integration of private law (or contract law) in the framework of the European Union? While it is easy to see the need for harmonization of the rules of conflict of laws, the harmonization of substantive private law requires deeper analysis and reasoning. To be more precise: harmonization of mandatory rules of substantive private law (e.g. in the field of consumer protection) does indeed directly promote the removal of barriers in favour of the fundamental freedoms of the European Union. The harmonization of these norms through Directives (lacking a better method) is by all means worthy of support. The Europe-wide debates among the legal profession around the creation and implementation of the Directive on consumer sales show that the harmonization efforts can have a modernizing effect too. The unqualified demand for harmonization of permissive rules of substantive private law does not, however, seem to be as urgent. The prerequisite for comprehensive harmonization is the creation of the institutional infrastructure and thereby the establishment of the necessary democratic legitimacy required for collective law-making. With all due respect to those representing a different view, in my opinion a facultative, optional

[16] In Osnabrück, Study Group on European Civil Code (see von Bar, in: *Festschrift Henrich* (2000), pp. 1–11); in Pavia, Academia of European Civil Law Scholars (see Giuseppe Gandolfi (ed.), *Code européen des contrats – Avant-projet*, (2001)); in Trento, Common Core Project; the Acquis Group; the Society of European Contract Law (SECOLA); the project on 'Common Principles of European Private Law' *im Rahmen des TMR-Programms der Europäischen Kommission* (see Schulze and Ajani (eds.), *Gemeinsame Prinzipien des Europäischen Privatrechts – Common Principles of European Private Law* (2003)); further the project 'Uniform Terminology for European Private Law' (see Ebers, Uniform Terminology for European Private Law – *Ein neues Forschungsnetzwerk der Europäischen Union*, *ZEuP* 2003, 185).

European contract law can serve only as the Esperanto of European harmonization.[17] While the harmonization of European private law does seem to be essential for the future, it is unnecessary and unrealistic to complete this task too quickly. My understanding is that the 2003 Action Plan of the European Commission also seems to propose a longer-term harmonization strategy.[18] A longer preparatory period offers excellent opportunities for digging a deeper academic foundation, with the strong academic forces of Europe put to good and efficient use. A deeper foundation is indeed very much needed when the task is no less than the harmonization of significant areas of private law on a European scale.

The above considerations offer the following conclusions to the former socialist new Member States. They must complete their reforms and their new codification efforts still in their national legal systems. If there is a possibility, they must also include the private law norms of EU law in their new codes, and they must have regard to the achievements of European harmonisation efforts, above all the European Principles and the excellent Rules worked out by the Study Group on European Civil Code.

2. As regards the question of monist or dualist codification, we may observe that the 20th century shows a marked decline in the creation of independent commercial codes. Italy integrated most of the content of its commercial code into the new *Codice Civile* in 1940–42. The Dutch legislator followed a similar pattern during the creation of the new *Burgerlijk Wetboek* between 1946–92.[19] Austria is about to set aside its commercial code (HGB), and wants to integrate a part of its rules relating to contracts into the ABGB.[20] The content and role of individual commercial codes have been transformed both in Germany and France; however, these countries do want keep these codes independent for the sake of legal tradition. Germany modernized the

---

17 Criticized also by Ott and Schäfer, '*Die Vereinheitlichung des europäischen Vertragsrechts, Ökonomische Notwendigkeit oder akademisches Interesse*?', in: Ott and Schäfer (eds.), *Vereinheitlichung und Diversität des Zivilrechts in transnationalen Wirtschaftsräumen* (2002), pp. 203–245. See however Grundmann, *Harmonisierung, Europäischer Kodex, Europäisches System der Vertragsrechte*, *NJW* 55 (2002), pp. 393–396 and on the field of insurance law Basedow, Insurance Contract Law as Part of an Optional European Contract Act, *ERA-Forum* 2/2003, pp. 56–65.

18 12 February 2003, COM(2003) 68, final, OJEC 2003/C 63/01; see also Council Resolution on 'A More Coherent European Contract Law', OJEC 2003/C 246/01; and also the communication from the commission to the Council and the European Parliament on European Contract Law, 11 July 2004.

19 See Hartkamp, *Das neue niederländische Bürgerliche Gesetzbuch aus europäischer Sicht*, *RabelsZ* 57(1993) pp. 664–684; further van Dijk, Hondius, Hartkamp and Vranken in Bydlinski, Mayer-Maly and Pichler (eds.), *Renaissance der Idee der Kodifikation. Das neue niederländische Bürgerliche Gesetzbuch* (1991).

20 See Schauer, '*Integration des Handels- und Unternehmensrechts in das ABGB*?', in Fischer-Czermak, Hopf and Schauer, *Das ABGB auf dem Weg in das 3. Jahrtausend* (2003), pp. 137–156.

provisions relating to carriage contracts in the HGB, and introduced accounting rules into this code. During the reform of the HGB in 1998, the definition of trader (Kaufmann) was also changed in a way that brought the HGB and the BGB closer together.[21] In 1978 the French included general commercial law provisions in their *Code Civil* that were at the same time applicable to the companies of the *Code de Commerce* as well.

Even the commercial codes that are still in use today are not made up of rules relating to special rules of commercial transactions. Some of the special rules on commercial contracts like the obligation of the entitled party to examine, have in the meantime become general requirements of contract law.

The wide-scale recognition of private autonomy and of contractual freedom, the lack of formal constraints and the primarily permissive way of rule making – except for consumer contracts – have become general characteristics of private law legislation.

The codification of consumer protection regulations also support the monist interpretation. If consumer contracts make their way into civil codes, as it is rightly suggested by many authors, and if this gains more acceptance in the legislative process as well, keeping individual commercial codes will be less and less required. One party to a commercial contract is always a company deemed as the trader; Grundmann rightly points out that consumer contracts can be regarded as unilateral commercial transactions.[22] On the other hand, the other party to most traditional and most typical commercial contracts, such as carriage contracts or consignment contracts, is the consumer. We might also say that instead of individual commercial contracts, it is the consumer contracts that increasingly stand out from the rest of general private law.

As we have seen before, the first former socialist country where a commercial code that included the law on commercial contracts (together with company law, regulation of the commercial register, some competition law provisions), was created in the then still united Czechoslovakia. Contract law is composed of general rules and special rules on particular types of contract. The Czechoslovakian code is still in force in both the Czech Republic[23] and

21 HRefG, *Gesetz zur Neuregelung des Kaufmanns- und Firmenrechts und zur Änderung anderer handels- und gesellschaftsrechtlicher Vorschriften*, v. 22 June 1998, BGBl. I, pp. 1474–1484; see Treber, *Der Kaufmann als Rechtsbegriff im Handels- und Verbraucherrecht, AcP* (1999), pp. 525–590.

22 Grundmann, Generalreferat, '*Internationalisierung und Reform des deutschen Kaufrechts*', in Grundmann, Medicus and Rolland (eds.), *Europäisches Kaufgewährleistungsrecht – Reform und Internationalisierung des deutschen Schuldrechts* (2000), pp. 281–321, (284); Grundmann, *Verbraucherrecht, Unternehmensrecht, Privatrecht – warum sind sich UN-Kaufrecht und EU-Kaufrechts-Richtlinie so ähnlich?*, *AcP* 2002, 40–71, p. 68.

23 Law Nr. 513/1991, with the modification, e.g. by Law Nr. 370/2000. Criticized by Kanda, *Zur Rekodifizierung des tschechischen Privatrechts*, *WiRO* 12 (1997), pp. 441–443; Verny, *Die Entwicklung des Zivilrechts in der Tschechischen Republik*, in Horn (ed.), *Neugestaltung*, pp. 89–110.

Slovakia,[24] albeit with necessary modifications in place. This dualist codification system is set to change in the Czech Republic (and probably in Slovakia also) when the proposed civil code is completed. In the creation of a new code, the overlapping provisions of the commercial code will be cancelled out, and thus the rules in the commercial code will be restricted to corporate and company law.[25] We must note here that also the Bulgarian Commercial Code, created in the 1990s, includes contract law: the first part accepted in 1991 contains the law relating to traders and corporate entities; the second part accepted in 1994 contains the law on bankruptcy; and the third part accepted in 1996 contains a complete contract law (general rules and special types of contract).[26] Estonia created its commercial code in 1995 without regulating contract matters: the code regulates the law relating to individual companies and corporate entities, including rules concerning a commercial register, but it does not contain special rules relating to commercial contracts. We have seen that Poland and Hungary have both voted in favour of the monist codification. In Poland the 1934 commercial code temporarily entered into force again, but it contained only one rule relating to contract law. When a new law on commercial companies entered into force in 2001, the old commercial code was repealed altogether. In Hungary there was a lively academic debate after the collapse of the old regime about the need for an independent commercial code. The result of these debates was that the underlying principles of the new Hungarian civil code now reject the dualist interpretation. This means that the law of commercial entities is not included in the new civil code (unlike Switzerland or the Netherlands) but the law of contracts will appear uniformly in the new code. We can also note that the Lithuanian civil code of 2000 follows a monist interpretation, having consciously chosen the Italian and Dutch codes as an example.[27]

Without emphasizing the structural questions of codification too much, we can observe that the former socialist states of Central Europe tend to follow the monist view of codification, despite some minor exceptions. It seems obvious that these countries do not want to make separate laws for commercial contracts, but want to regulate contract law in a uniform way outside the consumer protection sphere.

---

24 Modified e.g. by Law Nr. 500/2001. See Andova, *Osteuropa Recht* (2001), p. 580.

25 See Tichý, in Zemánek and Paschke (eds.), *Das tschechische Privat- und Wirtschaftsrecht unter dem Einfluss des europäischen Rechts* (2004), pp. 13–18; Verny, '*Die Entwicklung des Zivilrechts in der Tschechischen Republik*', in Horn (ed.), *Neugestaltung*, pp. 89–110; Lazar, *Kodifikation und Europäisierung des slowakischen Privatrechts*, in Fischer-Czermak, Hopf and Schauer (eds.), *Das ABGB auf dem Weg in das 3. Jahrtausend*, pp. 229–231.

26 *WOS*, III/2, Bulgarien (I.), IV. 2a, 1-84. See Stalev, *Transformation der Rechts- und Wirtschaftsordnung Bulgariens*, *ZEuP* (1996), pp. 444–451.

27 See Valentinas Mikelenas, *Unification and Harmonisation of Law at the Turn of Millennium, the Lithuanian Experience*, *Unif. L. Rev/Rev. dr. unif.* V (2000), pp. 243–261 (249).

3. In the past decade and half, codification of consumer protection law has brought up particular problems. The implementation of European Directives on the subject raises a question of substantial gravity whether to include the special rules relating to consumer contracts in the civil code or whether separate rules have to be made for them.

Similarly to the practice of the old Member States in the first period, the countries of Central Europe also decided in favour of creating separate rules for the implementation of consumer protection Directives. That was the way the Product Liability Directive, the Contracts Negotiated Away from Business Premises Directive and the Distance Contracts Directives were implemented into national law. The implementation of the Unfair Terms Directive and the Consumer Sales Directive was, however, achieved by integrating them into the civil codes. It was done similarly in Hungary and in Slovakia as well.[28] This was the way these Directives took their central position and everyday practical importance within the law of contract. This was what happened in some old Member States as well, for example in Austria[29] and in Germany,[30] and as regards the implementation of the proposal for the Consumer Sales Directive, in France too.[31] The solution of the integration of these Directives into national civil codes was preferred despite the fact that the mandatory rules of consumer protection place a burden on the rules of traditional contract law, and integration causes other conceptual and systematic difficulties as well.

The advantages and disadvantages of the two different methods of implementation can be defined very clearly today. Integration by way of individual legislation expresses the European law origin of the rules in a much clearer and simpler way. This in turn satisfies the requirement of uniform interpretation, and makes it clear that it is possible to bring a case before the European Court of Justice, and to ask for a preliminary ruling. The individual rules, on the other hand, shatter civil law into pieces, and do not fit into a codified legal system. Another solution is when consumer protection Directives are implemented in a unified consumer code, as it was done in Austria and in France until recently. This method ensures the transparency required by consumer protection, but it does not pay sufficient attention to the different character (civil, administrative, procedural, criminal law character, etc.) of these consumer protection norms; instead it combines all the

[28] See Vékás and Paschke (eds.), *Europäisches Recht im ungarischen Privat- und Wirtschaftsrecht* (2004), pp. 12–68; Tichý, in Zemánek and Paschke (eds.), *Das tschechische Privat- und Wirtschaftsrecht unter dem Einfluss des europäischen Rechts* (2004), pp. 13–55.

[29] Lurger, *Integration des Verbraucherrechts in das ABGB*?, in Fischer-Czermak, Hopf and Schauer, *Das ABGB auf dem Weg in das 3. Jahrtausend*, pp. 110–136.

[30] See Grundmann, Medicus and Rolland (eds.), *Europäisches Kaufgewährleistungsrecht – Reform und Internationalisierung des deutschen Schuldrechts* (2000).

[31] See to the draft proposal Frizberg, *Die französische Umsetzung der Richtlinie* 1999/44/EG *zum Verbrauchsgüterkauf – Ein neuer Maßstab im Verbraucherschutz? ZfRV* 44 (2003) pp. 203–220.

rules concerning consumer protection in a single law. The requirements of the unified nature of civil law rules and the codification needs are best satisfied by integrating consumer protection Directives into national civil codes. In the last two cases (i.e. integration into a consumer code and into the civil code respectively) we must be careful to indicate the European law origin of the norms. This is a prerequisite for uniform interpretation.

After having assessed the advantages and disadvantages above, we believe that in a codified legal system it would be most practical to integrate, if possible, the consumer protection private law norms of European origin into the civil code of each state. The field of consumer protection law is far too important today to be left out of the civil code. Apart from that, integration into the code also has the advantage that the contradictions encountered in different Directives (e.g. different time limits for consumer rescission, etc.) could be most easily eliminated by using this method. These advantages can be given further effect in the creation of a new code as well.

A further question arises about whether to implement consumer protection Directives only having regard to consumer issues or whether to implement them with a general scope. This question can be answered only after looking at particular Directives individually. The Hungarian legislator, for example, implemented the Consumer Sales Directive with a general scope (*überobligatorisch*), because it wanted to avoid the multiplication of sales provisions within the Hungarian civil code. The Unfair Terms Directive had a similar fate. Of course, the implemented rules are classified as mandatory rules only within consumer contracts. The Hungarian legislator – like his German counterpart – sought to modernize the law on the sale of goods at the same time. This solution, however, seems to demand uniform interpretation flowing from its European law origin to the whole regulation, although this would be a requirement only as regards consumer contracts. The unity of rule making, however, requires a uniform interpretation of the implemented Directives.

III. CONCLUSION

The above arguments present the opportunity to make a few concluding remarks.

First of all, it is possible to establish that the recently joined Central European Member States tend to follow the examples set by the old continental countries, rather than Central European states offering an example for the old ones to follow. This is understandable if we take into account the diversity of the tasks to be undertaken almost simultaneously by the Central European legislator in the process of codification of private law, in countries currently trying to fall into line with the state of development of the old Member States of the European Union. This observation does, of course, only relate to the whole codification process, but not to detailed regulations.

In this latter respect, we can expect similar innovation in the Central European codes too.

As regards the detailed regulations, the Principles provided by the international model statutes seem most appropriate to provide an example to follow for the new codes.

It is also obvious that the relationship between a common European law and national laws shows the same kind of problems in the new member states of Central Europe as in the old ones. The conclusions to be drawn are similar in this respect, and they may serve as models or standards to be used mutually.

Chapter 7

Das Konsumentenschutzgesetz – Beginn der Europäisierung des Kroatischen Vertragsrechts

Tatjana Josipović

Abstract: *This article describes the already existing Croatian Consumer Contract Code. Most directives have been transposed here. Its systematic order is discussed and may even help in the task of systemizing parts of consumer related directives on the EC level. This article also analyses the legislative reform steps taken in 2004 which lead to a Civil Code, into which the Consumer Code material is not integrated. This Civil Code does, however, contain the core directive – the Sales Directive – although this directive is, formally, a consumer directive. It also contains directives such as the Product Liability and the Sales Agent Directives. Croatia thus opts for a dualist approach but with some effort to build coherent sub-systems of private law.*

I. EINLEITUNG

Die Republik Kroatien schloss am 7 Dezember 2001 mit den Europäischen Gemeinschaften und deren Mitgliedsstaaten das Stabilisierungs- und Assoziierungsabkommen (SAA) ab.[1] Im Juni 2004 wurde Kroatien der

[1] Das Gesetz über die Bestätigung des Stabilisierungs- und Assoziierungsabkommens zwischen der Republik Kroatien und den Europäischen Gemeinschaften und deren Mitgliedsstaaten, 'Narodne Novine' – Amtsblatt der Republik Kroatien (im weiteren Text: *NN*) Internationale Verträge, 14/01.

S. Grundmann, M. Schauer (eds), *The Architecture of European Codes and Contract Law*, 129–151

Status eines Beitrittskandidaten der Europäischen Union eingeräumt. Im Artikel 69 des SAA verpflichtete sich Kroatien dazu, die allmähliche Anpassung der geltenden Gesetze und der künftigen Gesetzgebung an den *acquis communautaire* sicherzustellen. Die Anpassung hat am Tag der Unterzeichnung des Vertrags begonnen und wird schrittweise auf alle Elemente des Rechtsbesitzstandes aus dem SAA ausgeweitet und spätestens innerhalb von sechs Jahren ab dem Inkrafttreten des SAA abgeschlossen sein (article 69/2).[2] In der frühen Phase konzentrierte sich die Angleichung auf diejenigen grundlegenden Teile des Rechtbesitzstandes der Gemeinschaft, die sich auf den Binnenmarkt und auf andere handelsbezogene Bereiche beziehen. Im Rahmen dieser Prioritäten war die Angleichung der kroatischen an die europäischen Standards des Verbraucherschutzes ein besonders wichtiger Bereich im Hinblick darauf, dass ein wirksamer Verbraucherschutz für ein angemessenes Funktionieren der Marktwirtschaft unentbehrlich ist. Die Verpflichtung zur Angleichung des Verbraucherschutzes hat Kroatien ausdrücklich aus dem article 74/2 des Abkommens übernommen. Kroatien hat sich verpflichtet:

- die Anpassung der Gesetzgebung und die Angleichung des Verbraucherschutzes in Kroatien an den Schutz, der in der Union in Kraft ist, sicherzustellen;
- eine Politik des aktiven Verbraucherschutzes einschließlich einer besseren Information und der Entwicklung unabhängiger Organisationen zu führen;
- einen wirksamen gesetzlichen Verbraucherschutz mit dem Ziel einer Qualitätsverbesserung der Konsumwaren und dem Erhalt der entsprechenden Sicherheitsstandards zu gewährleisten.

Zum Zeitpunkt der Unterzeichnung des SAA und der Übernahme der Verpflichtungen zur Anpassung der nationalen Gesetzgebung an den *acquis communautaire* war der Verbraucherschutz in Kroatien nicht systematisch und umfassend durch eine Vorschrift geregelt. Die Bestimmungen über den Verbraucherschutz waren in zahlreichen Sondervorschriften aus verschiedenen Rechtsbereichen enthalten.[3] Der Verbraucherschutz wurde erst durch das Konsumentenschutzgesetz (KSchG)[4] aus dem Jahre 2003 systematischer und umfassender geregelt. Mit der Verabschiedung dieses Gesetzes beginnt innerhalb der kroatischen Rechtsordnung die Entwicklung eines neuen

---

2 Die Vertragsparteien werden das Abkommen im Einklang mit ihren entsprechenden Verfahren genehmigen (ratifizieren). Das Abkommen tritt am ersten Tag des zweiten Monats in Kraft, der nach dem Tag folgt, an dem sich die Parteien gegenseitig über die Beendigung dieser Verfahren in Kenntnis gesetzt haben (art. 129 Abkommen).

3 Die für den Verbraucherschutz relevanten Bestimmungen sind z.B. im Handelsgesetz, Postgesetz, Gesetz über die Kommunalwirtschaft, Normierungsgesetz, Energiegesetz, Gesetz über den Markt der elektrischen Energie, Gesetz über das Staatsinspektorat und in vielen anderen Gesetzen enthalten.

4 *NN* 96/03.

Rechtsbereichs – des Verbraucherschutzrechts – und in seinem Rahmen ebenfalls des Verbrauchervertragsrechts.

Das Konsumentenschutzgesetz wird ab dem 8 September 2003 angewandt und gilt als grundlegende und allgemeine Vorschrift über den Verbraucherschutz in der Republik Kroatien. Im KSchG sind – gemäß den durch das SAA übernommenen Verpflichtungen – zahlreiche Richtlinien über den Verbraucherschutz in die nationale kroatische Gesetzgebung übernommen worden. Der Großteil dieser Richtlinien bezieht sich auf die Vertragsverhältnisse zwischen Kaufleuten und Verbrauchern, auf einzelne Verbraucherverträge oder einzelne Aspekte dieser Verträge. Die KSchG-Bestimmungen, in welche diese Richtlinien eingebaut wurden, haben bedeutende Auswirkungen auf das positive kroatische Vertragsrecht. Durch die Verabschiedung des KSchG haben die Europäisierung des kroatischen Vertragsrechts und seine Angleichung an die europäischen Trends bei der Entwicklung des Vertragsrechts begonnen.

II. DAS VERBRAUCHERSCHUTZRECHT

1. Der Anwendungsbereich des Konsumentenschutzgesetzes

Durch das Konsumentenschutzgesetz werden die grundlegenden Verbraucherrechte beim Kauf von Produkten und Dienstleistungen, sowie bei anderen Formen des Produkt- und Leistungserwerbs auf dem Markt geregelt (article 1 KSchG). Die grundlegenden Verbraucherrechte sind im KSchG in fünf Gruppen unterteilt: (1) das Recht auf den Schutz wirtschaftlicher Verbraucherinteressen; (2) das Recht auf den Schutz vor Lebens-, Gesundheits- und Vermögensgefahren; (3) das Recht auf den Verbraucherrechtsschutz; (4) das Recht auf Information und Belehrung der Verbraucher und (5) das Recht auf Verbrauchervereinigung zum Schutz der Verbraucherinteressen, das Recht auf Verbrauchervertretung und auf Teilnahme des Verbrauchervertreters bei der Arbeit der Stellen, welche die im Interesse der Verbraucher liegenden Fragen klären. Diese Rechte können in Ausnahmefällen durch Gesetze und in gesetzlich geregelten Fällen eingeschränkt werden, d.h. zum Schutz der Interessen und Sicherheit der Republik Kroatien, der Natur, der menschlichen Umwelt und der Gesundheit der Menschen (article 1/3 KSchG).[5]

Als *Verbraucher* gilt gemäß dem KSchG jede natürliche Person, die ein Rechtsgeschäft auf dem Markt zu Zwecken abschließt, die weder für ihren Beruf, noch für ihre Geschäftstätigkeit oder unternehmerische Tätigkeit bestimmt sind (article 3 Punkt 1 KSchG). Als *Kaufmann* im Sinne des KSchG gilt jede Person (sei es nun eine natürliche oder eine juristische Person, eine

[5] Die Einschränkungen müssen auf die Weise gesetzlich geregelt werden, dass der Verbraucher nicht in eine ungleichberechtigte Lage versetzt wird (art. 1/3 KSchG).

öffentliche oder privatrechtliche Person), die Rechtsgeschäfte anbietet oder abschließt, beziehungsweise im Rahmen ihres Berufes oder ihrer Tätigkeit auf dem Markt auftritt (article 3 Punkt 2 KSchG). Als Kaufleute werden Handelsgesellschaften und Einzelhändler angesehen, aber auch alle anderen natürlichen und juristischen Personen, die im Rahmen ihres Berufes oder ihrer Tätigkeit auf dem Markt auftreten (Landwirte, Gewerbetreibende, öffentliche Institutionen, Einheiten lokaler und regionaler Selbstverwaltung, freie Künstler, Architekten, Rechtsanwälte u.Ä.).[6] Auf Grund einer solch weit gefassten Definition des Begriffs des Kaufmanns ist auch der Anwendungsbereich des KSchG sehr ausgedehnt. Das KSchG wird auf alle auf dem Markt geschlossenen Rechtsgeschäfte angewandt, bei denen der Verbraucher eine Vertragspartei darstellt, und die andere Seite eine Person ist, die im Rahmen ihrer Tätigkeit solche Geschäfte professionell abschließt, ohne Rücksicht darauf, ob es sich um Verkaufsverträge für Produkte oder Dienstleistungen oder um Vermittlungsverträge handelt.

Das Konsumentenschutzgesetz wird auf alle Rechtsverhältnisse zwischen Verbrauchern und Kaufleuten angewendet, die durch den Erwerb von Produkten und die Erbringung von Dienstleistungen auf dem Markt entstehen (article 1/1 KSchG). Es regelt die Verpflichtungen der Kaufleute durch die allgemeinen Bestimmungen über den Einzelhandelsverkauf,[7] die Verpflichtungen der öffentlichen Dienstleister gegenüber den Verbrauchern,[8] die Werbung für Produkte und Dienstleistungen,[9] die Träger des

6 Z. Pogarčić, 'Obveze trgovaca u zaštiti potrošača: opća pravila o trgovanju u Obveze trgovaca u sustavu zaštite potrošača' (Die Verpflichtungen der Kaufleute beim Verbraucherschutz: allgemeine Handelsregeln) in: M. Dika und Z. Pogarčić (eds.), *Die Verpflichtungen der Kaufleute im System des Verbraucherschutzes* (2003), 8; M. Baretić, 'Nepoštene odredbe u potrošačkim ugovorima u Obveze trgovaca u sustavu zaštite potrošača' (Missbräuchliche Klauseln in Verbraucherverträgen) in: M. Dika und Z. Pogarčić (eds.), *Die Verpflichtungen der Kaufleute im System des Verbraucherschutzes* (2003), 65.

7 Im Rahmen der allgemeinen Verkaufsregeln für den Einzelhandel sind die Verpflichtungen des Kaufmanns bezüglich der Bedingungen für den Verkauf und die Dienstleistungserbringung, des Preisaushangs, der Tilgung von Verpflichtungen, der Rechnungsausstellung, der Verpackung, der Produktdeklaration, des Ausverkaufs usw. geregelt (art. 7-21). Die Verpflichtungen des Kaufmanns bezüglich des Preisaushangs des Produkts sind nach dem Vorbild der Richtlinie 98/6 geregelt.

8 Als öffentliche Dienstleistungen gelten der Verkauf von elektrischer Energie, Gas aus dem Verteilungsnetz, Wärmeenergie, öffentlichen Telekommunikationsdienstleistungen, Postdienstleistungen, Dienstleistungen der Überführung von Reisenden im öffentlichen inner- und außerstädtischen Verkehr an die Verbraucher, sowie die Trinkwasserversorgung, die Abwasserabführung und die Erhaltung der Sauberkeit (art. 22/1 KSchG). Die Verpflichtungen des Kaufmanns bei der Erbringung von öffentlichen Dienstleistungen sind derart geregelt, dass allen die Erreichbarkeit von Dienstleistungen zu den im Vorhinein bekannten und vereinbarten Bedingungen und Preisen ermöglicht wird (art. 22-27).

9 Die Bestimmungen über die Werbung für Produkte und Dienstleistungen sind nach dem Vorbild der Richtlinie 84/450/EWG des Rates zur Angleichung der Rechts- und Verwaltungsvorschriften der Mitgliedstaaten über irreführende Werbung geregelt (ABl. L 1984, 250, S. 17).

Verbraucherschutzes,[10] die Inspektionsaufsicht und die Haftung für Ordnungswidrigkeiten gegen die Verbraucherrechte.

Nach dem Vorbild der europäischen Richtlinien über den Verbraucherschutz werden einige Verbraucherverträge durch das KSchG besonders geregelt: der Vertragsabschluss außerhalb der Geschäftsräume des Kaufmanns, der Vertragsabschuss im Fernabsatz, der Verbraucherkredit, der Vertrag über das Teilzeitnutzungsrecht an Immobilien und über unfaire Klauseln in Verbraucherverträgen.[11] Diese Bestimmungen stellen die grundlegende Rechtsquelle für das Verbrauchervertragsrecht dar, das seine eigenen Besonderheiten und Prinzipien hat, auf Grund welcher es sich vom allgemeinen Vertragsrecht unterscheidet.

2. Merkmale des Verbrauchervertragsrechts

Der grundlegende Zweck des Verbrauchervertragsrechts ist, dem Verbraucher – der schwächeren Vertragspartei bei Verbraucherverträgen – einen stärkeren Schutz zu gewährleisten. Dem Verbraucher wird bereits im Verhandlungsstadium, beim Vertragsabschluss sowie während seiner Erfüllung bzw. seiner Auflösung ein besonderer Rechtsschutz gewährleistet. Deshalb wird bei der Regelung der Vertragsverhältnisse zwischen Kaufmann und Verbraucher der Schwerpunkt insbesondere auf die ausdrückliche Regelung der Verbindlichkeiten des Kaufmanns in den Verbraucherverträgen, beziehungsweise auf die ausdrückliche Regelung der besonderen Verbraucherrechte in der Phase des Vertragsabschlusses, der Vertragserfüllung und -auflösung gelegt. Von diesen besonderen Verbraucherrechten bleiben jedoch die Rechte der Verbraucher, die ihnen auf Grund anderer Gesetze zustehen, unberührt (article 2/1 KSchG).

Die Verpflichtungen der Kaufleute gegenüber den Verbrauchern befinden sich in zahlreichen KSchG-Bestimmungen. Es ist ausdrücklich vorgeschrieben, dass der Kaufmann gegenüber dem Verbraucher zur Erfüllung des Vertrags im Einklang mit den Vertragsbestimmungen und den Schuldrechtsvorschriften

[10] Träger des Verbraucherschutzes sind die Verbraucherschutzvereine, der Verband der Verbraucherschutzvereine, das kroatische Parlament und die Regierung der Republik Kroatien.

[11] Durch die KSchG-Bestimmungen über Verbraucherverträge und missbräuchliche Klauseln in Verbraucherverträgen wurde die Richtlinie 97/7/EG über den Verbraucherschutz bei Vertragsabschlüssen im Fernabsatz (ABl. L 1997, 144, S. 19), die Richtlinie 87/102/EWG zur Angleichung der Rechts- und Verwaltungsvorschriften der Mitgliedstaaten über den Verbraucherkredit (ABl. L 1987, 42, S. 48), die Richtlinie 94/47/EG zum Schutz der Erwerber im Hinblick auf bestimmte Aspekte von Verträgen über den Erwerb von Teilzeitnutzungsrechten an Immobilien (ABl. L 1994, 280, S. 83) und die Richtlinie 93/13/EWG über missbräuchliche Klauseln in Verbraucherverträgen (ABl. L 1993, 95, S. 29) in die kroatische Gesetzgebung implementiert.

verpflichtet ist (article 5). An diese Bestimmung knüpft die ausdrückliche Bestimmung über die Verpflichtung des Kaufmanns oder Herstellers, der eine Garantie ausgestellt hat, sich an die gesetzlichen und an die durch die Garantie übernommenen Pflichten zu halten (article 6 KSchG). Der Kaufmann kann nur aus besonders gerechtfertigten Gründen den Abschluss eines Vertrags über den Verkauf eines am Verkaufsort ausgestellten Produktes ablehnen, selbst dann, wenn die Ausstellung der Produkte am Verkaufsort nach den Allgemeinvorschriften des Schuldrechts nicht als Angebot gilt (article 7 KSchG). Der Kaufmann ist verpflichtet, den Betrag des festgelegten Einzelhandelspreises der Produkte oder Dienstleistungen klar, sichtbar und lesbar anzugeben (article 8 KSchG) und für das verkaufte Produkt eine Rechnung auszustellen (article 12 KSchG). Der Kaufmann hat ebenfalls besondere Verpflichtungen im Hinblick auf die Verpackung der Produkte, die Produktdeklaration und die Organisation des Ausverkaufs (article 15, 17-20 KSchG). Beim Abschluss eines Vertrags über die Erbringung öffentlicher Dienstleistungen sind die Verpflichtungen des Kaufmanns durch strenge zwingende Bestimmungen geregelt, welche die Anbieter dieser Dienstleistungen zum Vertragsabschluss, zum Erhalt der Qualität bei der Erbringung der Dienstleistungen, zur Abrechnung der Dienstleistungen und zur Vorauszahlung verpflichtet (article 22-28 KSchG). Der Kaufmann hat in der Phase, die dem Abschluss eines Verbrauchervertrags vorangeht, ebenfalls spezifische Verpflichtungen. Der Kaufmann ist zum Zweck eines stärkeren Verbraucherschutzes vor oder während des Vertragsabschlusses verpflichtet, den Verbraucher besonders über sein Recht auf die Auflösung des Vertrags aufzuklären, und ihm auch andere vorausgehende Auskünfte über den Gegenstand und Inhalt des künftigen Vertrags sowie über seine künftigen Verbindlichkeiten zu geben.[12] Eine den KSchG-Bestimmungen entgegenstehende Vorgehensweise des Kaufmanns führt dazu, dass er sich für eine Ordnungswidrigkeit verantworten muss (article 109 *et seq.* KSchG).

Die spezifischen Verbraucherrechte beim Abschluss von Verbraucherverträgen werden an den Rechten der Verbraucher auf eine Belehrung über ihre Rechte, den Inhalt und die Bedingungen des Vertrags, bereits in der Verhandlungsphase, insbesondere am Recht auf eine einseitige Vertragsauflösung ohne Anführung von Gründen erkennbar.[13] Im Falle einer solchen Auflösung haftet der Verbraucher nicht für Schäden, welche der Kaufmann auf Grund der Vertragsauflösung erlitten hat. Der Kaufmann ist verpflichtet, ihm den eingezahlten Gesamtbetrag samt Verzugszinsen

[12] Vgl. dazu z.B. art. 31 KSchG für außerhalb der Geschäftsräumlichkeiten des Kaufmanns abgeschlossene Verträge, art. 42 KSchG für den im Fernabsatz abgeschlossenen Vertrag, art. 74 KSchG für den Vertag über das Teilzeitnutzungsrecht an Immobilien.

[13] Vgl. dazu art. 32 KSchG für den außerhalb der Geschäftsräumlichkeiten des Kaufmanns abgeschlossenen Vertrag, art. 44 KSchG für den im Fernabsatz abgeschlossenen Vertrag, art. 77 KSchG für den Vertag über das Teilzeitnutzungsrecht an Immobilien.

zurückzuerstatten.[14] Der Verbraucher hat ebenfalls das Recht auf einen besonderen kollektiven Verbraucherschutz. Dieser wird im öffentlichen Interesse durchgeführt und von der Republik Kroatien gesichert (article 98/1 KSchG). Die Verbraucherschutzvereine sind beispielsweise befugt, Gerichtsverfahren einzuleiten, um die Einstellung der entgegen den KSchG-Bestimmungen über den Vertragsabschuss im Fernabsatz (article 102/1/ Spiegelstrich 7 KSchG) stehenden Geschäftspraxis, die Untersagung der Verwendung unlauterer Vertragsbestimmungen in Standardverträgen (article 102/1/Spiegelstrich 8 KSchG), und die Beendigung der irreführenden beziehungsweise unzulässigen vergleichenden Werbung (article 102/1/ Spiegelstrich 9 KSchG) zu erwirken. Es besteht ebenfalls die Möglichkeit einer sog. alternativen Beilegung von Streitigkeiten durch Schiedssenate, die vom Verband der Verbraucherschutzvereine errichtet werden (article 101/8 KSchG).

Die besonderen Rechte und Verpflichtungen der Verbraucher in den Verbraucherverträgen bestimmen auch die spezifischen Merkmale des kroatischen Verbrauchervertragsrechts:

- Das Verbrauchervertragsrecht aus dem KSchG hat als lex specialis Vorrang vor dem allgemeinen Vertragsrecht, das im Gesetz über die Schuldverhältnisse (SchuldG)[15] – der Rechtsquelle des Schuldrechts in der Republik Kroatien – geregelt ist. Das SchuldG wird lediglich subsidiär angewandt – sofern und soweit für ein bestimmtes schuldrechtliches Verhältnis im KSchG keine Sonderregelung bestimmt ist (article 2/2 KSchG).
- Das Verbrauchervertragsrecht aus dem KSchG stellt kein ganzheitliches Verbraucherschutzsystem beim Abschluss von Verbraucherverträgen dar. Der Verbraucherschutz auf dem Gebiet des Abschlusses von Verbraucherverträgen ist lediglich fragmentarisch, so dass im Übrigen auch weiterhin die allgemeinen Bestimmungen des Schuldrechts oder andere Sondervorschriften zur Anwendung kommen. Das KSchG regelt nur bestimmte Verbraucherverträge bzw. nur bestimmte Aspekte einzelner Verbraucherverträge, d.h. einzelne Rechte, die dem Verbraucher beim Abschluss des jeweiligen Verbrauchervertrags zustehen. Für einzelne Verträge (z.B. Timesharing) ist jedoch die rechtliche Natur der Rechte, die der Verbraucher erwirbt, nicht gesetzlich geregelt, obgleich davon in einem großen Maße abhängt, auf welche Art und Weise der Verbraucher seine auf Grund des Vertrags zustehenden Rechte schützen kann. Der kroatische Gesetzgeber hat sich für die Implementierung der

[14] Vgl. dazu art. 34/2,3 KSchG für den außerhalb der Geschäftsräumlichkeiten des Kaufmanns abgeschlossenen Vertrag, art. 47/2,3 KSchG für den im Fernabsatz abgeschlossenen Vertrag, art. 77/4 KSchG für den Vertag über das Teilzeitnutzungsrecht an Immobilien.

[15] *NN* 53/91, 73/91, 111/93, 3/94, 107/95, 7/96, 91/96, 112/99, 88/01.

Verbraucherschutzrichtlinien durch die Übernahme in die nationale Rechtsordnung und die nahezu wörtliche Übersetzung entschieden, ohne sie zu einer systematischen und konsistenten Einheit zu verbinden. Hinsichtlich der Verbraucherverträge stellt das KSchG lediglich eine spezifische Kompilation von Bestimmungen einzelner Verbraucherschutzrichtlinien in einzelnen Verbraucherverträgen dar. Deshalb unterscheidet sich auch die Geltendmachung der jeweiligen Verbraucherrechte aus einzelnen Verbraucherverträgen, welche Rechte in allen Verbraucherverträgen gleich sind (z.B. unterschiedliche Fristen für die einseitige Auflösung).

- Durch das Verbrauchervertragsrecht wird im Einklang mit den europäischen Richtlinien lediglich der Mindestschutz geregelt, der den Verbrauchern zum Zweck eines wirksamen Funktionierens des Marktes gewährleistet werden sollte. Der kroatische Gesetzgeber hat sich nicht für die Ausweitung dieses Schutzes über das Minimum hinaus entschieden, welches durch die Implementierung der Richtlinien umgesetzt werden sollte.
- Für die Verbraucherverträge gilt die besondere Regel über die Vertragsauslegung. Zweideutige oder unverständliche Vertragsbestimmungen werden in dem für den Verbraucher günstigeren Sinne ausgelegt (article 86/1 KSchG).
- Zum Zweck eines stärkeren Verbraucherschutzes besteht ebenfalls eine besondere Kollisionsregel. Durch die Auswahl des maßgebenden Rechts kann einem Verbraucher, der seinen Aufenthaltsort in der Republik Kroatien hat, nicht der Schutz, auf welchen er nach dem KSchG Anspruch hat, entzogen werden. (article 4 KSchG).[16]
- Im Verbrauchervertragsrecht sind außer privatrechtlichen Elementen auch zahlreiche öffentlichrechtliche Elemente enthalten, da der Verbraucherschutz im öffentlichen Interesse durchgeführt wird (article 98/1 des KSchG). Die öffentlichrechtlichen Elemente kommen beispielsweise in den besonderen Zwangsbestimmungen des KSchG über die Verpflichtungen des Kaufmanns bei der Dienstleistungserbringung, in den Bestimmungen über die Werbung für Produkte und Dienstleistungen,[17]

[16] Im kroatischen internationalen Privatrecht bestehen jedoch keine besonderen Kollisionsregeln für Verbraucherverträge, wie z.B. in art. 5 Römisches Übereinkommen über das aus vertraglichen Schuldverhältnissen anwendbare Recht (19 Juni 1980). Es bestehen nicht einmal besondere Bestimmungen über die gerichtliche Zuständigkeit und die Vollstreckung von gerichtlichen Entscheidungen bezüglich der Verbraucherverträge, wie z.B. die in art. 15–17 Verordnung (EG) Nr. 44/2001 über die gerichtliche Zuständigkeit und die Anerkennung und Vollstreckung von Entscheidungen in Zivil- und Handelssachen (ABl 2001, L 12, S. 1).

[17] Vgl. dazu z.B. art. 31 KSchG beim außerhalb der Geschäftsräumlichkeiten des Kaufmanns abgeschlossenen Vertrag, art. 42 KSchG beim im Fernabsatz abgeschlossenen Vertrag, art. 74, 75 KSchG beim Vertag über das Teilzeitnutzungsrecht an Immobilien.

in der Delikthaftung des Kaufmanns auf Grund eines Verstoßes gegen die Verbraucherrechte u.Ä. zum Ausdruck.

- Im Verbrauchervertragsrecht sich zahlreiche Zwangsbestimmungen enthalten, welche die Vertragsparteien durch Vereinbarungen nicht ändern können. In zahlreichen Fällen ist die Möglichkeit der freien Verfügung über einzelne Rechte aus dem Vertrag – etwa durch abweichende Vereinbarung einzelner Vertragsbestimmungen oder den Verzicht auf einzelne Vertragsrechte – ausgeschlossen.[18]
- Obwohl es sich bei einem Verbrauchervertrag um ein zweiseitig verpflichtendes Verhältnis zwischen Kaufmann und Verbraucher handelt, welche in der Regel *inter partes* gelten, entfalten Verbraucherverträge ex lege bestimmte Rechtswirkungen auch gegenüber Dritten, mit denen der Verbraucher andere Rechtsgeschäfte abgeschlossen hat, insbesondere etwa im Falle einer einseitigen Vertragsauflösung.[19]
- Das Verbrauchervertragsrecht führt ebenfalls neue Regeln über die Beweislast in Rechtsstreitigkeiten ein, die gegen den Kaufmann geführt werden. Zum Zweck der Erleichterung der Lage des Verbrauchers bei Rechtsstreitigkeiten mit dem Kaufmann, liegt die Last des Nachweises zahlreicher relevanter Tatsachen beim Kaufmann.[20]
- Die Möglichkeit des gerichtlichen Schutzes der Verbraucherrechte wurde ausgeweitet. Durch die Anerkennung des Rechts der Verbraucherschutzvereine gerichtlichen Schutz zu verlangen, wenn die Verbraucherrechte durch Verbraucherverträge verletzt werden, wandte man sich merklich von der individualistischen Konzeption des Rechts auf den Gerichtsschutz ab. Das Recht auf den Schutz wird nicht nur demjenigen Verbraucher zuerkannt, dessen Recht im konkreten Fall gefährdet oder verletzt wurde, sondern es ist durch eine Kollektivklage möglich, gruppenbezogene, kollektive Verbraucherinteressen zu schützen.[21]

Alle angeführten Merkmale des Verbrauchervertragsrechts wirken sich stark auf das kroatische allgemeine Vertragsrecht aus. Zu diesem Zeitpunkt bestehen

[18] Vgl. dazu z.B. art. 82 KSchG über einzelne Vertragsbestimmungen, die als missbräuchlich gelten können.

[19] Vgl. hierzu z.B. art. 49, 50 KSchG über den Einfluss der Auflösung des im Fernabsatz abgeschlossenen Vertrags auf das gewährte Darlehen, art. 68 KSchG beim Vertrag über das Verbraucherdarlehen über die Verantwortung des Darlehensgebers für den Verkäufer und über den Einfluss der Auflösung des Kaufvertrags auf den Darlehensvertrag, art. 79 KSchG über den Einfluss des Vertrags über das Teilzeitnutzungsrecht an Immobilien auf den Kreditvertrag.

[20] Vgl. hierzu z.B. art. 55 für den im Fernabsatz abgeschlossenen Vertrag, art. 78 für den Vertrag über das Teilzeitnutzungsrecht an Immobilien.

[21] M. Dika, 'Pravosudna legitimacija udruga za zaštitu potrošača u Obveze trgovaca u sustavu zaštite potrošača' (Die juristische Legitimation der Verbraucherschutzvereine) in: M. Dika und Z. Pogarčić (eds.), *Die Verpflichtungen der Kaufleute im System des Verbraucherschutzes* (2003), 130.

zwei Rechtsregelungen für Vertragsverhältnisse – die Rechtsregelung für die durch das KSchG ausdrücklich geregelten Verbraucherverträge und die allgemeine im SchuldG festgelegte Rechtsregelung für alle übrigen Vertragsverhältnisse, die subsidiär auch für Verbrauchervertragsverhältnisse gilt.

III. DAS VERBRAUCHERSCHUTZRECHT UND DAS ALLGEMEINE VERTRAGSRECHT

1. Rechtsquellen des allgemeinen Vertragsrechts

Die Hauptrechtsquelle des Schuldrechts in der Republik Kroatien ist das Gesetz über die Schuldverhältnisse (GSV) aus dem Jahre 1978. Dieses war zuerst ein Bundesgesetz, welches das Schuldrecht (allgemeiner Teil und Verträge) auf dem Gebiet der ehem. SFRJ regelte. Zum Zeitpunkt, als es in Kraft getreten ist, stellte es eine sehr gelungene Kodifizierung des Schuldrechts dar. Nach der Unabhängigkeitserklärung übernahm die Republik Kroatien 1991 das Gesetz über die Schuldverhältnisse in ihre nationale Gesetzgebung. Das Gesetz über die Schuldverhältnisse ist mit seinen 1108 Artikeln und bestimmten Änderungen und Ergänzungen immer noch die Hauptquelle des kroatischen vertraglichen und außervertraglichen Schuldrechts.[21a]

Das Gesetz über die Schuldverhältnisse besteht aus zwei großen Teilen: 1. 'Allgemeiner Teil' (article 1-453) und 2. 'Verträge' (article 454–1098). Im 'Allgemeinen Teil' sind die Grundsätze der Schuldverhältnisse geregelt, auf denen die Regelung des kroatischen Schuldrechts beruht. Das sind der Grundsatz der Gestaltungsfreiheit der Schuldverhältnisse, des dispositiven Charakters der Gesetzesbestimmungen, der Gleichberechtigung der an Schuldverhältnissen Beteiligten, der Grundsatz von Treu und Glauben, des Verbots des Rechtsmissbrauchs, der Gleichwertigkeit der Leistungen, das Verbot der Schadensverursachung, der Grundsatz der Vertragserfüllungspflicht und der Anwendung guter Sitten. Zusätzlich zu den Grundsätzen sind im 'Allgemeinen Teil' auch die Entstehung (vertraglicher und außervertraglicher) Schuldverhältnisse, die Vertretungsarten, der Vertragsabschluss, die Vertragsauslegung, die Gründe für die Nichtigkeit des Vertrags und die allgemeine Rechtswirksamkeit des Vertrags geregelt. Von den außervertraglichen Schuldverhältnissen ist die außervertragliche Schadenshaftung, die ungerechtfertigte Bereicherung, die Geschäftsführung ohne Auftrag normiert. Im 'Allgemeinen Teil' sind auch Bestimmungen über die Rechtswirksamkeit der Verbindlichkeiten, allgemeine Bestimmungen über die Geltendmachung der Ansprüche von Gläubigern und die über die Pflichterfüllung des Schuldners, Bestimmungen über unterschiedliche Arten des Erlöschens der Verbindlichkeiten, über den Gläubiger- und

[21a] Ab 1. Januar 2006 ist das neue Gesetz über die Schuldverhältnisse in Kraft getreden (*NN* 35/05). Die Ausführungen im Text bleiben zur Gänze unberührt.

Schuldnerwechsel in einem schuldrechtlichen Verhältnis sowie über verschiedene Arten von Verbindlichkeiten (Geldverbindlichkeiten, Verbindlichkeiten mit mehreren Schuldnern oder Gläubigern, Verbindlichkeiten mit mehreren Gegenständen) enthalten. Die Bestimmungen des 'Allgemeinen Teils' gelten für sämtliche Schuldverhältnisse (sowohl vertragliche als auch außervertragliche), die durch das SchuldG geregelt sind. Sie stellen auch eine subsidiäre Rechtsquelle für die Regelung aller sonstigen schuldrechtlichen Verhältnisse dar, die durch andere Sondervorschriften geregelt sind.

Der zweite Teil des SchuldG regelt besondere Arten von Verträgen. Einige dieser Verträge gelten als typische Verträge des bürgerlichen Rechts und andere als solche des Handelsrechts. Für jede Vertragsart werden ausdrücklich der Begriff des Vertrags und dessen Merkmale und wesentliche Bestandteile (die Verbindlichkeiten der Vertragsparteien und die Beendigung des Vertrags) festgelegt. Auf all diejenigen Fragen, die nicht ausdrücklich durch die besonderen Bestimmungen über den einzelnen Vertrag geregelt sind, werden die Bestimmungen des 'Allgemeinen Teils' angewandt. In der Republik Kroatien besteht kein Dualismus bei der Regelung der Schuldverhältnisse, je nachdem, ob es sich um Verträge des Handelsrechts oder des bürgerlichen Rechts handelt. Das SchuldG regelt ebenfalls typische Handelsgeschäfte, da nach kroatischem Recht die monistische Theorie gilt, gemäß welcher die Handelsgeschäfte durch die einheitliche und allgemeine schuldrechtliche Vorschrift geregelt werden. Die Grundregel ist, dass unabhängig davon, wer die Vertragsparteien sind, bzw. ob die Vertragsparteien Kaufleute oder Subjekte des bürgerlichen Rechts sind, dieselben Regeln des Schuldrechts gelten (article 25 des SchuldG). In Fällen, in denen wegen der Besonderheit der Rechtsverhältnisse zwischen den Kaufleuten die Vertragsverhältnisse anders geregelt werden müssen (strenger oder elastischer), regelt das SchuldG ausdrücklich Ausnahmen von den allgemeinen Regeln, indem es vorschreibt, dass bestimmte Bestimmungen nur dann gelten, wenn die Vertragsparteien Kaufleute sind. Das SchuldG kennt zahlreiche Verträge, die als typische schuldrechtliche Verträge angesehen werden können (Verkauf, Pacht, Mandatsvertrag u.Ä.) sowie zahlreiche Verträge, die vorwiegend gerade zwischen Kaufleuten abgeschlossen werden (Lagerung, Kommission, Vermittlung, Gesellschaft des bürgerlichen Rechts, Spedition, Versicherung, Bankverträge u.Ä.) geregelt.

Neben dem SchuldG, als grundlegende Rechtsquelle des Schuld- und Vertragsrechts in der Republik Kroatien, bestehen auch andere Sondervorschriften, die einzelne Vertragstypen, wie z.B. das Wohnungsmietgesetz, das Gesetz über die Verpachtung von Geschäftsräumen u.a., regeln. Im Verhältnis zum SchuldG stellen sie eine *lex specialis* dar und haben Vorrang bei der Anwendung. Das SchuldG wird nur angewandt, sofern durch diese Sondervorschriften über die einzelnen Vertragsarten nicht etwas Besonderes oder Ausdrückliches festgelegt ist. In der Regel werden durch die Sondervorschriften über die einzelnen Vertragsarten diejenigen Fragen geregelt, die angesichts der Natur des Vertrags eine Sonderregelung erfordern, wie z.B.: besonderer Schutz des Mieters in Mietverträgen, die Bestimmungen über die Zahlung des Miet- und Pachtzinses, die Bestimmungen über die Beendigung von Verträgen, das Vorkaufsrecht des Mieters ü.Ä.

Obwohl das SchuldG ca. 30 verschiedene Verträge des Handelsrechts und des bürgerlichen Rechts regelt, wobei für einige Verträge Sondervorschriften bestehen, werden manche Vertragstypen noch immer nicht durch positivrechtliche Vorschriften umfasst. Daher bestehen beispielsweise keine besonderen gesetzlichen Bestimmungen über den Schenkungs- und den Leihvertrag. Auf diese Verträge werden ebenfalls die Bestimmungen des 'Allgemeinen Teils' des SchuldG über die Verträge, sowie die Bestimmungen anderer Vorschriften (z.B. des Erbgesetzes) angewandt. Es sind jedoch die Rechtsvorschriften des österreichischen Allgemeinen Bürgerlichen Gesetzbuches (ABGB), welches vor Inkrafttreten des SchuldG als grundlegende Rechtquelle des Schuldrechts in der Republik Kroatien[22,23] gedient hat, weiterhin die grundlegende Rechtquelle der Rechtsregelung des Schenkungs- und Leihvertrags geblieben.

Nach ihrer Unabhängigkeitserklärung führte die Republik Kroatien bedeutende wirtschaftliche, politische und rechtliche Reformen zum Zweck der Anpassung ihres Rechtssystems an die Anforderungen der Marktwirtschaft durch. Im Rahmen dieser Reformen wurde auch das SchuldG einige Male geändert und ergänzt. Am SchuldG wurden nur die notwendigsten Veränderungen zwecks Anpassung an die neuen wirtschaftlichen Verhältnisse vorgenommen. So wurden z.B. 1994 die besonderen Bestimmungen über die Gesellschaft des bürgerlichen Rechts hineingefügt und die Bestimmungen über die Verzugszinsen und der ungerechtfertigten Bereicherung geändert. Die Institute, Grundsätze und Bestimmungen, die auf der sozialistischen Rechtsordnung, der Planwirtschaft und dem gesellschaftlichen Eigentum gründeten, wurden geändert. Damit hat die Wiedereingliederung des kroatischen Schuldrechts in den Kreis der modernen europäischen Rechtsordnungen begonnen. Die Basis für die Entwicklung des sog. klassischen Schuldrechts, das sich in erster Linie an die germanischen Rechtsordnungen anlehnt, an welchen sich die gesamte kroatische privatrechtliche Ordnung ohnehin orientiert hatte, wurde wiederhergestellt. Dabei wurde auch weiterhin an den Grundsätzen festgehalten, auf denen bis dahin die Regelung des kroatischen Vertragsrechts basierte. Ferner wurde an der einheitlichen Regelung der Vertragsverhältnisse, unabhängig davon ob es sich um Verträge

[22] Diese werden als Rechtregeln auf Grund des Gesetzes über die Anwendung der vor dem 6. April 1941 verabschiedeten Rechtsvorschriften angewandt (*NN* 73/91).

[23] In der Geschäftspraxis erscheint immer häufiger eine Reihe von sog. unbenannten Verträgen (Leasing, Franchising, Factoring, Consulting u.Ä.), die ebenfalls noch nicht ausdrücklich durch positive Vorschriften geregelt sind. Auf sie werden in entsprechender Weise die Bestimmungen des allgemeinen Teils des SchuldG sowie die Bestimmungen des SchuldG über Verträge, die ihrer Natur und ihrem Zweck nach dem wesentlichen Inhalt der unbenannten Verträge entsprechen, angewandt (z.B. kommen auf Leasingverträge die Bestimmungen über die Pacht zur Anwendung).

des Handelsrechts oder des bürgerlichen Recht handelt, festgehalten. Schließlich gilt auch weiterhin der Grundsatz, dass im 'Allgemeinen Teil', das auf sämtliche Verträge angewandt wird, nahezu alle wesentlichen Fragen bezüglich des Vertragsabschlusses, der Pflichterfüllung, der Beendigung des Vertrags, der Ungültigkeit des Vertrags, der vertraglichen und vorvertraglichen Schadenshaftung u.A. geregelt sind. In den besonderen Bestimmungen über einzelne Verträge werden lediglich die Besonderheiten des jeweiligen Vertrages, sowie jene Aspekte eines Vertrags geregelt, welche auf Grund dessen Natur eine Sonderregelung erfordern.

2. Elemente des Verbraucherschutzes im allgemeinen Vertragsrecht

Das SchuldG schützt nicht die Verbraucher als eine besondere gesellschaftliche Gruppe, sondern als eine der Vertragsparteien.[24] Der Verbraucherschutz bei den Vertragsverhältnissen kann jedoch ebenfalls durch die Berufung auf zahlreiche Bestimmungen des SchuldG verwirklicht werden, welche die klassischen Rechtsinstitute des vertraglichen und außervertraglichen Rechts regeln.

Der Verbraucher, als Vertragspartei, kann sich bei Verhältnissen mit einem Kaufmann auf zahlreiche Grundsätze des Schuldrechts berufen, auf Grund welcher er seinen Schutz in Bezug auf den Kaufmann verwirklicht, wie z.B. auf den Grundsatz von Treu und Glauben (article 12 SchuldG), den Grundsatz des Verbots des Rechtsmissbrauchs (article 13/1 SchuldG), den Grundsatz der Gleichwertigkeit von Leistungen (article 15, 139 SchuldG), das Verbot der Schadensverursachung (article 16 SchuldG), den Grundsatz der Vertragserfüllungspflicht (article 17 SchuldG) und den Grundsatz betreffend die Verhaltensweise bei der Pflichterfüllung und bei der Geltendmachung von Rechten (article 18 SchuldG).

---

[24] Obwohl des Gesetz über die Schuldverhältnisse zur Zeit des Selbstverwaltungssozialismus, der auf dem kollektivistischen Konzept der Wirtschaftsverwaltung, der gesellschaftlichen Eigentumsordnung und der Planwirtschaft beruhte, enthielt es zum Zeitpunkt seiner Verabschiedung im art. 8 eine besondere Bestimmung mit der Überschrift 'Verpflichtungen gegenüber den Bürgern als Verbrauchern und Dienstleistungsnutzern'. Diese schrieb vor, dass juristische und natürliche Personen (im Einklang mit der damaligen Nomenklatur der Formen der Rechtssubjekte in der Wirtschaft) bei der Begründung von Schuldverhältnissen und der Geltendmachung der Rechte und Pflichten aus diesen Verhältnissen, wenn sie durch die Ausübung ihrer Tätigkeit die Bedürfnisse der Bürger unmittelbar befriedigen, verpflichtet sind, ihre Rechte und Pflichten derart zu regeln und auszuüben, dass eine regelmäßige und zufriedenstellende Befriedigung der Ansprüche der Bürger zu möglichst günstigen Bedingungen für die Befriedigung dieser Ansprüche gewährleistet wird. An sie knüpfte art. 9 SchuldG, der unter anderem den am Rechtsverkehr Beteiligten die Schadenszufügung gegenüber Marktteilnehmern, Verbrauchern und der gesamten Gesellschaft verbot. Die zitierten Bestimmungen wurden am 8. Oktober 1991, d.h. bei der Übernahme des SchuldG in die Gesetzgebung der Republik, außer Kraft gesetzt.

Es bestehen ebenfalls zahlreiche besondere Bestimmungen im SchuldG, die dem Verbraucher, als der schwächeren Vertragspartei, einen besonderen Schutz gegenüber dem Kaufmann gewähren. Durch die Berufung auf einige dieser Bestimmungen können in der Praxis gleichfalls sehr günstige Wirkungen des Verbraucherschutzes erreicht werden:

- Der Verbraucher kann sich gegenüber dem Kaufmann, der seinen Pflichten aus dem Verbrauchervertrag nicht nachkommt, auf den allgemeinen Grundsatz der Vertragserfüllungspflicht (article 17/1 SchuldG) berufen. Das SchuldG regelt ausdrücklich, dass die an einem Schuldverhältnis Beteiligten auf Erfüllung ihrer Verbindlichkeiten verpflichtet und für diese verantwortlich sind. Bei der Erfüllung der Verbindlichkeiten aus dem Verbrauchervertrag hat der Kaufmann mit der Sorgfalt eines gewissenhaften Fachmanns vorzugehen. Gemäß article 18/2 SchuldG ist der an einem Schuldverhältnis Beteiligte bei der Erfüllung einer Verbindlichkeit im Bereich seiner professionellen Tätigkeit verpflichtet mit erhöhter Sorgfalt, gemäß den Berufsregeln und guten Sitten, zu agieren.
- Im SchuldG bestehen Bestimmungen über den obligaten Vertragsabschluss. Sofern jemand dem Gesetz nach zu einem Vertragsabschluss verpflichtet ist (z.B. öffentliche Dienstleistungserbringer), kann der Interessent verlangen, dass ein solcher Vertrag unverzüglich geschlossen wird. (article 27/1 SchuldG).
- In welchem Fall, die von einer Vertragspartei bestimmten allgemeinen Vertragsbedingungen die andere Vertragspartei verpflichten, und in welchem Fall die allgemeinen Bedingungen nichtig sind, wird durch eine besondere Regel festgelegt. Die allgemeinen Bedingungen verpflichten die andere Vertragspartei, sofern sie dieser zum Zeitpunkt des Vertragsabschlusses bekannt waren oder sein mussten (article 142/3 SchuldG). Deshalb müssen die allgemeinen Bedingungen auf die übliche Art und Weise bekannt gegeben werden, während im Falle einer Nichtübereinstimmung der allgemeinen Bedingungen mit besonderen Vereinbarungen die besonderen Vereinbarungen gelten (article 142/2,4 SchuldG). Die allgemeinen Geschäftsbedingungen sind nichtig, sofern sie im Widerspruch zum Zweck des abgeschlossenen Vertrags oder zu den guten Sitten stehen, selbst wenn die allgemeinen Bedingungen von einer zuständigen Behörde genehmigt wurden (article 143/1 SchuldG). Zusätzlich kann das Gericht die Anwendung einzelner Bestimmungen der allgemeinen Bedingungen ablehnen, welche es der anderen Partei unmöglich machen, Einreden zu erheben, oder auf Grund welcher sie die Ansprüche aus dem Vertrag oder die Fristen verliert, oder die sonst unzumutbar oder ihr gegenüber übertrieben streng sind (article 143/1 SchuldG).
- Der Verbraucher kann sich gleichfalls auf zahlreiche Bestimmungen des SchuldG über nichtige und anfechtbare Rechtsgeschäfte berufen, um

seine Rechte zu schützen. Verbraucherverträge, die im Widerspruch zur Verfassung der Republik Kroatien, zu den zwingenden Vorschriften und der Moral der Gesellschaft stehen, sind nichtig (article 103 SchuldG) und entfalten keine Rechtswirkungen. Der Verbraucher könnte die Annullierung eines Vertrags wegen Betrugs fordern, wenn der Kaufmann ihn irregeführt hat oder ihn mit der Absicht, ihn so zum Vertragsabschluss zu verleiten, im Irrglauben belassen hat (article 65 SchuldG). Ferner ist es möglich, die Vertragsannullierung wegen einer erheblichen Irreführung zu fordern, wenn der Verbraucher bezüglich wesentlicher Eigenschaften zur Sache, der Person, mit der er den Vertrag abschließt, der Umstände, die nach den Verkehrssitten oder nach der Absicht der Parteien als entscheidend gelten, im Irrglauben war (article 61 SchuldG). Jedoch wird die Vertragsannullierung lediglich dann möglich sein, wenn der Verbraucher während des Vertragsabschlusses mit der Sorgfalt, die im Geschäftsverkehr geboten ist, verfahren ist. Die Möglichkeit einer Vertragsannullierung besteht außerdem wegen einer übermäßigen Schädigung, d.h. wenn zum Zeitpunkt des Vertragsabschlusses ein offenbares Missverhältnis zwischen dem Wert der Leistung und der Gegenleistung bestand, und die geschädigte Partei dies nicht wusste und nicht wissen musste (article 139 SchuldG).

- In denjenigen Fällen, in welchen der Kaufmann seine Pflichten nicht ordnungsgemäß erfüllt, kann sich der Verbraucher auf die Bestimmungen des SchuldG über die Vertragsauflösung wegen Nichterfüllung berufen (articles 124–132 SchuldG). Sofern sich nach dem Vertragsabschluss die Umstände geändert haben, auf Grund welcher der Zweck des Vertrags nicht mehr realisiert werden kann (*clausula rebus sic stantibus*), so kann der Verbraucher wegen veränderter Umstände die Auflösung oder Änderung des Vertrags fordern (article 133 SchuldG).
- Das SchuldG enthält gleichfalls Sonderregeln über die Auslegung strittiger vertraglicher Vereinbarungen. Die Grundregel dabei ist, dass man sich nicht an die wortwörtliche Bedeutung der verwendeten Ausdrücke halten muss, sondern dass man der gemeinsamen Absicht der Vertragsparteien auf den Grund gehen, und die Bestimmung so verstehen sollte, wie dies den Grundsätzen des SchuldG entspricht (article 99 SchuldG). Sofern der Vertrag nach einem vorgedruckten Inhalt abgeschlossen wird, oder wenn die andere Vertragspartei (z.B. der Kaufmann) den Vertrag auf eine andere Art und Weise vorbereitet hat, so werden die strittigen Bestimmungen zu Gunsten der anderen Partei (z.B. des Verbrauchers) ausgelegt.
- Die Verantwortung wegen des Ausbleibens der Benachrichtigung ist besonders geregelt. Diejenige Vertragspartei, welche verpflichtet ist, die jeweils andere Partei über die Tatsachen, die von Bedeutung für ihr gegenseitiges Verhältnis sind, zu benachrichtigen, haftet für den Schaden, den die andere Partei erlitten hat, weil sie nicht rechtzeitig verständigt wurde (article 268 SchuldG).

- Das SchuldG enthält ebenso Bestimmungen über die Verantwortung des Herstellers von zu bemängelnden Sachen (article 179 SchuldG), obwohl im SchuldG die Richtlinie 85/347 über die Verantwortung für fehlerhafte Produkte noch nicht implementiert wurde. Wer Sachen, die er hergestellt hat in Umlauf bringt, und die wegen eines Mangels, dessen er sich nicht bewusst war, eine Schadensgefährdung für Personen oder Gegenstände darstellen, haftet für den Schaden, der auf Grund dieses Mangels entsteht. Der Hersteller haftet auch für gefährliche Eigenschaften von Sachen, sofern er nicht alles Erforderliche unternommen hat im Hinblick auf den Schaden, den er vorhersehen konnte, z.B. durch eine Warnung, durch eine sichere Verpackung oder eine andere entsprechende Maßnahme zur Schadensvermeidung. Die Verantwortung des Herstellers ist objektiv. Er haftet unabhängig von einem Verschulden.
- Der Verbraucher kann sich gegenüber dem Kaufmann, der eine Produktgarantie ausgestellt hat, ebenfalls direkt auf die Bestimmungen der articles 501–507 SchuldG über die Haftung des Verkäufers und des Herstellers für ein fehlerfreies Funktionieren der verkauften Sache berufen. Ihre Haftung ist gesamtschuldnerisch, die Regeln über die Haftung des Verkäufers für die Mängel des verkauften Sache bleiben dadurch unberührt.
- Auf die Höhe und Weise des Schadensersatzes, zu dessen Leistung der Kaufmann gegenüber dem Verbraucher verpflichtet ist, werden die allgemeinen Regeln des Schuldrechts angewendet. Im Falle einer außervertraglichen Schadenshaftung sieht das SchuldG eine volle Genugtuung vor – eine Entschädigung im Betrag, der dafür nötig ist, die materielle Situation des Geschädigten in die Lage zurückzuversetzen, in welcher sie sich befunden hätte, wäre es nicht zu der schädigenden Handlung oder dem Versäumnis gekommen. Bei der vertraglichen Schadenshaftung wird die volle Genugtuung geleistet, sofern die Verletzung einer Vertragsverpflichtung durch Betrug, vorsätzlich oder grob fahrlässig herbeigeführt wurde (article 266/2 SchuldG). Sofern es durch leichte Fahrlässigkeit zur Vertragsverletzung gekommen ist, hat die geschädigte Partei den Anspruch auf einen sog. voraussichtlichen Schaden – ein Schaden, der zum Zeitpunkt des Vertragsabschlusses als mögliche Folge der Vertragsverletzung vorhergesehen werden musste (article 266/1 SchuldG).
- Zum Zweck des Schutzes der schwächeren Vertragspartei begrenzt das SchuldG den dispositiven Charakter der Bestimmungen des Gesetzes bei der Vereinbarung einzelner Vertragsbestimmungen. Obwohl die Vertragsparteien einvernehmlich die Anwendung bestimmter Bestimmungen des SchuldG auf ihr Vertragsverhältnis ausschließen können, ist diese Möglichkeit beschränkt, um die schwächere Vertragspartei zu schützen. Beispielsweise können die Vertragsparteien die Haftung des Verkäufers für Sachmängel an der verkauften Sache (article 486/1 des SchuldG) und die Haftung des Verkäufers für Rechtsmängel (article

513/1 SchuldG) begrenzen oder völlig ausschließen. Diese Regel wird auf eine entsprechende Art und Weise auf alle entgeltlichen Verträge angewandt (article 121 SchuldG). Das SchuldG schreibt jedoch ausdrücklich vor, dass eine Bestimmung über die Beschränkung oder den Ausschluss der Haftung nichtig ist, falls dem Verkäufer der Mangel bekannt war, und er den Käufer darüber nicht in Kenntnis gesetzt hat. Dies gilt auch dann, wenn der Verkäufer dem Käufer diese Bestimmung aufgezwungen hat, indem er sich seine besondere Monopolposition zu Nutze gemacht hat (article 486/2, 513/2 SchuldG). Eine ähnliche Regelung besteht auch für die vertragliche Schadenshaftung bzw. die Haftung für einen Schaden, der durch eine Vertragsverletzung entstanden ist. Die Vertragsparteien können die Haftung für einen Schaden, der durch eine Vertragsverletzung entstanden ist im Vorhinein vertraglich ausschließen. Die Haftung für vorsätzliches und grob fahrlässiges Verhalten kann jedoch nicht im vorhinein ausgeschlossen werden (article 265/1 SchuldG). Es ist möglich im Gerichtswege selbst für leichte Fahrlässigkeit die Annullierung der Vertragsbestimmung über den Ausschluss der vertraglichen Haftung zu fordern, sofern eine solche Vertragsbestimmung aus der Monopolposition einer Vertragspartei oder überhaupt aus einem nicht gleichberechtigten Verhältnisses der Vertragsparteien hervorgegangen ist (article 265/2 SchuldG). Ist jedoch die Haftung auf einen bestimmten Betrag begrenzt, hat der Gläubiger dennoch das Recht auf volle Genugtuung, sofern die Unmöglichkeit der Erfüllung der Verbindlichkeit durch den Schuldner vorsätzlich oder grob fahrlässig herbeigeführt wurde (article 265/4 SchuldG). Der dispositive Charakter der Bestimmungen des Gesetzes ist auch bei der Vereinbarung einer Vertragsstrafe – Pönale – begrenzt. Das Gericht mindert auf Antrag des Schuldners den Betrag der Vertragsstrafe, wenn es feststellt, dass diese – bezogen auf den Wert und die Bedeutung des Gegenstands der Verbindlichkeit – unverhältnismäßig hoch ist (article 274 SchuldG).

Durch die Berufung auf die genannten und zahlreichen anderen Bestimmungen des SchuldG können Verbraucher bereits im Rahmen des allgemeinen Vertragsrechts ein hohes Maß an Rechtschutz aus den Verbraucherverträgen geltend machen. Das SchuldG enthält jedoch weder besondere Bestimmungen, die sich ausdrücklich und ausschließlich nur auf den Verbraucherschutz in Vertragsverhältnissen beziehen, noch bevorzugt es ausdrücklich den Verbraucher als eine der Vertragsparteien. Die Parteien sind gemäß dem SchuldG bei Schuldverhältnissen gleichberechtigt (article 11). Die schwächere Vertragspartei wird nur in denjenigen Fällen geschützt, welche ausdrücklich durch das SchuldG vorgeschrieben sind. Der besondere Rechtsschutz aus den Verbraucherverträgen wird daher durch das Konsumentenschutzgesetz geregelt, durch welches der Schutz des Verbrauchers als Vertragspartei durch bestimmte Neuerungen gestärkt wird, die sich wiederum erheblich auf das allgemeine Vertragsrecht auswirken.

3. Auswirkungen des Verbrauchervertragsrechts auf das allgemeine Vertragsrecht

Durch das Konsumentenschutzgesetz wurde ein besonderes System des Verbraucherschutzes in den Verbraucherverträgen geschaffen, welches parallel zu dem durch das Schuldgesetz geregelten System des Schutzes des Verbrauchers als eine der Vertragsparteien existiert. Diese zwei Schutzsysteme überschneiden sich inhaltlich teilweise, wobei das SchuldG als subsidiäre Quelle teilweise das System des Verbraucherschutzes ergänzt, welches im KSchG geregelt ist. In dem Teil, in welchem die gleichen Fragen geregelt werden und sich die Fragen überschneiden, hat für die Verbraucher das Konsumentenschutzgesetz als *lex specialis* Vorrang. Jedoch regelt das KSchG nicht alle Verbraucherschutzfragen in den Vertragsverhältnissen, bzw. regelt es einige Fragen lediglich teilweise. In diesem Falle kann ein abgerundetes Schutzsystem erst durch die entsprechende Anwendung der Bestimmungen des SchuldG realisiert werden.

Der Einfluss der Anwendung des Konsumentenschutzgesetzes auf die Möglichkeit der Anwendung der Bestimmungen des allgemeinen Vertragsrechts erstreckt sich von den Fällen, in welchen die Anwendung einzelner, sehr spezifischer Bestimmungen des SchuldG ausgeschlossen wird, bis hin zu den Fällen, in denen die Wirkung einiger grundlegender, traditioneller Grundsätze des Vertragsrechts ausgesetzt wird. Beispielsweise sind einige KSchG-Bestimmungen bezüglich der Verbindlichkeiten der Kaufleute gegenüber den Verbrauchern rein deklaratorischer Natur, während die Rechtswirkungen des Verstoßes gegen diese Bestimmungen durch das SchuldG geregelt ist (die Verpflichtung der ordentlichen Pflichterfüllung, die Einhaltung von durch Bürgschaft übernommen Verbindlichkeiten, article 5,6 KSchG). Einige KSchG-Bestimmungen begrenzen die Freiheit der Gestaltung der Schuldverhältnisse, indem sie den Kaufmann auf den Vertragsabschluss verpflichten (article 7, 22 *et seq.* KSchG). Die dritte Gruppe der KSchG-Bestimmungen regelt ausdrücklich die Erfüllung der Vertragsverpflichtungen oder die Rechtsverhältnisse nach Vertragsauflösung entgegen den Bestimmungen des SchuldG (die Zahlungsleistung, den Ausschluss der Haftung des Verbrauchers für den Schaden, der durch die Auflösung entstanden ist, den Einfluss der Auflösung auf Nebenverträge). Durch die Bestimmungen über den zwingenden Inhalt einzelner Verbraucherverträge wurde im Vergleich zum SchuldG der Katalog der wesentlichen Vertragsbestandteile erheblich ausgeweitet. Dabei führt ihr Fehlen im Vertrag nicht zur Nichtigkeit des Vertrags, sondern lediglich zum Recht des Verbrauchers auf eine einseitige Auflösung (z.B. bei Timeshare-Verträgen). Es wurde ein besonderes Institut betreffend die missbräuchlichen Bestimmungen in Verbraucherverträgen eingeführt; das Unterlassen der Vereinbarung solcher Bestimmungen kann auch durch eine Verbraucher-Klage im Namen der Allgemeinheit gefordert werden.

Der wichtigste Einfluss des KSchG auf das allgemeine Vertragsrecht zeigt sich daran, dass sich im Verhältnis zu einer bestimmten gesellschaftlichen Gruppe die klassische Auffassung des Grundsatzes *pacta sunt servanda*, des Grundsatzes der Autonomie der Parteien und die ausschließlich privatrechtliche Natur der Vertragsverhältnisse, deren Verletzung im klassischen Vertragsrecht nur durch ein privatrechtliches Instrumentarium sanktioniert wird (Vertragsauflösung, Schadensersatz, Rückgabe der erhaltenen Leistung, Rückzahlung mit Verzugszinsen), geändert hat. Die größte Neuerung im Hinblick auf das allgemeine Vertragsrechts ist auf jeden Fall die Abweichung von der allgemeinen Regel, dass Verträge verbindlich sind, und dass sich die Vertragsparteien an sie halten müssen. Wenngleich diese Regel grundsätzlich auch für Verbraucherverträge gilt, wurde von dieser Regel entscheidend abgegangen durch die Anerkennung des Rechts der Verbraucher auf eine einseitige Vertragsauflösung ohne Anführung eines Grundes, selbst wenn der Kaufmann seine Vertragsverpflichtungen nicht verletzt hat. Andererseits wurde durch die Vorschreibung eines Pflichtinhalts einzelner Verbraucherverträge und den Ausschluss der Möglichkeit, dass einige der Bestimmungen durch eine Vereinbarung der Parteien geändert werden können, entscheidend von der Autonomie, der Freiheit der Gestaltung der Schuldverhältnisse, abgewichen (article 10 SchuldG). Die Vertragsverhältnisse zwischen Verbraucher und Kaufmann werden somit durch eine viel größere Anzahl von zwingenden Normen geregelt, als dies beim allgemeinen Vertragsrecht der Fall ist. Schließlich ist der öffentlich-rechtliche Einfluss auf die Vertragsverhältnisse zwischen Verbraucher und Kaufmann sehr stark, insbesondere in den Fällen einer Verletzung der Vertragsverpflichtungen durch den Kaufmann. In einem solchen Fall ist zwar die Anwendung der allgemeinen Regeln über die Vertragsauflösung wegen Nichterfüllung nicht ausgeschlossen, allerdings wurde ebenfalls die Haftung für Ordnungswidrigkeiten bzw. Straftaten, die öffentlichrechtliche Sanktionierung für die Verletzung der Vertragsverpflichtungen, eingeführt (article 109 KSchG). Eine solche Sanktionierung von Ordnungswidrigkeiten kann eine vorbeugende Rolle bei der Verhinderung der Verletzung von Vertragsverpflichtungen spielen. Ihre Begründetheit geht zweifellos aus der Tatsache hervor, dass das KSchG vorschreibt, dass der Verbraucherschutz im öffentlichen Interesse durchgeführt wird (article 98/1 KSchG). Die Verbraucherverträge sind dennoch von privatrechtlicher Natur, durch sie werden privatrechtliche Verhältnisse auf dem Markt eingegangen, welche in erster Linie durch die Autonomie der Parteien und zivilrechtliche Sanktionen bestimmt sein sollten. Die privatrechtliche Natur der Verbraucherverträge wird auf Grund starker öffentlichrechtlicher Elemente und Zwangselemente immer häufiger in Frage gestellt, sowohl bei ihrem[25] Abschluss als auch bei der Sanktionierung ihrer

[25] *NN* 37/2004.

Erfüllung. Das Maß, in welchem die öffentlichrechtlichen Elemente des Verbrauchervertragsrechts in der Praxis tatsächlich zum Ausdruck kommen werden, wird größtenteils gerade davon abhängen, wie hoch der Grad der Bildung und der Information der Verbraucher über ihre Rechte, über den Inhalt, den Sinn und die Rechtwirksamkeit der Verträge ist, die sie abschließen möchten. Für die Weiterentwicklung des Verbrauchervertragsrechts im Rahmen der privatrechtlichen Ordnung wäre es deshalb besonders wichtig den Schwerpunkt des Schutzes auf die Entwicklung derjenigen Methoden zu legen, durch welche bereits in der vorvertraglichen Phase die maximale Information des Verbrauchers gewährleistet wird. So könnten Voraussetzungen geschaffen werden, dass die Verbraucher frei und mit der Kenntnis aller relevanten Tatsachen zu aktiven Marktteilnehmern werden, die frei und mit den Kaufleuten gleichberechtigt Vertragsverhältnisse im Einklang mit ihren Interessen gestalten können.

IV. PERSPEKTIVEN DER ENTWICKLUNG DES VERTRAGSRECHTS

Der Republik Kroatien steht noch eine Reform des allgemeinen Vertragsrechts bevor, um die Angleichung an den *acquis communautaire* durchführen zu können. Bis jetzt sind durch das Konsumentenschutzgesetz diejenigen Richtlinien in die kroatische Rechtsordnung implementiert worden, welche ausschließlich oder überwiegend den Schutz von Personen regeln, die auf dem Markt als Verbraucher gelten. Diejenigen Richtlinien, welche sich nicht ausschließlich auf den Verbraucherschutz, sondern auch auf den Schutz von Interessen und Rechten anderer Marktteilnehmer beziehen, müssten in die neue allgemeine Vorschrift über die Schuldverhältnisse, d.h. in das neue Gesetz über die Schuldverhältnisse und in andere Sondervorschriften implementiert werden. Durch das Nationalprogramm der Republik Kroatien zur Assoziierung an die Europäische Union für das Jahr 2004 ist die Verabschiedung des neuen Gesetzes über die Schuldverhältnisse für das Ende des Jahres 2004 vorgesehen. In das neue Gesetz über die Schuldverhältnisse werden zahlreiche Richtlinien implementiert, durch welche die Materie des Schuldrechts geregelt wird.[26] Durch ihre Implementierung wird die

[26] Die Implementierung folgender Richtlinien in das neue SchuldG ist vorgesehen:

Die Richtlinie 1999/44/EG zu bestimmten Aspekten des Verbrauchsgüterkaufs und der Garantien für Verbrauchsgüter (ABl. L 1999, 171, S. 12), die Richtlinie 85/374/EWG zur Angleichung der Rechts- und Verwaltungsvorschriften der Mitgliedstaaten über die Haftung für fehlerhafte Produkte (ABl. L 1985, 210, S. 29), die Richtlinie 1999/34/EG zur Änderung der Richtlinie 85/374/EWG des Rates zur Angleichung der Rechts- und Verwaltungsvorschriften der Mitgliedstaaten über die Haftung für fehlerhafte Produkte (ABl. L 1999, 141, S. 20), die Richtlinie 1999/34/EG zur Änderung der Richtlinie 85/374/EWG des Rates zur Angleichung der Rechts- und

Europäisierung des kroatischen Vertragsrechts fortgesetzt, die durch das Konsumentenschutzgesetz begonnen hat. Neben der Implementierung der Richtlinien sieht der Plan für die Schuldrechtsreform Folgendes vor: die bestehenden Grundsätze des Schuldrechts und die monistische Regelung der Vertragsverhältnisse wird beibehalten, einzelne Rechtsinstitute werden ausführlicher und genauer geregelt und modernisiert, einige neuen Verträge werden geregelt u.Ä.[27]

Im Nationalprogramm zur Assoziierung an die Europäische Union ist jedoch die Einbeziehung des Verbrauchervertragsrechts in das künftige Gesetz über die Schuldverhältnisse nicht vorgesehen. Die Verabschiedung eines Bürgerlichen Gesetzbuches, welches die Materie des Privatrechts in einem einheitlichen Kodex vereinen würde, ist gleichfalls nicht vorgesehen. Die vorherrschende Tendenz ist, dass auch weiterhin an der jetzigen gesonderten Regelung des Verbrauchervertragsrechts in einer Sondervorschrift über den Verbraucherschutz neben der subsidiären Anwendung des SchuldG festgehalten wird, und dass einzelne Bereiche des Privatrechts auch weiterhin durch Sondervorschriften geregelt werden, wodurch diese Bereiche an die modernen Tendenzen im europäischen Recht angeglichen werden.[28]

Verwaltungsvorschriften der Mitgliedstaaten über die Haftung für fehlerhafte Produkte (ABl, L, 1999, 141, S. 20), die Richtlinie 90/314/EWG über Pauschalreisen (ABl. L 1990, 158, S. 59), die Richtlinie 86/653/EWG zur Koordinierung der Rechtsvorschriften der Mitgliedstaaten betreffend die selbstständigen Handelsvertreter (ABl. L 1986, 382, S. 17) und die Richtlinie 2000/35/EG zur Bekämpfung von Zahlungsverzug im Geschäftsverkehr (ABl, L 2000, 200, S. 35).

Die Bestimmungen des SchuldG werden ohnehin an die Richtlinie 1999/93/EG über gemeinschaftliche Rahmenbedingungen für elektronische Signaturen (ABl L 2000, 13, S. 12) und die Richtlinie 2000/31/EG über bestimmte rechtliche Aspekte der Dienste der Informationsgesellschaft, insbesondere des elektronischen Geschäftsverkehrs, im Binnenmarkt – 'Richtlinie über den elektronischen Geschäftsverkehr' (ABl L 2000, 178, S. 1) angepasst. Diese beiden Richtlinien wurden durch die Verabschiedung der neuen Sondervorschriften bereits zur Gänze implementiert (das Gesetz zur digitalen Signatur, *NN*, 10/02 und das Gesetz über E-Business, *NN* 173/03).

27 P. Klarić, 'U susret zakoniku o obveznim odnosima', *Pravo u gospodarstvu* (In Erwartung des Gesetzes über die Schuldverhältnisse, Das Recht in der Wirtschaft), 3/2003, 35 *et seq.*

28 Die Reform verschiedener Bereiche des Privatrechts wurde bereits durch die Verabschiedung zahlreicher Sondervorschriften durchgeführt. Dies sind z.B.: das Gesetz über das Eigentum und andere dingliche Rechte (1996, geändert: 1998, 1999, 2000, 2001), das Grundbuchsgesetz (1996, geändert: 1996, 1998, 1999, 2001, 2004), das Arbeitsgesetz (1995, geändert: 1998, 2001, 2003, 2004), das Gesetz über Handelsgesellschaften (1993, geändert: 1999, 2000, 2003), das Familiengesetz (2003, geändert: 2004), das Erbgesetz (2003, geändert: 2003), die Zivilprozessordnung (1977, geändert: 1980, 1982, 1984, 1987, 1989, 1990, 1991, 1992, 2001, 2003), das Konkursgesetz (1996, geändert: 1999, 2000, 2003), das Zwangsvollstreckungsgesetz (1996, geändert: 1999, 2000, 2003). Darüber mehr in N. Gavella, 'Građanskopravni sadržaji u hrvatskom pravnom sustavu i njihova promjena', *Zbornik Pravnog fakulteta u Zagrebu* (Zivilrechtliche Inhalte im kroatischen Rechtssystem und ihre Veränderung, Sammelband der Juristischen Fakultät in Zagreb), 6/2001, 1230 u.a.; J. Barbić, *Europeizacija hrvatskog prava u Hrvatska-kako dalje* (Europäisierung des kroatischen Rechts in Kroatien–was nun?) (eds. Kregar/Puljiz/Ravlić), (2004), 98 *et seq.*

In der Praxis wird sich herausstellen, ob die Ausgliederung des Verbrauchervertragsrechts als besondere Rechtsregelung den Marktanforderungen entsprechen wird, und in welchem Maß dies für die Entwicklung des Vertragsrechts im Ganzen förderlich sein wird. Entgegen zahlreicher Besonderheiten des Verbrauchervertragsrechts, ja sogar Abweichungen von einigen privatrechtlichen Grundsätzen, ist es nämlich unstrittig, dass durch das Verbrauchervertragsrecht die Voraussetzungen für die Entwicklung eines völlig unterschiedlichen Vertragsrechts geschaffen werden, welchem Konkurrenz und Wettbewerb auf dem gemeinsamen Markt zugrunde liegen.[29] Letztendlich ist das europäische Verbrauchervertragsrecht auch aufgrund der Errichtung eines optimalen Gleichgewichts zwischen den Interessen am freien Waren-, Dienstleistungs- und Kapitalverkehr auf dem gemeinsamen Markt und den wirtschaftlichen und sozialen Interessen der Verbraucher als Marktteilnehmer entstanden.

Die Einbeziehung der Regeln über die Verbraucherverträge in eine allgemeine Vorschrift, durch welche die Schuldverhältnisse geregelt werden, und die Erhebung einzelner Regeln über diese Verträge auf die Ebene einer allgemeinen Regel für alle Verbraucherverträge, eventuell auch für alle anderen Verträge, könnte sich positiv auf die weitere Modernisierung des Vertragsrechts auswirken. Sie würde auch dazu beitragen, dass dem Verbraucherschutz in Vertragsverhältnissen größere Bedeutung geschenkt wird. Dieser Schutz wird heutzutage in der Praxis immer noch marginalisiert. Die Vereinigung des allgemeinen Vertragsrechts und des Verbrauchervertragsrechts zu einer Einheit müsste hingegen nicht unbedingt auch die Erhebung aller Regeln über Verbraucherverträge auf die Ebene der allgemeinen Regeln des Vertragsrechts mit sich ziehen. Andererseits wäre es ebenfalls möglich einige Institute des Verbrauchervertragsrechts mehr an die rechtlichen Institute des allgemeinen Vertragsrechts anzupassen. Die Beibehaltung der getrennten Normierung des Verbrauchervertragsrechts und des allgemeinen Vertragsrechts wird die Errichtung eines ganzheitlichen und beständigen Systems des Vertragsrechts, welches den Marktverhältnissen entspricht, erschweren.

Es ist zu erwarten, dass die Republik Kroatien in Zukunft bei der Errichtung eines solchen abgerundeten Systems des Vertragsrechts den Trends in der Entwicklung des europäischen Vertragsrechts folgen wird. Wie sich jedoch das Vertragsrecht auf europäischer Ebene weiterentwickeln wird, wird größtenteils von den Befugnissen der Gemeinschaft abhängen, mit ihren Akten auf die Harmonisierung des Vertragsrechts der Mitgliedsstaaten einzuwirken.

[29] H. Schulte-Nölke, 'EC Private Law and the German Civil Code' in R. Schulze, G. Ajani (eds.), *Gemeinsame Prinzipien des Europäischen Privatrechts* (2003), 221; H. W. Micklitz, 'Perspektiven eines Europäischen Privatrechts', *Zeitschrift für Europäisches Privatrecht*, 1998, 257–259; T. M. J. Möllers, 'European Directives on Civil Law – The German Approach: Towards the Re-codification and New Foundation of Civil Law Principles', *European Review of Private Law*, 6/2002, 788,789; M. Gebauer, *Grundfragen der Europäisierung des Privatrechts* (1998), 111.

Das europäische Vertragsrecht hat im Vergleich zu den anderen privatrechtlichen Bereichen wahrscheinlich die besten Perspektiven im Vergleich zu den übrigen Bereichen des Privatrechts. Das Vertragsrecht spielt eine besonders wichtige Rolle für das effektive Funktionieren des gemeinsamen Marktes, d.h. der freie Verkehr von Waren, Dienstleistungen und Kapital. Der Beginn des Prozesses einer ganzheitlichen Harmonisierung des Vertragsrechts, bis hin zur Schaffung eines gemeinsamen europäischen 'Vertragskodex' könnte somit mit den Befugnissen der Gemeinschaft konform sein, die das effektive Funktionieren des gemeinsamen Marktes anstreben, und die im Einklang mit dem Grundsatz der begrenzten Einzelermächtigung, dem Subsidiaritäts- und dem Proportionalitätsprinzip verwirklicht werden.[30]

[30] Siehe art. 5 Vertrag zur Gründung der Europäischen Gemeinschaft.

Chapter 8

Discussion and Panel Discussion: Lessons for an Optional European Code?

Markus Hoffmann, Erlangen University

Lessons for an Optional European Code? This question is – maybe not solely – meant to be considered in the context of the reports given on the 'old' European codes, as well as on the more recent developments of the central European codes. These were also the basis for this wide-ranging and profound discussion.

Professor Rebhahn (Vienna) began his submission by stating that an Optional Code should cover the law of obligation or – if not possible – the law of contract; the category of juristic act could be left out. He pointed to the Austrian ABGB and the fact that the absence of a general part in this code did not hinder the development of spanning rules. Then he pointed to another aspect of abstraction: the accuracy of statutes. He argued again by comparison with the ABGB and its vital sections on the law of obligation, which only give a minor normative guidance, i.e. one can interpret these sections in many ways. This relative imprecision has contributed to the 'success' of the ABGB – had it been written more precisely, many more alterations would have been necessary. Since changes could also come from doctrine, the rather long legislative process on the European level could be circumvented. According to Professor Rebhahn, more abstract rules would contribute more to legal unity and be better accepted by national legislators and/or private individuals.

Dr. Zoll (Cracow) talked about the current legal situation in Poland and the intense discussion about a new civil code. In this context, he raised the question of whether a European codification should contain the current

S. Grundmann, M. Schauer (eds), *The Architecture of European Codes and Contract Law*, 153–156

directives or – more generally – if this would actually be possible. Professor Tichý (Prague) elicited the problems in context with consumer protection. As numerous directives today deal with various aspects of this area and because of its importance, he asked if those should be integrated into a European codification. First summarizing some of the introduced facets, Professor Collins (London) then amplified some of the structural issues, i.e. first of all the relationship of contract/private law to public law, with its individual rights drawn from constitution. He then continued by talking about the general contract law system and the special codes. Thirdly, he pointed to the level of abstraction of rules and their amendment in the future, but also argued that there should be general guidelines for judges on their application. In his last point, he reminded the audience that freedom of contract while generally being a good starting point should be balanced against good faith, fairness and solidarity.

Professor Josipović (Zagreb) gave an insight into the recent developments in the law of obligation in the Republic of Croatia. She pointed out that Croatia follows a monistic theory, meaning that commercial and civil law are both regulated in the Obligations Act. Special laws for various other kinds of contract do exist. Aiming to harmonize its law with European law, Croatia has also adopted various directives into a Consumer Protection Act. The problem, according to Professor Josipović, is however that Croatia is lacking a comprehensive and elaborate plan for the development of the complete private law system. The absence of principles on which such a system should be based and of concept for the codification of special segments of the private law might complicate the integration into a comprehensive civil code.

Professor Vékás (Budapest) stressed that a European code should be on an optional basis, either with an opt-in or opt-out system. He also observed that the development of private law will still take place primarily in the member states in the near future, despite the foreseeable perspectives in harmonization. In his opinion a European code should fulfill – in a positive sense – the function of an Esperanto but, if optional, also risks sharing its fate of minor success. Professor Grundmann (Berlin) stressed that a European code should be on an optional basis rather than being exclusive; however, the European code should be fully-fledged, i.e. it should be an extensive one, so that the parties would be able to choose it as a complete set of default rules. He argued that this would lead to competition among legislators. In considering the period to establish this, Professor Grundmann thought about less than a decade. Professor Gatt (Naples) also talked about the optional system and that a lot of work in creating optional codes has already been done. In his statement Professor Howells (Sheffield) focussed on the optionality of a common European code. Professor Lurger (Graz) commented on the abstract principles of party autonomy as well as fairness and especially on their relationship to each other. Further, she discussed the problems of choice in the context of consumers and consumer legislation. Professor

Wilhelmsson (Helsinki) on the other hand favoured a restatement approach over an optional European code, which would be static and difficult to amend. Restatements to the contrary, he argued, would contribute to the dynamic nature of the European legal system and could function as a common legal language.

A more critical statement on a European code was given by Dr. Röttinger (European Commission), who asked if there would actually be a demand for such a code especially as the current legal systems did rather well in the past 200 years. He also accentuated other problems, e.g. interpretation of legal terminology in various countries and the fact that there hardly is any European dogmatic, but rather a lot of patchwork. Professor Ranieri (Saarbrücken) mentioned that the discussion on approximation of the laws of contract and obligation is generally viewed in light of a legislative task. However, written statues are only one part of the '*droit appliqué*'. There is also a tradition of adjudication, of legal education and of legal argument that is inextricably linked with the legal background; therefore there are not only differences between 'civil' and 'common' law, but also within the continental legal systems. The way towards a European code needs to primarily take legal education into consideration. Professor Ranieri emphasized the need for a European legal education, meaning that future jurists need to gain experience in various European legal systems. He backed his thought by looking at legal history, e.g. of the French Code Civil or the German BGB. Both were not possible until a uniform university education and cultural unity was achieved. The BGB codifies mainly the teaching of legal scholars in Roman law of the second part of the 19th century. The unity of private law was therefore already established at university level before work on the BGB began. Professor Ranieri concluded by stating that also for a European civil code a 'European' jurisprudence spanning national borders is yet to be established.

Professor Kerber (Marburg) said that in his opinion an Optional code as the starting point would be a realistic and pragmatic approach. This codification could then be developed step-by-step. Moreover, however, he stressed that many economic arguments also speak in favour of maintaining such a system in the long run. Mr Hertel (German Notary Institute) summarized that in the majority of the contributions a general part on Juristic Act, which would also deal with unilateral transactions, property law, etc., was not deemed necessary; instead there should only be one section that would cover general rules of the law of contract. He agreed with this as it would facilitate the application of law in the new and unaccustomed European contract law by having all corresponding rules together in one place. He pointed to the Dutch contract law; its general rules partly govern unilateral transactions as well. Concerning the level of abstraction, he stated that the European legislature would not only have to draft the code, but a commentary as well – similar to the Lando-Principles or the US-Restatements, which exemplify the application to the principles further. This is necessary as the European legislator cannot build on an existing legal position like the national legislators.

While those commentaries would give useful examples for general understanding, scholars and practitioners could deal with border cases. According to Mr Hertel, it is essential to involve practitioners in the work on the codification as well. As a test, specialists from various countries could be asked how they would solve typical cases according to the draft. If their answers correspond, the codification would seem to be well drafted. It is important, however, that those steps are taken ahead of the legislative proceeding; otherwise they might come too late.

Part III
Consumer Law – Forerunner for or Part of a European Contract Law Code?

Chapter 9

Civil Contract Law and Economic Reasoning – An Unlikely Pair?

*Aristides N. Hatzis**

> 'If the soil of Europe is so much less fertile for economic analysis than that of the United States, how is one to explain the rapid growth of the field in Europe?'[1]

It is a well-known fact that 'law and economics', i.e. 'economic analysis of law', is an American product. Its founding fathers are all American, working in American law schools, and writing about American law in American law reviews. Therefore, it is hardly surprising to find an abundance of literature

---

* Assistant Professor of Philosophy of Law & Theory of Institutions, University of Athens, Department of Philosophy & History of Science (LL.B. 1989, LL.M. 1993, Aristotle University of Thessaloniki, Faculty of Law; LL.M. 1994, J.S.D. 1999, University of Chicago Law School). Earlier versions of this paper have been presented in the European School on New Institutional Economics (Cargèse-Corsica, May 2004), the conference on the 'Architecture of European Codes and Contract Law' organized by the Society of European Contract Law (Vienna, June 2004), in the workshop on the 'Co-evolution on Law & Economics' organized by the European Association of Evolutionary Political Economy (Rethymno-Crete, October 2004) and in an invited lecture at the University of Siena (April 2005). I am indebted for helpful discussions and comments to Eric Brousseau, Bruce Chapman, Massimo D'Antoni, Bruno Deffains, Stefan Grundmann, Antonio Nicita, Ugo Pagano, Matteo Rizzolli, Alessandra Rossi, Aspasia Tsaoussis, Richard Zerbe and the participants in my lectures and workshop presentations. I gratefully acknowledge financial support from the University of Athens ("Kapodistrias" research grant). For comments, please send me an email: <ahatzis@phs.uoa.gr>.

1 Posner, 'The Future of the Law and Economics Movement in Europe', *International Review of Law & Economics* 17 (1997) pp. 3–14 (5).

S. Grundmann, M. Schauer (eds), *The Architecture of European Codes and Contract Law*, 159–191

in American law and economics and in common law and economics in general. At the same time, it can prove to be extremely difficult to find papers on European themes in the established journals of the field.[2]

However, there are a growing number of European scholars working on law and economics since at least the early 1980s and a growing number of younger scholars for the past 10 years. Even though the number of their publications is not analogous to the number of scholars (which is due in great extent to the aforementioned 'jurisdictional' bias in the major journals), one could safely say that there is a sizeable corpus of law and economics literature written by European scholars. Nevertheless, again, the majority of these papers do not use economic tools to treat specific European institutions and legal systems, but they either discuss theoretical problems or they treat institutions as generic. In addition, the papers discussing European themes choose either to analyze European Union law or areas of economic law, where European legal theory follows Anglo-Saxon law closely (e.g. competition law, corporate law, securities law, etc.).[3]

As a result, there are very few studies to discuss contracts, torts, property and unjust enrichment, i.e. the problems which are dealt with by common law in the USA and by civil codes in continental Europe. These four areas constitute the basis of private law and they are the areas where US law and economics scholars have shifted their attention almost exclusively for many years. It is characteristic that even today most US law and economics textbooks cover only these fields.[4] The reason is that they have elaborated these fields to exhaustion and they are more than illustrative of what law and economics can offer to classical legal theory. Unfortunately, the respective published work in continental Europe is minimal. Moreover, comparative law and economics is still at a nascent stage, despite some important contributions to the field.[5]

And yet, the underdevelopment of the economic analysis of civil law should not be taken to signify that civil law is not amenable to economic analysis or that it is inefficient, or at least less efficient than common law.

---

2 I am referring to the two leading journals in the field: the *Journal of Law & Economics* (founded in 1958 by Aaron Director) and the *Journal of Legal Studies* (founded in 1972 by Richard Posner) both published by the University of Chicago Law School. See also the *Journal of Law, Economics, & Organization*, the *Supreme Court Economic Review* and the *American Law & Economics Review*. The *International Review of Law & Economics* and the *European Journal of Law & Economics* are more hospitable to papers written by European authors.

3 See e.g. the papers published in the *IRLE* and the *EJLE*.

4 With the possible addition of criminal law. See e.g. Polinsky, *An Introduction to Law and Economics* (2003); Cooter and Ulen, *Law and Economics* (2004) and Shavell, *Foundations of Economic Analysis of Law* (2004).

5 But see Mattei, *Comparative Law and Economics* (1997); Hatzis (ed.), *Economic Analysis of Law: A European Perspective* (2005) and a new journal that will be launched in 2007 under the title: *Civil Law & Economics Review* – and will specialize in the economics of Civil law.

Actually, as I am going to argue, rather the opposite is true, especially in what concerns civil contract law. In a series of papers, I have attempted to show that civil contract law is a fertile ground for economic analysis and, what is more, is more efficient than common contract law.

In this paper I will present my work in the area,[6] to organize my findings and to suggest directions for future research. In the first part of the paper I will briefly present an economic model of civil contract law, and also try to clarify some common misconceptions, especially the accusation that economic analysis is anti-consumerist. In the second part of the paper, I am going to present some findings from my ongoing research. These findings might appear to be controversial and counterintuitive. My basic point is that civil law is not only friendlier, but also more amenable to economic analysis than common law. In the third, fourth and fifth parts of the paper, I will use efficient breach and penalty clauses as examples, supporting my thesis on the efficiency of civil law. At the same time, I will demonstrate how helpful economic analysis can be in the interpretation and construction of a civil code, but also show its instrumentality for the genuine protection of consumers in standard form contracts.

I. AN ECONOMIC THEORY OF CIVIL CONTRACT LAW

The most common misconception about economic analysis of law is that it glorifies money and material wealth and that it is anti-consumerist. Supposedly, economists are only interested in maximizing wealth, without caring about the weak parties in transactions and with no concern for distributive effects. I believe that this picture is unfair, but I will not be discussing it in this paper. My concern in this section is to show that the concept of economic efficiency as applied to contracts can be compatible with the aims of civil contract law but also of consumer contract law. Despite the critique that economists are indifferent to the asymmetries in a contractual relationship, I will demonstrate that economists share the lawyers' concerns.

The following passage by Milton Friedman is characteristic:

---

6 My work in the area can be found in Hatzis, *An Economic Theory of Greek Contract Law* (Unpublished; Ph.D. Thesis – University of Chicago) (1999); 'Rights and Obligations of Third Parties', in: *Encyclopedia of Law and Economics Vol. III*, Bouckaert and De Geest (eds.). (2000) pp. 200–222; 'Having the Cake and Eating It Too: Efficient Penalty Clauses in Common and Civil Contract Law', *International Review of Law & Economics* 22 (2003) pp. 381–406; 'The Anti-Theoretical Nature of Civil Law Contract Scholarship and the Need for an Economic Theory', *Commentaries in Law & Economics* 2 (2003) pp. 1–64; 'The Economics of Contract Law', in: *Economic Analysis of Law: A European Perspective* (2005). I borrow extensively from some of the above papers. However, one should refer to them for a more detailed and nuanced treatment of the particular issues and arguments.

> 'The possibility of coordination through voluntary cooperation rests on the elementary – yet frequently denied – proposition that both parties to an economic transaction benefit from it, provided the transaction is bilaterally voluntary and informed.'[7]

Let's see what the above statement entails. In a contract, two rational actors promise to limit their future actions with the objective of deriving, from the present or future actions of the other party, a benefit that will be greater than the cost of restricting their actions. The presumption of economic analysis is that the contracting parties are rational, in that they always devise the most effective way to satisfy their preferences. In a contract, there is the initial assumption that the parties can efficiently regulate the contractual relationship they have engaged in and that they can solve all the potential problems stemming from the development of this relationship. Thus, the role of contract law is primarily to enforce people's promises, since these promises are by default (initially) value-enhancing and the purpose of the law is, in this instance, to encourage and facilitate the maximization of the well-being of the members of society[8] by enforcing the wishes of contracting parties,[9] as they are expressed in their agreements recognized as contracts.

However, the fact that the parties decide for themselves what will be the benefit and what will be the cost of their future actions does not imply that they will always and necessarily make the right decisions. Even though it is widely accepted that the parties know best where their interests lie, it is also true that the parties can make mistakes, due to imperfect information and/or uncertainty about the future. This is especially true for weaker parties in consumer contracts (but is the exception in business contracts). There is a chance that (at least) one of the parties will make a miscalculation of the cost or the benefit, based on inaccurate information. Another potential and more common problem is the likelihood of a change in circumstances that will overturn the previous calculation of costs and benefits and will create a new situation which is, sometimes, totally different from the one the parties took as a given when constructing their relationship.[10] Yet another problem, added

---

7 M. Friedman, *Capitalism and Freedom*, (1962), p. 13.

8 The parties will arrive at a Pareto optimal point after the performance of the contract and only then will the utility of the parties increase. However, this does not necessarily mean that the increase in utility will be distributed equally.

9 'The desirable effects from exchange all derive from the fact that each person receives, by subjective valuation, goods and services that are more valuable than those which are surrendered.' (Epstein, 'Are Values Incommensurable, or Is Utility the Ruler of the World?', *Utah Law Review* (1995) pp. 683–715 (694 and 701). See also Stephen, *The Economics of the Law*, (1988), pp. 155 and especially 157: '[c]ontract law can be seen as ensuring that the optimal number of contracts is entered into'; compare Kronman and Posner, *The Economics of Contract Law* (1979) pp. 1–2.

10 The parties tend not to specify terms for low probability events, because the expected cost from this exclusion will be minimal, whereas the cost of including the terms is borne with certainty.

on to those of imperfect information and 'unforeseen contingencies', is the opportunistic behaviour[11] of one of the parties, which is also a result of the sequential character of the performance[12] and is pertinent to the problem of unforeseen contingencies due to asymmetric information.

Let me now turn to the relation between economic analysis and contract law, in order to determine how the former can help the latter solve the problems we have pointed to. Thus, I will examine the problems of contract law as economic problems, given that contracts constitute the cornerstone of any market economy.

In a perfect world of perfect competition, a contract could be perfect.[13] A perfect contract is 'a promise that, if enforceable, is ideally suited to achieving the ends of the promisor and the promisee'.[14] In such a 'complete contingent contract', every possible contingency would be foreseen and regulated by the parties. In this ideal world of perfect information and competition, opportunism would wane, given the existence of reputational effects (since information is costless) and the possibility of private sanctions. In such a utopia, the only function of contract law would be the enforcement of contracts – but even this would be redundant since market forces would

---

[11] See Muris, 'Opportunistic Behavior and the Law of Contracts', *Minnesota Law Review* 65 (1981) pp. 521–590 and Trebilcock, *The Limits of Freedom of Contract* (1993) p. 16. In conditions of perfect competition, opportunism would be extremely expensive given the full information and the consequent effects in reputation ('[b]ecause [market transactions] are repetitive, they usually make deceit and nonfulfilment of promises unprofitable', Stigler, *The Economist as Preacher and Other Essays* (1982) p. 22. However, a contract modification is not always the result of opportunism. As relational contract theory (and more generally the theory of the firm) have shown, on many occasions the parties consider that a modification of the initial terms of their contract will be mutually beneficial or at least will be a better alternative than one ensuing from judicial intervention.

[12] Indeed, the temporal element is an essential part of the definition of contract. See Kronman/Posner (n. 9), p. 3.

[13] See especially Craswell, 'Freedom of Contract', in: E. Posner, (ed.), *Chicago Lectures in Law and Economics*, (2000), pp. 81–99, for a description of such an environment and a non-technical explanation of why, in a perfect market, only the efficient clauses survive.

[14] Cooter and Ulen, *Law and Economics* (1988) p. 230. In this section, we rely extensively on the model that is presented by Robert Cooter and Thomas Ulen in the first edition of their introductory book (see Cooter & Ulen (n. 14), pp. 229–242) as the 'economic theory of contract', with some minor modifications. Cooter and Ulen's summarization of the work of legal and economic scholars into a coherent, systematic and impressive model constitutes a very useful basis for the presentation of a similar (or rather parallel) theory for civil contract law. See Trebilcock (n. 11), pp. 15–21 for a different, but also in many respects similar, exposition. See also Schwartz, 'Justice and the Law of Contracts: A Case for the Traditional Approach', *Harvard Journal of Law & Public Policy* 9 (1986) pp. 107–116 (pp. 110–113); Gensler, 'The Competitive Market Model of Contracts', *Commercial Law Journal* 99 (1994) pp. 384–398; Burrows 'Contract Discipline: In Search of Principles in the Control of Contracting Power', *European Journal of Law & Economics* 2 (1995) pp. 127–147 and finally Craswell (n. 13), for a model resembling the one presented here, but emphasizing the problem of imperfect information.

assure contractual performance – and any intervention by the state would be inefficient.[15]

Given that actual markets are merely the 'reflection' of the idea of perfect markets with perfect competition and perfect (and thus symmetric) information, we should cope with the fact that imperfect information entails imperfect contracts. Nevertheless, in a basically free market economy, where the distance between the theoretical concept of perfect competition and the reality of real markets is not so great, there is a good chance that many of the contracts will be nearly perfect, i.e. that they will serve the intentions of the parties adequately.[16] This is especially true for business contracts but also for consumer contracts in competitive markets. The fact that the great majority of contracts are performed without any significant problems constitutes empirical proof of this hypothesis.

Nonetheless, some 'incomplete' contracts end up in court. Apparently, these are the contracts that suffer heavily from the 'imperfection' of the market; consequently, contract law must deal with the problems stemming from this imperfection, especially in the area of consumer contract law.[17] The gravest circumstances of a 'malfunctioning' market are 'market failures', where the distance between imperfect and perfect competition is so great as to create serious problems in many aspects of economic life and, in our case, in the formation or performance of contracts.

What is the function of contract law under such unfortunate circumstances? It is again to help the parties achieve their ends, but as they would have formulated them had the market been perfect. The only thing courts have to do is to mimic the (perfect) market,[18] by restructuring contracts in a way that the parties would have done if there were no market failures.

There are six conditions that must be met in order for the market (and consequently for the contract) to be perfect:[19]

15 See e.g. the famous remarks by Sir George Jessel in *Printing and Numerical Registering Co. v. Sampson*, L.R. 19 Eq. (1875) pp. 462, 465.

16 Or, rather, slightly imperfect (or imperfect in respects of slight significance). 'No system has to be perfect to survive' (Epstein, 'Contracts Small and Contracts Large: Contract Law Through the Lens of Laissez-Faire', University of Chicago Law School, Law & Economics Working Paper, 2d series, No. 49 (1997) 3.

17 I consider a contract clause to be imperfect, i.e. inefficient, when 'the harm it inflicts on buyers is greater than the savings it creates for sellers', Craswell (n. 13), p. 85.

18 See generally Posner, *Economic Analysis of Law* (2003) p. 251, for the very useful distinction between 'settings in which the cost of voluntary transactions is low' and 'settings in which the cost of allocating resources by voluntary transactions is prohibitively high, making the market an infeasible method of allocating resources.'

19 This does not mean that there will always be a problem when one of the conditions doesn't apply in a particular situation. In many cases, the 'failure' is not so critical as to justify an intervention by the state, or the parties do not perceive it as being so important as to merit the initiation of legal action or the termination of an amicable long-term relationship, or 'government failure' is worse than market failure.

(1) **Rational agents.** Decision makers must have stable (i.e. rational) preferences. Their behaviour must be rational,[20] not random or irrational, and they must try to maximize their utility, given the constraints, by finding the best feasible outcome.
(2) **Unconstrained choice.** The parties must be constrained only by the factor of scarcity (in their income, time, energy, consumer demand, technology, etc.) in the materialization of their preferences.[21] Their choice must be free and not subject to any other kind of restriction by private parties (e.g. threat) or by the state (e.g. regulation).
(3) **Absence of transaction costs.** The cost of engaging in any transaction should be minor for the parties. Problems arise from an absence of or an inefficiently low amount of bargaining because of high transaction costs.
(4) **Absence of externalities.** The contract must not have negative third party effects. The cost of the transaction in its entirety must be borne by the parties and not by any other third party that has nothing to do with the contract.
(5) **Perfect information.** The parties must be fully informed as to the nature and consequences of their choices. This does not mean that there should be no (primary) uncertainty as to future events, but that there should be no severe informational asymmetries or symmetric informational imperfections, distorting the choice of either party.
(6) **Perfect Competition.** There must be enough potential contractors, e.g. many buyers and many sellers (that is no monopolies, monopsonies or oligopolies). None of the parties should have great market power in the particular market and use it to extract monopoly rents. More accurately, the party that has the market power should not exploit it to his/her favour, thus making the bargain overly one-sided.

If all the aforementioned requirements are met,[22] then the contract is perfect and it must be strictly enforced. But if one of them is not, then the contract is imperfect and there is a good chance that the parties will end up in court or that one party will be burdened by this imperfection so severely as to make future contracting parties inefficiently cautious. Contract law can provide solutions to this problem by creating doctrines that are suitable for

---

[20] See Williamson, 'Revisiting Legal Realism: The Law, Economics, and Organization Perspective', *Industrial & Corporate Change* 5 (1996) pp. 383–420 (398), for the three versions of rationality: strong form (hyper-rationality-maximization-comprehensive contracting), semi-strong (bounded rationality-farsighted contracting), and weak (bounded rationality-myopic contracting). Although this distinction is relevant, it has the defect of not being continuous – a defect shared by many types of categorization. I would choose 'rational spirit', a term Williamson himself uses and prefers.

[21] But see Trebilcock (n. 11), pp. 79–84.

[22] These conditions are not as absolute as they seem. For example, the total absence of transaction costs is impossible, but this does not signify that all contracts will be imperfect by default. The concepts are relative (or rather, I am using them relatively), especially in real world situations, such as commercial transactions in a given modern capitalist economy.

correcting the defects of the market. These doctrines, embodied in default rules, will provide a 'perfect-contract environment' for the parties, by reducing the probability of problematic situations. At the same time, parties will save time and money, i.e. economize on transaction costs (with both optional and mandatory default rules) and they will have a better chance of elaborating on more intricate aspects of their relationship, thus further reducing the likelihood of problems, since the cost of bargaining will be lower.

The majority of default rules should be subject to the will of the parties, who must reserve the right to alter them if they wish to. The insertion of mandatory rules in the context of a civil code and the specialized legislation on consumer contracts and sales is essentially a public policy choice. Every distribution of rules, into mandatory and optional, has its own social benefits and costs. The most efficient distribution would be the one more faithfully based on the aforementioned market failure analysis.

Contract law has responded quite successfully to the demands of given markets and, as a result, there are a number of legal doctrines, in both common and civil law (as well as in EU consumer law), that correspond to the imperfections of markets and can be seen as legal answers/solutions to the market failures just mentioned.

The table that follows is characteristic:

Table 1: Contract Imperfections

Imperfection	Contract Doctrine
1. Irrationality	Majority, Incompetency, Transactional Incapacity
2. Constrained Choice	Coercion, Duress, Necessity, Unconscionability, Contracts of Adhesion, Impossibility, Rules of Good Faith and against Opportunistic Behaviour
3. Negative Externalities	TORT LAW, Mandatory rules (rules of public policy)
4. Imperfect Information	Fraud and Misrepresentation, Frustration of Purpose, Mistake, Mutual Mistake, Duty of Disclosure, Unconscionability, Impossibility, Commercial Impracticability, Rules of Good Faith and against Opportunistic Behaviour
5. Monopoly	Necessity, Contracts of Adhesion, Unconscionability, Rules of Good Faith and against Opportunistic Behavior, ANTITRUST LAW DOCTRINES, REGULATORY LAW

Table 1: (cont.)

6. Transaction Costs	Default rules, Impossibility, Commercial Impracticability, QUASI CONTRACTS AND UNJUST ENRICHMENT DOCTRINES, Rules of Good Faith and against Opportunistic Behavior

Adapted from Cooter & Ulen (1988)

I hope that the above exposition has made clear that economics can help us understand the economic rationale of legal rules. For economics, the market is not perfect. Law can greatly help in correcting its failures and this is the basic function of contract law. Promoting economic efficiency basically means correcting the market.

This surely sounds paternalistic. What if the parties agree on something which an economist would find inefficient? Richard Posner opts for the parties' wishes, as shown in the following famous passage:

> 'Now consider what to do about cases in which the parties' intentions, as gleaned from the language of the contract or perhaps even from testimony, are at variance with the court's notion of what would be the efficient term to interpolate into the contract? If the law is to take its cues from economics, should efficiency or intentions govern? Oddly, the latter. The people who make a transaction – thus putting their money where their mouths are – ordinarily are more trustworthy judges of their self-interest than a judge [. . .] who has neither a personal stake in nor first-hand acquaintance with the venture on which the parties embarked when they signed the contract. So even if the goal of contract law is to promote efficiency rather than to enforce promises as such [. . .] enforcing the parties' agreement insofar as it can be ascertained may be a more efficient method of attaining this goal than rejecting the agreement when it appears to be inefficient.'[23]

Before we proceed, we will deal briefly with the question of contract law's suitability for pursuing and achieving social justice. Although this is an almost exhausted issue,[24] which we will not scrutinize here, we wish to call attention to two points:

- Contract is primarily an ingenious mechanism for the transfer of scarce resources. The role of contract law and the state's function in general

[23] Posner (n. 19), pp. 96–97.

[24] For an overview of the issues of paternalism and freedom of contract, see Kronman/Posner (n. 9), pp. 230–267; and for further elaboration, see Kennedy, 'Distributive and Paternalist Motives in Contract and Tort Law, With Special Reference to Compulsory Terms and Unequal Bargaining Power', *Maryland Law Review* 41 (1982) pp. 563–658 and Kronman, 'Paternalism and the Law of Contracts', *Yale Law Journal* 92 (1983) pp. 763–798.

should be to help this mechanism operate smoothly, and nothing else beyond that. The most reliable method for a contract law to achieve efficiency is for it to enforce the parties' deals and to 'reconstruct' these deals when this is necessary, employing the standards of 'trade usage' and 'business ethics'.

These observations should not be taken to mean that there is no place for the intervention of the state and of judges in particular. This intervention seems necessary and inevitable in those cases where the disparities in bargaining power are conspicuous (in consumer contracts). But this intervention should have as its only purpose to enforce and thus facilitate exchanges and to create, to the greatest extent possible, a 'perfect market environment', by helping the market correct its failures and not by patronizing the parties. It is true that on many occasions the failures of the market can lead to unfair outcomes, resulting from highly unequal bargaining positions. But this is not always so. Most of the time, this inequality does not have any effects on the contractual relationship, especially in conditions of (practically) perfect competition or in the case of business contracts. As Allan Schwartz[25] put it: If '[consumer markets] do work well, there is little to worry about in terms of justice – that is, justice in the sense of allowing people to do the best they can for themselves under given circumstances.'

– The state has numerous other opportunities for correcting injustices and pursuing 'social justice' without distorting the market and harming people.[26] It is generally accepted that contract law is not a suitable tool for achieving social justice and that other methods may be more efficient and more equitable, like taxation. '[J]udges can, despite appearances, do little to redistribute wealth [. . .] Legislatures, however, have by virtue of their taxing and spending powers powerful tools for redistributing wealth.'[27] Without any doubt, the pursuit of social justice by legislative bodies and not by the courts is not only more efficient, but also more comprehensive, democratic and impartial. This clearly sets some boundaries in the power of consumer contract law to protect weak parties in consumer contracts. This protection will be efficient and desirable when it deals with market failures. But when the goal of consumer law is distributive justice and not economic efficiency, the results could be harmful for the weaker parties it has set out to protect.

---

25 Schwartz, *Harvard Journal of Law & Public Policy* 9 (1986) p. 110.

26 The prevailing view among economists is that contract law is not the right vehicle for social justice: 'Why is that? Because not enforcing contract clauses, which is all judges can do, tends to make people poorer rather than richer.' Schwartz, *Harvard Journal of Law & Public Policy* 9 (1986) p. 115.

27 Posner, *The Problems of Jurisprudence* (1990) pp. 359–360.

II. CIVIL LAW AND ECONOMIC REASONING

I will now turn to our second question. Economic analysis of law is an American innovation and it was first applied in Common law. Is there any economic reasoning behind Civil law as there supposedly is behind Common law?[28] In other words, is Civil law efficient or at least as efficient as Common law? To answer this question, I have decided to use contract law as the area of comparative analysis. The idea of my research project is very simple. In the areas where there is a significant difference between Common and Civil law, which law is more efficient? Which legal family is closer to economic reasoning?[29]

When I started working on comparative contract law 12 years ago, my first observation was the total absence of theoretical discussion and the parallel lack of contemporary *grand* theories developed for civil contract law. By grand theories, I mean theories which purport to describe, interpret and even modify contract law in congruence with major philosophical, sociological, historical, political or economic theories claiming universality. On the other hand, if we look over the impressive literature published on contract law over the last two decades in the numerous common law (especially American) journals and law reviews, we will discover that the purely doctrinal studies have been confined to the low-ranking journals. Nearly all the well-known American contract scholars (and there are many) can be easily categorized according to their adherence to a specific theory, most of them to law and economics. All of them discuss broad theoretical issues, even when they set out to solve particular doctrinal problems.[30]

On the other hand, contract scholars in civil law countries adopt a very different approach. The great majority of studies are purely doctrinal, there are very few references to philosophical, economic or other theories – and these few are largely outdated. Moreover, the topics are quite restricted, since the discussion on many issues seems to have come to a conclusion and the interpretation of the statutes appears to be exhausted. With the exception of certain 'new' issues of some interest, like collective bargaining agreements, standard form contracts and electronic commerce, the rest of the law review articles are analogous to their counterparts in the low-ranking American law reviews.

---

28 The prevalent theory in law and economics maintains that the common law process is the primary reason for the generation of efficient rules. See characteristically Rubin, 'Why Is the Common Law Efficient?', *Journal of Legal Studies* 6 (1977) pp. 51–63; and the work of Richard Posner in general, mainly his treatise *Economic Analysis of Law* (2003).

29 This section draws heavily from Hatzis, 'The Anti-Theoretical Nature of Civil Law Contract Scholarship and the Need for an Economic Theory', *Commentaries in Law & Economics* 2 (2003) pp. 1–64, where the interested reader can find a more sophisticated presentation of the argument.

30 Barnett, 'The Richness of Contract Theory', *Michichan Law Review* 97 (1999) pp. 1413–1429.

What is the reason behind this almost total absence of theoretical discussion on contract law in civil law countries? How can we account for such stagnation when there is such an intellectual hype in the common law? Are theoretical problems considered resolved in continental Europe? Is there an indifference towards theory and a predilection towards results in the civil law countries, or is this just a sign of technical conservatism?

One reason for the absence could be the major differences in intellectual legal traditions. But this cannot explain such disparity, especially if we take into consideration the intellectual resurgence in 19th century European legal thought. Another explanation could be that contract law was gradually divested of its substance by commercial law, insurance law, labour law, etc. But this is at least as true for common law as it is for civil law. In any case, it remains the core of any civil code and the model of most legal relationships. In addition, it seems that a renaissance of contract law has occurred in the last 15 years for two reasons: 1) the triumph of free market and capitalism in Europe at large which led, in Eastern Europe, to a drafting or revision of civil codes (especially contract and property law) that are better-suited to free market economies and more conducive to economic development; and 2) the growing concern of the European Union for the unification of European private law in general[31] and contract law in particular, as well as the trend toward the internationalization of contract law.

However, the continuing absence of general theories developed in Europe or influenced by the ones developed in common law domains may at first seem puzzling for common law scholars, until they realize what the most plausible explanation for this phenomenon is: in civil law there is no need for theories since the legislator, mainly through the codes, has proclaimed what the law is and the judge is (supposedly) a mere interpreter, useful only for accommodating trivial twists of facts. In such a static universe, where is the need for theory?

By contrast, in common law, theory is necessary even today, since there are no codes capable of offering not only solutions to particular problems, but also – and most significantly – a unified approach. Common law has for centuries been (and today continues to be) in the process of its formation and common law judges have tried to resolve issues by borrowing ideas, rules, and even theories, from multiple sources. With the advent of the industrial revolution and the pressure applied by novel commercial relations, and society in general, judges and scholars increasingly felt the need to inject the law with a theory that would provide a sense of stability and security to the contracting parties.[32]

---

31 See the essays in this volume and also Grundmann and Stuyck (eds.), *An Academic Greenpaper on European Contract Law* (2002). See also Grundmann, 'Information, Party Autonomy and Economic Agents in European Contract Law', *Common Market Law Review* 39 (2002) pp. 269–293 (270–272), for the role of party autonomy in European contract law. For some legitimate concerns, see Lurger, 'Austrian Consumer Law', in this volume.

32 See generally Atiyah, *The Rise and Fall of Freedom of Contract* (1979).

A typical characteristic of common law theories, that is also a good illustration of our point, is the desperate attempt of common law scholars to prove that their theories and their approaches are not only better normative theories, but also perfect positive ones. As a result, a rather strange phenomenon occurs in common contract law review articles: after the exposition of a theoretical framework, the rebuttal of opposite theories and the discussion of several cases which are characteristic for their 'compatibility' with the theory expounded, the author examines a number of controversial cases with the purpose of demonstrating that, deep down, these 'irregular' cases are compatible with his theory, despite the opposite wording or even outcome.[33]

Only in extreme cases is a decision characterized as forthrightly wrong or (at least) opposed to the theory developed, and is consequently dismissed. Of course, another scholar may easily support a theory that is in diametric contradiction, and may interpret the decisions accordingly. This need for an 'approval' by the already adjudicated cases (!) signifies the insecurity and the desperate need for coherence in common law and is telling of the definitive power of precedent even today. This phenomenon of 'procrusteanism' in common law theory leads, according to one of the leading legal historians and common law scholars, A. W. B. Simpson, to a sort of 'doctrinal monism':[34]

> '[T]here has always in the common law been a tendency towards a sort of doctrinal monism – there must be one test for the formation of contract (offer and acceptance), one principle governing possession, one test for the actionability of promises.'[35]

In stark contrast with common law's century-long struggle for coherency, Roman law in continental Europe was so comprehensive, successful and coherent as to offer judges useful guidelines for the regulation of economic activities with no serious conflicts with the needs of economic life, despite the age of the statutes.[36] It is characteristic that the history of contract theory developed by common law within the last two centuries was, to a great

---

33 See e.g. Hillman, *The Richness of Contract Law: An Analysis and Critique of Contemporary Theories of Contract Law* (1997) pp. 60–74. A characteristic historical example of this problem is the famous scene between Samuel Williston and Arthur Corbin in a session of the first *Restatement* drafting committee, as described by Gilmore, *The Death of Contract* (1974) pp. 62–63. See also the excellent observations in Weir, 'Contracts in Rome and England', *Tulane Law Review* 66 (1992) pp. 1615–1648.

34 'Monotheorism' for Weir (*Tulane Law Review* 66 (1992) pp. 1615–1648).

35 Simpson, *A History of the Common Law of Contract: The Rise of the Action of Assumpsit* (1975) p. 325.

36 James Whitman has developed a theory according to which this compatibility was to a great extent 'helped' in the 19th century by the theoretical constructs of a number of German professors of liberal political ideology, mainly of Rudolf von Jhering. See Whitman, *The Legacy of Roman Law in the German Romantic Era: Historical Vision and Legal Change* (1990), *passim* and also pp. 229–243. See also Rolland, 'The Role of the Law of Obligations in the Legal System of a Free Industrial Society', in: Harmathy/Németh (eds.), *Questions of Civil Law Codification* (1990) pp. 142–154 (143–145).

extent, the history of the adoption and development of concepts that were part of civil law's contract theory and practice since Roman times (or at least since the major codifications in Western Europe).[37] The codification of Roman law by Justinian and the subsequent development of this law, always within the boundaries of the great codifications, and, at the same time, the successful and uninterrupted application of civil law in continental Europe and elsewhere, has offered the contracting parties in civil law countries a stable, coherent and positive legal framework, including a set of default rules that they can bargain around – and thus further develop.

Its usage has also created a tradition of a particularistic elaboration of issues and economic relations, which is based not on a case-by-case treatment that needs a general theory in order to remain stable and coherent, but on a regulation of special types or categories of contractual relationships by means of a unified set of rules imprinted in the civil codes. Alan Watson describes Roman law as comprised of numerous self-contained 'blocks'.[38] These rules have for centuries been the object of further treatment, elaboration and improvement by judges, scholars, and of course, the contracting parties themselves. This 'fermentation' process has shaped legal orders that are time-honoured and thus highly sophisticated. Therefore, it is no coincidence that Roman law was a decisive factor for the creation of the first commercial societies in Europe and for the rise of capitalism. After all, the Roman economy was essentially a market economy. According to Andreas Wacke:

> 'The ground rule of the Roman emperors with regard to private economic activity may be described [. . .] as laissez-faire liberalism, which only sought to regulate to a limited extent the production of mainly agrarian and household goods, as well as their distribution on the predominantly small-scale markets [. . .] The market-economy principle of free competition remained, by and large, undisturbed by these state activities, which were important, but which remained peripheral to the general economic system.'[39]

---

37 See esp. the work of R. H. Helmholz ('Continental Law and Common Law: Historical Strangers or Companions?', *Duke Law Journal* (1990) pp. 1207–1228; 'Use of the Civil Law in Post-Revolutionary American Jurisprudence', *Tulane Law Review* 66 (1992) pp. 1649–1687). See also recently Perillo, 'Robert J. Pothier's Influence on the Common Law of Contract', *Texas Wesleyan Law Review* (Pothier exerted an enormous influence on the Common law of contract) and Appleman, 'The Rise of the Modern American Law School: How Professionalization, German Scholarship, and Legal Reform Shaped Our System of Legal Education', *New England Law Review* 39 (2005) pp. 251–306 (she examines German educational influence on American nineteenth-century reformers and details the effect of the German scientific method on elite American law schools, 11 (2005) pp. 267–290).

38 Watson, *The Making of the Civil Law* (1981) pp. 18–20.

39 Wacke, 'Freedom of Contract and Restraint of Trade Clauses in Roman and Modern Law', *Law & History Review* 11 (1993) pp. 1–19 (2).

As a result, Roman law was developed in order to meet commercial needs and to regulate an advanced commercial society and its transactions. It is illustrative of the contribution of Roman law to the economic development and the modernization of European legal systems that the enemies of Roman law in Germany attacked it as a law that was 'rationalistic', 'commercial' and 'materialistic'.[40] In a series of papers and books, Prof. James Whitman[41] has established the close relationship between the re-emergence of Roman law and the birth of the first commercial society in Holland.[42]

The major codifications that started in the beginning of the 19th century and ended in the early 20th century offered a modernized version of Roman law. These codifications rendered the law more compatible, in certain respects, with the economic developments of the period. Further, they were the product of an extensive theoretical discussion and were greatly influenced by the social and economic theories that prevailed at the time, which were not very different from the present mainstream ones.

Following the tradition of Roman law,[43] the new civil codes have not espoused any particular theory, especially in the area of contract law. The main concern for the codifiers was to solve all major theoretical and practical problems by choosing the best possible solution for the welfare of the parties, as this welfare was perceived under the liberal ideology of the day, which was also heavily influenced by Christian ethics, and certainly within the boundaries set by the rules, standards and principles that had proven successful for many centuries.

Consequently, in the civil codes one can find answers to almost all the doctrinal and theoretical problems that have preoccupied and still preoccupy common law theory (e.g. the basis of contract, the rigidity of the 'privity' doctrine, the enforcement of penal clauses, liquidated damages or third-party beneficiary contracts, the choice between different types of damages and specific performance, the problem of quasi contracts and unjust enrichment, the puzzle of precontractual liability, the controversial unconscionability defense, the nature of the 'good faith' requirement, the compensation paradox, the differentiation between commercial impracticability with other similar cases of frustrations of contract, etc.). Civil law thus provided definitive and authoritative solutions to all the aforementioned problems, without restricting the parties by heavily regulating their contract.

---

40 Whitman, 'The Disease of Roman Law: A Century Later', *Syracuse Journal of International Law & Commerce* 20 (1994) pp. 227–234 (228).

41 Whitman (n. 37; n. 41; 'The Moral Menace of Roman Law and the Making of Commerce: Some Dutch Evidence', *Yale Law Journal* 105 (1996) pp. 1841–1889.

42 According to Whitman, *Yale Law Journal* 105 (1996) pp. 1841–1889 (1845), 'Roman law did not cause the rise of a new commercial morality in seventeenth-century Holland; it helped justify the rise of a new commercial morality'.

43 For Dawson, 'Book Review: *The Making of the Civil Law* by Alan Watson', *University of Chicago Law Review* 49 (1982) pp. 595–612 (596), problem solving rather than high-level speculation was the great skill of Roman jurists (as this is evident in the *Digesta*).

In addition, most of the clauses in civil law codes are default, non-mandatory (i.e. optional) rules. The codes routinely endow the judges with broad discretion by way of a series of general standards. Regardless of the practice of civil law judges, their independence is not similar in nature to that of their common law colleagues, since they need not be creators but interpreters of the law. Consequently, there is no urgent need for unifying theories resembling those that were developed in common law, since civil law judges are not expected to create law in the manner required of common law judges.

This particularistic approach of civil law has proven quite successful for a long time, if one judges by the absence of major intellectual controversies among civil law scholars (at least in the area of contract law), similar to those taking place in common law. Since this is a phenomenon common to nearly all European civil law systems, one could safely say that it is not the outcome of a consensus based on 'intellectual laziness', conservatism or ignorance, but the result of:

(a) the lack of major doctrinal problems created by the rise and fall of opposing philosophical paradigms;
(b) a parallel absence of major economic or social distortions created by the application of rigid legal theories; and finally
(c) a shared common-sense pragmatism (a Roman law legacy) that has guided interpretation as a technical skeleton key.

As early as 1960, Ernst Cohn, a London barrister practising in both Germany and England, writes:

> 'A practitioner who has grasped the rules of the first book of the German Civil Code and those of the first part of the second book is thereby alone well equipped to deal satisfactorily with an astonishingly large number of everyday problems. A question which would require a common law practitioner to search in books of reference for one or several quarters of an hour could be solved by his Continental colleague completely satisfactorily in as many minutes.'[44]

Similarly, in a letter to the editor from 'a retired American lawyer living in France':

> 'French contracts tend to be extraordinarily short and simple by American standards [. . .] This is partly because parties to business contracts

---

[44] Cohn, 'The German Attorney', *International & Comparative Law Quarterly* 9 (1960) pp. 580–587 (586); see also recently Hill and King, 'How Do German Contracts Do As Much With Fewer Words?', *Chicago-Kent Law Review* 79 (2004) pp. 889–926 (in Germany, legal and extra-legal forces combine to make the costs of 'stopping sooner' in the contracting process lower than they are in the USA).

usually don't try to anticipate every situation that could conceivably arise but are content to abide by the Code Civil.'[45]

An indication of the superiority of civil law, especially in the field of contracts, is that over the last two centuries, common law has incessantly copied the institutions of civil law. According to one of the major figures in comparative law and economics, Ugo Mattei, '[T]he influence [of the Napoleonic Code Civil] in England and the United States was far from superficial but reached deep and long lasting layers of the law'.[46]

All the above could indicate that civil law is more efficient that common law. However, one would need more evidence. Even today, common law and civil law are quite dissimilar in the field of contract law. These should not be exaggerated, since the similarities between them are numerous and more important, given the tendency of the Common law to borrow solutions from Civil law. Nevertheless, it would be interesting to explore the differences in the light of economic analysis in order to test the success of both systems. Which system of law is more efficient in those areas where such differences exist?

In my work, I have explored five areas where there are marked differences between civil and common contract law. These areas are: contract formation;[47] the enforcement of liquidated damages and penal clauses;[48] third party beneficiaries;[49] frustration of performance;[50] and efficient breach.[51] As my research showed, the solution provided by the civil law systems in these five areas where major differences are observed is more congenial to the one advocated by economists as the most efficient one. This is extremely important given the influence that common law has exerted on the economics of contracts, as Eric Brousseau[52] has aptly demonstrated.

The particularistic (casuistic) and pragmatic approach of Roman and civil law has proven to be more efficient than that of the rigid theoretical common law, whose reluctance to adopt all the successful solutions given by the civil law (although it has already adopted most of them) is primarily due to the futile attempt of common law scholars to create unified theories, based not on economic efficiency (the real and primary purpose of contract

45 Himel, 'Resolving Disputes the French Way' [Letter to the Editor], *Business Law Today* 6/3 (1997) p. 5.

46 Mattei, 'Why the Wind Changed: Intellectual Leadership in Western Law', *American Journal of Comparative Law* 42 (1994) pp. 195–218 (202).

47 Hatzis, n. 6 (1999).

48 Hatzis, *International Review of Law & Economics* 22 (2003) pp. 381–406.

49 Hatzis, n. 6 (1999); n. 6 (2000).

50 Hatzis, n. 6 (1999).

51 Hatzis, n. 6 (1999); n. 6 (2000).

52 Brousseau, 'Did the Common Law Biased the Economics of Contract . . . and May It Change?', in: Deffains/Kirat (eds.), *Law and Economics in Civil Law Countries* [*The Economics of Legal Relationships*, Vol. 6] (2001) pp. 79–105.

law), but on philosophical and moral ideals that are irrelevant to the parties' wishes and welfare.

This does not necessarily mean that civil law's underlying logic is economic (a feature that R. Posner and other law and economics scholars attribute to Common law). But it *does* make the point that the long process from Roman law times to the modern civil codes and the parallel testing of its rules by a host of legal scholars, judges and lay people in diverse social and economic settings, has shaped institutions that regulate the market efficiently.

My hypothesis also does not imply that countries with civil law systems are wealthier or more efficiency-oriented than common law countries. The evidence suggests that rather the opposite is true. According to Paul Mahoney,[53] common law countries experienced faster economic growth than civil law countries during the period 1960–1992; the difference reflects common law's greater orientation toward private economic activity and civil law's greater orientation toward government intervention. However, I believe that this disparity should rather be attributed to different cultural traditions and historical circumstances.[54]

III. TESTING THE THEORY – PRELIMINARY COMMENTS

In the following sections, I will present two examples where common and civil contract law have a major difference: the availability of efficient breach and the enforcement of penalty clauses. In essence, we are dealing with the question of contractual freedom and the need to protect parties paternalistically, which is basically an issue for consumer law. As we will see, these two problems are not unrelated. In the case of efficient breach, the promisor should be able to breach since he is ignorant of the future and he might be trapped in a one-sided contract. For the breach to be efficient he should also fully compensate the other party, including the penalty clauses. However, as we are going to show, these clauses should only be enforced if they are efficient, i.e. not abusive. These are not real issues in business contracts. However, they are very important in consumer contracts, especially in standard form contracts. The efficient solution for all the parties (including the third party offering a better deal) is the optimal allocation of resources which

53 Mahoney, 'The Common Law and Economic Growth: Hayek Might Be Right', *Journal of Legal Studies* 30 (2001) pp. 503–525.

54 See esp. Glaeser and Shleifer, 'Legal Origins', *Quarterly Journal of Economics* 117 (2002) pp. 1193–1230, for a related discussion (not friendly to our conclusions) which gives emphasis to differences in procedure and the role of the judiciary and not to substantive differences. According to the authors, civil law can become a control instrument of a bad government with adverse consequences for the security of property rights.

sometimes can be achieved only through the breach. For the breach to be efficient, the compensation must cover the subjective value of the performance (the consumer surplus) and any other hidden or idiosyncratic value. But this is possible only with the parallel enforcement of penalty clauses.

As we will demonstrate, civil law offers the rules that are necessary for these distinctions. However, if these rules are to function adequately, they should be interpreted with the help of economics. In addition, a clear distinction between business and consumer contracts should be made, since the intervention of a judge in a contractual dispute is often necessary in consumer contracts (to correct market failures) and redundant (if not catastrophic) in cases where both parties are sophisticated economic agents.

IV. TESTING THE THEORY – THE CASE OF EFFICIENT BREACH

To test my hypothesis, I am going first to discuss a problem that has preoccupied law and economics scholarship for many years: 'efficient breach' induced by a third party.[55]

In certain cases, the breach of a contract is more efficient than its performance. 'Breaching is more efficient than performing when the costs of performing exceed the benefits to all parties.'[56] According to R. Posner, this means that '[i]n many cases it is uneconomical to induce completion of performance of a contract after it has been broken'. Thus, the law should not compel adherence to a contract, but it should let the contracting parties decide whether they want to perform the contract or compensate the other party for the injuries incurred by non-performance. This is not a new idea. According to Oliver Wendell Holmes, Jr.:

> 'The only universal consequence of a legally binding promise is that the law makes the promisor pay damages if the promised event does not come to pass. In every case it leaves him free from interference until the time for fulfillment has gone by, and therefore free to break his contract if he chooses.'[57]

More recently, in *Patton v. Mid-Continent Sys.*,[58] Richard Posner writes:

> 'Even if the breach is deliberate, it is not necessarily blameworthy. The promisor may simply have discovered that his performance is worth

55 For a more detailed elaboration, see Hatzis, n. 6, (1999), pp. 170–194; n. 6 (2000).

56 Cooter and Ulen (n. 4), 254. See the introductory discussion of the problem in Cooter and Ulen (n. 4), 254–261. See also Posner (n. 19), 119 and Farnsworth, *Contracts*, (2004), pp. 735–738.

57 Holmes, Jr., *The Common Law* (1881) p. 301.

58 841 F.2d 742 (7th Cir. 1988).

more to someone else. If so, efficiency is promoted by allowing him to break his promise, provided he makes good the promisee's actual losses.'

For the breach to be efficient (i.e. socially desirable), the compensation must be full, i.e. the non-performing party should pay expectation damages, thus placing the victim of the breach in as good a position as he would have been in if the breaching party had performed – otherwise the breaches will be inefficiently deterred.

Nevertheless, even law and economics scholars acknowledge that expectation damages which are actually awarded by courts are typically imperfect. Determining the extent of damages in litigation is a specific form of what economists call the 'problem of preference revelation', i.e. closing the gap between objective prices and subjective values. As we will see below, the only satisfactory solution to the problem of idiosyncratic values could be the enforcement of liquidated damages (i.e. damages stipulated by the parties).

Sometimes efficient breach is the result of a third party's interference in a contractual relationship, an interference that takes the form of a better offer by the third party to the promisor. This interference has been characterized as tortuous in common law, especially in US law, but also in other jurisdictions. This 'criminalization' of the better offer by a third party has been widely disputed by lawyers and economists as creating inefficiency.[59]

The essential legal question appears to be the following: given the practical problem of calculating expectation damages, the corresponding high administrative costs and the parallel (and consequent) appearance of opportunism, in most situations, should we allow efficient breach or should we adhere to a theory that sanctifies promise, consent and/or good faith? The ethical dilemma which surfaces is that the two regimes can lead to quite different distributive outcomes. In a regime where efficient breach is not

[59] E.g. Wexler, 'Intentional Interference with Contract: Market Efficiency and Individual Liberty Considerations', *Connecticut Law Review* 27 (1994) pp. 279–328; Hatzis, n. 6 (2000). As Remington ('Intentional Interference with Contract and the Doctrine of Efficient Breach: Fine Tuning the Notion of the Contract Breacher as Wrongdoer', *Buffalo Law Review* 47 (1999) pp. 645–711 (646)) correctly points out, "[t]he view of breacher as wrongdoer is quite inconsistent with modern contract law. When the tort of interference with contract is founded on this view it leads to the spectacle of tort law seeking to deter the very same behavior that contract law encourages." Contract law encourages investment by enforcing promises and ensures full compensation for the aggrieved party in case of a breach. This latter compensatory goal of contract law would be undermined by the "deterrence" model of a tortious approach to the problem of breach (based on a tort-like conception of contract). If we accept that the basic goal of contract law is the efficient allocation of resources in a society and the ensuing wealth maximization and not the enforcement of promises for moral reasons (as some libertarians would argue, see esp. Fried, *Contract as Promise: A Theory of Contractual Obligation* (1981), but also Scanlon, 'Promises and Practices', *Philosophy & Public Affairs* 19 (1990) pp. 199–226 (205–209) for similar views) or the protection of the sanctity of contract, then the choice is obvious. The pursuit of both goals would lead to serious indeterminacy.

allowed, the new surplus (by the better offer) will be shared by the third party and the promisee, but in a damages/efficient-breach regime the surplus will be divided between the third party and the promisor.

In a seminal paper, Goetz and Scott[60] emphasized the proof problems inherent in fully recovering idiosyncratic values. These problems prevent the non-breaching party from recovering his subjective expectations, if recovery is limited to legally determined 'objective' remedies. Accordingly, efficiency will be enhanced, under many circumstances, by the enforcement of liquidated damage clauses that represent the most efficient means by which parties can insure against the otherwise non-compensable consequences of breach.

Promisees can always ask for penal clauses or high liquidated damages, reflecting their subjective valuation of the contract or their risk-aversion respectively. Those who are risk averse or value performance higher than its market price can insure themselves or can ask for either a penal or a 'liquidated damages' clause to be included in the contract. This way, the promisee who has concluded an ordinary contract in a competitive market will be less protected than the one who struck a deal that he considers unique for personal reasons.

The essence of the free market is competition and this includes offering someone a better deal. The 'criminalization' of competition can bring about only distorted effects, since the incentives to search would be diminished and the outcome cannot be Pareto optimal. Contract is a mechanism invented to be used for better allocating resources. If this allocation can be improved with the non-performance of a contract and without injury to anyone, i.e. if there is a way to a Pareto improvement, then the purposes of contract law have been achieved.

As I mentioned before, the mainstream approach in Common law today has led to the tortification of efficient breach. A third party cannot offer a better deal without putting itself in danger of being liable for 'inducing breach'. According to Joseph M. Perillo, the author of the most widely-used American contract law textbook: '[R]egardless of the soundness of efficient breach theory in economic science, it is not, and should not be, the basis of normative determinations in the legal system.'[61]

The Romano-Germanic family of civil law proves to be more compatible with the economic approach. A contract is just a promise to perform or to pay damages instead. It does not transfer any property right to the promisor and a tort for the 'inducement to breach' sounds exotic to most civil lawyers.

---

60 Goetz and Scott, 'Liquidated Damages, Penalties, and the Just Compensation Principle: Some Notes on an Enforcement Model and a Theory of Efficient Breach', *Columbia Law Review* 77 (1977) pp. 554–594.

61 Perillo, 'Misreading Oliver Wendell Holmes on Efficient Breach and Tortious Interference', *Fordham Law Review* 68 (2000) pp. 1085–1106 (1106).

According to the principle of the 'relativity of obligations' (the counterpart of the 'privity doctrine' under common law), a contract creates a personal bond between the two contracting parties that binds only the two of them. Third parties cannot obtain rights or be burdened with duties from this two-party contractual relationship. Thus, a contract – or a juridical act in general – can only be considered a covenant between the two contracting parties and does not constitute a legal rule that is to be respected by third parties.

One of the results of this principle is that only the contracting parties have the obligation to comply with the contract and only the parties can be held liable for its breach. A third party cannot 'breach' a contract; even when he is an accomplice to its breach, he cannot be held liable and his acts cannot be considered unlawful as such. The creditor in a contract does not have an absolute right to the performance of the debtor or to the object of performance – let alone any power on the debtor himself.

Thus, according to the associate principle of 'separability' (*Trennungsprinzip*) in the exchange of a good (especially of an immovable good), two contracts are necessary for the transfer. 'There is a difference, between transferring of Right to the Thing; and transferring, or tradition, that is, delivery of the Thing itself.' (Thomas Hobbes, *Leviathan*, I, 14). For the movement of a good from the property of the seller to the property of the buyer, two different contracts must be concluded: a wholly executory 'promissory' contract, that creates an obligation to the seller to perform (i.e. to transfer the ownership of a property right) and is essentially an agreement to sell, and a dispositive 'performance' contract, that transfers the ownership (the property right) permanently to the buyer and constitutes the actual performance.

In the example of a sale, the promissory contract creates an obligation on the part of the seller to transfer ownership of the object of sale and to deliver it to the buyer. In a second stage, another juridical act, regulated by property law, needs to take place for the sale to be concluded, i.e. the actual transfer of the right. This act is also considered a contract, even though it is essentially the performance of a promissory contract.

However, the parties in everyday transactions most often use one single contract for the promise to transfer and the actual transfer of a right or a good. Nevertheless, the theoretical (and practical) importance of the principle is enormous. The 'legal fiction' of the explicit separation of promise from performance (although it could be characterized as outdated and impractical, or even as antithetical to the principle of freedom of contracts), solves a number of problems that have plagued common law scholarship and have created a tension between US contract law scholarship and economics. The most persistent of these problems is the restraint to efficient breach created by the tortification of its inducement by a third party and the simultaneous problematic nature of 'promise' that is often treated as a property in a system where there is nothing similar to the principle of separation.

The problem of the tortification of efficient breach is essentially non-existent in Romano-Germanic legal scholarship. A contracting party can freely breach a wholly executory promissory contract. The creditor only has a claim for damages and does not have any right to the object of performance or to performance itself. Even the wording of the articles in most European civil codes does not essentially diversify between culpable and non-culpable impossibility of performance.[62] Finally, the creditor cannot have any claim against the third party, since his inducement of the 'efficient' (or inefficient) breach *per se* is not characterized as a tort.

Thus, Romano-Germanic legal theory and practice, following an old and successful Roman law fiction that has been preserved by the Romano-Germanic law family as part of its legal heritage, has managed to deal effectively and concurrently with the problems generated by externalities from contracts, efficient breach and protection of idiosyncratic values.

V. TESTING THE THEORY AGAIN – THE CASE OF PENALTY CLAUSES

This is going to be more clearly illustrated in the example of agreed damages and especially of penalty clauses.[63] Common law judges are quite reluctant to enforce liquidated damages, especially if they believe that they include penalty clauses which are not enforceable.[64] On the other hand, in almost all European contract laws, liquidated damages are readily enforced, as are penalty clauses when they are not extravagant (sometimes even then) and purely gambling.

Although most law and economics scholars have criticized common law courts for the non-enforcement of penalty clauses,[65] there is a sizable minority of scholars who defend the common law 'non-enforcement' policy on the ground that penalty clauses are inefficient because they hinder efficient breach; that is, breaches that confer a greater benefit on the contract breaker than on the victim of the breach, in which event breach plus compensation for the victim produces a net gain with no losers and should be encouraged.[66] If this were true, then Common law would be more efficient than civil law in this particular area. However, and despite the merits of the arguments deployed by scholars who advocate the non-enforcement of penalty clauses, we believe that common law's rejection of penalty clauses is inefficient. We further

[62] Stathopoulos, *Contract Law in Hellas* (1995) pp. 262–263.

[63] This section is based on Hatzis, *International Review of Law & Economics* 22 (2003) pp. 381–406, where one can find a more detailed analysis.

[64] Farnsworth (n. 58), pp. 811–815; Beatson, *Anson's Law of Contract* (2002) pp. 624–629.

[65] Goetz and Scott, *Columbia Law Review* 77 (1977) pp. 554–594.

[66] De Geest and Wuyts, 'Penalty Clauses and Liquidated Damages', in: *Encyclopedia of Law and Economics*, Bouckaert and De Geest (eds.) (2000) pp. 141–161.

argue that the civil law solution to the problem is not only comparatively more efficient, but can also put to rest the worries of scholars who are afraid that efficient breaches will be deterred.

In the USA today, the parties may negotiate a clause providing for compensation in the form of a specified amount of damages in case of breach or of defective performance. These contract clauses are usually scrutinized by the courts which compare them to conventional damages. If the difference is substantial (if liquidated damages are 'unreasonably' high or grossly disproportionate to the actual injury, according to the court) the relevant provisions of the contract are considered as penalty clauses and are not enforceable. The courts then award a conventional remedy to the injured party as if the contract was silent and there were no agreed damages to be paid in the event of a breach.

It seems that the main reason for this distrust of stipulated damages by common law judges lies in their aim to avoid the introduction of any form of punitive damages (in addition to compensatory damages) for the breach of a contract.[67] The reason is that supposedly,

> 'the mere availability of such a remedy would seriously jeopardize the stability and predictability of commercial transactions, so vital to the smooth and efficient operation of the modern American economy.'[68]

According to Farnsworth,[69] 'it is a fundamental tenet of the law of contract remedies that an injured party should not be put in a better position than had the contract been performed.'

English law is also quite ambivalent towards liquidated damages and penalties. English courts have, like their American counterparts, 'retained the jurisdiction' to control the content of similar clauses. Liquidated damages are accepted to the extent that they are purely compensatory and not punitive. Even though English courts are not as unfriendly to liquidated damages as the US courts, they have formulated a similar test to the one employed in US case law to separate liquidated damages from penalty clauses.

However, the common law non-enforcement of penalty clauses incited the critique of economists quite early. This critique was not only rooted in the traditional economists' distrust of any kind of paternalistic judicial intervention in economic relations in general, but also in the very important economic role played by penalty clauses in commercial transactions.[70]

---

[67] See e.g. *Restatement (Second) of Contracts* § 356, comment a: 'The central objective behind the system of contract remedies is compensatory, not punitive'.

[68] *General Motors Co. v. Piskor*, 281 Md. 627, 381 A.2d 16 (1977).

[69] Farnsworth (n. 58), p. 760.

[70] According to Farnsworth (n. 58, pp. 812–813): 'Today the trend favors freedom of contract through the enforcement of stipulated damage provisions as long as they do not clearly disregard the principle of compensation.'

For economists, liquidated damages are far superior to the conventional damages awarded by the courts since they have been designed by the parties themselves. The parties have the incentives to stipulate damages that are not under- or super-compensatory, but serve the purpose of full compensation. In most cases where the liquidated damages appear to be under- or super-compensatory, this is a mirage. The parties know better than anyone else their subjective valuations of goods and performances and their stipulations serve their idiosyncratic values.[71] But even when the damages are in fact under- or supercompensatory, this might mean, respectively, that the parties decided to share the risk of a future change in circumstances (undercompensatory damages)[72] or to include an insurance premium (supercompensatory damages).

Thus, when one contracting party is risk-averse and/or places a high subjective valuation on performance of the contract and the other party is the best possible insurer against his loss, then it is only rational for the parties to include an insurance ('penalty') clause in the contract. The reason why a promisee often prefers a penalty clause which is essentially an insurance clause to a third-party insurance contract (besides the fact that he economizes on transaction costs) is that quite often the insurance compensation cannot adequately cover damages that are non-pecuniary. Additionally, a subjective value which is much higher than the market price may require a very high premium.

On the other hand, with a slight increase in contract price (due to the inclusion of the penalty-insurance clause) the promisor will take extra care in his performance. Since most of the time both parties wish just that (a more than average-quality credible performance in return for a more than average-price), the non-enforcement of these clauses by the courts is certainly inefficient and leads to undercompensation. At the same time, the court does precisely what it tries to avoid: By prohibiting a supposed windfall to the injured party, it awards an actual windfall to the breaching party, since the penalty clause reflects an above-the-market-rate contract price since it includes an insurance premium. The breached contract embodies an insurance policy written by the promisor in favor of the promisee – which is never going to be compensated![73]

Moreover, the enforcement of liquidated damages solves a number of problems of contract remedies, but also of real-world contract relations:

---

71 Goetz and Scott, *Columbia Law Review* 77 (1977) pp. 554–594 (558–577).

72 See esp. D. Friedman, *Law's Order: What Economics Has to Do with Law and Why It Matters* (2000) p. 151: it may be perfectly reasonable to choose a penalty clause, in the expectation that it will rarely be invoked, over the alternative of giving the court a free hand to decide damages.

73 According to Collins, *Regulating Contracts* (1999) p. 260: '[W]e cannot determine the issue of unfairness without investigating thoroughly the issue of whether advantages have been paid for in the price.'

- It solves the paradox of compensation (efficient breach versus efficient reliance[74]) in a better way than the conventional remedies, producing the socially optimal solution, since reliance and breach are chosen efficiently.
- It facilitates the calculation of risks, since it eliminates uncertainty and helps future planning by the contracting parties. In fact, the damages stipulated by the parties will always allocate the contract risk optimally when the parties are risk averse, because the liquidated damage payment will equal the optimal damage payment.
- It discourages opportunistic behaviour by the promisor and inefficient contract renegotiation and modifications.
- It reduces transaction costs (measurement problems for expectation damages and reliance damages, litigation and administrative costs, the cost of legal error when the miscalculation of the expectation damages leads to inefficient behaviour, the cost of circumventing an inefficient rule by the parties and their attorneys, direct policing costs, etc.), especially in cases where the damages are not readily ascertainable.
- It simplifies efficient breach since the breaching party, knowing exactly the amount of damages that he has to pay to the promisee in the event of a breach, can easily determine if he would be better off after the breach. At the same time, it precludes inefficient breaches caused by a hidden subjective valuation that is higher than the market (contract) price. In any case, post-breach bargaining is always available and can reduce the likelihood of an inefficient performance. The stipulated remedy provision in the contract would serve as a 'bargaining entitlement', encouraging the breaching party to share the benefits of an efficient breach with the injured party.[75]
- It helps young or inexperienced professionals to convey information about their reliability by offering a kind of 'penal bond', i.e. a risk premium. A penalty clause is the least costly way (or the only way) for a promisor to communicate credibility to a skeptical promisee by signaling his commitment to perform.

For all the above reasons, most economists criticize common law's penalty doctrine as inefficient. The non-enforcement of penalty clauses undercompensates parties with idiosyncratic values, leads to inefficient breaches and complicates efficient breach. Furthermore, it precludes parties signaling their reliability, it substantially increases administrative and litigation costs, it encourages opportunistic behaviour, it leads to inefficient renegotiation, it disregards the allocation of risk by the parties, etc. For all these reasons, the penalty doctrine discourages contracting and is one of the main reasons why some value-maximizing contracts are never concluded.

---

[74] Shavell, 'Damages Measures for Breach of Contract', *Bell Journal of Economics* 11 (1980) pp. 466–490.

[75] Macaulay, Kidwell, Whitford and Galanter, *Contracts: Law in Action* (1995) p. 104.

However, some economists are concerned that the enforcement of penalty clauses might deter efficient breaches.[76] When the liquidated damages are higher than the actual losses, then they are certainly inefficient, since they compel the promisor to perform even when the cost of performing exceeds the net benefits for everyone involved. Thus, when efficient breach is possible and an award of expectation damages could cover all actual losses, a penalty or a stipulated sum which is significantly larger than the amount required to compensate the injured party for his loss may operate in terrorem on the breaching party, deterring breach and compelling inefficient performance.[77]

There are also significant distributive consequences: in the case of a possible efficient breach, a penalty clause serves only to increase the expected surplus of the original contractors relative to the incumbent. It does not increase the overall expected surplus and it creates a barrier to entry. Thus, a limit on liquidated damages in this case enhances efficiency by preventing the parties from overcommitting (from a social perspective) to the original contract.

These arguments against efficient breach are valid to a certain degree and are rarely rejected by the scholars who support the enforcement of penalty clauses. However, this critique does not differentiate between the three different kinds of stipulated damages:

(a) There are arbitrary liquidated damages set high enough to compel performance and deter breach without the genuine consent of the promisor and without relation to the actual damages ('shotgun clauses'). The particular stipulated sum is not the result of a bargain between the two contracting parties, but it is usually inserted in the contract without the knowledge or consent of the promisor. Similar clauses are quite frequent in standard form consumer contracts. Of course, the contract price does not reflect the penalty or the excessive liquidated damages. In these cases, there is no real agreement between the parties concerning the penalty clause, which is the result of a monopoly environment or of the presence of any of several formation defects. The enforcement of this penalty clause, which is an inefficient contract term, will not enhance efficiency, since (besides being abusive) similar contract terms deter efficient breaches.[78]

---

[76] For the efficient breach and the importance of remedies in the decision between performance and breach, see the remarks by Posner in *Patton v. Mid-Continent Systems, Inc.*, 841 F.2d 742 (7th Cir. 1988).

[77] See also Talley, 'Contract Renegotiation, Mechanism Design, and the Liquidated Damages Rule', *Stanford Law Review* 46 (1994) pp. 1195–1243 (the non-enforcement of contractual liquidated damages clauses is the economically efficient means of treating such clauses to encourage renegotiation and account for transaction costs); and Che and Chung, 'Contract Damages and Cooperative Investments', *Rand Journal of Economics* 30 (1999) pp. 84–105 (reliance damages are more efficient than liquidated damages if ex post renegotiation is possible).

[78] See similar thoughts in Collins, *The Law of Contract* (2003) p. 378, for the case of consumer contracts.

(b) There are penalty clauses (or higher liquidated damages) which are inserted in a contract because they serve a specific economic role. In these cases, the penalty clause is freely accepted by the parties, especially when the market is competitive and/or the contracting parties are sophisticated enough, which is always the case in commercial contracts. The non-enforcement of the stipulated damages which are the result of bargaining between the parties is inefficient and it hurts the very people it wishes to protect by offering them an alternative they do not want to retain (possibility of efficient breach) and expropriating from them an alternative they wish to have (adding an enforceable penalty clause to their contract). Efficient breach is not really an issue when a penalty clause plays an important economic role and the liquidated damages compensate actual losses.

(c) There is also a third category of penalty clauses (which is essentially a sub-category of the second) which might require special treatment: penalty clauses which are economically efficient and reasonable ex ante, but seem quite excessive ex post. These clauses are usually protective of risk-averse promisees or they play an informational role, substituting the lack of reputation.

According to Clarkson et al,[79] the enforcement of these penalty clauses may create a 'moral hazard' problem, i.e. incentives for inefficient behaviour by the parties when the damages calculated *ex ante* and included into the contract as liquidated damages are much greater than the actual losses. This situation is quite frequent, especially after a price fall.

Indeed, here overcompensation is due to the fact that the determination of damages was difficult or impossible *ex ante* and the actual losses are far lower. However, the stipulated amount in these cases constitutes the 'expected value' of damages, a value that could also be much lower than the actual losses. Then the excess is not a penalty, but the result of the previous allocation of risk to the least cost avoider (who is usually the least risk-averse party). The non-enforcement of the risk allocation agreed by the parties themselves is not only inefficient, but it undermines the economic role of contract as a risk-allocation mechanism.

Some of these caveats originated from economists who seem to overlook the fact that although one of contract law's main purposes is coping with market failures, its primary goal is simply to enforce the parties' wishes.

The problem of penalty clauses is one of the very few in contract law and economics to incite considerable disagreement among economists, but also among legal scholars. Most economists and most legal scholars might be in favour of the enforcement of penalty clauses, but we should acknowledge that the (sizeable) minority has developed several strong and valid arguments

[79] Clarkson, Miller and Muris, '*Liquidated Damages v. Penalties: Sense or Nonsense?*' *Wisconsin Law Review* (1978) pp. 351–390 (366–378).

against the enforcement of penalties. The reason for the existence of these conflicting arguments, which often cancel each other out, is that there are apparently two categories of penalty rules: efficient and inefficient. Efficient rules (second and third category) are the ones which serve an economic purpose. Inefficient penalty rules (third category) are purely gambling, unconscionable penalties. But these are almost by default scarce in commercial contracts between sophisticated parties (especially among corporations) and in most consumer (even standard form) contracts concluded in competitive markets.

The policy of non-enforcement has costs for the contracting parties: the non-enforcement of penalty clauses which function as performance bonds undermines efficient new firms which are not able to compete with inefficient established firms by offering higher bonds.[80] Additionally, besides doing harm to the sophisticated contractual parties, the non-enforcement of efficient penalty clauses does not adequately protect weaker parties since the rule can be easily evaded.

Thus, there seems to be no reason for common law courts to adhere so strongly to enforcement authority. The most efficient policy is one that would differentiate between inefficient (abusive) and efficient penalty clauses. Courts should enforce penalty clauses in general and they should annul only those clauses that are abusive and do not appear to play a specific economic role. This is impossible under the rigid penalty doctrine of common law. But it is exactly what most civil codes permit, if not invite judges to do.

Penalty clauses have been enforceable in Europe since Roman times.[81] They were employed in conjunction with all sorts of transactions and Roman lawyers toiled laboriously in drafting them. Not only were they enforced by the courts, but the rationale behind their enforcement was to help the promisee recover his actual losses (especially securing non-pecuniary interests), to reduce transaction costs, and to compel the promisor to perform according to the terms of the contract.

Today continental contract laws still abide by Roman law and enforce penalty clauses, even excessive ones. Under civil law systems, there is no reason to distinguish penalty clauses from liquidated damages since they are both enforceable. However, when a penalty clause is excessive (i.e. disproportionately high), courts have retained the discretion to reduce it to a reasonable amount – but only if the promisor asks for it. Nevertheless, the courts generally resort to this power only in exceptional cases.

The turning point in the shift from the unlimited penalties of classical Roman law to the contemporary 'equitable' approach was the final draft of the German Civil Code (BGB), where, after much deliberation and opposition by the adherents of the old liberal Pandectist doctrine, the power of the

80 Dnes, *The Economics of Law* (2005) p. 107.

81 Zimmermann, *The Law of Obligations: Roman Foundations of the Civilian Tradition* (1990) pp. 95–113.

judge to limit excessive penalty clauses was instituted. According to § 343 BGB, when the reasonableness of a penalty clause is judged by the courts, non-pecuniary losses and idiosyncratic values should be taken into consideration.

French law is more faithful to the Roman law's liberal approach. It is characteristic that the old article 1152 of the French (Napoleonic) Civil Code provided (following classical Roman law) that if the contract stipulates 'a certain sum of damages, no larger or smaller amount can be awarded.' This clause was amended as late as 1975. Under the amended statute, judges can at their discretion 'reduce or increase the agreed penalty if it is either derisory or manifestly excessive'; thus, the new statute brings the French *Code Civil* in line with other European Civil Codes. However, in making this decision (which is in their *pouvoir souverain*), judges should take into account, as in the BGB, the purpose of the penalty clauses as stated by the parties and they should state the reason for the reduction.

The members of the Commission on European Contract law managed to combine the best elements of the two different European legal families in article 9.509 ('Agreed Payment for Non-Performance') of the Principles of European Contract Law:[82]

> '(1) Where the contract provides that a party who fails to perform is to pay a specified sum to the aggrieved party for such non-performance, the aggrieved party shall be awarded that sum irrespective of his actual loss.
>
> (2) However, despite any agreement to the contrary the specified sum may be reduced to a reasonable amount where it is grossly excessive in relation to the loss resulting from the non-performance and the other circumstances.'

Judges have the power to intervene only when there is a 'gross disparity' between the stipulated sum and the actual losses. But the court cannot reduce the award to the actual loss; it can only fix an intermediate figure.

It is clear that civil law is not only more efficient, but it also has the potential to accommodate the more sophisticated economic critique to penalty clauses. G.H. Treitel laments the common law policy in his *Remedies for Breach of Contract*:

[82] There is no provision on penalty clauses in the Vienna convention. This means that the parties will be able to enforce penalty clauses if the law of jurisdiction permits enforcement (Macaulay et al. [n. 78], 110). According to § 7.4.13 of the UNIDROIT Principles: an aggrieved party is entitled to recover a specified sum 'irrespective of its actual harm', though the sum may be 'reduced to a reasonable amount where it is grossly excessive in relation to the harm resulting from the non-performance and to the other circumstances.' This rule is identical to the one found in various Civil codes and in the *Principles of European Contract Law*.

> 'The common law rules for distinguishing between penalties and liquidated damages manage to get the worst of both worlds. They achieve neither the certainty of the principle of literal enforcement, since there is always some doubt as to the category into which the clause will fall, nor the flexibility of the [civil law] principle of enforcement subject to reduction, since there is no judicial power of reduction.'[83]

My analysis has shown that civil contract law is more efficient, or at least closer to the views of mainstream economic scholarship in its treatment of penalty clauses than common law. As stated earlier, the most efficient policy on stipulated damages would require a differentiation between inefficient (abusive) and efficient penalty clauses. Courts should enforce penalty clauses in general and they should annul only those clauses which are abusive and do not appear to play a specific economic role. This 'efficiency test' is possible in every Civil contract law, provided that judges will accommodate economic theory in their interpretation of contracts. There is no other criterion for differentiating between 'reasonable' and 'abusive' penalty clauses than the one offered by economic theory.

Economic theory will make the interpretation more sophisticated by offering the judges a perspective that is absolutely necessary for their treatment of problems such as (but not restricted to) the opportunistic deterrence of an efficient breach, the problem of credibility of young professionals and the impact of their decision on all kinds of transaction costs.

VI. CONCLUSION

The European civil codes have proven overall successful after many decades of constructive implementation. Their particularistic approach towards contract law and the absence of rigidity contributed to the facilitation of economic life and to the realization of the parties' wishes more successfully than in the Common law.[84] This was the result of a natural evolution of legal rules and practices that threw into disuse a number of worthless institutions and insignificant formalities. It was also the outcome of the judges' respect for the principle of freedom of contracts and the absence of an activist judiciary, similar to the one in the USA.

The main obstacle to economic analysis in civil law countries might be the absence of an intellectual tradition similar to that of common law countries

[83] Cited by Whincup, *Contract Law in Practice (The English System and Continental Comparisons)* (1992) p. 261.

[84] For a similar conclusion, see Tullock, *The Case Against the Common Law* (1997) pp. 53–59: European procedures are far superior in clarity, precision and implementation to common law procedures; and Deffains, 'Efficiency of Civil Law', in Hatzis (ed.), *Economic Analysis of Law: A European Perspective* (2005): those who build and implement civil codes contribute towards realizing an efficient regulation of human activities.

(i.e. a tradition of respect for individualism and/or economic efficiency). But we should not overestimate these culturally-specific conditions, especially after taking into consideration the trends in international economic relations, the globalization of economic activity, the deregulation influx and the discrediting of political theories that could create a hostile environment for the growth of economic analysis.

We dare suggest that a civil law country has even better prospects for the application of such theories than a common law country.[85] Currently, in most civil law countries (at least in Europe) any attempt to deregulate economic life and to create an economically efficient law comes primarily from the state and not from the judicial system or legal scholarship. Thus, the timing is perfect for the sophistication of contract law in these countries. Specifically, as concerns the European Union, the attempt to unify the private law of member states in recent years, the publication of tentative drafts and the enactment of many EU directives on consumer contracts, present a golden opportunity for modernization based on economic analysis.[86]

In this paper I argued that the absence of theories developed for Roman contract law and the absence of grand theories developed in civil contract law scholarship were outcomes of a particularistic approach to the problems created by the deficiencies of markets. This approach was driven by the need for a construction of a legal framework conducive to economic progress. The generation of efficient results by civil law through the selection of efficient rules and standards was completed over the course of several centuries and stabilized after the great codifications.

Common law had for centuries attempted to develop a similar construct that would be stable enough to facilitate economic relations. The borrowing of ideas and solutions from civil law was the easy way out. Despite the numerous legal transplants, common law fought hard to preserve a false independence and a parallel dilapidated coherence by building unified, conclusive, but dogmatic theories. The mimicking of civil law has no doubt led to some efficient results, but with many islands of 'inefficiency' in the sea of rigid theories.

In a recent decision,[87] appellate judge, Richard Posner, the father of law and economics and the one who first developed the theory of the efficiency of common law, has had to enforce the rigid penalty doctrine of common law although he thinks it is inefficient! He writes:

---

85 See also the recent views of Richard Posner in Posner, 'Law and Economics in Common-Law, Civil-Law, and Developing Nations', *Ratio Juris* 17 (2004) pp. 66–79.

86 See esp. Grundmann, 'Consumer Law, Commercial Law, Private Law: How can the Sales Directive and the Sales Convention be so Similar?', *European Business Law Review* 14 (2003) pp. 237–257.

87 *XCO International Inc. v. Pacific Scientific Co.*, 369 F. 3c 998 (7th Cir. 2004).

> 'The reason for the rule is mysterious; it is one of the abiding mysteries of the common law. At least in a case such as this, where both parties are substantial commercial enterprises (ironically [in this case], it is the larger firm, that is crying "penalty clause"), and where damages are liquidated for breach by either party, making an inference of fraud or duress implausible, it is difficult to see why the law should take an interest in whether the estimate of harm underlying the liquidation of damages is reasonable. Courts don't review the other provisions of contracts for reasonableness; why this one?'

He will give the answer some pages later: 'The slow pace at which the common law changes makes it inevitable that some common law rules will be vestigial, even fossilized.'

On the other hand, civil law scholarship and practice is going to find it increasingly difficult to respond to the fast-changing economic circumstances. For the first time in history, economic relations have become so complicated that it is impossible for a judge endowed only with common sense to solve problems created by the dysfunctions of markets. Economic expertise is not merely helpful; it is indispensable.[88] Of course, judges are not expected to invent the wheel – but they should definitely learn how to use it. A responsive economic theory of contract law is imperative if civil law is to continue playing the role that it has successfully performed for centuries: providing the legal framework that helps the economy function.

[88] *Cf.* Grundmann, 'The Optional European Code on the Basis of the *Acquis Communautaire* – Starting Point and Trends', *European Law Journal* 10 (2004) pp. 698–711 (711).

Chapter 10

La place du Code de la consommation en droit contractuel français

*Judith Rochfeld**

Abstract: *In a first section, this contribution discusses the French Code de la consommation of 1993 and does so rather critically: The Code is seen as a mere compilation, with large lacunae and no coherent order, and not as a real codification in the sense of system building as had been intended initially. Moreover the Code was aimed at putting together the consumer law materials, thus making them more accessible. The paper argues that this goal has also been missed, due to large lacunae, and that a coherent order is missing too. In a second section, the paper discusses the question as to whether we can learn from this experience for Europe. The conclusion is evident: consumer law is too much a part of general contract law and also influences it too much, for instance with information duties, to make segregating them from one another possible. The author rather sees two modes of thinking: those who rather stress liberal party autonomy, are happier with the Code Civil, whilst those who rather stress trends to materialize contract law favour the Code de la consommation. Examples from the history of transposition of directives are given for this 'clash of cultures'.*

* Université du Miane, Le Mans-Laval.

S. Grundmann, M. Schauer (eds), *The Architecture of European Codes and Contract Law*, 193–204

I. INTRODUCTION

Je remercie chaleureusement, tout d'abord, la Société de droit européen des contrats de me faire l'honneur de m'inviter à m'exprimer devant elle et de célébrer le Code civil à l'occasion de son bicentenaire. Le chauvinisme des Français n'est pas le moindre de leurs défauts et ils ne peuvent que se sentir honorer de cette attention.

Pour autant, en fait de chauvinisme, il faudra s'arrêter là. En effet, si l'on franchit désormais le seuil du sujet qui fait l'objet de cette présentation – celui de la place du Code de la consommation dans le droit français – et l'insère dans notre débat – déterminer la nécessité d'un tel code dans la perspective de la construction d'un droit européen des contrats –, il serait illégitime d'afficher la même fierté. L'approche, immédiatement, doit se faire plus critique. Autant, d'ailleurs, prévenir de suite les organisateurs comme le public que s'ils avaient espéré un intervenant positif, supporter d'un tel Code, c'est un autre qu'il aurait dû choisir!

En effet, je voudrais démontrer, tout d'abord, que la réalisation française en la matière, le Code français de la consommation, soulève beaucoup plus d'ambiguïtés qu'il ne résout de problèmes de par ses défauts intrinsèques et spécifiques (II). Ensuite, sur le fondement de cette expérience, mais au-delà des spécificités de la réalisation française, je voudrais esquisser les difficultés d'ordre général, inhérentes à une telle entreprise, auxquelles peuvent conduire l'institution, aux côtés d'un code général, de ce type de Code (III).

II. LES INCONVENIENTS DE LA CODIFICATION FRANÇAISE

Tout d'abord, résumons les inconvénients de la codification française en la matière.

Certes, la France peut s'enorgueillir d'avoir été le premier pays, en 1993, à se doter d'un tel outil.[1] Mais cela ne fut pas fait sans maladresses. En effet, que ce soit de par la nature spécifique de ce Code, ses objectifs, les critères établis pour la sélection des textes à y inclure, ou les lacunes résultant de l'ensemble de ces présupposés, le Code de la consommation français s'impose comme un outil très imparfait.

Maladresses, en premier lieu, quant à la nature de ce Code. L'idée d'une codification du droit de la consommation s'est imposée en raison de l'éparpillement des textes intéressant le consommateur, qui ne s'inséraient dans aucun code existant. Une Commission de refonte fut instituée, chargée de proposer un projet de Code.[2] Elle s'était orientée vers un code conceptuel,

1 Loi n° 93-949 du 26 juillet 1993, *JO* 27 juillet 1993; ajoutée de la partie réglementaire par le décret n° 97-298 du 27 mars 1997, *JO* 3 avr. 1997, p. 5123.

2 Sur cette Commission et les différentes étapes de son travail, *cf.* l'historique succinct, *Infra.*

dans la grande tradition française des 'Codes-innovation'. A cet effet, elle avait proposé les définitions des notions devant servir de base au droit de la consommation et s'était attachée à formuler et à organiser ce dernier en un ensemble cohérent. Malheureusement, pour des raisons de politiques législatives et face à la complexité du travail entrepris, une autre voie fut finalement choisie. Ce fut celle du simple accolement des textes existants, c'est-à-dire une codification à 'droit constant' ou 'administrative'. La nature du Code se modifiait alors, revêtant celle de 'Code-compilation'. Dès lors, était délaissé tout effort de rationalisation et de cohésion du droit de la consommation. N'en résultait – c'est donc le seul apport du Code institué – qu'un classement des différents textes existants en cinq livres, subdivisés en titres, et pensés selon une approche chronologique cheminant en cinq thèmes: (1) Information des consommateurs et formation des contrats; (2) Conformité et sécurité des produits et des services; (3) Endettement; (4) Associations de consommateurs; (5) Institutions.

Mais alors, et en second lieu, du fait de ce changement de nature, il fallait bien constater que les objectifs du Code de la consommation se trouvaient modifiés. Parti de la volonté de créer une nouvelle matière et de définir ses notions élémentaires – donc d'une conceptualisation d'un corps de règles devenues homogènes –, le travail accompli aboutissait à délaisser ces impératifs pour en privilégier de nouveaux: ceux d'accessibilité et de lisibilité du droit existant. Priorité était ainsi donnée à une cohérence formelle et à l'exigence de divulgation des textes de la matière. Certes, le classement opéré devait également combler les lacunes, écarter les ambiguïtés, supprimer les contradictions ou les redondances, voire les conflits entre les textes. Mais, la mise à l'écart de tout travail conceptuel et de définition des notions sur lesquelles chacune des règles repose devait obérer cette cohérence.

Le travail fut d'autant moins cohérent, en troisième lieu, que le champ matériel du nouveau code, censé s'organiser autour de l'idée d'un droit général de la consommation, fut borné par trois critères[3] restrictifs, qui éloignèrent encore le résultat de l'outil attendu:

- tout d'abord, ne s'y trouvèrent insérées que les dispositions présentant un haut degré de généralité, c'est-à-dire celles intéressant uniquement l'ensemble des biens et des services;
- ensuite, ne s'y trouvèrent comprises que les règles présentant une nature législative ou réglementaire nationale;
- enfin, ne s'y trouvèrent insérées que les règles qui, 'constatant un déséquilibre au détriment des consommateurs', y remédient.

En effet, chacun de ces critères recèle une sélection qui rejette nombre de textes hors du Code de la consommation alors que l'on se serait attendu à les y trouver.

[3] Sur ces critères, *cf.* E. Petit, 'La codification du droit français de la consommation', *Revue européenne de droit de la consommation*, 1993, 213 *et seq.*, 215.

Ainsi, l'application du critère de la généralité des textes a rejeté hors du Code les réglementations spéciales, telles celles relatives à l'enseignement à distance, au courtage matrimonial ou aux voyages à forfait proposés par les agences de voyage. De même, celles intéressant les denrées alimentaires ou les produits pharmaceutiques en sont absentes.[4] Le contrat médical, également, reste en dehors de ces préoccupations et du regard consumériste. Toutes ces dispositions présentent, pourtant, une importance pratique non négligeable pour la protection du consommateur.

Dans le même ordre d'idée, du fait de l'application du critère de la nature législative ou réglementaire des textes, se sont trouvées rejetées:

- la synthèse des solutions jurisprudentielles;
- la reprise des textes internationaux relatifs à la compétence et à la loi applicable;[5]
- ainsi que celle des textes communautaires. Il est vrai, cependant, que la plupart de ces derniers apparaissent dans le Code sous leur forme transposée. Mais il n'en pas moins été regretté par certains qu'une annexe, dressant en fin de Code la liste de l'Acquis communautaire, n'ait été dressée;[6]
- enfin, les sources conventionnelles et les accords négociés entre les associations de consommateurs et les professionnels, certes rares en France, n'ont pas été considérés.

Mais c'est certainement l'application du critère finaliste, celui de l'inclusion des seuls textes qui, 'prenant acte d'une situation déséquilibrée au détriment du consommateur, cherchent à la corriger', qui a occasionné le plus d'ambiguïtés lors de sa mise en œuvre. En effet, il a entraîné une sélection très discutable des textes à inclure dans le nouveau Code.

Ainsi, d'une part, certains textes du Code civil, pourtant très protecteurs du consommateur, n'ont pas été reproduits, dès lors qu'ils ne pouvaient pas être considérés comme constatant spécifiquement un 'déséquilibre au détriment' de ce dernier et comme cherchant à y remédier à son égard spécifiquement. Une technique était, pourtant, à même de servir cette insertion: celle des 'articles suiveurs', venant en reproduction d'un Code dans l'autre. Il est, d'ailleurs, d'autant plus étonnant de ne pas la trouver utilisée à cette fin qu'elle aurait parfaitement servi les objectifs de la codification entreprise, à savoir l'accessibilité et la lisibilité des textes relatifs au droit de la consommation. On peut ainsi regretter l'absence, dans le Code de

---

4 En pratique, ces textes sont parfois annexés au Code par les groupes d'édition privés qui se chargent de sa publication, *cf.* Code Dalloz.

5 On pense évidemment aux règles de la Convention de Bruxelles du 27 septembre 1968 concernant la compétence judiciaire et l'exécution des décisions, ainsi qu'à celles de la Convention de Rome sur la loi applicable aux obligations contractuelles du 19 juin 1980 (art. 5).

6 *Cf.* J.-P. Pizzio, *Code de la consommation commenté* (1995), n° 26, 17.

la consommation, de la reproduction des textes relatifs aux vices du consentement. Ils intègrent, en effet et notamment, dans l'application jurisprudentielle qui en est faite actuellement, les obligations d'information et de loyauté. De même, ils servent de base à une évolution vers la protection de parties subissant une violence économique de la part de leur partenaire.[7] Dans le même ordre d'idée, on s'étonne de ne pouvoir lire dans le Code de la consommation les dispositions relatives à la responsabilité des fabricants pour les produits défectueux.[8]

En outre, d'autre part, l'ambiguïté est accrue lorsque l'on constate que certaines dispositions de cette texture y figurent bien, quant à elles, par le biais de cette technique des 'articles suiveurs'. C'est le cas des dispositions relatives à la garantie des vices cachés pesant sur le vendeur. Elles ont, en effet, été reproduites dans le Code de la consommation[9] au vu de l'interprétation jurisprudentielle très favorable au consommateur qui leur est donnée. En revanche, les règles concernant l'obligation de délivrance conforme du même vendeur, très proches de celles relatives à la garantie des vices cachés, quant à elles, n'y figurent pas.[10] Force est alors de constater que l'utilisation des 'articles suiveurs' s'est effectuée de manière incohérente et sans logique apparente.

Enfin, on est plongé dans une réelle perplexité lorsque l'on sait que certains textes du Code de la consommation ont pour champ d'application l'ensemble des 'personnes physiques' et s'appliquent, ainsi, bien au-delà du constat du 'déséquilibre au détriment du consommateur'. On citera à titre d'exemple, certaines dispositions relatives à la protection entourant la caution qui ont, depuis une loi du 1er août 2003, étendu cette dernière à toute caution personne physique contractant avec un créancier professionnel.[11] La mise en œuvre stricte du critère de la protection du seul consommateur achève alors de perdre en cohérence.

C'est alors qu'on en arrive, enfin et en quatrième lieu, au problème central de cette codification. Cette sélection peut en effet apparaître chaotique parce qu'elle ne s'est pas accompagnée d'une réflexion et d'une définition des notions fondamentales du droit de la consommation. Pour surprenant que cela puisse paraître, ce Code ne porte ainsi nulle définition des contrats qu'il régit, des sujets qu'il intéresse, et plus généralement de son objet.

---

7 *Cf.* les évolutions connues, en matière de sanction du dol ou de violence économique; pour une synthèse du droit français sur ces questions, *cf.* F. Terré, P. Simler et Y. Lequette, *Droit civil. Les Obligations* (2002), n° 228 *et seq.*, 229 *et seq.*

8 Art. 1386-1 *et seq.*, Code civil.

9 Art. L. 211-1, Code cons.

10 On a pu remarquer, d'ailleurs, que l'ambiguïté existait jusque dans les intitulés des titres du Code: le Titre I du Livre II s'appelle 'conformité' alors qu'il reproduit, la copiant du Code civil, la seule notion de garantie des vices cachés et exclut, précisément, l'obligation de délivrance conforme qui sert de base à l'obligation de conformité actuelle.

11 Loi n° 2003-721 du 1re août 2003 pour l'initiative économique, *JO* 5 août 2003, intégrée au Code de la consommation, notamment aux articles L. 341-3 *et seq.*

Ainsi, tout d'abord, on y chercherait vainement une définition du contrat de consommation. Il apparaît évoqué dans un seul article – l'article L. 211-1, disposant que les 'règles relatives à la garantie des vices cachés dans les contrats de consommation sont fixées par les articles 1641 à 1648 . . .' –, mais à aucun moment sa définition n'en est fixée,[12] ni sa spécificité affirmée.[13]

De même, ensuite, on ne trouvera nulle définition du consommateur. La codification s'étant réalisée à droit constant, chacune des règles a été reprise avec la définition du consommateur qui lui était propre. Il n'y a donc eu aucune uniformisation et l'on se trouve face à un accolement des définitions existantes. Le fait est d'autant plus notable et problématique qu'en droit français cette notion est le critère prédominant de la protection: plus que d'autres droits européens qui peuvent s'attacher au mode de conclusion du contrat – selon que celle-ci s'effectue avec ou sans négociation entre les parties –, ou au déséquilibre du contenu contractuel, le droit français, dans une approche subjective, s'attache à la qualité des parties. Or, on ne compte pas moins de trois approches. La première se caractérise par une définition négative, s'attachant à exclure les professionnels du champ de la protection. C'est le cas des textes applicables au démarchage à domicile[14] ou de ceux relatifs aux opérations de crédit.[15] La seconde approche privilégie, quant à elle, une définition positive, centrée autour du consommateur *stricto sensu*. C'est le cas des textes relatifs à l'information.[16] Des textes, enfin, sont applicables à toute personne physique,[17] voire à tous, professionnels inclus, tels ceux relatifs à la fraude et à la falsification,[18] ainsi qu'à l'usure. Il est vrai,

---

12 Au vu de ce texte, certains auteurs se sont interrogés sur la création d'un nouveau genre de contrat, qui aurait été institué par le Code de la consommation. En effet, la garantie des vices cachés ne s'applique, classiquement (dans le Code civil), qu'à la vente. On aurait donc pu lire, ici, une extension. Néanmoins cette ambition apparaît absente des travaux parlementaires et l'on doit conclure à un nouveau défaut du Code de la consommation.

13 La question aurait pu être, cependant, des plus intéressantes. En effet, il existe en France des conceptions remettant en cause la vision traditionnelle du contrat. Par exemple, il a été soutenu que le droit de la consommation donnerait naissance à un nouveau rapport d'obligation, qui ne lierait plus deux, mais trois parties: un rapport triangulaire entre un créancier, un débiteur et les différentes commissions créées pour la défense des consommateurs et qui sont à même d'intervenir à ce titre dans la vie du contrat, de donner leur avis ou de le faire modifier, *cf.* D. Bureau, Remarques sur la codification du droit de la consommation, *D.* 1994, chr., 291 *et seq.*, 296.

14 Art. 121-21 *et seq.*, C. cons. Plus précisément, l'article L. 121-22 4°, exclut les 'opérations qui ont un rapport direct avec une activité professionnelle'. Le critère est interprété strictement, contre le professionnel, *cf.* par exemple Cass. civ. 1re, 10 juil. 2001, *Bull. civ.* I, n° 209, p. 132: un chômeur qui avait rempli un bon de commande de matériel, après démarchage à domicile, n'a pu se rétracter, ce droit lui ayant été dénié car l'objet du contrat a été regardé comme ayant un 'rapport direct' avec son activité (future).

15 Art. L. 311-3, 3° et L. 312-3, 2°, C. cons., sont exclues 'les opérations destinées à financer les besoins d'une activité professionnelle'.

16 Art. L. 111-1, C. cons.

17 Art. L. 341-1 *et seq.* relatif au cautionnement, *cf. supra.*

18 Art. L. 213-1 *et seq.*, C. cons.

néanmoins, que, s'il y a une ambiguïté dans les textes, la jurisprudence a tendance à unifier le champ de la protection accordée en adoptant l'approche négative: l'exclusion du professionnel dont le contrat a un rapport direct avec son activité.[19] Mais cette approche pluraliste n'en est pas moins extrêmement gênante et génératrice de doutes.

Enfin, le Code de la consommation n'a pas défini clairement son objet, oscillant entre une protection générale de toute personne subissant un contenu contractuel déséquilibré et celle du seul consommateur. Nous retrouvons ultérieurement ce problème de façon plus générale.

En définitive, tirer le bilan de cette codification aboutit à émettre deux remarques. D'une part, le Code de la consommation ne contient pas tout le droit de la consommation. On ne peut, en droit français, assimiler l'un à l'autre: le premier – le droit de la consommation – ne se trouve pas tout entier contenu et repris dans le second – le code de la consommation. D'autre part, et en conséquence, ce code, loin d'atteindre ses objectifs d'accessibilité et de lisibilité du droit applicable, fait à l'inverse naître des doutes sur ce dernier.

Mais, plus profondément, sur le fondement de l'expérience française, eût-elle été menée de meilleure façon, ne peut-on entrevoir les ambiguïtés intrinsèques et inhérentes à ce type de codification.

III. LES DIFFICULTÉS D'ORDRE GÉNÉRAL POSÉES PAR L'INSTITUTION D'UN CODE DE LA CONSOMMATION EN DROIT EUROPÉEN DES CONTRATS

On en arrive ainsi, et ce pour tenter d'alimenter le débat relatif à la pertinence de la création d'un tel instrument en droit européen des contrats – à sonder les difficultés d'ordre général posées par cette dernière.

A l'instar de tout nouveau code, celles-ci résident dans l'articulation problématique du droit spécial créé et du droit général existant et dans la délimitation de la spécificité du premier à l'égard du second. Dans cette réflexion, on remarquera que l'exemple français permet d'aller en profondeur, le droit français, très attaché à une théorie générale du contrat, ayant toujours conçu le Code de la consommation comme l'instrument d'un droit spécial. A cet égard, il permet de poser plusieurs constats.

Le premier réside en ce que l'autonomie du droit contractuel de la consommation n'est pas telle que le Code de la consommation puisse être

---

[19] C'est le cas en matière de lutte contre les clauses abusives, où la Cour de cassation semblerait être plus large, accueillant dans la protection toute personne dont les clauses du contrat sont sans 'rapport direct' avec son activité professionnelle, *cf.* Cass. civ. 1re, 24 janv. 1995, *Bull. civ.* I, n° 54; Mais où, en réalité, l'application de ce critère conduit à une limitation très stricte de la protection, qui ne s'étend que très rarement à des professionnels.

suffisamment efficient et complet et se passer des règles de droit commun de la formation ou de l'exécution du contrat. Spécialement, le contrat 'de consommation' n'a aucune autonomie réelle.[20] Néanmoins, cela n'étant pas propre au Code de la consommation, on pourrait admettre qu'une distinction des deux droits soit faite afin d'imprimer aux règles une certaine spécificité.

Or, c'est justement à l'égard de cette dernière que réside le point crucial: quelle spécificité attribuer au Code de la consommation? Est-il l'instrument d'un droit catégoriel en fonction de ses sujets? On penche alors vers une approche subjective, tendant à la protection d'une catégorie de personnes, les consommateurs, en raison des déficiences qu'on leur attribue en termes d'absence de compétence ou de faiblesse. Ou, à l'inverse, est-il l'instrument d'une protection spécifique en fonction de son objet, indifféremment des personnes protégées? On adopte alors une vision objective, au sein de laquelle il s'agit de réagire à tout déséquilibre, des forces de négociation ou de contenu contractuel. Le droit français a refusé de mener un travail de conceptualisation et de répondre à cette question. Ce faisant, il s'est alors organisé autour du cumul des deux lignes directrices[21] – visant le consommateur et les règles qui tendent à restaurer un équilibre des forces ou du contenu contractuel[22] – et a laissé perdurer l'ambiguïté de départ.

Mais, aurait-il mené ce travail, serait-il parvenu à une solution satisfaisante? On peut en douter et, ce, pour deux raisons. En premier, se serait-il fondé sur le critère subjectif exclusivement, il en aurait rencontré les limites, connues. Elles résident dans la pénétration de l'idée que toute personne en situation de faiblesse ou de contrainte par rapport à son partenaire contractuel, quelle que soit sa qualité, de consommateur ou de professionnel, semble légitime dans sa revendication de protection. C'est pourquoi, à l'égard de cette approche, il apparaît difficile de soutenir encore la spécificité des deux droits et de tracer une frontière satisfaisante entre eux. Il l'apparaît d'autant plus que le droit civil actuel revendique désormais des impératifs de protection de la partie faible[23] et se dissocie, en conséquence, encore plus malaisément du droit de la consommation. En second lieu, et à l'inverse, aurait-il entrepris une approche objective, visant toute situation de déséquilibre, des forces de négociation ou des contenus contractuels, sans discrimination, il aurait mal affirmé, de nouveau, sa spécificité. En effet, cette préoccupation n'est plus propre au droit de la consommation. Elle le déborde largement pour atteindre le droit civil commun. Cela se vérifie *rationae materiae* comme *rationae per-*

[20] *Cf.*, par example, la formulation selon laquelle le consommateur 'peut renoncer à l'engagement' (art. L. 121-25 C. cons.), que l'on ne peut comprendre que par mise en relation avec le droit commun (elle renvoie alors, soit à la destruction d'un contrat formé, soit à la formation du contrat par étapes).

[21] *Cf.* D. Mazeaud, 'Droit commun du contrat et droit de la consommation', dans *Liber amicorum Jean Calais-Auloy, Etudes de droit de la consommation* (2003), 702 *et seq.*

[22] Aussi appelé critère 'téléologique', *cf.* D. Mazeaud, *op. cit.* en n. 21, 701 *et seq.*

[23] On retrouve même cette préoccupation en droit français de la concurrence, qui en vient à réglementer les relations déséquilibrées entre professionnels.

sonae. Rationae materiae, d'une part, on peut constater que nombre de notions portées par le droit de la consommation ont désormais intégré le droit contractuel en général. Il en va ainsi, par exemple, des idées d'inégalités et de déséquilibre, imposées au rebours des postulats classiques de liberté et d'égalité abstraite des parties; de l'appréciation du contrat et de sa validité en fonction de leur rapport de forces (économiques ou intellectuelles); de l'attention portée à la période pré-contractuelle, ignorée dans le Code civil;[24] de la généralisation de l'exigence d'information[25] et de la nouvelle approche de la formation du contrat,[26] renouvelant celle effectuée en termes d'offre et d'acceptation; de la remise en cause de l'intangibilité du contrat.[27] De façon plus prospective, on pourra peut-être bientôt mettre à l'actif du Code de la consommation le développement en droit commun du principe de proportionnalité,[28] voire de cohérence.[29] L'influence du Code de la consommation a essaimé également à l'égard des techniques. On a ainsi vu l'importation des délais de réflexion et de rétractation hors de leur domaine initial, en l'occurrence dans des contrats opposant deux non-professionnels,[30] ainsi que la systématisation de la sanction de l'élimination des clauses abusives, entre professionnels.[31] On en est ainsi venu à présenter le droit de la consommation comme 'un droit spécial à vocation générale'.[32] Indirectement, en conséquence, l'extension se produit également *rationae personae*, sur le fondement de l'idée que les professionnels, soit qu'ils agissent hors de leur domaine de compétence, soit qu'ils se trouvent dans les mêmes conditions de contrainte que les consommateurs, doivent bénéficier des mêmes protections. On n'aperçoit plus guère, en définitive, où réside encore la spécificité au Code de la consommation.

---

[24] Elle est ultra-réglementée dans le Code de la consommation (notamment en termes d'informations, art. L. 111-1 à L. 111-3 C. cons.), au point qu'on a pu voir ce dernier comme 'le laboratoire d'expérimentation de techniques nouvelles à partir desquelles doit s'élaborer un droit général nouveau', J.-L. Aubert, *Le contrat* (1996), 70 *et seq.*

[25] *Cf.* Art. L. 111-1 C. cons., renforçant les obligations du professionnel.

[26] *Cf.* Art. L. 312-1 *et seq.* C. cons., instituant un délai de réflexion en cas de crédit immobilier ou un droit de repentir; art. L.121-25, en cas de démarchage.

[27] *Cf.* Art. L. 331-1 *et seq.* C. cons., relatifs au traitement du surendettement.

[28] *Cf.* Art. L. 341-4 C. cons., relatif au cautionnement; pour une réflexion sur sa place en droit commun, *cf.* Dir. M. Béhar-Touchais, 'Existe-t-il un principe de proportionnalité en droit privé? Colloque 20 mars 1998', *Petites affiches*, 1998, n° 117.

[29] *Cf.*, pour une synthèse de tous les changements induits par le Code de la consommation sur le fond du droit, J. Calais-Auloy, 'L'influence du droit de la consommation sur le droit des contrats', dans *Droit du marché et droit commun des obligations*, RTD com. 1998, 95 *et seq.*, 115 *et seq.*

[30] *Cf.*, en matière de promesses de vente immobilière: Art. L. 271-1, Code de la construction et de l'habitation.

[31] *Cf.* Cass. com., 22 octobre 1996, *Bull. civ.* I, n° 261: sur le fondement de l'absence de cause, instillée par une clause privant de sanction l'obligation fondamentale du transporteur rapide de colis, la jurisprudence est venue implanter la sanction de l'éradication d'une clause dans les contrats entre professionnels. C'est le fameux arrêt *Chronopost*, qui a bouleversé le paysage contractualiste français.

[32] J. Beauchard, 'Remarques sur le Code de la consommation', *Ecrits en hommage à G. Cornu* (1995), 9 *et seq.*, 15.

En réalité, la justification de son existence réside peut-être ailleurs, la dualité des codes masquant une autre dichotomie. En grossissant un peu le trait, on pourrait la regarder comme révélatrice d'une opposition entre deux conceptions du contrat. D'un côté, celle classique, encore assise sur les présupposés de liberté contractuelle et d'égalité, aurait été conservée dans le Code civil, comme l'expression de la théorie générale du contrat. D'un autre côté, la conception plus moderne et réaliste, intégrant les idées de déséquilibre des forces ou de contenu contractuel, ainsi que celles de standardisation et de collectivisation des contrats, aurait été recueillie dans le Code de la consommation, ce dernier se trouvant appelé par là même à recueillir les évolutions et pour ainsi dire la modernité du droit contractuel. L'existence de ces deux codes ne ferait ainsi qu'incarner l'opposition de ces deux conceptions du droit des contrats. Certes, la vision est volontairement caricaturale car le droit civil, nous l'avons vu, a énormément puisé aux nouvelles techniques et conceptions du droit de la consommation. Néanmoins, il n'est peut-être pas étonnant que le Code de la consommation ait vu le jour en France, pays où une partie importante de la doctrine reste particulièrement attachée à la vision classique du contrat et tient à la conserver. *A minima*, quoi qu'il en soit, on peut voir dans le Code de la consommation un instrument stratégique de transition: en cantonnant les changements de la théorie générale à un Code circonscrit, on permettait ainsi de les faire admettre à ceux qui les refusaient tout en les faisant apparaître comme limités.[33] Cependant, il n'en devenait pas moins cet instrument peu maniable, toujours à la limite du débordement de ses frontières, le contrat en général ne pouvant être laissé en dehors du mouvement de protection contre les déséquilibres.

D'ailleurs, ce débat trouve une nouvelle résonance aujourd'hui, en ce qu'il est sous-jacent à l'âpre discussion relative à la transposition de la directive du 25 mai 1999 sur la garantie dans les ventes de biens de consommation. On sait que celle-ci est considérablement retardée. Or, ce retard s'explique par l'opposition des uns, plaidant pour une transposition dans le Code de la consommation,[34] à des autres, soutenant son insertion dans le Code civil.[35]

33 Un débat existe en France entre les tenants d'une vision d'un droit de la consommation, droit spécial, venant compléter le droit général sur les points où ce dernier est insuffisamment protecteur, *cf.* J. Ghestin, *Traité de droit civil. Le contrat. La formation* (1993), n° 77, 53; et d'autres auteurs, pour qui le droit de la consommation serait un révélateur de l'inadaptation actuelle de la théorie générale des contrats aux situations contractuelles modernes, *cf.* G. Rouhette, 'Droit de la consommation et théorie générale des contrats', dans *Etudes offertes à René Rodière* (1981), 247 *et seq.*

34 *Cf.* G. Paisant et L. Leveneur, 'Quelle transposition pour la directive du 25 mai 1999 sur la garantie dans la vente de biens de consommation?', *JCP* 2002 I 135; O. Tournafond, 'De la transposition de la directive du 25 mai 1999 à la réforme du Code civil', *D.* 2002, chr., 2883.

35 *Cf.* G. Viney, 'Quel domaine assigner à la loi de transposition de la directive européenne sur la vente?', *JCP* 2002 I 158, l'auteur ayant pris la tête de la Commission chargée de présenter un avant-projet en vue de cette transposition; P. Jourdain et D. Mazeaud, *D.* 2003, point de vue, 4 *et seq.*

Les premiers, avocats d'une conception étroite, justifient leur position, entre autres raisons,[36] par une volonté de limiter la protection au seul consommateur. A l'inverse, les tenants de l'insertion du texte dans le Code civil font valoir que ce dernier doit s'appliquer à tout acquéreur déçu,[37] pour des raisons de protection et de simplicité du droit.[38] On retrouve donc, pour partie, la même opposition très caractéristique, entre droit protecteur, limité au consommateur, et réforme générale du droit. Dans le dernier état des discussions, la première thèse l'aurait emporté.

IV. CONCLUSION

En définitive, le Code français de la consommation apparaît comme un instrument d'accessibilité au droit assez imparfait et ambigu, tant ses rapports avec le Code civil et la théorie générale des contrats n'ont pas été éclaircis. Transposés à l'échelle européenne, dans le débat relatif à la place d'un Code de la consommation dans le futur droit des contrats, les apports de l'expérience française résident dans la démonstration que la question ne semble pas tant se situer dans la pertinence de cette création en tant que telle, que dans le niveau de protection du contractant faible que le droit européen des contrats est prêt à mettre en place. En ce sens, instituer un Code de la consommation aux côtés d'un droit contractuel général apparaîtrait, alors, comme le choix d'un outil de limitation à une protection minimale et circonscrite.

Historique succint de la conception du Code français de la consommation

- Commission de refonte du Code de la consommation, créée par le décret du 25 février 1982 et présidée par Jean Calais-Auloy.

---

36 Sont en outre avancés comme arguments:
- le respect du domaine catégoriel de la directive communautaire invitant à créer un 'socle minimal de protection du consommateur', et non à réécrire le droit dans son ensemble;
- le fait que la protection ne pourrait pas être à la fois élevée et générale;
- le maintien de la distinction, qui existe dans le Code civil, entre non conformité et vice caché. Celle-ci disparaîtrait si la notion unitaire communautaire devait s'y implanter.
- le maintien de la liberté contractuelle des professionnels de pouvoir prévoir des clauses contraires
- la simplicité du processus de transposition.

37 Est ici avancé l'argument que le dépassement du domaine assigné par la directive est possible, celle-ci prévoyant un 'socle minimal' et ayant été prise sur le fondement de l'article 153 (qui appelle les Etats à garantir 'un niveau élevé de protection du consommateur'). Cet élargissement n'exposerait ainsi pas la France à la même censure que celle subie relativement à la Directive de 1985.

38 Il y aurait disparition de l'opposition des actions issues du Code civil et élimination du risque de voir, en cas de transposition dans le Code de la consommation, naître une nouvelle opposition.

- Rapport final: 'Pour un nouveau droit de la consommation', 1985, *La documentation française*, collection des rapports officiels, avril 1985.
- Commission pour la codification du droit de la consommation, présidée par Jean Calais-Auloy.
- Second rapport: 'Proposition pour un code de la consommation', 1990, *La documentation française*, collection des rapports officiels, avril 1990.
- Refus de faire voter un Code nouveau et décision en faveur d'un Code 'compilation', à 'droit constant': loi du 18 janvier 1992 renforçant la protection des consommateurs.
- Elaboration par la Commission supérieure de codification.
- Promulgation le 26 juillet 1993.
- Code: 316 articles,
  - numérotés de L. 111-1 à L. 562-1, pour la partie légale;
  - numérotés de R. 112-1 à R. 551-1, pour la partie réglementaire;
  - ordonnés en 5 livres.
- Mission donnée au Gouvernement de déposer tous les deux ans sur le bureau de l'Assemblée nationale un rapport dressant l'état des modifications législatives et réglementaires apportées au Code.

Chapter 11

Consumer Law – Forerunner for or Part of a European Contract Law Code? The Case of Austrian Consumer Law

Brigitta Lurger, University of Graz

I. THE AUSTRIAN STATUS QUO OF CONSUMER CONTRACT LAW

1. Development before 1995

Austria – like the majority of EU Member States[1] – possesses a codified contract law which is part of the general codification of civil law, the 'ABGB' (*Allgemeines Bürgerliches Gesetzbuch*). Like in a number of other countries, this codification dates back to times when consumer protection was not an issue: the ABGB entered into force in 1811.

The first individual measures of consumer protection were adopted as early as around the end of the 19th century.[2] However, most of the Austrian autonomous consumer protection legislation which, over time, developed into a more comprehensive protection system was not adopted earlier than in the 70s and 80s of the former century. In 1979 the Austrian 'Consumer

[1] Like in France, Belgium, Italy, Spain, Portugal, Greece, Netherlands, Germany.

[2] An example is Austria: Schuhmacher, *Verbraucher und Recht in historischer Sicht* (1981) pp. 55 *et seq.*; Kalss and Lurger, *Rücktrittsrechte* (2001) pp. 35 *et seq.* with further references.

S. Grundmann, M. Schauer (eds), *The Architecture of European Codes and Contract Law*, 205–217

Protection Act', the '*Konsumentenschutz-Gesetz*',[3] entered into force, in which the legislator tried to collect together more or less all protection measures in favour of consumers. This Consumer Protection Act has the following characteristics:

- For quite some time it successfully avoided the splitting up of legal sources in the field of consumer protection: We do not have separate statutes for credit sales transactions, doorstep selling, unfair terms, consumer guarantees, etc., but only one Consumer Protection Act. This effect was, however, weakened after 1995, due to the implementation of EC Directives.
- The Consumer Protection Act is more a compilation than a comprehensive or systematic codification of rules that apply to consumer transactions. It states mandatory modifications of the general ABGB contract law rules for certain situations and certain types of contracts. The ABGB contract law rules are applicable also to consumer contracts and form the general basis on which they rest. Special rules for commercial contracts are found in the Austrian Commercial Code, the 'HGB' ('*Handelsgesetzbuch*').
- The provisions of the Consumer Protection Act are not arranged in a stringent system, but seem to be rather accidental additions to the general contract law. There is no systematic approach to information duties, or rights of withdrawal or to the question of which types of contract seem more dangerous for consumers than others and therefore need special protection.
- The system is arranged along the lines of rule and exception: The Austrian Civil Code does not mention consumers at all. All provisions pertaining to consumers are collected in the Consumer Protection Act or are found in other separate legislation for timesharing, bank transactions, travel agencies and others. The strict separation of ABGB rules and consumer protection rules seems to reflect the anachronistic idea that consumer protection provisions are still an exceptional phenomenon which cannot be allowed to enter the 'holy grail' of general rules and principles of private law in the Civil Code.
- What is remarkable, however, and is mentioned here as the fifth characteristic of the Austrian Consumer Protection Act, is that the Austrian legislator has always been very active in the field of consumer protection, even long before the Austrian accession to the European Union in 1995. Together with the Scandinavian countries and partly also Germany, Austria already had a very high level of consumer protection when the EC directives were adopted and still now has a lot of additional consumer protection which is not mentioned in the directives.

---

3 *Bundesgesetz vom 8.3.1979, mit dem Bestimmungen zum Schutz der Verbraucher getroffen werden, BGBl Nr 140/1979.*

Therefore, in many cases, the EC directives cannot be seen as effecting major improvements in the system.

– The notion of a consumer in the Austrian Consumer Protection Act is a bit wider than that in the directives: It encompasses not only natural but also legal persons under appropriate circumstances and contracts concluded in preparation of the start of a new business. But it does not protect small enterprises against big and experienced ones as quasi-consumers.

2. The Implementation of the EC-Directives in Austria

In implementing the EC consumer protection directives the Austrian legislator experimented with a lot of different, partly opposite approaches.

a. Different Approaches with Respect to the Location

Many directives led to amendments of the Austrian Consumer Protection Act: The provisions of the Doorstep Selling Directive,[4] the Package Travel Directive,[5] the Unfair Contract Terms Directive,[6] the Distance Selling Directive,[7] the Injunctions Directive,[8] and the Consumer Guarantees Directive[9] were wholly or partly included in the Consumer Protection Act.

But unfortunately a considerable number of Directive provisions can be found outside the Consumer Protection Act in separate legislative instruments: This is the case for timesharing contracts, consumer credits, package travel arrangements, doorstep selling of financial services and the broad field of directives that do not only protect consumers but also business customers: like in insurance contracts, product liability, misleading and comparative advertising, credit transfer and e-commerce transactions.

b. Different Approaches with Respect to the Method

In some cases, like for instance with the Doorstep Selling Directive or the Consumer Credit Directive, a number of the piecemeal exceptions of the

---

4 Directive 85/577/EEC of 20 December 1985 to protect the consumer in respect of contracts negotiated away from business premises, OJ L 372/31, 1985.

5 Directive 90/314/EEC of 13 June 1990 on package travel, package holidays and package tours, OJ L 158/59, 1990.

6 Directive 93/13/EEC of 5 April 1993 on unfair terms in consumer contracts, OJ L 95/29, 1993.

7 Directive 97/7/EC of 20 May 1997 on the protection of consumers in respect of distance contracts, OJ L 144/19, 1997.

8 Directive 98/27/EC of 19 May 1998 on injunctions for the protection of consumers' interests, OJ L 166/51, 1998.

9 Directive 1999/44/EC of 25 May 1999 on certain aspects of the sale of consumer goods and associated guarantees, OJ L 171/12, 1999.

Directives were ignored by the implementation provisions. This widened the protective scheme of the respective directives and led to certain improvements of the system of the provisions.

However, in other cases not the slightest attempt to systematically streamline the scope of application of the directive's provisions was made and the respective Directive with all its piecemeal exceptions was put almost word by word into the Consumer Protection Act or some other statute: examples are the implementation of the Distance Selling Directive and the E-Commerce Directive.

The Unfair Contract Terms Directive necessitated only a few changes in the already existing rules on unfair contract terms in the Consumer Protection Act. The grey list of the Annex of the Directive was integrated into our already existing list of unfair clauses in § 6 Consumer Protection Act. The transparency rule was already partly covered by § 864a ABGB and by § 915 ABGB, the latter of which provides for an interpretation of ambiguous contract clauses formulated by one party in favour of the other party. Nevertheless a much disputed rule was added in § 6 (3) CPA which generally invalidates unclear and incomprehensible terms. It should be construed narrowly and be restricted to those unclear terms that cannot be already repaired by § 915 ABGB.

Of all the consumer protection directives the Consumer Guarantees Directive provoked the strongest spill-over (or spin-off) effects[10] for Austrian Contract Law: The Austrian Law of Guarantees (the *Gewährleistungsrecht*) in the ABGB was amended in accordance with the rules of the directives.[11] It applies not only to consumer contracts, but also to business to business contracts and to consumer to consumer contracts, and it not only applies to sales contracts but also to other contracts like the sale of land, service contracts and the assignment of claims. In the case of consumer contracts these guarantee rights of the consumer cannot be restricted by party agreement. This massive over-implementation of the directive helped to preserve the key idea of the Austrian system with one law of guarantees for all purposes and all contract types and was welcomed by all Austrian commentators.

---

[10] Weatherill, 'Prospects for the Development of European Private Law Through "Europeanization" in the European Court – the Case of the Directive on Unfair Terms in Consumer Contracts', *European Review of Private Law 3* (1995) p. 320; Reich, 'Diverse Approaches to Consumer Protection Philosophy', *Journal of Consumer Policy 14* (1991) p. 273; Wilhelmsson, 'Consumer Protection and the Rules and Principles of General Contract Law', in: Wilhelmsson, *Twelve Essays on Consumer Law and Policy* (1996) p. 133; W-H Roth, 'Transposing "Pointillist" EC Guidelines into Systematic National Codes', *ERPL* 2002, III.3; Lurger, '*Integration des Verbraucherrechts in das ABGB*?', in: Fischer-Czermak, Hopf, Schauer (eds.), *Das ABGB auf dem Weg in das 3. Jahrtausend*, (2003) pp. 111 (123 *et seq.*).

[11] Faber, *Handbuch zum neuen Gewährleistungsrecht* (2001); Welser/Jud, *Die neue Gewährleistung – Kurzkommentar* (2001).

3. Defects and Problems

The implementation of the two directives that affect the general principles of contract law most directly, namely the Unfair Terms Directive and the Consumer Guarantees Directive, can be considered quite a successful integration into the already existing system of contract law. But the experience with the other directives clearly reveals all of the much discussed negative effects of the fragmentary and unsystematic character of the directives and its disintegrative forces for the national system.[12] Their implementation led to a multiplication of legal sources for consumer protection law, which could be only partially avoided by an integration of provisions in the Consumer Protection Act. In most cases, the unsystematic and incoherent approach of the directives to issues like information duties or rights of withdrawal was not repaired by the Austrian legislator but just copied from the directives. The diversity of fragmentary and unsystematically arranged protection instruments was simultaneously augmented by autonomous additions to the protection system by the Austrian legislator.

An example of the disintegrative effects of directive provisions is the European Court of Justice decision in the Austrian case *Simone Leitner*:[13] The decision concerns the traveller's right to claim damages from the organizer in case of improper performance. The ECJ stated that the notion of 'damages' in article 5 of the Directive encompasses also the immaterial damages suffered by the consumer because she was prevented from enjoying her holidays. This kind of immaterial damages for a loss of enjoyment is completely unknown to the Austrian law of damages, which recognizes the compensation for immaterial damages only in exceptional cases: like in the case of compensation for pain and suffering due to physical injuries or mental illness. As a consequence the ECJ decision does not only necessitate an amendment of the law of package travel contracts, but moreover puts a fundamental principle of Austrian tort law in question: its restrictive attitude with respect to the compensation of immaterial losses. This may be a bad attitude, but should the European package travel standards really compel a Member State to fundamentally reform its law of contractual and delictual damages?

---

[12] Joerges, '*Desintegrative Folgen legislativer Harmonisierung: ein komplexes Problem und ein unscheinbares Exempel*', in: Schulte-Nölke and Schulze (eds.), *Europäische Rechtsangleichung und nationale Privatrechte*, (1999) pp. 205 *et seq.*; Christoph Schmid, '*Desintegration und Neuordnungsperspektiven im europäischen Privatrecht*', in: *Jahrbuch Junger Zivilrechtswissenschaftler* (2000) pp. 33 (34 *et seq.*); Lurger (n. 10) pp. 111 (118 *et seq.*).

[13] ECJ 12 March 2002 (*Simone Leitner*) Case C-168/00, *ECR* 2002, I-2631.

II. PROTECTION ONLY FOR CONSUMERS?

Before developing my final conclusions on where the law of consumer protection is going to lead us in the future, I would like to draw your attention to yet another important aspect: Protective provisions for contractual relationships are probably most evident in the case of consumer protection, but they are equally present in a lot of other contractual settings, as follows.

1. Protection of Customers and Businesses

First of all a lot of autonomous national provisions and a lot of EC directives not only protect consumers but also businesses as customers. Among those are: the Advertising Directives,[14] the Product Liability Directive,[15] the Insurance Directives,[16] the Package Travel Directive,[17] the Credit Transfer Directive[18] and the E-Commerce Directive.[19] A few Directives even contain protective provisions only in favour of entrepreneurial parties, such as the Commercial Agents Directive[20] and the Late Payment Directive.[21]

The most common reason for the introduction of protective measures in favour of business clients is the lack of specialized knowledge in the respective branch of business on the side of the customer who is confronted with a

[14] Directive 84/450/EEC of 10 September 1984 relating to the approximation of the laws, regulations and administrative provisions of the Member States concerning misleading advertising, OJ L 250/17, 1984; Directive 97/55/EC of 6 October 1997 amending Directive 84/450/EEC concerning misleading advertising so as to include comparative advertising, OJ L 290/18, 1997.

[15] Directive 85/374/EEC of 25 July 1985 on the approximation of the laws, regulations and administrative provisions of the Member States concerning liability for defective products, OJ L 210/29, 1985, amended by Directive 99/34/EC of 10 May 1999, OJ L 141/20, 1999.

[16] Directive 92/49/EEC of 18 June 1992 on the coordination of the laws, regulations and administrative provisions of the Member States relating to direct insurance other than life assurance and amending Directives 73/239/EEC and 88/357/EEC, OJ L 228/1, 1992 (third non-life insurance Directive); Directive 92/96/EEC of 10 November 1992 on the coordination of the laws, regulations and administrative provisions of the Member States relating to direct life assurance and amending Directives 79/267/EEC and 90/619/EEC, OJ L 360/1, 1992 (third life assurance Directive); since 19 December 2002 Directive 2002/83/EC of 5 November 2002, OJ L 345/1, 2002, is in force and replaces Directive 92/96/EEC.

[17] Directive 90/314/EEC of 13 June 1990 on package travel, package holidays and package tours, OJ L 158/59, 1990.

[18] Directive 97/5/EC of 27 January 1997 on cross-border credit transfers, OJ L 43/25, 1997.

[19] Directive 2000/31/EC of 8 June 2000 on certain legal aspects of information society services, in particular electronic commerce, in the Internal Market, OJ L 178/1, 2000.

[20] Directive 86/653/EEC of 18 December 1986 on the coordination of the laws of the Member States relating to self-employed commercial agents, OJ L 382/17, 1986.

[21] Directive 2000/35/EC of 29 June 2000 on combating late payment in commercial transactions, OJ L 200/35, 2000.

contract party who is an expert in the field. Sometimes also the market power or the superior negotiating power of the other party is the reason behind a protective provision.

This expansion of protection of parties in European contract law – and also in national contract law – which reaches far beyond the protection of consumers, has led Grundmann to reconsider the term of 'consumer protection' altogether: He suggested renaming the whole field of consumer or customer protection and calling it simply 'market law' or 'exterior business law' ('*Marktrecht*' or '*Unternehmensaußenrecht*').[22] He considers this market or exterior business law, which deals with the contractual relations of businesses with other market actors – consumers or others – to be part of general civil law. Franz Bydlinski argues on the same lines when he denies the notion of the consumer and the idea that consumer protection has the ability to produce the necessary interior and exterior system for the formation of a special sub-discipline of private law.[23] The same conclusion is reached by a recent study by Krejci.[24]

2. Party Protection in General Contract Law

I think these authors are perfectly right in drawing these conclusions. The outright protection of one party's interests in certain situations is not a speciality of consumer law, but a much wider phenomenon at the heart of market relations and contract law. The idea of a more or less one-sided protection of the interests of one of the parties can also be found in various parts of the traditional contract law of the codifications:[25] in the general principles of good faith, 'good morals' and unconscionability ('*Treu und*

[22] Grundmann, '*Verbraucherrecht, Unternehmensrecht, Privatrecht – warum sind sich UN-Kaufrecht und EU-Kaufrechts-Richlinie so ähnlich*?', *Archiv für die civilistische Praxis* 202 (2002) pp. 40 (43, 56 *et seq.*); Grundmann, '*Europäisches Handelsrecht – vom Handelsrecht des laissez faire im Kodex des 19. Jahrhunderts zum Handelsrecht der sozialen Verantwortung*', *Zeitschrift für das gesamte Handelsrecht und Wirtschaftsrecht* 163 (1999), pp. 635 (668 *et seq.*); Grundmann, 'The Structure of European Contract Law', *European Review of Private Law* 2001, pp. 505 (515 *et seq.*); as '*Unternehmensaußenrecht*' (exterior business law) in Grundmann, *Europäisches Schuldvertragsrecht*, (1999), part 1, note 14 *et seq.*

[23] F. Bydlinski, *System und Prinzipien des Privatrechts* (1996) pp. 718 *et seq.*

[24] Krejci, '*Ist das Verbraucherrecht ein Rechtsgebiet*?', in: Eccher, Nemeth and Tangl (eds.), *Verbraucherschutz in Europa, Festgabe für Heinrich Mayrhofer* (2002) pp. 120 *et seq.*

[25] For the German BGB see: Dörner, '*Integration des Verbraucherrechts in das BGB*', in Schulze and Schulte-Nölke (eds.), *Die Schuldrechtsreform vor dem Hintergrund des Gemeinschaftsrechts* (2001) pp. 177 (178) with further references; for the Austrian ABGB: Lurger, *Vertragliche Solidarität* (1998) pp. 85, 133 *et seq.*; Lurger, *Grundfragen der Vereinheitlichung des Vertragsrechts in der Europäischen Union* (2002) pp. 353 *et seq.*

Glauben',[26] '*bonne foi*',[27] '*buona fede*',[28] '*regole della correttezza*',[29] '*redelijkheid en billijkheid*',[30] '*gute Sitten*',[31] '*bonnes moeurs*',[32] '*buon costume*',[33] '*goede zeden*',[34] §§ 33, 36 of the Nordic Contract Law,[35] etc.), in the '*laesio enormis*' provision (§§ 934, 935 Austrian ABGB), the change of circumstances provisions, the notice of termination in long-term contracts and the breach of contract rules.[36] The principle is not restricted to mandatory legal provisions. Dispositive law is not a set of neutral fall-back rules, but secures the material balance, the regard and fairness in contractual relations. It has guiding and justice functions.[37] In the area of control of unfair clauses in general or pre-formulated contract terms, the dispositive contract law develops – at least according to the Austrian and German doctrines – indirectly mandatory effects:[38] therefore, a party may depart less from the dispositive model the bigger the difference in power between the parties is.[39]

3. The Evolution of the Guiding Principles of Contract Law

As a third point I would like to mention that consumer, customer and party protection are one key element of a larger spectrum of innovations in con-

26 § 242 German BGB; § 241 BGB establishes the general duty of the parties to show regard ('*Rücksicht*') for the rights, legal 'goods' ('*Rechtsgüter*') and interests of the other party.
27 Art. 1134 French *Code Civil*.
28 Arts 1337, 1366, 1375 Italian *Codice Civile*.
29 Art. 1175 Italian *Codice Civile*.
30 Book 6 Art 248 Dutch NBW.
31 § 138 German BGB, § 879 Austrian ABGB.
32 Art. 1133 French *Code Civil*.
33 Art. 1343, 1418 Italian *Codice Civile*.
34 Book 3 art. 40 Dutch NBW.
35 § 36 Contract Act serves as a basis for Wilhelmsson's theory of 'social force majeure': Wilhelmsson, '"Social Force Majeure" – A New Concept in Nordic Consumer Law', *Journal of Consumer Policy* 13 (1990) pp. 1 *et seq*.; Wilhelmsson, 'Need-Rationality in Private Law?', *Scandinavian Studies in Law* 33 (1989) pp. 227 *et seq*.
36 Lurger (n. 25) pp. 141 (155 *et seq*.); Lurger (n. 25) pp. 353 *et seq*.
37 "*Leit-, Ordnungs- und Gerechtigkeitsfunktionen*": Kramer, '*Funktion, rechtliche Problematik und Zukunftsperspektiven der Innominatverträge*', in: Kramer, *Zur Theorie und Politik des Privat- und Wirtschaftsrechts* (1997) pp. 147 (162 *et seq*.); Raiser, *Das Recht der Allgemeinen Geschäftsbedingungen* (1935) Neudruck (1961) pp. 293 *et seq*.; Ennecerus and Nipperdey, *Allgemeiner Teil des Bürgerlichen Rechts* I/2, Vol.15, (1959/60) pp. 1011 *et seq*.; Lurger (n. 25) pp. 85, 116.
38 Kramer, '*Die "Krise" des liberalen Vertragsdenkens*', in: Kramer, *Zur Theorie und Politik des Privat- und Wirtschaftsrechts* (1997) pp. 69 (113 *et seq*.); P. Bydlinski, '*Beschränkung und Ausschluss der Gewährleistung*', *Juristische Blätter* (1993) pp. 560 *et seq*.; Basedow, '*Über Privatrechtsvereinheitlichung und Marktintegration*', in: Immenga, Möschl and Reuter (eds.), *FS für Mestmäcker* (1996) p. 355.
39 Kramer, ('*Die "Krise" des liberalen Vertragsdenkens*', in: Kramer, *Zur Theorie und Politik des Privat- und Wirtschaftsrechts* (1997) pp. 69 (114)) calls this phenomenon '*relative Geltungsintensität*' (relative intensity of applicability).

tract law that has developed over the last decades:[40] The process of rationalization, materialization and policy orientation in contract law was caused by EC law and consumer protection law as well.[41] What counts are not traditions of regulation and formal or abstract concepts, but the functional orientation of the norms with respect to the internal market and the protection goals. Another general characteristic of modern contract law is the care for the material balance of the contract during the time of contract conclusion and during performance. The binding force of the contract is often unilaterally loosened in favour of a weaker party. Transparency and information occupy a central role in contract law. Third parties are integrated in the distribution of contractual responsibility.[42] These latter developments relativize the central idea of the traditional contract doctrine, the principle of *pacta sunt servanda*. They give rise to a flexible contract law which intensifies the competition between the different enterprises, and has been, for that reason, called 'competitive' contract law.[43] Additionally, the traditionally very sharply drawn line between the moment of contract conclusion and the stage of contract performance gets blurred. The legal interests protected by contract law are expanded to cover all financial interests and the substantive freedom of decision of the weaker party.[44] This elevation of the substantive freedom of decision of the weaker party to an officially protected value of contract law was recently laid down expressly in the new § 241 (2) of the German BGB in the form of an obligation of the other party to show regard for this freedom.

This leads me to the conclusion that consumer protection is not a singular or exceptional development, but one aspect of a more general principle of modern contract law, which I called the 'principle of regard and fairness' ('*Prinzip der Rücksichtnahme und Fairness*').[45] When the market mechanism

---

[40] Lurger, 'The "Social" Side of Contract Law and the New Principle of Regard and Fairness', in: Hesselink, Hartkamp et al. (eds.), *Towards a European Civil Code*, 3rd ed., (2004) pp. 279 (293 *et seq.*).

[41] Lurger, '*Konflikte um Macht und Wissen als Grundelemente von Vertragstheorie und Verfassungswirkungen*', in: *Jahrbuch Junger Zivilrechtswissenschaftler*, Stuttgart (1995, 1996) p. 17 (36); Hesselink, *The New European Legal Culture*, (2001) pp. 73 *et seq.*; Joerges, '*Die Europäisierung des Privatrechts als Rationalisierungsprozess und als Streit der Disziplinen*', *Zeitschrift für europäisches Privatrecht* (1995) p. 181; Christoph Schmid (n. 12) p. 35.

[42] Three or more party contracts (and network contracts), as e.g. several banking transactions, credit sales agreements, are extremely important in practise, but are (almost) ignored by the traditional civil codes. There is a definite necessity for legislative action.

[43] Micklitz, '*Der Vertragsbegriff in den Übereinkommen von Brüssel und Rom*', in: Schulte-Nölke and Schulze (eds.), *Europäisches Vertragsrecht im Gemeinschaftsrecht*, (2002) pp. 39 (41 *et seq.*); Micklitz, '*Ein einheitliches Kaufrecht für Verbraucher in der EG?*', *Europäische Zeitschrift für Wirtschaftsrecht* (1997) p. 236; Micklitz, '*Die Fernabsatzrichtlinie 97/7/EG*', *Zeitschrift für Europäisches Privatrecht* (1999) pp. (875) 885; Kalss and Lurger (n. 2) p. 30.

[44] Kalss and Lurger (n. 2) p. 129.

[45] Lurger (n. 25) pp. 376 *et seq.*; Lurger, '*Das vertragsrechtliche Prinzip der Rücksichtnahme und Fairness zwischen Sozial- und Wirtschaftspolitik und privatrechtlichem Interessenausgleich*', in: *Die soziale Dimension des Zivilrechts – Jahrbuch Junger Zivilrechtswissenschaftler* (2004) pp. 9 *et seq.*; Lurger (n. 40) pp. 279 (294 *et seq.*).

or other factors do not motivate one party to treat the other party fairly and considerately, this fairness and regard must be imperatively prescribed by the law. Thereby, the freedom of contract of one party is limited for the benefit of the other party. The two principles of contractual freedom and party protection and fairness are in partial conflict with each other: Mandatory protective provisions, especially information duties, can succeed in restoring the full substantive freedom of contract of the weaker party and thereby render any further intervention into the contractual stipulations unnecessary. Additionally, the exercise of regard and fairness can also be in the interest of and thus intended by the entrepreneur, who wants to win new and keep old customers. If this is not the case (no restoration of contractual freedom, no self-interest of the business to comply with fairness standards) mandatory protective provisions must intervene directly in order to compensate the weaker party's restricted freedom at the expense of the freedom of the entrepreneur. Only in this latter situation does a direct conflict between the two principles arise.[46]

III. THE ROLE OF CONSUMER LAW FOR A EUROPEAN CONTRACT CODE

I will not discuss the question here of whether a European Contract Code is desirable or not in the first place. My following remarks are based on the assumption that such a Code is principally desirable and on the fact that preparations for it are on their way.

And I now ask the question: What is therefore the role of consumer law with respect to a future European Contract Code?

1. Status Quo of Austrian and European Consumer Contract Law

First of all, the status quo of national as well as European consumer protection law is not satisfactory: The rules are fragmentary, unsystematic, sometimes even contradictory; they are hard to find and they lack a general dogmatic and plausible justification on the level of principles. They therefore often appear intransparent and illegitimate to those subjected to them. Both the national and the European legislator are to blame for that unpleasant diagnosis.

From an Austrian point of view you could ask why many of the directives were not implemented in the existing statutes, namely the ABGB and the Consumer Protection Act, and why they were not implemented in a more

[46] Lurger (n. 40) pp. 279 (292).

systematic way. And more generally: Why are consumers and also customer protection still systematically excluded from the general contract law rules of the ABGB? As mentioned above, all arguments seem to speak against such an anachronistic isolation of consumer law. Consumer and customer protection law should be an integrated part of general contract law and should contribute to its evolution and modernization.[47] In that sense they could be forerunners of a modernized and coherent contract law; yet, in Austria they are not.

At the European level, the EC's interest in consumer and customer contract law and in consumer and customer protection by restricting unfair trade practices was always closely tied to the functioning of the internal market. The protection of regard and fairness in contractual relations is never seen as an end in itself, as a general constitutive element and important principle of contract law as a whole, whereas party autonomy is seen as such an element and important principle. This constitutes a serious defect in the EC legislator's approach to contract law, because it leads to a strong imbalance[48] between the two fundamental values on which contemporary contract law rests: contractual freedom *and* regard and fairness. The idea that consumer and customer protection cannot be separated from the development of the general principles of contract law in the Member States and in the European Union is only slightly indicated in EC Commission's 2003 action plan on a more coherent contract law[49] and will still need some time to grow.

2. Academic Projects of Drafting European Contract Law Rules

Equally, many of the academic projects of drafting European contract law rules have not yet freed themselves of the already outdated view that consumer and customer protection should not interfere too much with the general rules of contract law: Examples are the Gandolfi Code, the Lando Principles and also most of the recent drafts of the von Bar Study Group on

[47] For further suggestions how this systematic integration of consumer and customer protections law into the general contract law could look like see: Lurger (n. 25) pp. 61 *et seq.*; Lurger (n. 12) pp. 111 (152 *et seq.*); Lurger (n. 40) pp. 279 (298 *et seq.*). I do not want to abolish the notion of consumer altogether and to extend the existing protection to all kinds of parties or customers, but suggest that each protective provision and instrument should be analysed as to its goals and the existing needs for protection and contractual freedom. As a result of this analysis it should be restricted to consumers or extended to all customers or parties or abolished altogether.

[48] Lurger (n. 25) pp. 287 *et seq.*; Lurger, '*Die Europäisierung des Vertragsrechts aus vertragstheoretischer und verfassungsrechtlicher Perspektive*', in: Marko and Poier (eds.), *Festschrift Wolfgang Mantl* (2004), pp. 305 (323 *et seq.*); Lurger, (n. 46) pp. 279 (290).

[49] Action Plan of the EC Commission 'A More Coherent European Contract Law', 12 February 2003, COM(2003) 68 final.

a European Civil Code. They not only hesitate to integrate most of the consumer and customer protection law into their draft rules, but they have failed to also develop a principled approach to party protection in general and the limits of contractual freedom.[50]

3. Key Questions for a Future European Contract Law Code

The key questions for a future European Contract Code are the following:

> How could the *Acquis Communautaire* of consumer and customer protection law be improved and integrated into such a European Code? How can we develop the fragmentary and incoherent directive provisions into a systematic, transparent and legitimate body of rules that well co-operates with all the other rules of contract law?

A satisfactory solution to this problem can be only found if we simultaneously work at both levels: the level of rules and also the level of underlying principles and basic values of our market order.[51] What are the justifications for the protection of certain market players (consumers, customers or others)? What are its political implications for the shaping of our market order and our societies? What is the essence and what are the limits of the principle of regard and fairness in contract law? And in the light of these basic assumptions: How can we formulate the dogmatic framework, the categories of protection and the details of fairness and protection rules?

4. Conclusion

If the preparatory drafts for a European contract law continue to avoid the above-mentioned questions, if they continue to separate and underestimate consumer protection law and the level of underlying principles, they will leave the impression that they are incoherent and arbitrary and will have little chance of convincing the relevant political players in the European Union and the Member States of their quality and desirability.

This short analysis of Austrian and European consumer contract law leads me to the clear conclusion that consumer protection law must definitely be part of this European Contract Code. Consumer law is a straight-forward

---

50 Lurger (n. 41) pp. 279 (301).

51 For the relationship between the fundamental human rights of the national and the EU Constitution and the European contract law rules see: Lurger (n. 40) pp. 279 (290 *et seq.*); Lurger (n. 48) pp. 305 (318 *et seq.*); Lurger (n. 25). pp. 49, 53 *et seq.*; Hesselink, 'The Horizontal Effect of "Social Rights" in European Contract Law'; Paper presented at the conference '*Diritti fondamentali e formazione del diritto privato europeo*' at the Università Roma III, on 18 June 2002.

and instructive expression of the principle of regard and fairness in contract law. It will have to be reformed and integrated into the general contract law rules. And it can teach the drafters of a European Contract Code an important lesson.

Chapter 12
The Greek Consumer Law

Elisa Alexandridou, University of Thessaloniki

I. INTRODUCTORY NOTE

As long as traders and consumers are subjects of the market law, it is a common theme that they must be 'equally' protected. The protection foreseen may be guided by the yardstick of 'corrective justice', that is to say, the justice that must be applied in everyday transactions to re-establish equity in a disturbed balance of interests.[1] So the main goal of the legislator must be to protect the weaker of the two contracting parties, which is usually the consumer.

The efforts to harmonize the consumer law of the EU Member States were in recent years successful and this has given hope to the euro-optimists that a unified contract law in Europe could be developed for the years to come. Important in that respect is the general consensus for the necessity of the harmonization of consumer law. The reasons, which are socio-political on the one hand and economic on the other, are, *expressis verbis*, referred to in the Treaty of the EC. In fact the Interior Market would not be able to function satisfactorily if equal consumer protection for European citizens did not exist across all 25 EU Member States.

The following question was put at first to the legislators of the various Member States. Should they introduce a system where contract law and

---

1 This is the Aristotelian point of view in Ethika Nikomachia, *Oxford Classical Texts*, Book V (1970); see also Radbruch, *Rechtsphilosophie* (1970), para. 4, 125 who refers to the '*ausgleichende Gerechtigkeit*'.

S. Grundmann, M. Schauer (eds), *The Architecture of European Codes and Contract Law*, 219–233

consumer contract law exist in parallel *or* a system of integrated contract law applying to all players? Most of the national legislators have followed the first system. Nevertheless, the national legislative Acts that have been harmonized with the relevant directives on consumer law had a considerable impact on the national contract law of the Member States. The question now pending is, if, and how soon, national legislators may integrate consumer law into the national contract law. On that issue there are still a variety of opinions, whereas the mentality and the position of the traditional private lawyers of Member States is obviously fixed; they are often against any 'invasion' of European law in their national civil codes!

With respect to Greece, the national legislator in 1991 chose to adopt the first system, so he promulgated the Act (1961/1991) on Consumer Protection.[2] In 1994, he drafted the Act 2251/1994, which replaced the previous Act. An important legislative framework which offers consumers a specialized shield of protection, equal to those already existing at that time in other Member States of the European Union (e.g. Denmark, Germany, France, Belgium, etc.) has been adopted and all directives on consumer protection existing at that time have been transposed into national law.

This was the situation until the 'earthquake' that rocked national private laws: D 99/44/EC on certain aspects of the sale of consumer goods and associated guarantees. Between the two solutions, i.e. either adopting a specific text for the transposition of the directive or integrating the provisions of the directive in the corpus of the Civil Code in the chapter on 'sale', the legislator this time chose the second option. The reasons expressed in the Explanatory Memorandum of the relevant Act[3] are that it had been oriented towards a European evolution and towards the vision of a supranational law of obligations. By harmonizing the national law on sale with the relevant directive and with the Vienna Convention on the International Sale of Goods, as well as with the principles of European contract law, it intended to assure that Greece would participate in the common efforts of the countries of Europe to achieve a unified contract law. Such a contract law may be a factor of facilitating and simplifying transactions in the Internal Market. Besides, the Greek legislator considered that, as the rules introduced by the relevant directive are aimed at the protection of consumers, and comply with the contemporary conditions of the market, the same rules may be adopted for all players for every sale of goods (including also real estate). Besides, as referred to in the Explanatory Memorandum, the danger of fragmentation of the regulations on basic subjects ruled by the provisions of the Civil Code, such as the sale of goods, had to be taken seriously into account and be avoided.[4] The so-called 'small solution', e.g. the amendment mainly of the

[2] See Alexandridou, 'The Greek consumer protection Act of 1991', *ECLJ* (1992) 4, pp. 20–31.

[3] Act 3043/2002 on the liability of the seller of goods.

[4] See the Explanatory Memorandum of the Act, No. 3.

provisions of the Civil Code on sale[5] and not of the whole legislation on obligations, was finally chosen.[6]

Various relevant provisions are found across legal texts dealing with more specific issues. Specific consumer contracts are regulated in separate Decrees supplementing the legal framework on consumer protection. These are: the Decree on consumer credit which is harmonized with the D 87/02/EEC as amended by the D 90/88/EEC on consumer credit; the Decree on package travel harmonized with the D 90/314/EEC on package travel and package holidays; the Decree on time sharing harmonized with the D 94/47/EEC on time sharing; the Decree on e-commerce harmonized with the D 2000/31/EC on e-commerce and others.

II. CONTENT OF THE ACT ON CONSUMER PROTECTION

The Act 2251/1994 on Consumer Protection, which is the core regulation of the Greek consumer protection law, is structured under three major chapters. The first chapter contains the general provisions, which determine the meaning of the terms 'consumer' and 'supplier'. The second chapter contains provisions harmonized with the directives on consumer protection as following: article 2 regulates unfair terms in consumer contracts; article 3 regulates doorstep selling; article 4 provides for rules on distance selling; article 5 regulates after sale services and guarantees for consumer goods; article 6 regulates product liability; article 7 refers to product safety; article 8 regulates liability for the supply of services (following the second and last Proposal D on services of 1992) and article 9 provides for rules on misleading and unfair advertising. The third chapter of the Act on consumer protection contains organizational provisions which provide for enforcement through institutionally established associations.

The impact of the EC Internal Market Programs on Greek consumer law was very positive. As there was previously no extensive tradition on consumer protection policy, the national legislator might not have proceeded that far without the interference of the aforementioned Programs and the relevant directives.

III. THE NOTION OF THE TERM 'CONSUMER'

The notion of 'consumer' is of crucial importance, as it plays a key role for the application of the Act on Consumer Protection. According to this Act a

5 Arts 534–537 and 540–561 CC.

6 For the transposition of this directive into national law, see below.

'consumer' is a person for whom the products and services offered on the market are intended or the person who uses such products or services as long as he is their final recipient. So consumers are, according to the Greek law, not only natural but also legal persons. A consumer is also regarded as any person who is the recipient of an advertising message.[7] It is thus debatable whether a multinational company, a bank or a ship-owner who are supplying themselves with technical equipment for their business can be excluded from the notion of 'consumer'. Or should we share the view that those physical or legal persons need the protection provided by the Act on Consumer Protection?

An essential argument which can be brought against the broad meaning of the notion of 'consumer' is that courts may differentiate in interpreting the provisions of the Act when those provisions apply to consumers in the strict sense of the term and when they apply them to persons who are professionals, purchasing products and services as their final recipient. The broad definition of the term 'consumer' may finally create problems in the application of the Regulation EC 44/2001 (Brussels I) on the recognition and performance of foreign judgments (see article 15) and of the Rome Convention on the applicable law on the contractual obligations (see article 5). Both define the consumer as the person who concludes contracts for purposes that are outside his trade or profession.

It must be pointed out that in the Greek CC there is no provision defining the term 'consumer' as it is the case, for example, in the German '*Bürgerliches Gesetzbuch*'.

IV. UNFAIR TERMS IN CONSUMER CONTRACTS

The rules on unfair terms in consumer contracts of the Act on Consumer Protection are generally in line with the D 93/13/EEC.

Article 2 (1) of the Act, which partially reflects the Greek legal tradition on contract issues, stipulates the conditions under which terms in consumer contracts are binding on the consumer. Such terms are not regarded as part of the contract if, through no fault of his own, the consumer ignores them at the time of the conclusion of the contract and the supplier does not indicate their existence or deprives him of the possibility of real knowledge of their content. Contract terms must be drafted in a comprehensive way in an obvious place within the text of the contract. These regulations reflect also the transparency requirement of article 5 of the D 93/13/EEC.

In case that contract terms are binding on the consumer, courts must proceed to the next step of control which is their interpretation. A rule of

---

7 See Alexandridou, 'The Greek Consumer Protection Act of 1994', in: *Festschrift für F.-K. Beier zum 70. Geburtstag* (1996), pp. 400–440.

interpretation is that ambiguous contract terms are interpreted in favour of consumers in application of the principle *ambiguitas contra preferentem.*[8] When G.C.T. are subject to control of their fairness after a collective action though, the interpretation which is less favourable for consumers must prevail so that the use of those terms in the consumer contracts be forbidden.

After the aforementioned indirect control over contract terms[9] they must be subject to an unfairness assessment. Terms formulated in advance for a single contract are also subject to control of their fairness. The relevant provision is to be applied to every contract term which has not been individually negotiated. Terms which have been individually negotiated between the supplier and the consumer take precedence over the respective standard contract terms. It is obvious that there is always the risk of exploitation of an ignorant consumer who needs a product or service and is forced to accept additional terms. The rules of the Act are anyway the same as in the D 93/13/ EEC.

The list of terms regarded as unfair, which is a long list of 31 clauses, includes the examples in the Annex to the relevant Resolution [(76) 47] of the Council of Europe and also a few examples of standard contract terms from the Annex of the relevant directive. Those terms refer to fundamental consumer rights and are unfair, *per se*, in the Greek law consisting of a 'black list',[10] whereas the terms of the indicative list in the Annex of the D 93/ 13/EEC consist of a 'gray list'.

The law has not adopted the exclusion from the unfairness assessment of the terms relating to the main subject matter of the contract and to the relationship between price and quality. Although those are matters of crucial importance for consumers they are nevertheless excluded from the scope of the D 93/13/EEC (article 4 (2)). The Greek legislator has deviated from the European model on that issue and his choice is more in favour of the consumers' interests than of Member States who have adopted the above exclusion. The national legislator has ensured more effective protection for consumers on that point too.

A consumer having a legal interest may bring action demanding the control *in concreto* of the terms of the contract that he has concluded. If the terms are regarded as unfair they are null and void and not binding on the consumer. Besides consumer associations which fulfill the necessary legal requirements may bring a collective action demanding the assessment of whether contract terms drawn up for general use by a certain enterprise are *in abstracto* unfair and also demanding the issue of a cease and desist order.

---

8 See Alexandridou, 'Implementation of the EC directive on unfair contract terms in Greece', *EurRevPrL* (1997), pp. 173 *et seq*. (175).

9 This concerns the fulfillment of the transparency requirement and the way they are interpreted.

10 For examples see Alexandridou, *EurRevPrLaw* (1997) p. 177.

Chambers of Commerce and Industry and generally Chambers of Professionals have also the standing to sue suppliers.[11]

It is important to stress the fact that in the Greek Civil Code (CC) there are no specific provisions concerning unfair contract terms. The only *ad hoc* regulation concerning the fairness assessment is the one stipulated in the Act on Consumer Protection for consumer contracts. Courts have to fill this gap by applying the general clause on good faith found in the CC. (In severe cases the judicial control of such terms might lead to the pronouncement of their invalidity.) In order to take advantage and apply the provisions of the Act on Consumer Protection, courts tend to interpret the already very broad definition of the term 'consumer' in a broad sense. The multi-member Court of First Instance of Athens[12] has pronounced that an enterprise (a limited company by shares) excavating and selling marble, which had concluded a contract with a bank for the supply of financial services (a loan), is to be deemed a consumer! The question was whether the terms of the contract concluded between the above company and the bank could be subject to control under the provisions on unfair terms in consumer contracts of the Act on Consumer Protection. The court applying article 2 of the Act pronounced the unfairness of the terms of the aforementioned loan contract which imposed compound interests on interests in arrears, calculated every six months.[13] Those terms were deemed to fall also under letter (l) of the indicative list of unfair terms included in the Act on Consumer Protection.[14] In order to apply the general clause and the indicative list of unfair terms of the Act the Court has regarded the enterprise selling marble as a consumer!

V. DOORSTEP SELLING

The provisions on doorstep selling are in line with D 85/577/EEC. Contracts concluded away from the business premises of the trader must be in writing or are otherwise null and void.[15] The supplier has the obligation, among

11 In conformity with the directive and the spirit of consumer protection, the Act provides that the provisions of this article are applicable when the contract between a consumer and a seller has a close connection with Greece or the territory of another Member State by virtue of the choice of the law of a non member country.

12 Decision No. 6795/99.

13 The contract had been concluded in 1973 and the plaintiff had already paid seven times the equivalent of the capital of the loan.

14 This is equivalent to letter (e) of the indicative list of D 93/13/EEC stipulating that a term which requires that the consumer who fails to fulfill his obligation has to pay a disproportionately high sum in compensation is unfair.

15 The relevant provisions apply to contracts which have been settled after a visit to the consumer's dwelling or working place upon the initiative of the supplier and without an invitation from the consumer (art. 3, para. 1).

others, to inform the consumer that he has the right of withdrawal. A separate written form of withdrawal is to be handed to him together with a written form of the sale contract. The consumer may complete the form of withdrawal and send it to the supplier by registered letter. The cooling-off period is ten working days from the date of receipt of the product and not seven working days as in the directive 85/577/EEC. The consumer's renunciation of this right is null and void.[16]

As there is no specific (narrower) definition of the term 'consumer' in this provision, the general broad notion is to be applied. All final recipients of goods, natural as well as legal persons are also protected, although the main reason for the aforementioned protection is the quick and superficial decision making of the consumer due to the persuasion exercised during an unexpected visit of a supplier to his door. Of course such circumstances do not exist when the purchaser is a legal person.

VI. DISTANCE SELLING

The next provision of the Act (article 4) regulates contracts negotiated at a distance. The text is in line with D 97/7/EC.

The supplier has the obligation to inform the consumer of all necessary items foreseen in law.[17] If that information is not provided, the contract negotiated at a distance is null and void in favour of the consumer. The same rule applies if the consumer does not receive in due time, during the performance of the contract or at the latest when the goods are delivered, also *in writing* all necessary information in the same language as the contract. Information in writing must be given about the trade name and the address of the closest supplier's store to the consumer, the way the price is to be paid and the relevant terms, the consumer's right to withdraw, the after-sale services and the guarantees and also the terms of denunciation of the contract when the contract is of indefinite duration or of a duration longer than one year. The supplier must provide him with a separate written form of withdrawal in order to use it in case he makes up his mind to withdraw from the contract.

In some issues the Greek Act goes beyond the Directive in favour of the interests of consumers. It is provided for example, that before the delivery of the product or the supply of the service total or partial payment is not permitted, not even in the form of a guarantee. Besides, it is stipulated that all means of distance communication (and not only the two means included in article 10 of the directive) must not be used unless the consumer has

16 See Alexandridou, '*Neue Entwicklungen in der griechischen Verbraucherschutzgesetzgebung*', *VuR* 6/95, p. 390.

17 E.g. to inform him about the identity of the supplier, the main characteristics of the good or service, the cost of the distance communication, the minimum duration of the contract, etc.

expressed his consent. It is also provided that distance communication techniques should not be used in a way to disturb the private life of consumers. Those rules, which are not found in D 97/7/EC, improve the legal position of consumers.

The right of withdrawal can be exercised within a period of *10 working days* starting from the date of the receipt of the purchased good or the receipt of the documents for the conclusion of the contract for supply of services.

The supply of goods or services without their being ordered by the consumer beforehand, where such supply involves a demand for payment, is prohibited. The sanction for the infringement of this rule is that the consumer has no obligation to either pay for or to return the good. *On the contrary he may dispose it on his own discretion.* The last stipulation, providing for a sanction which is not included in article 9 of the relevant directive, may have positive preventive effect.

Distance-selling enterprises have to be included in a specific register and they have to disclose their register number to the other contracting party. The Minister of Development may deny the registration if this is justified. He may also cancel the existing registration provisionally or definitely if the supplier violates the provisions on distance selling of the Act on Consumer Protection.

VII. SALE OF CONSUMER GOODS

The Greek legislator has chosen to integrate the regulations of D 99/44/EC on sale of consumer goods and associated guarantees in the Civil Code.[18] Besides, he amended the provisions of the Act on Consumer Protection, which already regulated the contractual obligations of the supplier for information and for supplying the so-called 'commercial guarantee'.[19]

The revised provisions on sale of the Civil Code now regulate the liability of the *seller* of goods without making any further distinction. Consequently, after the harmonization of the Greek law with D 99/44/EC, transactions of the seller concluded with every purchaser fall into the scope of the provisions on sale of the CC. As a result the situation of the purchaser has been improved, whereas the situation of the seller has got worse.[20]

[18] Act 3043/2002 on the liability of the seller of goods.

[19] For details see below.

[20] The provisions on sale of the CC now regulate the two sources of liability together. The former two articles of the CC with titles 'Defects existing' and 'Lack of qualities agreed' are concentrated in one. It is provided that the seller must deliver goods which are in conformity with the qualities agreed in the contract of sale and which are without defects (art. 534 CC). In respect to the conformity of the goods to the contract (as in art. 2 para. 2 of the D) it is provided that the seller shall not be deemed to have fulfilled his obligations if the delivered good is not in conformity with the contract and *particularly*: a) if it

When the consumer is one of the contracting parties the provisions are of a mandatory nature, whereas when both parties are traders the provisions are of a non-mandatory nature.

Article 2 paragraph 3 in combination with article 3 paragraph 1 of the D 99/44/EC are transformed into a positive description of the liability of the seller. It is provided that the seller is liable irrespective of fault for the existence of defects of the good or for lack of the qualities agreed if the above existed at the time that the risk passes to the purchaser, unless if at the time the contract was concluded the purchaser was aware of the lack of conformity to the contract.[21] The purchaser is in this respect better protected than in the Directive[22] because the exclusion of the liability of the seller for the case that the purchaser 'could not reasonably be unaware' of the defect or of the lack of the qualities agreed, has not been transformed to national law.

Under the title 'rights of the purchaser' it is provided that he may choose to start by exercising any of the four rights foreseen in law without the priority limitations stipulated in article 3 of the directive. But, in the case that he has exercised the right of withdrawal, if the withdrawal is not justified under the circumstances, the court may only order a reduction of the price or the replacement of the good.[23] By reason of some other defect or lack of qualities agreed which have been revealed subsequently, the purchaser may once again exercise one of the aforementioned rights.[24] If the agreed quality is lacking at the time that the risk passes to the purchaser, the latter is entitled to demand damages for non performance of the contract instead of the four aforementioned rights. He may also exercise this last right cumulatively with the other four, if his damage cannot be covered by the exercise of the four rights. The same rule shall apply if there is a defect in the delivered good which is due to fault of the seller.[25] The seller is not liable for damages due to lack of qualities agreed, if at the time the contract was concluded those qualities existed and disappeared without his fault before

---

does not comply with the description given by the seller or with the sample; b) if it is not fit for the particular purpose of the contract; c) if it is not fit for the purposes for which goods of the same type are normally used; and d) if it does not show the quality and performance that the purchaser can reasonably expect from goods of the same type taking into account any public statement of the seller, of the producer or of his representative particularly in advertising or in labelling unless the seller was not aware and could not be aware of the relevant statement (art. 535 CC). The consequence of the above formulation and of the expression 'particularly', is that the purchaser may prove that the good is not in conformity with the contract even in the case that only one of the four criteria is lacking and also even in case that the above four criteria have been fulfilled. (see the explanatory memorandum of the Act under II, No. 3).

21 Art. 537 CC.

22 Art. 2, para. 3.

23 Art. 542 CC.

24 Art. 541 CC.

25 Art. 543 CC.

the risk passed to the purchaser.[26] The consequence of the formulation of the above provision is the reversal of the relevant burden of proof in favour of the purchaser.[27]

The option foreseen for the Member States in article 5 § 2 of the D 99/44/EC has not been used by the Greek legislator. The requirement that in order to be able to benefit from his rights, the purchaser has to inform the seller of the lack of conformity with the contract within two months from the date on which he detected it, has been regarded as heavily against the interests of the purchaser.[28]

The final seller who is liable to the purchaser for lack of conformity with the contract is entitled to pursue remedies against a previous seller if this lack is resulting from his act or omission. The prescription period for the right of the final seller to pursue remedies against the person liable begins to run from the time he has completed the remedy required by his purchaser.[29] The same rule applies in the case that any previous seller in the contractual chain is exercising the aforementioned right. No reference is made to the liability of the producer towards the final seller of the good as in the D 99/44/EC (article 4). This could have an indirect negative effect on the interests of consumers.

A new article of the CC provides that the agreed guarantee for durable goods is legally binding on the seller or on a third party under the conditions laid down in the guarantee statement or in the associated advertising without prejudice of the rights provided by law in favour of the purchaser. The same rule is provided in the Act on Consumer Protection for consumers when buying durable consumer goods. So, on the subject of guarantees, the Greek law is split in two texts. Guarantees for all players are provided in the provisions on sale in the CC, whereas guarantees particularly for consumers are provided in the Act on Consumer Protection. This Act is now regulating the pre-contractual duty of the seller for information and the duties for offering a guarantee for durable consumer goods[30] and for ensuring after sale services (article 5).

---

26 Art. 544.

27 As the D 99/44/EC on consumer sales is a minimum directive (see art. 8, para. 2) the above provisions which are more stringent in favour of the purchaser may be maintained in force. In the case that the good has been destroyed or deteriorated *by reason of the existing defect*, the purchaser is still entitled to claim replacement of the good or to exercise the right of withdrawal or to have a reduction of the price. In the case that the good has been destroyed completely or to a large extent or it has been lost or has been substantially deteriorated *by reason of a fortuitous event*, (under the condition that the seller is liable for non-conformity with the contract) the purchaser is entitled only to a reduction of the price (art. 549). In case that the purchaser has taken the goods without reserve, although he was aware of the existence of the defect or of the lack of the qualities agreed, he is deemed to have accepted it with the above deficiencies (art. 545).

28 See the Explanatory Memorandum, under II No. 8.

29 Art. 560 CC.

30 The guarantee must be in conformity with the principle of good faith. Important is the rule that the effect of guarantees should not be negated by excessive exception clauses, a

Very important in the same provision of the Act on consumer protection is the rule that any resignation of the consumer from the protection foreseen in the provisions of the Civil Code on the liability of the seller, made before the lack of conformity is brought to his attention, is null and void.[31]

The rights of the purchaser are subject to a limitation period of two years from the time of the delivery of the good. The rule that the limitation period begins to run as from the time of the delivery of the good applies also in case that the defect or the lack of the qualities agreed have been detected by the purchaser in a subsequent date.[32]

The purchaser is entitled to exercise his rights by objection after they have expired. A prerequisite to that is that he has given notice to the seller about the defect or the lack of the qualities agreed before the expiration of the prescription period.[33]

In respect of second hand goods, the option for the Member States to allow agreements or contract terms providing that the rights of the purchaser will be subject to a shorter limitation period than that of two years has not been used.

The following are in brief the most important novelties introduced in the provisions on sale of the Civil Code:

> The introduction of the binding nature of advertising[34] is a novelty which may have considerable preventive effect. For the first time advertising is to be taken into account for determining the liability of the seller[35] and for the description of the guarantee.[36]
>
> The provision introducing in the Greek Civil Code a guarantee offered by the seller or a third party is also a novelty. The notion of 'guarantee' up till now in the CC has no relation to the so-called 'commercial guarantee' which is foreseen in article 6 of D 99/44/EC.

---

fact which is often the case in written guarantees. The supplier of new durable goods is obliged to ensure the maintenance and repair for the period of the product's normal life and also to furnish spare parts necessary for the use of the product during all its normal life-time. The Act mainly follows the Green Paper of the Community 'concerning warranties and after-sales services' (COM(93) 509 of 15.11.1993).

31 Art. 5, para. 5, subpara. 1.

32 Arts 554, 555 CC.

It is also provided that in the case that there has been an agreement concerning the limitation period for the liability of the seller for defects or lack of qualities agreed, if the above deficiencies become apparent during this period, in case of doubt, the prescription period shall begin to run as from the time they were revealed (art. 556).

The seller shall not be entitled to invoke the expiration of the limitation period if he has fraudulently hidden the defect or omitted to refer to it to the purchaser (art. 557 CC).

33 Art. 558 CC.

34 Details for the provisions on advertising see below.

35 Art. 535 CC.

36 Art. 559 CC.

New in the law on sale of goods is the right to demand the repair of the good.

The limitation period for the expiration of the rights of the purchaser, which was six months, has been altered to a two years period.

The right of the purchaser to demand damages for non-performance of the contract cumulatively with the other four rights, in case that his damage cannot be covered by the exercise of those rights, is also new.

VIII. MISLEADING AND UNFAIR ADVERTISING

1. Advertising Regulated by the Act on Consumer Protection

The provisions on misleading advertising are similar to those of the D 84/450/EEC.

As to *unfair* advertising, the Act has opted for the use of a general clause coupled with an indicative list of certain types of advertising which are regarded as unfair.[37] It is stipulated that advertising which is contrary to good morals is forbidden. The detailed indicative list of various sorts of unfair advertising which follows is useful both in terms of the guidance it offers to the Courts, as well as because of the preventive effect it may have in helping businesses plan their advertising campaigns so as to avoid violating the provisions of the Act. Some of the important sorts of advertising of the aforementioned list are the following:

- **Comparative advertising.** The relevant provision of the Act on Consumer Protection[38, 39] legislates positively under strict requirements. Such advertising must neither be misleading nor unfair and has to compare in an objective way material and verifiable details. Moreover it must not cause confusion with the trademarks and other distinctive signs of competitors of the advertised business and it must not be parasitic. The publication of comparative tests of goods and services is permitted by the Act under strict requirements.[40]
- **Advertising aimed at minors.** The legislator has been particularly sensitive towards the most vulnerable groups of the population and particularly towards minors. The indicative list of unfair advertising practices includes advertising which projects the impression of an attractive offer,

37 Art. 9 (8). See Alexandridou, Completion of the Internal Market and Consumer Protection in Greece, *JCP* 1994, 51 *et seq.* (55).

38 Art. 9 (8).

39 By drawing this provision, art. 4 of the once existed Proposal for a Directive concerning misleading and unfair advertising (OJ No. C 70 of 21.3.78, p. 4.) was taken into account.

40 Art. 9 (9).

especially directed to children and generally to more impressionable cross-sections of the population.[41] Also, television advertising for toys for children is prohibited during the time from 7 a.m. to 22 p.m.[42] It is interesting to see that the multinational enterprises that are importing toys to Greece have addressed to the Commission arguments against Greece with the contention that the above prohibition in the Greek law was infringing article 30 of the EC Treaty.[43]

- **Indirect advertising** is unfair and therefore prohibited. An advertisement is regarded as indirect if it does not explicitly reveal the company or the product to be promoted but projects certain data that seduce the consumer.[44] This method, apart from misleading consumers, results also in the distortion of 'best-offer competition' ('*Leistungswettbewerb*').
- **'Subliminal' advertising** is prohibited. The advertising message should not be addressed to the subconsciousness of the consumer in a way that his ability to criticize is disturbed and also should not try to provoke or to exploit his fears and superstitions in order to persuade him to conclude a contract.
- **Direct advertising.** The direct transmission of an advertising message to the consumer by telephone (cold-calling), fax, electronic mail (spamming), automatic calling machine or by other electronic media is permitted only under the condition that the consumer has given his clear consent in advance. If the consumer demands so, the supplier is obliged to stop any direct advertising and to delete the consumer's personal data from his catalogues. The more crucial issue is the introduction of the general principle that 'direct advertising must not prejudice the consumers' privacy'. The consumers' private life and personal data have to be respected. Finally, it is stipulated that any commercial communication must be recognizable, particularly in the case that it is an unsolicited commercial communication.[45]

---

41 Art. 9 (6) c of the Act.

42 Art. 14 (8) of the Act.

43 The case has never been determined.

44 A well known advertising of this sort is that of 'Benetton'.

45 A specific Act on 'the legal status of private television and local radio broadcasting' contains law harmonized with D 89/552/EEC as amended by D 97/36/EC 'on the pursuit of television broadcasting activities' (so-called 'television without frontiers directive'). In respect to advertising messages for alcoholic beverages it stipulates concrete conditions under which those messages are permitted. Strict conditions for advertising messages targeting directly to minors are also provided. Advertising of tobacco products on TV is totally prohibited. TV-programs that involve pornography or gratuitous violence are also prohibited. Scenes of violence are not permitted in the broadcasting of the 'News', when this is not necessary.

2. Advertising Regulated by the Act against Unfair Competition

The Act against Unfair Competition is combining a general clause on good morals with specific prohibitions.[46] In article 1 it is provided that any competitive behaviour in the course of commercial or industrial activity is prohibited if it is contra bonos mores. This general clause is to apply to any competitive behaviour, which violates the legal order and is not subject to any specific provision.[47] According to the predominant opinion of courts, when assessing the fairness of a competitive behaviour, the interests of the enterprise, the interests of the competitors and also the interests of the public have to be closely examined.[48]

Owing to the fact that consumers play a significant role in the functioning of competition, the provisions on consumer protection and the provisions against unfair competition are a bunch of rules which are interrelated, constituting the law of the market. That fact leads to the conclusion that when interpreting the general clause on good morals of the Act against unfair competition, the interests of consumers in particular must also be taken into account. The aforementioned specific rules on advertising of the Act on Consumer Protection obviously constitute the concretization of the general clause on good morals or on fair marketing practices. This idea is actually reflected today in the Proposal Directive on unfair commercial practices.[49]

In a separate provision the Act against unfair competition prohibits misleading advertising (It concerns particularly the advertising which 'creates the impression of a very favorable offer').

This Act also prohibits discount sales and the relevant advertising and permits them only in exceptional cases, for instance when they take place at 'the close of season'.[50] During seasonal sales prices ought to be truly reduced and the products sold ought to be not of a lower quality than those normally sold. If these conditions are not met, consumers may be deceived, so the general rule, which prohibits misleading advertising, comes into force. Special offers in relation to certain products, which are to be sold not at their

---

46 See Alexandridou, '*Die gesetzgeberische Entwicklung des Verbraucherschutz- und Wettbewerbsrechts in Griechenland*', GRUR Int (1992) pp. 120 *et seq.*; Kotsiris, *Competition Law* (2000) (in Greek) pp. 76 *et seq.*, 187 *et seq.*

47 See Alexandridou, *Das Recht des unlauteren Wettbewerbs in den Mitgliedstaaten der EWG*, Band VII, Griechenland (1994) pp. 21 *et seq.*

48 Alexandridou, *Das Recht des unlauteren Wettbewerbs in den Mitgliedstaaten der EWG*, pp. 22 *et seq.*

49 COM(2003) 356 final, in the meantime adopted – Directive 2005/28/EC.

50 See art. 7 of the Act against Unfair Competition.

current but at reduced prices independent of the season, are permitted with strict prerequisites.[51]

In addition, the Act against Unfair Competition contains specific rules on several forms of promotional marketing practices. For example bait and switch offers (so-called '*Lockvogelangebote*') are prohibited.[52] It concerns any advertising offering a limited number of products, usually those that have won a good reputation, which are sold at special discount prices in order to attract the public at the shop. This sort of advertising is regarded as unfair because it creates the false impression that all products in this specific store are sold at discount prices, whilst the rest of the products actually have normal or even higher than normal prices.

IX. FINAL REMARK

There are no intensive discussions in Greece concerning an eventual integration of the provisions of the Act on Consumer Protection in the general contract law.[53] With the exception of the provisions on sale in the CC harmonized with D 99/44/EC, the tendency continues to be in favour of the separate co-existence of the consumer contract law and the general contract law. Traditional private lawyers insist on preserving the systematic and conceptual 'clearance' of the Civil Code.

Nevertheless, having in mind the method that some Member States of the EU[54] have chosen in order to implement the Directive on the Sale of Consumer Goods, that is, the method of integrating the relevant provisions into the national Civil Code, the approach of the feasability of a European Civil Code or at least of a European Sale of Goods Act seems today more realistic than a few years ago.

---

51 Act 802/78 as amended by Act 1989/91. Permission for such sales is to be granted by decision of the competent prefect and the seller has to state the terms and conditions of the offers, the beginning and the closing date, the mode of retail used and any other details related to the subject. Signs for the 'special offers' have to be placed at visible locations in the shop indicating the 'before' and 'after' prices of every good involved.

52 See art. 7 (12) of the Act on Unfair Competition.

53 As it happened for ex. in Germany concerning the provisions on unfair terms in consumer contracts.

54 As for example Germany and Greece.

Chapter 13
Verbrauchervertragsrecht im tschechischen Recht

*Luboš Tichý**

Abstract: *This article discusses Czech consumer law in three parts: the general background of Czech private law, Czech consumer law and consumer protection in Czech law of contract with regard to the lege ferenda. Czech private law has formerly been based on the Austrian ABGB and HGB (Civil and Commercial Code). The communist Civil Codes first became much shorter (1950) and later largely eliminated institutions like private property and contract freedom (1964), with an exception for foreign trade regulation. In 1992, a major reform reintroduced most of contract freedom and – besides the Civil Code – a Commercial Code. In the second part, the author treats two issues: he deconstructs the generally accepted myth of the existence of consumer protection under communist law (without a market economy, real consumer protection cannot exist; and for ideological reasons any protection of an individual against the state is absurd) and analyzes the current situation where the European rules have been implemented. The latter problem is difficult and wide-ranging and has many ramifications: Czech legislator has been too "creative" in his transposition work. The wording of the Czech laws, especially in the cases where the European directives have been transposed into the Civil Code, is manifestly divergent from the European text. In sum, the level of private law consumer protection is below the standard of minimal harmonization. Finally, this paper addresses the core question as to whether consumers*

* Karls Universität Prag.

S. Grundmann, M. Schauer (eds), *The Architecture of European Codes and Contract Law*, 235–254

should be treated separately at all or whether protection of the weaker party is not rather of general private law issue. It opts for the second solution.

I. EINLEITUNG

Möchte man über die Konzeptionsfragen wie z.B. das Maß der Abstraktion einer privatrechtlichen Regelung sprechen, so muss man versuchen, entweder ein allgemeines Modell bzw. Leitlinien zu entwickeln oder eine eher konkrete Lösung in Hinblick auf bestimmte Rechtsordnung zu finden. Im zweiten Fall sollte man auch die Akzeptanz und daher auch die Effizienz der Durchsetzung einer solchen künftigen Regelung in Betracht ziehen. Dies setzt wiederum voraus, die Rechtskultur in ihrer Entwicklung zu berücksichtigen. Da wir nicht eine allgemeine, sondern eine 'tschechische' Darstellung vermitteln wollen, sollten wir zunächst eine breitere Perspektive des Privatrechts schildern (II), dann eine kurze Analyse des geltenden Verbraucherrechts verfassen (III) und schließlich eine Lösung skizzieren (IV).

II. DIE GRUNDLAGEN

1. Entwicklung der Gesetzgebung

Seit dem Jahre 1811 bis zum Ende des Jahres 1951 galt in Böhmen (und dann im tschechischen Teil der Tschechoslowakischen Republik) das Österreichische Allgemeine Bürgerliche Gesetzbuch (ABGB) in der Fassung dreier späterer Novellen. Daneben war auch das Handelsgesetzbuch Haus dem Jahre 1863 in Kraft.

In den dreißiger Jahren gab es den Vorentwurf eines tschechoslowakischen Zivilgesetzbuchs, das Züge des österreichischen ABGB trug, und auf denselben Grundgedanken und derselben Systematik beruhte. Das Ziel der neuen Kodifikation lag vor allem darin, ein einheitliches Zivilrecht auf dem ganzen Gebiet der damaligen 'ersten' Tschechoslowakischen Republik einzuführen; denn in der Slowakei und der Karpato-Ukraine galt bis dahin ungarisches Recht. Als Gesetz wurde dieser Vorentwurf niemals verabschiedet.[1]

Die kommunistische Machtübernahme hatte Änderungen im Zivilrecht zur Folge. Man entschied, eine neue Kodifikation der Hauptbereiche des 'neuen' Rechts vorzunehmen, die auch den Zivilprozess, das Strafrecht und das Strafprozessrecht umfasste.

---

[1] Siehe z.B. F. Rouček und J. Sedláček, *Komentář k československému obecnému zákoníku občanskému* (Kommentar zum tsch. ABGB) (Praha 1935–1937), I.-VI.Bd, und J. Švestka in O. Jehlička, J. Švestka und M. Škárová (eds.), *Občanský zákoník, Komentář* (ZGB, Kommentar) (2002) 3.

Dieses gewaltige Vorhaben wurde 'juristisches Zweijahr' genannt. Darunter wurde die Vollendung einer großen Reform innerhalb von zwei Jahren verstanden, welche unter der persönlichen Aufsicht eines der Prominenten des damaligen kommunistischen Regimes, des Justizministers A. Čepička, erfolgte.[2] Das Zivilgesetzbuch ist[3] mit 1. Januar 1951 in Kraft getreten und löste vorrangig das ABGB und HGB ab. Das Zivilrecht sollte, so hieß es, den Werktätigen näher gebracht werden, also, volkstümlich werden.

Obschon einige traditionelle Institutionen verschont geblieben sind und auch die Auffassung in einiger Hinsicht formale Züge trägt, bringt das ZGB tiefgehend gesellschaftliche Veränderungen zum Ausdruck und kürzte unter anderem den Text des ABGB auf ein Drittel.

Der Staat, der schon früher durch Verstaatlichung der größte Eigentümer im Lande geworden ist, ersetzte Marktwirtschaft durch Planung. Die fundamentalsten Veränderungen ereigneten sich im Rahmen des Sachenrechts. Der einheitliche Begriff des Eigentums wurde durch mehrere Eigentumsarten ersetzt. Dabei wurde das staatliche Eigentum in vielerlei Hinsicht bevorzugt; man beseitigte die konstitutive Wirkung der Grundbuchseintragung.

Die Parteiautonomie wurde erheblich eingeschränkt, u.a. durch bindende Rechtsakte. Die Wirtschaftsbeziehungen wurden anhand verschiedener Verordnungen und Bekanntmachungen außerhalb des ZGB geregelt. Dies stellt eine typische Handlungsweise des totalitären Staates dar.[4]

Die 'Sozialisierung' des Zivilrechts wurde in der ersten Hälfte der sechziger Jahre (1963, 1964) verwirklicht: der Widerspruch zwischen dem noch den Hauch der Tradition tragenden Zivilgesetzbuch einerseits und der das Recht vergewaltigenden Politik anderemits wurde beseitigt. So erzielte die damalige Tschechoslowakei ein Primat, sogar unter den sozialistischen Ländern. Das Erfindungswesen triumphierte, der Rest der traditionellen Rechtsinstitutionen verschwand oder wurde durch sozialistische Neuschöpfungen ersetzt.[5] Erst 12 Jahre später konnte die damalige DDR mit ihrem ZGB diesem Beispiel folgen. Die neuen Züge des sozialistischen Zivilrechts lassen sich wie folgt zusammenfassen:

- Man ging von den abstrakt gefassten Rechtsinstitutionen, die im römischen Recht ihre Wurzeln hatten, ab. Sie wurden allmählich durch Konstruktionen, die erheblich weniger abstrakt waren, ersetzt.
- Der schon beschädigte Begriff des Eigentums wurde weiter angegriffen und weiter zersplittert. Die einzelnen Formen und Typen des Eigentums

[2] Siehe z.B. F. Zoulík, 'Problematika rekodifikace soukromého práva v České republice' (Problematik der Rekodifizierung des Privatrechts in der Tschechischen Republik), *Právní praxe* 1996, 126 *et seq.*

[3] Siehe das ZGB, Gesetz Nr. 141/1950 Slg.

[4] Vgl. F. Zoulík, *op. cit.* in n. 2, 132 *et seq.*

[5] Vgl. § 151 *et seq.* ZGB/1950, und z.B. Dienstleistungen anstatt Obligationen, Verkauf im Laden anstatt Kaufvertrag, usw.

wurden nun selbstständig, sie bekamen eine Rechtsform, einen eigenen Schutz und Inhalt.

- Das bis dahin geltende allgemeine Obligationenrecht hörte auf zu existieren. Es gibt von jetzt an einerseits den Vertrag und die Obligationen im Wirtschaftsrecht; und andererseits einen Vertrag zwischen den Bürgern und schließlich einen Vertrag im Außenhandel; es gibt ferner einen Arbeitsvertrag entsprechend dem Gesetzbuch der Arbeit.[6]
- Das bürgerliche Recht wurde zum Vehikel des Staates und es wurde zur Richtlinie für die Rechtssubjekte. Die zwingenden Rechtsnormen gewannen die Oberhand über die dispositiven.

Diese neuen Züge, die das Zivilgesetzbuch kennzeichnen, sind allerdings im Rahmen des ganzen Zivilrechts sehr verschiedenartig angewendet worden; gezielt, sehr abgestuft und differenziert. Das Zivilrecht wurde in vier verschiedene Gesetzbücher geteilt, die jeweils eine eigenständige Regelung darstellen: ZGB, Wirtschaftsgesetzbuch, Gesetzbuch des Außenhandels[7] und Gesetzbuch der Arbeit, wobei das Wirtschaftsgesetzbuch die Beziehungen unter den sozialistischen Organisationen regelte, also fast das ganze Gebiet der Produktion und des Handels.

Die Parteiautonomie wurde minimalisiert, der ganze Bereich wurde dirigistisch geregelt. Auch im Rahmen des Arbeitsgesetzbuches gab es praktisch keinen Raum für die freie Rechtsgestaltung; das ZGB regelte die restlichen zwei Gruppen von Rechtsverhältnissen: zwischen den Bürgern einerseits und unter den sozialistischen Organisationen andererseits. Das Maß an Strenge im Sinne von Unabdingbarkeit galt ebenso im Wirtschaftsrecht und Arbeitsrecht wie im Rahmen des bürgerlichen Rechts bzw. im ZGB. Abseits dieser Entwicklung lag das Gebiet des Rechts des Außenhandels, denn für Außenbeziehungen behielt auch der totalitäre Staat die traditionellen Institutionen bei. Das Gesetzbuch des Außenhandels (AHGB) aus dem Jahre 1963 gab Haupttendenzen des Haager Kaufrechts wieder.

In dieser Fassung existierte das Zivilrecht mit Änderungen bis zur Wende im Jahre 1989. In den Jahren 1990 bis 1991 wurden einige Teiländerungen vorgenommen. Die grundsätzlichen Änderungen im ZGB sind anhand der großen Novelle, die am 1. Januar 1992 in Kraft getreten ist,[8] durchgeführt worden. Gleichzeitig wurde auch das Handelsgesetzbuch[9] geschaffen und das alte Wirtschaftsgesetzbuch abgeschafft. Trotz des Ausmaßes der Veränderungen gelten diese Reformen als provisorische Lösung. Das Provisorische ergibt sich evident aus der beschränkten Bedeutung dieser Änderung, bei aller Achtung, die wir ihr beimessen. Die Änderungen sind auf zwei Gebiete beschränkt: zunächst einmal Revidierung der Stellung des

---

6 Vgl. Gesetz Nr. 65/1965, welches nach vielen Novellen immer noch in Kraft ist.

7 Vgl. Wirtschaftsgesetzbuch, Gesetz Nr. 109/1964 Slg., Gesetzbuch des Außenhandels, Gesetz Nr. 101/1963 Slg.

8 Vgl. Gesetz Nr. 509/1991 Slg.

9 Vgl. Gesetz Nr. 513/1991 Slg.

Staates und seine Beziehungen zur Wirtschaft, indem alle seine Privilegien abschafft werden: also Begünstigungen des sozialistischen Eigentums, insbesondere Stellung der sozialistischen Organisationen. Zum anderen musste man einfach neue Institutionen einführen, wo sie zuvor nicht existierten. Der Grund der Einschränkung der Reform lag darin, dass der Markt noch sehr unterentwickelt war und daher eine umfassende Änderung verfrüht gewesen wäre.

2. Vertrag, Rechtsgeschäft

Eine der wichtigsten Kategorie des allgemeinen Teils des Zivilrechts ist zumindest in Deutschland nicht der Vertrag, sondern das Rechtsgeschäft. Es ist eine Unterart des Begriffs der Rechtshandlung, unter welcher man auch die rechtswidrigen Handlungen versteht.

Das Rechtsgeschäft war jedoch unter dem ABGB nur ein Begriff der Dogmatik, wobei das Gesetz selbst neben dem 'Vertrag' nur das Wort Rechtshandlung kannte. Kein Wunder, denn der Ausdruck 'Rechtsgeschäft' ist jung, und er war erst Anfang des 19. Jahrhunderts in die deutsche Rechtsprache von Hugo[10] eingeführt worden. So hatte das Preussische Allgemeine Landrecht als naturrechtliche Kodifikation schon die Lehre von der Willenserklärung gekannt, aber ohne das Wort Rechtsgeschäft zu benutzen. Es ist bei uns allerdings von Bedeutung, dass diese Terminologie erst durch das tschechoslowakische ZGB von 1950 eingeführt wurde.[11] Seither wird der Begriff Rechtsgeschäft sowohl positivrechtlich als auch dogmatisch verwendet.

Ähnlich wie im deutschen Recht ist die Lehre von der Willenserklärung die Grundlage des Rechtsgeschäftsbegriffs. Sie hat ihre Entstehung und Entwicklung der deutschen Pandektistik zu verdanken und hatte für die systematische Einordnung der beschriebenen Begriffe und Kategorie große Bedeutung.

Es bleibt jedoch an dieser Stelle festzustellen, wie der Begriff des Rechtsgeschäfts in das ZGB 1950 eingeführt wurde. Es sei nur hervorzuheben, dass das ZGB aus dem Jahre 1950 eine skurrile Mischung von einerseits traditionellen Rechtsfiguren, die zum Teil schon sehr verstümmelt wurden, und andererseits neuen totalitären Institutionen enthielt und als ein Vehikel des Übergangs zur Planwirtschaft diente.[12] Meine Erklärung dafür ist, dass das Rechtsgeschäft – also eine typische deutsche Kategorie – nicht direkt aus dem BGB importiert worden ist. Es ist vielmehr wahrscheinlicher, dass der

---

10 Dazu vgl. z.B. K. Zweigert und H. Kötz, *Einführung in die Rechtsvergleichung*, Band II (1969), 3.

11 Vgl. V. Špaček, *Projevy vůle a právní úkony v občanském právu* (Willenserklärungen und Rechtsgeschäfte im Zivilrecht) (1953), 102.

12 Siehe unten ad II und III. Und F. Zoulík, *op. cit.* in n. 2, 129 *et seq.*, so auch viele andere.

deutsche Einfluss sogar unbewusst war. Die Erklärung ist eine ganz andere. Die sowjetische zivilrechtliche Gesetzgebung führte schon diesen Begriff in das ZGB RSFSR im Jahre 1922 als 'sdjelka' ein. Was der tschechoslowakische Gesetzgeber im Jahre 1950 tat, war die Übernahme des sowjetischen Vorbilds. Rein quantitativ entstammt der größte Teil des Schuldrechts dem BGB oder dem sich auf das BGB stützenden Entwurf aus dem Jahre 1913.[13]

3. Zwingendes und nachgiebiges Recht

Insbesondere in der Entwicklung der Vertragspraxis in jüngster Zeit können wir in wachsendem Maße eine nahezu typische Erscheinung beobachten. Im Gegenteil zu früher sind die Vertragsparteien bemüht, ihr Verhältnis möglichst detailliert, direkt und komplex im Vertragstext zu gestalten. Jedoch lassen sie auch einige wenige Fragen ihrer Beziehungen offen. Der anglosächsischen Einfluss ist offensichtlich.[13a] Die Tendenz spricht sicherlich für ein höheres Maß an Sicherheit und Voraussehbarkeit. Dies ist jedoch unter der Voraussetzung möglich, dass die vertragliche 'autonome' und ausführliche Regelung erlaubt ist, bzw. nicht dem Recht widerspricht. Damit sind wir bei dem allgemeinen Problem der Nachgiebigkeit und der zwingenden Kraft der zivilrechtlichen Vorschriften angelangt.

An sich ist dies auch im deutschen BGB kein einfaches Problem. Man braucht an dieser Stelle nur in Erinnerung zu rufen, dass zwar die Vorschriften des BGB in erheblichem Umfang dispositiven Charakter haben, trotzdem ist es nicht leicht, diese Frage zu entscheiden. Indem das Gesetz den zwingenden Charakter bei einigen Normen ausdrücklich anmerkt, erklärt es nicht etwa alle anderen für dispositiv. Der zwingende Charakter ist insbesondere aus dem Zweck der Vorschrift zu erschließen.

Nach österreichischem Privatrecht galt und gilt noch der ungeschriebene Grundsatz, dass die zwingenden Normen eingreifen, soweit das allgemeine Wohl, die Verkehrssicherheit, das Wohl der Familie, der Schutz der wirtschaftlich Schwächerer oder die Obsorge für unerfahrene Personen, dies erfordern.[14] Gleichzeitig galt jedoch, dass durch den zwingenden Charakter eines Rechtssatzes seine privatrechtliche Natur nicht verändert wird, so dass der Begriff des zwingenden Rechts also keinesfalls mit jenem des öffentlichen Rechts gleichzusetzen ist.

Auch in der Zeit der Geltung des ZGB aus dem Jahre 1950 hatte man anerkannt, dass einige Rechtssätze des Obligationenrechts dispositiven

---

[13] Vgl. N. Reich, *Sozialismus und Zivilrecht* (1972) 185.

[13a] Es handelt es sich insbesondere um grössere Projekte, an denen sich ausländische (nicht nur anglosächsische) Investoren beteiligen. Stil, Terminologie, Umfang lassen kleinen Zweifel zu. Bezeichnend ist, dass vor allem die US-Vertragspraxis sich auch dort durchsetzte, wo das tschechischer Recht anwendbar ist.

[14] H. Krejci (ed.), *Handbuch zum Konsumenteschutzgesetz* (1981), 10.

Charakter haben.[15] Auch diese nachgiebigen Vorschriften des ZGB bringen das Interesse der Werktätigen zum Ausdruck, schrieb man damals.[16] Dies galt insbesondere dort, wo das Recht die Erfüllung des Wirtschaftsplanes des Staates sicherstellen sollte. Unter diesen Bedingungen konnte man mehr fordern, z.B. konnte man die Aufhebung des Vertrages verlangen, auch wenn die Sachmängel der Ware zu beseitigen waren. In der Tat handelte es sich um eine Regelung, die eine Partei bevorzugte, indem sie ihr einseitige Vorteile verschaffte. Die Nachgiebigkeit lag darin, dass die bevorzugte Partei nicht verpflichtet war, von diesen Rechten Gebrauch zu machen.

Im ZGB aus dem Jahre 1964 hatte die Mehrheit der Rechtsnormen des ZGB zwingenden Charakter. Die ganze Auffassung, führte, wie die offizielle Lehre einräumte,[17] zur Annahme, dass es sich in Bezug auf den Charakter der Rechtsvorschrift im Zweifel um zwingende Rechtsnorm handelt. Das WGB hatte sogar dem ganzen Obligationenrecht zwingenden Charakter beigemessen. Im AHGB galten andere Regeln. Nach seinem § 5 durften die Parteien eine vom Gesetz abweichende Regelung vereinbaren, es sei denn, dass ausdrücklich festgelegt wurde, dass die Rechtsätze unabdingbar sind. Im § 722 waren die konkreten Vorschriften mit zwingendem Charakter aufgezählt. Von den 726 Paragraphen des ganzen AHGB gab es 122 mit zwingendem Charakter.

Nach dem heute geltenden Recht sehen wir in mancher Hinsicht einen großen Unterschied zu früher. Das neue HGB blieb im Prinzip der Lösung des AHGB treu. Der dritte Teil des HGB, der die Schuldverhältnisse regelt, zählt die Rechtssätze auf, die die Parteien nicht ausschließen oder von denen sie nicht abweichen dürfen. Es sind von den 496 Paragraphen des Gesetzbuchs überraschend 104 Paragraphen, die immer zwingend sind. Die Entwicklung zu früher ist dennoch klar und man kann sie in verschiedener Hinsicht festhalten:

- Es gibt keine Kontrahierungspflicht außer der, die sich aus dem Vorvertrag ergibt; dies ist eine Vorschrift, verglichen mit dem WGB, welches das HGB abschafft, und den Parteien die Pflicht auferlegte, die Schuldverhältnisse abzuändern oder sogar aufzuheben.
- Die Parteien können auch andere Typen von Verträgen, als diejenigen, die im HGB geregelt sind, vereinbaren.

Die zwingenden Vorschriften des HGB im Teil über die Obligationen[18] sind nach dem Regierungsentwurf vor allem die Bestimmungen, die Interessen Dritter betreffen.[19] Wenn wir jedoch die einzelnen zwingenden Rechtsnormen

---

15 Vgl. V. Špaček, *op. cit.* in n. 11, 20 *et seq.*

16 Unter anderen vgl. V. Špaček, *op. cit.* in n. 11, 32 *et seq.*

17 V. Knapp, Š. Luby, *Občanské právo hmotné* (Materielles bürgerliches Recht), Band I (1974), 28 *et seq.*

18 Siehe § 263 HGB.

19 Vgl. den Regierungsentwurf (vládní návrh zákona) mit Begründung, 352.

näher analysieren, können wir feststellen, dass die Mehrheit von ihnen nicht die Rechte Dritter behandelt. Darüber hinaus kommen einige der bedeutendsten Autoren[20] in ihren Ausführungen zum Schluss, dass nicht nur die aufgezählten zwingenden Rechtssätze im Interesse der Rechtssicherheit aufgestellt sind und den Schutz der Dritten gewährleisten sollen, sondern dass man wegen dieser Prinzipien über den Rahmen dieser Bestimmungen hinausgehen und andere sonst nachgiebige Rechtssätze als zwingend anwenden sollte. Mit anderen Worten sollte das HGB eigentlich verstärkt zwingend sein als angenommen.

Unter dem ZGB gilt eine neue durch die große Novelle eingeführte Regel, nach der die Vertragsparteien eigene Rechte abweichend vom ZGB regeln können, falls dies das Gesetz nicht verbietet und aus dem Charakter seiner Bestimmungen nichts hervorgeht, dass man nicht abweichen darf. Die Parteien dürfen nicht anderes festlegen und vom Gesetz abweichen, wenn die zwingende Natur ausdrücklich festgelegt ist oder sich aus dem Charakter des Rechtsatzes ableiten lässt. Diese Regel wäre auch dann anzuwenden, wenn sie nicht ausdrücklich im Gesetz verankert wäre.

4. Verbraucherschutz unter Planwirtschaft?

Es hat sich gezeigt,[21] dass für das völlig rigide System der Volkswirtschaft eine spezifische Regelung der so genannte 'Lieferanten-Abnehmer' – Beziehungen des wirtschaftlich öffentlichen Charakters nötig war. Dieser Gedanke wurde im so genannten Wirtschaftsgesetzbuch zum Ausdruck gebracht. Neben den Rechtsnormen hat dieses auch die Planungsakte als Verhaltensregeln betrachtet. Weder technisch noch politisch (d.h. ohne Terror der Zuteilungswirtschaft) war es aber möglich, die Einwohner genauso einzuschränken wie die Wirtschaft. Dieser Umstand hat die Weiterexistenz des WGB ermöglicht. Dieses Gesetzbuch hat sich einerseits auf die Beziehungen zwischen den Bürgern und den sozialistischen Organisationen und andererseits auf die Beziehungen zwischen den Bürgern untereinander bezogen. Das Zivilgesetzbuch vom Jahre 1964 ist von der hier bislang existierenden Tradition am meisten abgewichen, sogar im Vergleich mit allen Kodifikationen, die entweder formell (mit ihrem Namen) oder zweckmäßig ähnlich gestaltet wurden, und auf dem Gebiet der europäischen Staaten entstanden sind. Es hat nicht nur die vorherige erste sozialistische Kodifikation vom Jahre 1950 überwunden, sondern es ist noch weiter gegangen als das wesentlich später entstandene (1975) Zivilgesetzbuch der damaligen DDR (ZGB). Diese Kodifikation hat die Vertragsautonomie sogar in manchen Hinsichten begrenzt (siehe oben II/1). Sie hat die Grundlage dieser Autonomie,

---

[20] Vgl. z.B. L. Kopáč, *Obchodní kontrakty* (Handelsverträge) (1993), Band I, 125.
[21] Nachweise bei F. Zoulík, *op. cit.* in n. 2, 141 *et seq.*

nämlich Eigentum, Eigentumsrechte und ihre Ausübung reduziert (bzw. hat sie die bereits in der Verfassung verankerten Beschränkungen durchgeführt). Um den staatlichen ('gesamtgesellschaftlichen', in der Praxis jedoch bloß parteipolitischen) Sektor zu begünstigen, hat das Bürgerliche Gesetzbuch das einheitliche römischrechtliche Institut des Eigentums in selbständige Typen nach den einzelnen Subjekten – Eigentümern – aufgeteilt, und zwar in das Staats-, Genossenschafts-, Personen- und zuletzt auch in das Privateigentum.

Es hat den einheitlichen Begriff der Rechtssubjektivität aufgehoben, denn ähnlich wie im Falle des Eigentums war es unerlässlich, die Stellung der einzelnen Subjekte zu unterscheiden und somit auch den sich daraus ergebenden Umfang der Rechte der Eigentümer. Beseitigt wurde auch das einheitliche Recht der Schuldverhältnisse, da es notwendig war, spezifischen Zielen zu dienen. Die Verträge wurden zur Erfüllung des Wirtschaftsplans, zur Gewährung bestimmter Dienstleistungen an die Bürger usw. abgeschlossen. Einen besonderen Charakter hatte der Arbeitsvertrag (geregelt in einem selbständigen Gesetzbuch [Arbeitsgesetzbuch]),[21a] der die Erfüllung der Volkswirtschaftspläne hinsichtlich des Personals sicherstellen sollte.[22] Das Zivilgesetzbuch ist nicht mehr eine Verhaltensanweisung, es wird zu einer Sammlung von Geboten und Verboten, die für den Bereich des Öffentlichen Rechts charakteristisch sind. Den einzelnen Rechtssubjekten steht ihre eigene Selbständigkeit, bzw. der Raum für eigene Entscheidungen, nicht mehr zur Verfügung.

Da die Bürger keine Möglichkeiten hatten, eigene Entscheidungen frei zu treffen, und eigener Mittel zur Sicherstellung ihrer Existenz beraubt wurden, sind sie in eine ökonomische Abhängigkeit vom Staatssektor geraten. Auch seitens des Staates bestand ein wirtschaftliches Interesse an der Sicherstellung eines bestimmten Niveaus als Minimalstandards für das Leben der Einwohner, welches zugleich das maximale Niveau darstellte. Vom Verbraucherschutz im Sinne des europäischen Rechts konnte allerdings keine Rede sein.

III. VERTRAGLICHES VERBRAUCHERSCHUTZRECHT

1. Allgemeine Bemerkung

Die Tschechische Republik gehört zu den neuen Beitrittstaaten, in wetsher einige Rechtsbereiche kaum diskutiert wurden. Das gilt auch für den Bereich des Verbraucherschutzes, insbesondere des privatrechtlichen Schutzes der Verbraucher. Die Ursachen dieser Tatsache sind verschiedener Natur. Sicher

---

[21a] Zákoník práce, Gesetz Nr. 65/1965 Slg.

[22] Siehe z.B. G. Howells 195, H.-W. Micklitz (ed.), *Rechtseinheit oder Rechtsvielfalt in Europa* (1996); H.-W. Micklitz, *Interim Report on Sales of Goods Law in the Phare Countries* (1995).

ist, dass die mangelhafte Diskussion auch auf den Zeitdruck mit der Umsetzung der europäischen Verbraucherschutzrichtlinien zurückzuführen ist. Hinsichtlich der Kodifikation des allgemeines Vertragsrechts oder aber des Verbraucherschutzrechts, erscheinen zwei überwiegende Tendenzen. Die erste Tendenz stellt vor allem eine Reaktion auf die nachweisbaren negativen Erfahrungen der sozialistischen bzw. kommunistischen Gesetzgebung dar, die allerdings gerade nach der Wende in Kodifikationsarbeiten jüngsten Datums bewahrt wurden. Die dualistische Auffassung der Regelung der privatrechtlichen Beziehung, das heißt Kodifikation des bürgerlichen Rechts einerseits und des Handelsrechts andererseits,[23] hatte geradezu bizarre Folgen. Diese Konsequenzen bestehen in einer doppelten Regelung eines Instituts auf die Art und Weise, die nicht nur den doppelten Grund erfasst, sondem manchmal auch dazu führt, dass die Regelung des bürgerlichen Rechts dem Verbraucher eine weniger günstige Stellung im Vergleich mit der Stellung des Unternehmers als nach den Bestimmungen des Handelsgesetzbuches gewährt. Es geht z.B. um das strengere Regime für einen Unternehmer, der als Vertragspartei gegenüber einem anderen Unternehmer für einen Schaden nach dem Handelsgesetzbuch haftet. Diese Haftung beruht auf dem Objektivprinzip,[24] im Vergleich mit dem milderen Regime eines Unternehmers gegenüber einem Verbraucher, dessen Haftung auf dem Subjektivprinzip beruht.[25] Die andere entscheidende Tendenz in der Theorie des gegenwärtigen Privatrechts knüpft an die traditionellen Gedanken der tschechischen Zivilrechtsschule (vor dem zweiten Weltkrieg) an. Diese gegenwärtige Orientierung der tschechischen Zivilrechtstheorie sieht den Weg (Methode zum besseren Privatrecht) nicht in der Diskussion, in der intellektuellen Tätigkeit, in einer Analyse, in der Rechtsvergleichung und in der Fortbildung des Rechts. Krönung ihrer Bemühungen wäre das schnellstmögliche Erreichen einer lückenlosen Kodifikation.[26] Eine solche erfordert ein komplexes Zivilgesetzbuch, dessen Grundlage der Entwurf des tschechoslowakischen bürgerlichen Gesetzbuchs von Jahre 1937 sein soll.[27]

---

23 Das römischrechtliche Konzept der Verträge und der Obligationen wurde lediglich im Gesetzbuch des internationalen Handels bewahrt, also in einem besonderen Regime, das auf handelsrechtliche Beziehungen mit ausländischen Subjekten mit der Ausnahme von Staaten des Rates der gegenseitigen wirtschaftlichen Hilfe (COMECON) angewandt wurde, da mit den sozialistischen Ländern innerhalb dieser Organisation besondere Vorschriften des zwingenden Charakters und 'der sozialistischen Herkunft' angewandt wurden. Die Häufigkeit der Anwendung des Gesetzbuches des internationalen Handels und seine allgemeine Bedeutung waren allerdings mehr oder weniger geringfügig.

24 Siehe oben unten II/1.

25 Vgl. § 373 HGB.

26 Vgl. § 420 ZGB.

27 Vgl. z.B. K. Eliáš, 'Poznámky k návrhu obecné části občanského zákoníku' (Anmerkungen zum Entwurf des allgemeinen Teils des ZGB), *Justiční praxe* 2002, 501.

2. Anfänge des Verbraucherschutzes

Die große Novelle des ZGB eus dem Jahre 1991 hat die Hauptursachen der Beschränkungen der Willensfreiheit beseitigt. Sie hat die in der Novelle der Verfassung bereits enthaltenen Änderungen konkret durchgeführt und hat wieder die einheitliche bürgerlichrechtliche Regelung eingeführt. Hingegen haben die bis dahin beträchtlich begünstigten staatlichen. bzw. öffentlich-rechtlichen Subjekte des Eigentums allmählich ein besonderes neues Regime gewonnen, das das Bedürfnis eines spezifischen, den Charakter des Eigentümers berücksichtigenden Kontrollsystems befriedigt hat. Klassische Vertragstypen wurden eingeführt bzw. entwickelt und das Recht der Schuldverhältnisse wurde restauriert. Eine Besonderheit der großen Novelle liegt darin, dass einige durch das sozialistische ZGB vom Jahre 1964 eingeführte Institute unberührt gelassen wurden, die neben den in der großen Novelle eingeführten traditionellen Instituten Anwendung finden (siehe z.B. § 612, der ausdrücklich eine parallele Existenz dieser Beziehungen verankert). Es handelt sich z.B. um die Regelung des sog. 'Verkaufes in einem Laden' (§ 612 *et seq.* ZGB), die neben den allgemeinen Bestimmungen über den Kaufvertrag anwendbar ist; in anderen Fallen gelten die neu eingeführte traditionelle Regelung einerseits und die alte immer noch geltende sozialistische Regelung andererseits im Rahmen eines Gesetzbuches nebeneinander. So findet z.B. der Mietvertrag als ein allgemeiner Vertragstyp seine Anwendung neben den Bestimmungen über die Wohnungsmiete, der Auftragsvertrag hat einen bestimmten Subtyp in Form des Vertrages über die Besorgung einer Angelegenheit, der Werkvertrag existiert gemeinsam mit dem Vertrag über die Herstellung einer Sache auf Bestellung und mit dem Vertrag über die Instandsetzung und Reparatur einer Sache. Auf ähnliche Weise gelten auf der einen Seite die allgemeine Regelung des Auftragsvertrages und auf der anderen die Regelung des Vertrages über die Besorgung einer Angelegenheit und Besorgung des Verkaufes einer Sache.

Die Ursache dieser Situation ist nur bei dem Kaufvertrag und seiner besonderen Modifikation – des Vertrages über den Verkauf in einem Laden – offensichtlich. In diesen Fällen unterscheidet das Gesetz ausdrücklich nach der Art des Subjektes, und für den Fall der Beziehung Unternehmer – Verbraucher behält (!) das Gesetz die 'alte' Regelung des 'Bürgers', der im vorliegenden Falle eigentlich ein Verbraucher ist. Die Bestimmungen des Vertrages über den Verkauf in einem Laden sind zwingender Natur. Diesen Charakter haben allerdings auch die Bestimmungen des ZGB, die auf das Verhältnis zu einem Verbraucher keine Anwendung finden. Der zwingende Charakter dieser Vorschriften (siehe § 2 Abs. 3 des ZGB) ist ihrem Wortlaut zu entnehmen. In dieser Hinsicht bleibt die geltende Regelung des ZGB im Rahmen der alten sozialistischen Regelung, die in Kraft geblieben ist. Im Übrigen wird auch das Handelsgesetzbuch durch die Tendenz der zwingenden Auffassung des Privatrechts gekennzeichnet, indem dieses Gesetzbuch mit einer enumerativen Aufzählung der zwingenden Bestimmungen (§ 263 HGB) sinnwidrig die Willensautonomie beschränkt.

Der Charakter der zwingenden Normen wurde auch in anderen vom ZGB geregelten Bereichen beibehalten. Diese Regelung konnte auf den ersten Blick auch dahin ausgelegt werden, dass sie nach ihrem Sinn und Zweck dem Verbraucher dienen soll, dessen Stellung dem Unternehmer gegenüber verbessert werden sollte. Die Bestimmungen des Zivilgesetzbuches finden jedoch auch in durchaus ausgeglichenen Beziehungen ihre Anwendung. Da der Verbraucherschutz als ein möglicher Zweck der Regelung nicht festzustellen ist, ist zu konstatieren, dass die zwingende Regelung zugunsten des Verbrauchers vom Gesetzgeber nicht beabsichtigt wird. Übrigens ist der Begriff des Verbrauchers im Zivilgesetzbuch überhaupt nicht definiert. Paradoxerweise befindet er sich in bestimmten Beziehungen Bürger – Bürger (Verbraucher) in einer schlechteren Position als in der Beziehung Bürger – Unternehmer (vgl. III/1), wie z.B. in den Vertragsverhältnissen, die durch das ZGB einerseits und durch das Handelsgesetzbuch andererseits geregelt sind.[28]

3. Besondere Fragen des Verbraucherschutzes im Zivilrecht

Um die vorherigen Erwägungen zu bewerten, muss man feststellen, dass sich die tschechische Regelung noch nicht vom bisherigen Konzept des sozialistischen bürgerlichen Rechts befreit hat, dessen Grundlagen bereits durch das Zivilgesetzbuch vom Jahre 1950 und vor allem durch das ZGB vom Jahre 1964 gelegt wurden. Indem die große Novelle bestimmte Eingriffe in die sozialistische Konzeption gebracht und neben dem ZGB die Grundlagen des modernen Handelsrechts geschaffen hat, wurden einerseits einige grundlegende Beschränkungen der privatrechtlichen Autonomie aufgehoben; auf der anderen Seite jedoch wurde der Zustand der Gesetzgebung infolge der doppelten Regelung (siehe die Regelung einiger Vertragstypen wie Mandatsvertrag, Kommissionsvertrag oder Kreditvertrag) unübersichtlich. Klarzustellen ist, dass es sich um eine weitere Art und Weise der Verdopplung der Regelungen handelt. Es geht also nicht um die parallele Regelung, auf die ich bereits oben kritisch aufmerksam gemacht habe und die sich innerhalb des ZGB befindet.

a. Eine zersplitterte Regelung

Alle Verbraucherschutzrichtlinien wurden bereits umgesetzt. Die Produkthaftungsrichtlinie wurde in einem besonderen Gesetz verankert, die Richtlinie für Haustürgeschäfte fand ihren Ausdruck im § 57 ZGB, die Richtlinie über

---

[28] Vgl. F. Zoulík, *op. cit.* n. 2, 133; K. Eliáš, *op. cit.* n. 19, 105 *et seq.*

missbräuchliche Klauseln wurde ein Teil des allgemeinen Teils des ZGB (§ 55 f.), die Fernabsatzrichtlinie wurden im allgemeinen Teil des Zivilgesetzbuches umgesetzt. Die Pauschalreiserichtlinie ist auch als ein besonderer Vertragstypus im ZGB geregelt. Auch die Verbrauchsgüterkaufsrichtlinie und Timesharing-Richtlinie wurden Teil des ZGB. Für die Umsetzung der Verbraucherkreditrichtlinie hat man ein neues Gesetz geschaffen.[29]

b. Begriff des Verbrauchers

Der Verbraucher ist ein Konsument, der Dienstleistungen benutzt und Waren für seinen persönlichen Gebrauch verbraucht. Ein auf diese Art und Weise definiertes Subjekt, das sich von dem im Gesetz über den Verbraucherschutz abgegrenzten Begriff unterscheidet, ist in manchen Hinsichten heutzutage benachteiligt. Seine Stellung ist zwar formell der Stellung eines geschädigten Unternehmers gleichgestellt, trotzdem besteht in der Position dieser beiden Subjekte ein wesentlicher Unterschied. Dieser Unterschied stellt sich in vielen Richtungen eindeutig heraus. Vornehmlich besitzt der Verbraucher eine ganz unterschiedliche Verhandlungskraft, sowohl beim Abschluss eines Vertrages, bei der Benutzung einer Dienstleistung oder beim Kauf einer Ware, als auch bei der Geltendmachung seiner Rechte im Zusammenhang mit der Haftung eines Unternehmers. Der Unternehmer stellt einen Spezialisten in seinem Bereich dar, ihm stehen manchmal ganze Teams von Angestellten und externen Beratern zur Verfügung. Bei dem Verbraucher[29a] handelt es sich dagegen in zahlreichen Fällen um eine unerfahrene Person sowohl bei den Verhandlungen mit dem Unternehmer, als auch bei dem Umgang mit der Dienstleistung bzw. den Waren. Seine Unerfahrenheit besteht unter anderem auch deshalb, weil ihm unvergleichbar weniger Informationen zur Verfügung stehen als dem Unternehmen und häufig erhält er die relevanten Informationen nicht. Der Verbraucher ist oft einem Überraschungsmoment ausgesetzt: infolge der oben beschriebenen Umstände wird er zum Adressaten einer Werbung, die auf seine emotionale Sphäre gerichtet ist. Manchmal wird der Verbraucher zum Konsumenten von Risikoprodukten und zum Adressaten von Dienstleistungen, die mit einem bestimmten, häufig hohen Risiko verbunden sind.

Die tschechische Gesetzgebung enthält bislang, insbesondere bezüglich der Zahl der einzelnen legislativen Akten, überwiegend einen verwaltungsrechtlichen (administrativen) Verbraucherschutz. Verkannt wird dabei die Unverzichtbarkeit des bürgerlichen Rechts und des zivilrechtlichen Verbraucherschutzes.

---

29 Siehe das Gesetz Nr. 634/1992 SIG., in der Fassung der späteren Gesetze.

29a Dazu vgl auch L. Tichý, Pojem spotřebitele českém a evropském právu (Begriff des Verbrauchers im tschechischen und europäischen Recht), in: CEFRES, Česká a francouská legislativa ochrany spotřebitele (Tschechische und Französische Gesetzgebung des Verbraucherschutzes), Praha 2003, 131–161.

Wie bereits oben erwähnt, kennt das ZGB den Begriff des Verbrauchers erst infolge der Novelle im Jahre 2000.[30] In der tschechischen Gesetzgebung wird der Begriff des 'Verbrauchers' im Verbraucherschutzgesetz[31] in § 2 Abs. 1 Buchst. a) dahin definiert, dass ein Verbraucher eine natürliche ader juristische Person ist, die Erzeugnisse einkauft, oder die Dienstleistungen benutzt zu einem anderen Zweck als zur unternehmerischen Tätigkeit mit diesen Erzeugnissen oder Dienstleistungen.

c. Die Art und Weise der Umsetzung der einzelnen EG-Richtlinien im Bereich des Verbrauchervertragsrechts in das tschechische Recht

i. Allgemeines

Aus den Erfahrungen der Mitgliedstaaten wissen wir, in welcher Weise, d.h. mit welcher Rechtstechnik, die Richtlinien des bürgerlichen Rechts in die nationalen Rechtsordnungen umgesetzt wurden.[32] In einigen Fallen wurden die Richtlinien auf eine eingehende, die Rahmenbestimmungen der Richtlinien ausführende, Art und Weise umgesetzt. Man kann von einer extensiven Form der Harmonisierung sprechen. In anderen Fällen kommt es praktisch zu einer wortwörtlichen Übernahme der Richtlinie, insbesondere, wenn die Richtlinie insoweit konkret und bestimmt ist, dass ihre weitere Konkretisierung, Ausführung oder sogar Abweichung von ihrem Wortlaut zum Risiko führen würden, dass die entsprechende innerstaatliche Norm mit der europäischen Vorschrift nicht vereinbar wäre. Die genannten Methoden sind für die Gesetzgeber der Mitgliedstaaten charakteristisch, z.B. hält sich der griechische Gesetzgeber in der Regel an die minimale Konzeption, während der deutsche, österreichische oder der niederländische Gesetzgeber eine sehr extensive Harmonisierung verwirklicht, falls es die Richtlinien ermöglichen und falls es im Einklang mit den jeweiligen Rechtsordnungen und ihrer Rechtspolitik steht.

Es ist zweifellos, dass diese zwei Methoden auch mit einer anderen Problematik zusammenhängen. Es geht um das Problem der Form bzw. der Rechtsquellen, in die die Richtlinien umgesetzt wurden. Wenn die Richtlinien in spezielle Gesetze umgesetzt werden, zeichnen sie sich durch die extensive Harmonisierung aus, während im Falle der Umsetzung der Richtlinien in Gesetzbücher von der minimalen Harmonisierung ausgegangen wird. Das ist mit der Tatsache verbunden, dass die einzelnen Rechtsquellen als selbständige Regimes funktionieren sollen, ohne eine subsidiäre Anwendung von anderen

---

[30] Vgl. Gesetz Nr. 367/2000 Slg.

[31] Vgl. Gesetz Nr. 634/1992 Slg.

[32] Siehe unter vielen auch E. Hondius, 'Consumer Law and Private Law: Where the Twain Shall Meet', in: L. Krämer *et al.* (eds.), *Liber amicorum Norbert Reich*, 315.

Vorschriften. Auch das erklärt die extensive Harmonisierung im Falle von besonderen Gesetzen und die minimale Harmonisierung bei der Eingliederung der Richtlinien in Kodizes. Die Gesetzbücher bilden die unmittelbare Rechtsstruktur und insbesondere ihre allgemeinen Teile werden zu einem komplementären Bestandteil der besonderen Bestimmungen, die die Umsetzung des Richtlinienrechts darstellen. Ein Beispiel ist das niederländische Bürgerliche Gesetzbuch, das die Richtlinien sehr 'sparsam' handhabt, während z.B. das Verbraucherkreditgesetz ein Beispiel einer extensiven Harmonisierung darstellt.[33]

ii. Die Haustürgeschäfte (Richtlinie Nr. 85/577)

In diesem Fall unterscheiden sich die tschechische und die europäische Regelung im Folgenden:[34] das tschechische ZGB (§ 57) gewährt beschränkteren Schutz im Falle, dass der Verbraucher den Unternehmer um einen Besuch gebeten hat, also um den Vertragsabschluss außerhalb von Geschäftsräumen, aber zur Zeit der Bitte wusste oder konnte der Verbraucher nicht wissen, dass die Lieferung bzw. die Gewährung von anderen Waren oder Dienstleistungen als denen, hinsichtlich deren er den Unternehmer[34a] um den Besuch gebeten hat, zur unternehmerischen oder anderen Erwerbstätigkeit des Unternehmers gehören.

Die Regelung dieses Schutzes im ZGB ist enger, da die Richtlinie auch auf die Verträge angewandt wird, die außerhalb von Geschäftsräumen abgeschlossen wurden, obwohl das Angebot für den Verbraucher vor der Annahme dieses Angebotes durch den Unternehmer verbindlich war.

Demgegenüber erweitert das tschechische ZGB den Schutz im Gegensatz zur Richtlinie auch auf juristische Personen.

Der tschechische Gesetzgeber hat hingegen keinen Gebrauch von der Möglichkeit der Einschränkung des Verbraucherschutzes gemacht, die darauf beruht, die Mindesthöhe der von dem Verbraucher gewährten Leistung zu beschränken, wobei der Wert dieser Leistung 60 Euro nicht überschreiten darf (Art. 3 Abs. 1 der Richtlinie).

Im Gegensatz dazu entsteht eine unklare Lösung, wenn die beschränkende Bestimmung im Zivilgesetzbuch, die die Anwendung des Gesetzes ausschließt (§ 57 Abs. 4 Buchst. d)), lediglich die Versicherungsgebühr betrifft, obwohl die Richtlinie diese Einschränkung für Versicherungsverträge festsetzt.

---

[33] Vgl. L. Tichý, 'Zivilrecht' in: J. Zemánek und M. Paschke, *Das tschechische Privat- und Wirtschaftsrecht unter dem Einfluss des Europäischen Rechts* (2004), 35 *et seq*.

[34] Vgl. K. Eliáš, M. Zuklínová, *Principy a východiska nového kodexu soukromého práva* (Prinzipien und Ansätze des neuen Gesetzbuchs des Privatrechts) (2001) 105.

[34a] In diesem Fall wendet der Gesetzgeber einen sehr unpräzisen Ausdruck an: nicht Unternehmer, sondern 'Lieferant', was eine wörtliche (sklavische) Übersetzung aus dem Englischen (supplier) ist.

iii. Schutz des Reisenden (Richtlinie Nr. 90/314)

Im Falle des Schutzes des Reisenden unterscheidet sich die tschechische von der europäischen Regelung vom systematischen Gesichtspunkt aus. Sie ist aber ausführlicher und relativ befriedigend. Allerdings im Gegensatz zu anderen europäischen Staaten, die diese Richtlinie übernommen haben, hat der tschechische Gesetzgeber ihren Inhalt in zwei Vorschriften umgesetzt, und zwar in das Gesetz Nr. 159/1999 SlG., über einige Bedingungen für Unternehmen auf dem Gebiet der Reiseverkehrs. Des Weiteren hat er das ZGB geändert, indem er in dieser Vorschrift den Reisevertrag neu geregelt hat (siehe Kapitel 21 des fünften Teiles, § 852a *et seq.*). Das erste der zitierten Gesetze enthält auch verwaltungsrechtliche Vorschriften, die nur einige mit der Richtlinie vergleichbare Erfordernisse sicherstellen. Im ZGB befinden sich lediglich Grundbestimmungen über den Reisevertrag ohne Bestimmungen über die Grundbedingungen dieses Vertrages. Aus diesem Grunde ist die Regelung gewissermaßen unübersichtlich.

Im Hinblick auf den persönlichen Anwendungsbereich ist der Schutz im tschechischen Recht beschränkter. Die EG-Richtlinie, zum Unterschied von anderen Regelungen auf diesem Gebiet, schützt nicht nur den Verbraucher als eine natürliche Person, sondern auch juristische Personen, die Dienstleistungen im Bereich des Reiseverkehrs vermitteln, daher auch Reisen für eigene Verbraucher – in der tschechischen Terminologie Kunden. Während der Betreiber eines Reisebüros ein Unternehmer ist, kann nach der Logik des ZGB ein Nichtunternehmer die geschützte Person werden, insbesondere eine natürliche Person. Deshalb kann die Regelung des ZGB den Vermittler der Reisedienstleistungen (einen Unternehmer) nicht schützen.

Eine der Bedingungen des Reisevertrages stellt der Katalog dar, der als eine allgemeine Auskunft über die angebotenen Dienstleistungen dient. Das tschechische und das europäische Recht unterscheiden sich hinsichtlich der Pflichten der Reisebüros betreffend den Inhalt des Katalogs voneinander. Die tschechische Regelung (§ 10 des Gesetzes Nr. 159/1999 SIG.) ist sehr ausführlich und enthält einige in der europäischen Regelung nicht verankerten Erfordernisse. Die europäische Regelung (Art. 3 Abs. 2) enthält wiederum einige auf den Katalog bezogene Bedingungen, die die tschechische Regelung nicht vorschreibt, wie etwa Preisbestimmungen. Dadurch unterscheiden sich beide Regelungen; auf der einen Seite ist die tschechische Regelung für den Verbraucher günstiger, von einem anderen Gesichtspunkt aus weniger günstig als die europäische Regelung.

iv. Missbräuchliche Vertragsklauseln (Richtlinie Nr. 93/13)

Die Übernahme dieses Regelung in die tschechische Rechtsordnung wurde auf eine seltsame Art und Weise verwirklicht. Ihr Text wurde im Allgemeinen Teil des Zivilgesetzbuches (§ 55 *et seq.*) umgesetzt. Aufgrund ihres Charakters gehören diese Bestimmungen zwar in den Allgemeinen Teil, jedoch an eine andere Stelle als dort, wo sie letztendlich eingegliedert wurden, nämlich zwischen den im Fernabsatz (Verbraucherschutz hinsichtlich des Vertragsabschlusses) und den außerhalb von Geschäftsräumen abgeschlossenen Verträge. Der Zweck der Richtlinie Nr. 93/13 ist es, die Verbraucher vor missbräuchlichen Klauseln zu schützen, d.h. vor den ohne eine Verhandlungsmöglichkeit abgeschlossenen Verträgen (sog. Adhäsionsverträge), falls der Inhalt dieser Verträge im Widerspruch mit dem Grundsatz des guten Glaubens zum Nachteil der Verbraucher ein wesentliches und unberechtigtes Missverhältnis zwischen den Rechten und Pflichten der Vertragsparteien (vgl. Art. 3 Abs. 1 der Richtlinie) verursacht.

Des Weiteren ist bemerkenswert, dass die 11 Artikel enthaltende Richtlinie nur durch Bestimmungen im Umfang von zwei Paragraphen umgesetzt wurde. Die tschechische Regelung unterscheidet sich in beträchtlichem Maß von der europäischen Bestimmung, sowohl durch die wesentlich weitere Festsetzung des Anwendungsbereichs der tschechischen Regelung, als auch durch die Nichteinhaltung von manchen wichtigen in der europäischen Vorlage festgesetzten Prinzipien.

Der Schutz kommt dem Verbraucher als Vertragspartei aller Vertragstypen zugute, die er mit dem Unternehmer abgeschlossen hat. Die tschechische Regelung der missbräuchlichen Klauseln bezieht sich nur auf die Verträge, bei denen der Verbraucher ihren Inhalt nicht beeinflussen konnte, sei es wegen der formulierten Standardverträge oder auch aus anderen Gründen (Art. 3 Abs. 2 der Richtlinie).

Der gesetzliche Schutz zeichnet sich neben dem oben genannten weiteren sachlichen auch durch den umfangreicheren persönlichen Anwendungsbereich aus. Unter einem Verbraucher wird nicht nur die natürliche Person verstanden, sondern auch eine juristische Person, die beim Abschluss und bei der Erfüllung des Vertrages nicht im Rahmen ihrer Handels- und unternehmerischen Tätigkeit handelt.

Der Unterschied besteht in der Formulierung des Grundinhaltes der Definition des Verbrauchers. Während die europäische Regelung vom Zweck des Vertrages ausgeht, erachtet die tschechische Regelung den Rahmen für wichtig, in dem die Person handelt, und der die Handelsverträge oder andere unternehmerische Tätigkeit nicht betrifft. Dies stellt eine bemerkenswerte Divergenz dar.

Eindeutig beträchtliche Nachteile für die Verbraucher bereitet die Tatsache, dass die Kriterien, nach denen die Missbräuchlichkeit der konkreten Bestimmungen beurteilt wird, nicht vorhanden sind. Die im Art. 4 der Richtlinie enthaltene Regel kommt im Zivilgesetzbuch nicht vor. Das stellt einen grundsätzlichen Mangel an Rechtssicherheit dar.

Das Zivilgesetzbuch ist im Verhältnis zum Verbraucher absolut zwingend. Der Verbraucher kann auf die ihm durch das Gesetz gewährten Rechte nicht verzichten oder sich mit einer Schmälerung seiner Vertragsposition einverstanden erklären (§ 55 Abs. 1 ZGB). Es stellt sich aber die Frage, inwieweit der Verzicht auf Rechte auch die Verschlechterung der Vertragsposition bedeuten kann. Der zwingende Charakter, der zugleich offensichtlich die absolute Ungültigkeit (Nichtigkeit) des Rechtsgeschäfts bewirkt, kann auch zum Nachteil der Verbraucher wirken.

Das Bürgerliche Gesetzbuch enthält keine Schutzregelung, die auf der Pflicht des Unternehmers (im Wortlaut des ZGB des Lieferanten), die Klarheit und Verständlichkeit von allen schriftlichen Vertragsbestimmungen zu beachten, beruht.

Einen weiteren Unterschied stellt das Grundkriterium des Ungleichgewichtes des materiellen Charakters dar. Die Grundvoraussetzung für die Beurteilung der Vertragsbestimmungen ist das Postulat des guten Glaubens. Die Charakteristik einer missbräuchlichen Klausel in einem Vertrag ist der Konflikt mit diesem Grundsatz, der ein wesentliches und unbegründetes Missverhältnis der Rechte und Pflichten der Vertragsparteien, zum Nachteil der Verbraucher verursacht. In dieser Hinsicht ist das ZGB eindeutig freundlicher dem Verbraucher gegenüber, da die Grundvoraussetzung für den missbräuchlichen Charakter einer Vertragsbestimmung nicht das wesentliche und unbegründete Missverhältnis, sondern lediglich ein beträchtliches Ungleichgewicht zwischen den Rechten und Pflichten ist.

v. Vertragsabschluss im Fernabsatz (Richtlinie Nr. 97/7)

Diese Richtlinie wurde in den Allgemeinen Teil des Zivilgesetzbuches (siehe § 52 *et seq.*) umgesetzt, da es sich um eine Kontrolle von den unter besonderen Umständen abgeschlossenen Vertragen handelt. Die Vertragsparteien sind nicht an einem Ort anwesend und darüber hinaus benützen sie Fernkommunikationsmittel. Der Schutz bzw. der Inhalt des in der tschechischen Rechtsordnung verankerten Schutzregimes unterscheidet sich kaum von der europäischen Vorlage.

Der Anwendungsbereich dieser Regelung bezieht sich auch auf die juristischen Personen, die ebenso als Verbraucher betrachtet werden, vorausgesetzt, dass sie nicht im Rahmen ihrer Handels- oder einer anderen unternehmerischen Tätigkeit handeln. Der Unterschied in beiden Regelungen, diesmal zugunsten des tschechischen Verbrauchers, besteht in der Regelung des Rechts auf Rücktritt (Widerruf). Die Rücktrittsfrist betragt gemäß der Richtlinie 7 Tage ab der Leistungsabnahme (vgl. Art. 6 Abs. 1 und 3), wogegen im tschechischen Zivilgesetzbuch diese Frist 14 Tage beträgt (siehe § 53 Abs. 6 des ZGB).

4. Der letzte Versuch des neuen ZGB: ein spezielles Verbraucherschutzgesetz?

Das Konzept des neuen ZGB geht davon aus, dass die Problematik der schwächeren Partei bzw. des Verbrauchers in einem speziellen Gesetz geregelt werden sollte. Mit anderen Worten soll diese Problematik nicht Teil des ZGB werden. Die Begründung ist salopp: wegen der Veränderlichkeit dieser Materie ist es angeblich einfacher, das normale Verbraucherschutzgesetz als das ZGB zu ändern, um das EG-Recht umzusetzen.

IV. LÖSUNGSANSATZ

Es stellt sich die Frage, ob man die Verbrauchschutzproblematik separat regeln und aus dem Zivilgesetzbuch aussondern, oder aber ob man ein einziges Zivilgesetzbuch schaffen sollte, das auch den Verbraucherschutz erfasst. Damit vermeiden wir aber die Hauptfragen: Ist der Verbraucherschutz tragbar, soll der Schutz nicht für jedermann gelten? Wie weit soll der Schutz gehen? Soll z.B. auch der Grundstückskauf erfassen werden?

Das Beispiel der Tschechischen Republik zeigt eine inkonsequente Lösung. Es ist weder eine französische noch eine eher deutsche Lösung.

Es ist nicht nur eine technische Frage, sondern auch eine Frage des Systemsdenkens und ein praktisches Problem. Bei der zersplitterten Regelung kann es natürlich zu Überlappungen kommen und vor allem eine Gefahr entstehen, dass man die einzelnen Gesetze isoliert und separat von einer allgemeinen Regelung anwendet.

Bei der Kodifikation des vertraglichen Verbraucherschutzrechts sollte man von einigen Charakteristiken des geltenden tschechischen Privatrechts ausgehen:

Man kehrte zur viel zu großen Abstraktion der Rechtssätze zurück. Für die Umsetzung mancher EG-Richtlinien ist Verkürzung und dadurch auch erhöhte Abstraktion bezeichnend. Als Beispiel kann der Schutz gegen missbräuchliche Klauseln dienen. Für den unerfahrenen und durch ständige Veränderungen der Rechtsordnung strapazierten Richter ist diese Lösung kein effizientes Instrument.

Rechtsfindung sowie Gesetzes- und Rechtsgeschäftsauslegung stellen ein chronisches Problem dar. Die Dogmatik ist vollkommen unterentwickelt und unterschätzt.[35] Rechtsfortbildung und Richterrecht werden z.T. als dem Rechtsstaatsprinzip widersprechend scharf verurteilt.[36] Die Kreativität der Richter wurde ständig beeinträchtigt. Der Richter wagte nicht die allgemeinen Klauseln, die Treu und Glauben oder den Prinzipien der guten Sitten entsprachen (der Grundsatz des sozialistischen Zusammenlebens), anzuwenden,

---

[35] Man verwechselt die Interpretation der Gesetze und Auslegung der Rechtsgeschäfte (vgl. J. Švestka, Kommentierungen zu § 35 ZGB in: O. Jehlička, J. Švestka und M. Škárová, *op. cit.* n. 2, 175 *et seq.* und das Lehrbuch des Zivilrechts (Knappová, Švestka, *Občanské právo hmotné*, 3. Aufl. (2002), 1352s), wo die Auslegung des Rechtsgeschäfts innerhalb eines Absatzes (!) behandelt wird.

[36] Vgl. z.B. E. Wagnerová, 'Precedent v právním řádu' (Zum Richterrecht), *Právní rozhledy*, 2001, 225 *et seq.*

um nicht den potentiellen Konflikt mit der kommunistischen Macht hervorzurufen.[37] Die Erfahrung und die Tradition einer eher passiven Einstellung stimulieren nicht zum kreativen Denken, sie schrecken eher davon ab. Dies ist einer der Faktoren, der den Gesetzgeber zu einer weniger abstrakten Ausdrucksweise verleiten sollte.

Der Gebrauch, die geltende Gesetzgebung und der Mangel an Ausbildung sowie relevanter Erfahrung haben die Tendenz zur Folge, die Parteiautonomie einzuschränken. Dies muss nicht notwendig mit dem Schutz der schwächeren Partei zusammenfallen. Die Kategorie, wie Treu und Glauben sind hier leere Gefäße.[38]

Die allgemeine Tendenz (Rechtstheorie, Rechtssprechung) bei der Behandlung der Störung und Mängel der Rechtsgeschäfte ist bezeichnend: nicht die Aufrechterhaltung, sondern ihre Beseitigung hat immer die Oberhand.

Dies ist für den Verbraucher nicht immer die beste Lösung.

Der Verbraucherschutz ist eine integrale Komponente des Zivilrechts. Es ist eine Kategorie, die auf unzählige Weise mit dem ganzen Organismus des Privatrechts verbunden ist. Wie die abschreckenden Beispiele der Anwendung der einzelne Gesetzbücher und andere die Selbstständigkeit beeinträchtigende Gesetze, durch die das Privatrecht zerstückelt wurde, zeigen, würde die Kumulation paralleler Regelungen nur dieselbe Gefahr darstellen. Dies spricht sehr mahnend und alarmierend gegen jegliche Absonderung des vertraglichen Verbraucherschutzes. Diese Regelung sollte auch formal ein Teil der Kodifikation des allgemeinen Privatrechts sein.

---

37 Zur sozialistischen Auslegungstheorie in der deutschen Literatur siehe J. Löbbe, *Sozialistische Rechtsanwendung* (1998) insbesondere 61 *et seq.* und B. Rüthers, 'Recht und Juristen in der Diktatur des Proletariats', *JZ* 1999, 1009 *et seq.*

38 Siehe J. Švestka, Kommentierung zum § 35/III in: O. Jehlička, J. Švestka und M. Škárová, *op. cit.* n. 2, 178. Zum Treu und Glauben Prinzip gibt es hier kein Wort (!).

Chapter 14

The Instrumentalist Conception of the *Acquis Communautaire* in Consumer Law and its Implications on a European Contract Law Code

Christoph U. Schmid,[1] *Bremen*

I. INTRODUCTION

It is frequently assumed that the consumer law *Acquis Communautaire* could be not only the forerunner to, but also a part of, a future European contract law code. Indeed, European consumer law directives now cover not only many different types of transactions such as doorstep sales, consumer credit, distance sales, package tours and time sharing rights. Also, there are two important horizontal directives, namely the unfair terms directive and the consumer sales directive, which are sometimes called a 'basic law for

[1] Prof. Dr., Ph.D. (EUI Florence), Director of the Centre for European Law and Politics (ZERP) at the University of Bremen. This contribution presents some results of my 'habilitation' thesis, '*Die Instrumentalisierung des Privatrechts durch die Europäische Union; Privatrecht und Privatrechtskonzeptionen in der Entwicklung der Europäischen Integrationsverfassung*', typescript, Munich, January 2004. It has benefited from the helpful comments of Geraint Howells and written observations by Jules Stuyck and Hugh Collins. The author is grateful to the Society of European Contract Law and its President Stefan Grundmann for their invitation to the annual 2004 conference in Vienna.

S. Grundmann, M. Schauer (eds), *The Architecture of European Codes and Contract Law*, 255–269

contracts' in Europe. Whereas about ten years ago European consumer law was often compared to scattered islands in an ocean of national private law, one might now speak of an archipelago – and with the plans for a European contract code, we may well be on the way towards a new European law continent surrounded by an ever smaller sea of national contract law. Also, as private law theorists and the German legislator in the 2002 reform of the law of contracts (which integrated all the major consumer contract law instruments into the *Bürgerliches Gesetzbuch*) have plausibly shown, a 'marriage of convenience' of consumer law and general contract law is possible.[2] The main problem perceived today as an obstacle to the further extension of the *Acquis* is its lack of coherence. Indeed, it does not possess an encompassing systematic concept. Instead its regulatory approach is selective and problem-oriented, which makes its interplay with national private law often very difficult.[3] Also, legal concepts such as damage are not used consistently; there are unfortunate gaps often due to political compromise. Many frictions, split-ups, overlaps and inconsistencies may be found among the various consumer law directives. It is the latter problems that the Commission wished to address in its latest strategy paper entitled: an 'Action Plan for A More Coherent Contract Law'.[4] But would a more coherent rewriting and possibly complementing of the *Acquis* really qualify as the basis for a new European contract law code? I would like to argue that this view is not entirely wrong, but is too simplistic. Indeed, it overlooks the significant conceptual divergence between the consumer law *Acquis* and traditional civil codes of continental European countries.

2 See J. Drexl, *Die wirtschaftliche Selbstbestimmung des Verbrauchers* (1998); H. Schulte-Nölke, *Europäisches Verbrauchervertragsrecht und deutsches bürgerliches Recht*, (2000). This 'marriage of convenience' is based on the assumption that an exclusively role-specific understanding of a consumer is too imprecise a basis for protective legal rules. Instead, it resorts to a situation-specific understanding of consumer law: protective rules are necessary to the extent that the functioning of private autonomy is hampered either by the complexity (e.g. time sharing contracts), the 'great temptations' of particular transactions (e.g. consumer credit), or by dangers typically arising from the particular circumstances of their conclusion (e.g. doorstep or distance sales). However, in a second and subordinate step, it still makes sense to ask whether such dangers typically exist for everyone or only for persons acting in a private capacity. Whereas the former seems to be true for sales law in general (every buyer runs the risk of getting goods with defects – with the effect that the consumer guarantee directive should not be limited to consumers), the latter may be correct for doorstep or distance sales (with the result that the limitation of these directives to consumers is plausible). Conceptually, defining consumer law primarily as a set of 'situation-specific' rules to re-establish private autonomy where it is threatened departs from the former understanding of a '*Sonderprivatrecht*' (a special protective regime for presumably weak subjects), but makes it an integral part of general private law.

3 For attempts at systematizing European private law see the contributions in S. Grundmann (ed.), *Systembildung und Systemdenken in Kerngebieten des Europäischen Privatrechts*, (2000).

4 COM(2003), 68 final.

II. THE CLASSIC CONCEPT OF EUROPEAN STYLE CIVIL CODES

Famously, classic European-style civil codes are based on three fundamental concepts: freedom and equality of all citizens, and justice as the key criterion to govern legal relationships – which in private law predominantly means commutative, not distributive justice.[5] Whereas freedom and equality are children of Enlightenment philosophies and the grand revolutions, the concept of justice is even older and famously originates from the Nikomachian Ethics by Aristotle. Freedom and equality require that every human being be capable of participating in legal relationships at his or her will and on equal terms. Capacity is no more restricted, and there is no more privileged treatment of certain individuals or social classes – in short, classic private law takes on a universal character. Commutative justice means in its strictest sense that the exchange of performances in contract law and the redress of damages in tort law shall be equivalent; in its weaker and perhaps more important version, it means that private law relationships shall be governed only by criteria originating in the relationship between the parties themselves – and not by reference to external political, social or economic goals.

This basic ethical concept of private law was shaped further in the evolution of the modern society, as a response to a changing social and economic environment, novel philosophical doctrines and alternating political convictions.[6] Thus, during the liberal era of the 19th century, the grand codifications such as the *Bürgerliche Gesetzbuch* were mostly restricted to commutative justice, largely without compensatory social mechanisms – which was often perceived as a usurpation of the bourgeoisie over the working class. Conversely, the active societal 'steering' and proliferation of compensatory mechanisms since about the 1920s, frequently labelled 'materialization', have increasingly transformed private law into a tool of social solidarity and distributive justice. Finally, the increased differentiation, complexity and fragmentation of modern societies, together with the rise of new technologies and communication media, have conferred upon contemporary private law the additional task of mediating among different social and economic systems and subsystems and ensuring the framework conditions for the effective realization of private autonomy and private ordering – a development which is captured in the buzzwords 'pluralization' and 'proceduralization'. In addition, the decline of centralized public law command and control tools, which are no longer able to cope with an ever more complex reality, has entailed a

5 On commutative and distributive justice in modern private law, see C.-W. Canaris, *Die Bedeutung der iustitia distributiva im deutschen Vertragsrecht*, (1997).

6 Classic accounts on the societal shaping of private law include F. Wieacker, *Industriegesellschaft und Privatrechtsordnung*, reprint, (1974), and J. Habermas, *Faktizität und Geltung* [English: Between facts and norms], 4th ed. (1994), pp. 468 *et seq.*

revival of decentralized ordering through private law or combined private–public arrangements.

Yet, throughout the evolutionary path of national private law, the weak version of commutative justice has always remained present. In fact, external social, economic and political goals – which may either favour one party such as workers or tenants or stand completely outside the party relationship as in the case of market integration concerns[7] – may and should be taken into consideration by lawmakers and interpreters. At any rate, however, the ordering of private law relationships must always respect the minimum requirements of justice among the parties. According to the famous Austrian author Franz Bydlinski, this means:[8] If one were to ignore the regulatory external dimension of a norm or decision hypothetically, it must still qualify as an outcome defendable on the grounds of justice alone – albeit other alternatives might serve justice even better. In summary, the party relationship must not be instrumentalised by external collective goals. This concept of private law and private autonomy is even constitutionally protected in some EU Member States. To quote but one example, the German *Bundesverfassungsgericht* has recently ruled that the high financial contributions which an employer is bound to make by way of maternity leave allowances granted to female employees under German labour law are unconstitutional[9] – ultimately because the employer does not receive an adequate counter-performance by the employee for these payments. Whilst it is socially highly desirable that women on maternity leave do not lose their income, the funding of it is a task of the community as a whole and not of the single employer, who should not have to sacrifice himself for it.

III. PRIVATE LAW USED AS AN INSTRUMENT FOR EUROPEAN INTEGRATION

As compared to the basic ethical-societal concept of national private law just described, the concept of European private law is very different. The Euro-

7 The protection of typically weak parties such as tenants and workers is principally characterised as an *external* goal here because it may go beyond commutative justice. In other words, it does not necessarily reflect the (true or hypothetical) will of the parties to a contract. However, in the perspective of economic analysis, certain socially motivated interventions into transactions are efficient – e.g. a certain degree of protection of a tenant against rent increase prevents the landlord from obtaining an undeserved monopoly rent corresponding to the tenant's removal costs (which may make him accept a higher rent than the market would otherwise allow in order to avoid moving). If one accepts this perspective, such social interventions may accordingly still be assigned to commutative justice. See e.g. H.-B. Schäfer/C. Ott, Die ökonomische Analyse des Rechts – Irrweg oder Chance der Rechtserkenntnis?, *JZ* 1988, 213, 218.

8 F. Bydlinski, *System und Prinzipien des Privatrechts*, (1996), 92 *et seq.*, 95 *et seq.*

9 See BVerfG JZ 2004, p. 354 with annotations by H. Kube.

pean Union is an integration project aiming at an ever closer union, the famous core of which is the institution of a single market.[10] By enabling the free circulation of goods, persons, services and capital and through undistorted competition, national markets are to be integrated, in order to enhance the production and distribution of goods through economies of scale. This integration programme is stipulated in the European treaties, often labelled constitution, and further operationalized and consolidated by secondary law. All law, irrespective of the traditional public-private divide, is accordingly used as a tool to achieve market integration objectives. As regards consumer policy and law, this was not even part of the original treaty of Rome, but was gradually added to the integration project from the 1972 Paris summit onwards. However, most legal measures could only be enacted after the introduction of qualified majority voting in the Single European Act of 1986. Even though consumer law also reflects early efforts to bring Europe closer to its citizens, it primarily constitutes genuine market regulation in fields typically involving transactions between businesses and non-professional final users of products and services. In line with this, there was no autonomous legal basis for consumer law until the Treaty of Amsterdam (and even the legal basis established there, article 153, paragraph 2, lit. b) TEC, has hardly ever been used since) and harmonization measures allegedly belonging to consumer law, including all consumer contract law directives, were normally enacted under the general basis for market regulation, articles 100 and 100a TEC (i.e. 94 and 95 TEC under the new numbering). As a consequence, the core objective of European consumer law is not social protection, but the establishment and the regulation of the Single Market.

Now, to what extent does this instrumentalist logic of European law in general, and of consumer law in particular, matter for the concept of private law? Fortunately enough, the ethical-societal concept of private law and the logic of market integration are to a large extent compatible and in many cases even mutually dependent and reinforcing. The European market, just as any other market economy, needs private law as its basic legal infrastructure – i.e. the legal framework enabling all kinds of market transactions. In contrast with most fields of economic regulation, the EC did not have to replace or harmonize core fields of private law such as contract or tort law in order to realize its integration project. Instead, it was able to make use of the existing national private law systems, which were similar enough to enable the realization of most market transactions without major obstacles.[11] Thus,

[10] The classic account on the development of the European legal constitution is J. H. H. Weiler, The Transformation of Europe, *Yale L.J.* 100 (1991/1992), p. 2423.

[11] In line with this, one of the first contributions on the harmonization of private law in Europe does not mention contract and tort law with a single word: See W. Hallstein, Angleichung des Privat- und Wirtschaftsrechts in der Europäischen Wirtschaftsgemeinschaft, *RabelsZ* 28 (1964), p. 211.

European consumer law is less about enabling than optimizing market transactions. Incidentally, this has been different in company law,[12] where the existing national institutions did not allow for sufficient compatibility among national systems – with the consequence that new European company forms (the Societas Europea, the European interest grouping and the European cooperative) had to be created and the compatibility of national ones established by means of the principle of mutual recognition (the *Centros*[13] jurisprudence).

On the other hand, private law itself, its scope and effectiveness are considerably enhanced through its integration into the common market.[14] This is true, first, in a territorial sense, in that the reach of private law instruments is extended beyond national borders. Moreover, as the European economic constitution forces Member States to do away with discriminating and restrictive national regulation ('deregulation'), the substantive scope left to societal self-regulation and private law as its principal tool considerably increases as well. In particular, as an effect of the deregulation of national monopolies, public undertakings and state aid, the re-regulation of the economy at the European level by means of private law is promoted ('private governance').[15]

Beyond that, in the field of private law, too, European law may play a positive constitutional 'moderating role', in that it controls the rationality and impartiality of national law and jurisprudence, and gives European citizens the right to second-guess their national sovereigns on common European grounds. Thus, in the recent *Heininger* follow-up case involving consumer credit and doorstep sales law, the ECJ is likely to reject the denial of the German *Bundesgerichtshof* to extend the effect of a consumer's withdrawal from a credit contract (concluded to acquire real property) to the interconnected purchase and mortgaging transactions.[16] Likewise, the *Centros*

---

12 On the evolution of European company law, see J. Wouters, European Company Law: Quo vadis?, *CMLR* 37 (2000), p. 257.

13 Case C-212/97, *Centros*, ECR 1999, I-1459 and the follow-up decision C-208/00, *Überseering*, ECR 2002, I-9919 and C-167/01, *Inspire Art*, of 30/9/03.

14 This finding has been explicated in the writings of P.-Ch. Müller-Graff, see *idem*, Basic freedoms-extending party autonomy across borders, in: S. Grundmann, W. Kerber and S. Weatherill (eds.), *Party autonomy and the role of information in the internal market*, (2001), 133.

15 See e.g. Ch. Joerges, 'The Market Without a State? States Without a Market?: Two Essays on the Law of the European Economy', *EUI Working Paper Law* No. 96/2.

16 Case C-350/03, *Schulte*. The reference decision of the Landgericht Bochum is reported in NJW 2003, 2612. Indeed, German jurisprudence had perverted effective consumer protection, because a consumer would be worse off after exercising the withdrawal right – he would then need to pay back the whole credit at once, as the installment arrangements would be void as a part of the credit contract. The original *Heininger* sage is well described by M. Franzen, 'Heininger' und die Folgen: ein Lehrstück zum Gemeinschaftsprivatrecht, *JZ* 2003, 321.

decision, in which the ECJ allowed European citizens to have companies established under a foreign law registered in their home states, is interpreted by some as a desirable correction of inadequate and inefficient national corporate capital rules – a correction not of market, but of Nation State failures, as Christian Joerges put it.[17]

Yet alongside these positive points, there is also a dark side to the use of private law as an integration tool. There is, indeed, a worrying tendency for private law to be excessively instrumentalized, which means that private parties are sacrificed to integration objectives. This may be illustrated by various examples drawn from consumer law.

IV. EXAMPLES OF EXCESSIVE INSTRUMENTALIZATION OF PRIVATE LAW BY THE EU

1. An Incoherent Consumer Model

The first examples deal with consumers' information rights. Of course, there is absolutely nothing wrong with information rights in themselves. As both economic analysis and contract practice show, information asymmetries among professional traders and consumers are a frequent type of market failure, which information rights are able to correct in many cases.[18] In line with this basic finding, information rights constitute the most prominent and frequent regulatory tool in European consumer law. This seems to be inspired by the model of an inadequately informed consumer who is able to make rational decisions only after adequate information. Thus, to quote but one example, in the recent *Cofidis* case,[19] the ECJ quashed national time limits restricting the exercise of consumer protection rights on the ground that consumers may ignore their rights completely, but needed to be protected all the same.

Conversely, as regards national information rights, these are often found to be inconsistent with the four market freedoms on proportionality grounds by the ECJ.[20] In particular, in the field of misleading advertising, national information rights requiring clear and unambiguous information are treated restrictively. In what boils down to an unrealistic assumption about market behaviour, consumers are for example supposed to recognize objectively

---

[17] See Ch. Joerges, Zur Legitimität der Europäisierung des Privatrechts. Überlegungen zu einem Recht-Fertigungs-Recht für das Mehrebenensystem der EU, *EUI Working Paper LAW* 2003/2.

[18] See generally, H. Fleischer, *Informationsasymmetrie im Vertragsrecht*, (2000).

[19] Case C-473/00, *Cofidis*, ECR 2002, I-10875.

[20] On the relationship of contract law and the market freedoms, see O. Remien, *Zwingendes Vertragsrecht und Grundfreiheiten des EGV*, (2003).

wrong, manipulative advertising statements[21] or foreign-language labels similar to well-known domestic products.[22] In this case, we seem to face a different model of a well-informed and intelligent consumer. As a result, consumer information requirements are construed widely in *European* consumer contract law, whereas *national* consumer protection-based limitations on the basic freedoms in national unfair competition law are construed narrowly. However, this distinction is by no means justifiable under private law, as –in the words of Stefan Grundmann – one should not require a lower degree of attention from a consumer entering into contractual negotiations than from a consumer reading advertisements in his armchair.[23]

The background to this jurisprudence seems to be that national consumer protection instruments, including information obligations, have been recognized as valid limitations of the basic freedoms in the famous *Cassis de Dijon*[24] decision. Therefore, a wide recognition of national information rights would reduce the *effet utile* of the market freedoms. At the end of the day, the different treatment of national and European information rights shows that the ECJ's true concern is not a uniform model of a consumer or even consumer protection as such, but the optimisation of the *effet utile* of Community law irrespective of its contents and objectives. Thus, consumer information in particular, and private law in general, are subordinated to integration purposes. Obviously, this approach prevents private law from adequately fulfilling its core task of realising justice between the parties.

2. Commercial Advertising Treated as Adequate Consumer Information in order to Override National Rules on Misleading Advertising: *GB-Inno*

In a similar, yet even more manipulative move, the ECJ has in the *GB-Inno*[25] case treated commercial advertising as information in the meaning of European consumer policy, so as to displace national rules on misleading advertising without having to balance them against market objectives in the first place: A Belgian supermarket chain was forbidden by a Luxembourg Court to distribute sales promotion leaflets in Luxembourg, which contained as advertising devices: (a) information on the limited duration of discounts on specific goods; and (b) comparisons of current with (higher) former prices

[21] Case C-470/93, *Mars*, ECR 1995, I-1923. In this decision, the ECJ argued that a consumer would not confuse the (larger) size of a '10% more' advertisement on a chocolate package with the actual (smaller) increase in quantity.

[22] Case C-369/89, *Piageme*, ECR 1991, I-2971.

[23] S. Grundmann, *Europäisches Schuldvertragsrecht*, (1999), 270, n. 106. For a similar critique, see H. Fleischer, Vertragsschlußbezogene Informationspflichten im Gemeinschaftsprivatrecht, *ZEuP* 2000, 791.

[24] Case 120/78, *Rewe/Bundesmonopolverwaltung für Branntwein*, ECR 1979, 649.

[25] Case C-362/88, ECR 1990, I-667.

(‘*Eigenpreisvergleiche*’ in German). Such market practices were at the time regarded as misleading and forbidden in Luxembourg and Germany, but allowed in all other Member States including Belgium. Consequently, a Belgian retail association challenged the Luxembourg prohibition as a violation of the free movement of goods. In its decision, the ECJ interpreted the free movement of goods in a passive dimension, as meaning not only that industries shall have the right to import goods to other Member States free of constraints, but that consumers also had the right to travel and shop freely in other Member States under the same conditions as the local population. According to the Court, this right had been negatively affected by the Luxembourg prohibition of the advertising leaflets, as this had deprived national consumers from access to advertising available in Belgium. In a further step, the ECJ rejected the justification of Luxembourg consumer protection law as a mandatory requirement in the general interest under the *Cassis de Dijon* doctrine. The main reason given by the Court was that EC consumer policy itself favoured unrestricted and accurate information over other consumer protection devices – as was evident already in the early EC consumer strategy papers. As a result, the ECJ has created a European consumer right to be protected against paternalistic national consumer protection (!), with the consequence that the restriction of free movement of goods by national consumer protection rationales is no longer justified.

In reality, this case is not about neutral consumer information as referred to in EC consumer policy, but about deliberately selective, and artificially created information for advertising purposes to stimulate consumers’ buying behaviour. The limited duration of the special offer generates a ‘now or never situation’, whereas the comparison with previous prices stresses the price difference, with the effect that the consumer’s attention will be diverted from considering the adequacy of the price. However, the national prohibition of such advertising not only protects consumers, but also (and perhaps even primarily) small- and medium-sized enterprises against the competition of large retailers – usually the only ones who can afford the market practices mentioned. Therefore, the true conflict in this case was not between a liberal European and a paternalistic national consumer model, but between the protection of consumers and small- and medium-sized enterprises (‘*Mittelstandsschutz*’) and market integration, that is economies of scale and uniform marketing practices in this case. This conflict might well have been legitimately decided in favour of economic efficiency, but not with the fake consumer protection argument relied upon by the Court. Instead, an honest and fair approach would have needed to balance the competing values and principles thoroughly – a task the ECJ has perhaps avoided because of its political implications. In summary, it is under the guise of general European consumer information policy (not even specific information rights laid down by European regulation) and commercial advertising treated as neutral information that market efficiency has trumped national protective regulation in this case.

3. National Information Rights Sacrificed to the Promotion of Market Access for Foreign Competitors: Axa Royale Belge

The previous cases have already shown that, even though information rights are the predominant tool of EC consumer law, they, too, may be displaced if counteracting higher-ranking market integration objectives. This tendency is confirmed by another instrumentalist line of case law in which information obligations have been considered violations of market freedoms, because they may dissuade consumers from specific market behaviour which is considered useful for integration purposes. As an example, one may quote the case *Axa Royale Belge*[26] decided by the ECJ in 2002, which deals with information rights under the Third Life insurance directive.[27] This directive contains an extensive catalogue of the information obligations of an insurer. Additional information, the directive stipulates, may only be required by national law to the extent that it is necessary to a proper understanding by the policy-holder of the essential elements of the contract. Now, a Belgian provision stipulated that life insurance policies had inter alia to inform the policy-holder that cancellation, reduction or surrender of an existing contract before its end date would generally be detrimental to his or her position. As regards this provision, the ECJ argued that it was not only too general and vague, but that it did not encourage the consumer to compare between insurance policies offered on the Single Market. Instead, it encouraged him to stick to existing agreements. In doing so – and this was the decisive rationale – the information duty under Belgian law negatively affected the access of foreign insurers to the domestic market. On these grounds, the ECJ found the Belgian provision incompatible with the insurance directive.

Whilst the Belgian provision may actually have such protectionist side-effects, one should not ignore its legitimate core objective. In fact, it addresses the notorious phenomenon that the termination of life insurance policies before the end date is normally economically to the detriment of the policy-holder. This is generally the case irrespective of the fact that foreign competitors may offer a certain insurance policy at better conditions. Unlike the rather redundant amount of information prescribed under the directive, which may even cause counterproductive information overload,[28] the Belgian information requirement is probably more appropriate in terms of making the consumer examine the consequences of an early termination of a life insurance contract. If this simple but effective information is forbidden, it

---

26 Case C-386/00, ECR 2002, I-2209.

27 Council Directive 92/96/EEC, OJEC 1992 L 360/1.

28 On the phenomenon of information overload in European consumer law, see M. Martinek, '*Unsystematische Überregulierung und kontraintentionale Effekte im Europäischen Verbraucherschutzrecht oder: Weniger wäre mehr*', in: S. Grundmann (ed.), *Systembildung und Systemdenken in Kerngebieten des Europäischen Privatrechts*, (2000), p. 511.

means that the ECJ prefers consumers to incur potentially high financial losses when prematurely terminating life insurance policies rather than to diminish market access opportunities for foreign insurance companies. In other words, contractual justice among the parties is again sacrificed to the promotion of the integration of the Single Market.

4. The Abolition of Minimum Harmonization and its Consequences: The Example of the Product Liability Cases of 25/4/2002

The issue of minimum harmonization provides another example of European consumer law tending to favour, not consumers, but European enterprises – in attempting to provide them with a uniform regulatory framework which reduces transaction and market access costs. This trend is visible in the current plans of the Commission to abolish the minimum harmonization principle[29] which is contained in most consumer contract law directives since 1990. This principle aims to grant consumers the best possible protection by allowing the Member States to retain stricter national consumer laws than those contained in European directives.

The effects of the planned abolition of this principle have already made themselves visible in recent court jurisprudence. As compared with most consumer contract law directives, the 1985 product liability directive[30] does not contain a minimum harmonization clause, though most commentators read such a clause into it on account of its framework character and the large number of gaps.[31] This is fully plausible as the fragmentary texture of the directive cannot reasonably be expected to do justice to this complex and socially highly sensitive matter governed by different national regulatory traditions.[32] However, in three cases decided on 25 April 2002, the ECJ found that no minimum harmonization principle could be read into the directive in the light of its paramount goal of establishing uniform regulation of product liability – so as to prevent market distortions when undertakings in one State are forced to pay more to victims of dangerous products than in

29 European Commission, Consumer Policy 2002–2006, (2002), approved by the Council of Ministers on 2 December 2002, OJEC 2002 C 11/1.

30 Council Directive 85/374/EEC, OJEC L 210/29, 1985.

31 See G. Brüggemeier, *Produkthaftung und Produktsicherheit*, *ZHR* 152 (1988), pp. 511, 531, 534; G. Howells, Product Liability – A History of Harmonization, in A. Hartkamp et al. (eds.), *Towards a European Civil Code*, 3rd ed. (forthcoming).

32 See H. Koch, '*Internationale Produkthaftung und Grenzen der Rechtsangleichung durch die EG-Richtlinie*', *ZHR* 152 (1988), p. 537; the incomplete character of the directive becomes visible also in its complex interplay with product safety law, see G. Howells, 'The Relationship between Product Liability and Product Safety – Understanding a Necessary Element in the European Product Liability Through a Comparison with the US Position', *Washburn L.J.* 39 (1999–2000), p. 305.

others.[33] In doing so, the ECJ deprived a Spanish plaintiff, whose health had been seriously affected by the transfusion of infected blood in a public hospi tal, of a claim for damages against the hospital existing under a Spanish product liability statute.[34] The reason for this was that – unlike under Spanish law which followed US law in this respect – the victim can only sue the producer of the defective product, but in general not another member in the commercial chain, such as the hospital which had not produced the infected blood itself in this case. Alongside the Spanish case, the ECJ convicted France and Greece of a treaty infringement procedure as they had not transposed the Directive word by word into national law, but had tried to remedy some of its apparent shortcomings such as the minimum threshold required for the restitution of damages (*Selbstbeteiligung* in German, and *franchise* or *franchigia* respectively in French and Italian).[35]

This jurisprudence is very unfortunate in that it sacrifices national consumer protection without any visible gain for European industries. Indeed, the narrow scope of application of the European directive and its many gaps render its objective to provide European undertakings with a uniform product liability regime absolutely illusory.[36] As a result, the ECJ has in this case

[33] The rejection of this jurisprudence seems to be quasi unanimous among European commentators: See G. Viney, '*L'Interprétation par la CJCE de la Directive du 25 Juillet 1985 sur la Responsabilité du Fait des Produits Défectueux*', *La Semaine Juridique*, (2002), I 177, 1945; J. Calais-Auloy, '*Menace européene sur la jurisprudence francaise concernant l'obligation de sécurité du vendeur professionel*', *Recueil Le Dalloz* (2002), No. 31, 1458; A. Palmieri and R. Pardolesi, '*Difetti del prodotto e del diritto privato europeo*', *Il Foro Italiano* IV, 2002, 296; Ch. Joerges (n. 17) pp. 30 *et seq*.; M. E. Arbour, 'Compensation for Damage Caused by Defective Drugs: European Private Law between Safety Requirements and Free-Market Values', *ELJ* 10 (2004) p. 87. A more positive assessment seems to underlie the comment by R. Schaub, '*Abschied vom nationalen Produkthaftungsrecht? Anspruch und Wirklichkeit der EG-Produkthaftung*', *ZEuP* 2003, 562.

[34] Case C-183/99, *González Sánchez*, ECR 2002, I-3901.

[35] Cases C-52/00, *Commission vs. France*, ECR 2002, I-3827 and C-154/00, *Commission vs. Greece*, ECR 2002, I-3879.

[36] See the telling comment by a leading German practitioner: J. Schmidt-Salzer and H. Hollmann, *Kommentar EG-Richtlinie Produkthaftung*, Vol. 1, (1986), Einl. IV Zweck der EG-Richtlinie, pp. 135 *et seq*., note 73 *et seq*., 79: '*Hält man sich die Milliarden und Abermilliarden von Produkten vor Augen, die jährlich innerhalb des Gemeinsamen Marktes veräußert werden, ist bereits bei Beschränkung auf den in der Richtlinie geregelten Bereich (Personenschäden, private Sachschäden) betriebswirtschaftlich der Nachweis, daß innerhalb der Europäischen Gemeinschaft die unterschiedlichen Haftungsregeln die Warenströme beeinflussen, abwegig. Dazu sind die Unterschiede des Haftungsrechts letztlich zu gering und treten Produkthaftungsansprüche relativ viel zu selten auf. Die Beobachtung des Anteils, den (unter Ausklammerung 1. der US-Schäden, 2. der gewerblichen Sachschäden und 3. der Produkt-Vermögensschäden die sog. konventionellen Produktschäden innerhalb der Betriebshaftpflichtversicherung haben, belegt eindeutig, daß es sich im Vergleich zu den Warenvolumina um eine quantité négligeable handelt (. . .) Die vorgenannten Beispiele belegen, daß ein Unternehmen (. . .) schlichtweg fahrlässig handeln würde, wenn es seinen Warenstrom-Dispositionen und -Kalkulationen die Haftungsregelungen der EG-Richtlinie zugrunde legen würde*.' Paradoxically, it seems to be exactly the ineffectiveness of the directive which has made it an attractive model for legislators worldwide. See M. Reimann, Product Liability in a Global Context: the Hollow Victory of the European Model, *ERPL* 2003, p. 128.

strengthened a nearly 20 year-old piece of legislation already infused with massive shortcomings. In doing so, it prevents Member States from adequately fulfilling their responsibility of providing industry and consumers with a socially and economically adequate and consistent product liability law.[37] In a most unusual resolution, the Council of Ministers has in the meantime explicitly criticized this jurisprudence and reminded the ECJ of the European Union's mandate of consumer protection.[38]

In summary, whilst the four examples just described cannot of course do justice to the whole body of European private and consumer law, they represent a threatening instrumentalist tendency, in which the *effet utile* of market integration is placed above all else – including above justice among the parties.

V. CONCLUSIONS

What are the lessons which one may draw from the instrumentalist conception of the private and consumer law *Acquis* for a future European contract code? To start with, it is evident that the *Acquis* cannot simply be extended into a code, but would need to undergo a huge move back to a more justice-oriented conception. However – and this is the good news – I would argue that with the enactment of a code encompassing the entire field of contract law and not merely selective issues, as the current *Acquis* does, such a conceptual change appears probable. First, it would seem politically unrealistic to envisage Europe agreeing on an instrumentalist code with a clear preponderance of market integration rationales over justice among the parties. Moreover, if the entire field of contract law is to be covered, a code would almost inevitably need to follow the European tradition, shared by both Common and Civil Law, of a justice-oriented non-instrumental private law. Indeed, a European code could not be restricted to information rights, nor could it do without other corrective instruments such as mandatory law, judicial review of contracts, prohibitions of certain forms of market behaviour and general clauses on fairness and good faith. The danger which became visible in *GB-Inno*, that information rights claim supremacy over

---

37 It may be added that this case law also leads to a different treatment of various Member States: art. 13 of the directive explicitly allows the application of competing national liability regimes based on contract or tort. However, in the lack of legislative action, national courts for example in Germany have developed traditional tort law into a fully fledged product liability regime. As a result, those Member States which – more or less by chance – have developed a product liability regime formally still based on fault (though in practice converted into one close to liability without fault by the inversion of the burden of proof and similar judicial devices) would probably be allowed to keep it, whereas others, such as Spain, whose legislatures have opted for a strict liability regime, have to accept the primacy of the Directive.

38 OJEC C 26/1, 2003; for a comment, see P. Rott, '*Produkthaftung und Vollharmonisierung – der Rat kartet nach*', RIW 2003/4, editorial.

further-reaching national consumer protection, would then be ruled out. Instead, all regulatory instruments would be placed again on an equal European law footing. This prognosis is confirmed by the Lando Principles of European Contract Law, which may be regarded as a sort of precursor, and perhaps even the hardcore, of a future contract law code. Indeed, even if these principles may be accused of ignoring the European consumer law *Acquis* to a large extent, they do constitute a traditional justice-oriented draft code without any instrumentalist flavour.

However, one could object that a European code, even if non-instrumentalist in its wording and conception, might still be interpreted in an instrumentalist way by a European judiciary. Indeed, it was the ECJ who often aggravated instrumentalist tendencies present in European law by a one-sided, excessively *effet utile*-oriented interpretation. However, I would like to argue that this danger remains limited with a contract law code. First, it is technically unthinkable that a centralised judiciary would administer in detail a contract or civil code for 25 states with about 400 million people; necessarily, national courts would need to play a major role. As I have argued elsewhere, such a centralized interpretation of the code is not even desirable, because a national margin of interpretation would be needed to render a uniform instrument compatible with diverse social and economic conditions and political preferences.[39] This flexibility is in my view more important than the ensuing problems of different national interpretations. But even if a last instance European high court for private law (possibly divided into several senates or divisions located in several Member States) were to be created, its situation would be different from that of the ECJ. After the enactment of a European code, a European court would no longer have the necessity of imposing the *effet utile* of some scattered European law texts on a reluctant national system. Instead, it would itself be responsible for administering the coherence and impartiality of an encompassing contract law committed to the new European constitution and its fundamental rights charter – and this increased responsibility might possibly also counteract a one-sided emphasis on the *effet utile*.

However, a set of additional 'legitimacy conditions' would need to be fulfilled to make a European code a success: First, one would of course need to ensure that such a code enjoys not only high technical quality and coherence, but also a balanced internal structure. This implies in particular that it should integrate consumer and general contract law to a much wider extent than is the case in the current academic draft compilations such as the Lando principles – so as to ensure that autonomy and solidarity as the core principles of contract law enjoy equal status in a new European contract law.[40]

39 *MJ* 8 (2001) p. 277.

40 This is a central thesis of the work of B. Lurger, *Grundfragen der Vereinheitlichung des Vertragsrechts in der EU*, (2001).

Whilst, moreover, the option of maximal harmonization would seem to be legitimate for an encompassing code, much more than for the present piecemeal consumer contract legislation, a higher standard of protection might still be allowed in the case of some particularly controversial norms.[41] Beyond that, the elaboration of a code should be carried out in a democratically more accountable way – which means that the de facto delegation of this task to an academic expert group which operates with little transparency and is hardly accessible to outsiders should at least be complemented by other institutional devices.[42] Moreover, a European contract law code should, as envisaged in the last Action Plan, be enacted only alongside national codes. It would indeed be detrimental to the acceptance and legitimacy of such an instrument, were it to be imposed on unwilling Member States by majority decision (which would also entail the de facto abolition of the existing national codes on pre-emption grounds). Notwithstanding that, it would be desirable that national parliaments adopt the European code also for internal cases on their own motion.

In summary, if the European bodies were able to master these legitimacy problems, the potential for a European contract law code could be promising. Indeed, it might not only do away with the lack of coherence of European private law directives, but also – and this has apparently been completely overlooked by its opponents as well as its supporters up until now – a European code might end once and for all the current tendency of downgrading private law to a mere integration tool; a slave of the *effet utile* so to speak. Private law justice would be constitutionalized in the European system, and it would finally receive a voice of its own in the concert of European legal disciplines.

---

41 This approach would be similar to making available various options to Member States at controversial junctures of the code, as did the American Uniform Commercial Code.

42 Against this background, one should welcome the recent initiative of the European Commission of establishing a network composed of legal practitioners, which is supposed to support and control the Study Group on a European Civil Code in the drafting of the text. However, it is still questionable that academics who are not part of the Study Group do not have access to that network and that no institutionalized links to civil society seem to exist. Therefore, I still think that a European Law Institute modelled on its famous and successful US counterpart would be the best solution.

Chapter 15
The Role of the *Acquis Communautaire* in Consumer Law for a European Contract Law Code – A Comment

Geraint Howells, Lancaster University

Christoph Schmid presented some concerns about the present state of the *Acquis* – namely the over-reliance on information as a method of protection (which is connected to a preference for market integration) and the petrification of the *Acquis* through the maximal harmonization doctrine. Yet he still ends up as being a rather optimistic proponent of a European Contract Law Code. I will agree with his criticisms of the current *Acquis*, but sound a perhaps more cautionary note about the development of such a European Contract Law Code.

I. INFORMATION STRATEGY

It is true that information is the Community's favoured form of intervention. One might indeed derive from the case law a feeling that provision of information is always a good thing. An exception might be made for misleading information, but unless blatantly false it will only be treated as misleading if it is so misleading that it would mislead someone of average intelligence who pays careful attention. As well as the *GB-Inno-BM v. Confederation du commerce luxembourgeois*[1] case cited by Schmid, this basic stance in favour of

[1] C-362/88 ECR [1990] I-667.

S. Grundmann, M. Schauer (eds), *The Architecture of European Codes and Contract Law*, 271–280

liberalizing what can be said about products is evident in the well-known cases under which the Germans have been required to re-orientate their understanding of what amounts to misleading advertising.[2]

Those of less than average intelligence or who do not pay attention are sacrificed in the interests of integration. One could say in the interests of the majority, but I suppose half of us must be less than averagely intelligent and even those with above average intelligence are unlikely to pay careful attention at all times.

Jules Stuyck made a useful intervention during the debates pointing out that cases like *GB-Inno* were actually removing rules that had little to do with consumer protection and more to do with protectionism. My response is that this may be an instance of 'hard cases making bad law'. Indeed many of the judgments of the European Court of Justice in this area can be defended on their facts or at least one can see that the arguments were finely balanced. One might even conclude the impact of Europe has been beneficial in countries like Germany that had previously sought to wrap their consumers in cotton wool. Certainly the approach of the UK courts has traditionally been rather more hard-nosed and more in line with the thinking of the European Court of Justice.[3] Such correction might be valuable for German consumer policy and necessary for the internal market to work. However, Schmid is right to point out that the underlying message is dangerous. The European Court of Justice has signified that it will be unsympathetic to national rules restricting the supply of information, because consumers are taken to be able to process the information and act on it rationally. The ways in which consumers handle information is far more complicated and probably sector/situation sensitive than seems sometimes to be appreciated by the European Court of Justice.[4] National legislators in some countries may be working with old fashioned views of consumer protection, but in many countries sophisticated rules on information provisions have been worked out; simply to disturb that balance because of needs of the internal market seems to show a lack of respect for national traditions and the ability of national

2 E.g. C-315/92 *Verband Sozialer Wettbewerb e.V./Clinique Laboratories SNC and Estée Lauder Cosmetics GmbH* (1994) ECR-I-317; *Verein Gegen Unwesen in Handel und Gewerbe Köln v. Mars Gmbh.* Case C-470/93 [1995] 3 C.M.L.R.1; *C-210/96 Gut Springheide GmbH/Oberkreisdirektor des Landkreises Steinfurt* (1998) ECR-I-4657.

3 See *Burleigh v. Van den Berghs and Jurgens Ltd.*, a case under the Trade Descriptions Act 1968, where Judge Gower QC said: 'the court must be sure that . . . [the description] was likely to mislead the average reasonable member of the public, and that means, of course, the shopping public. It is important that we should remember that we are dealing with the average person. It is not enough that we should be sure that an unusually careless person might be misled . . . [or] a person who is dyslexic, illiterate, short-sighted, or of less than average intelligence.'

4 See G. Howells, A. Janssen and R. Schulze (eds.), *Information Rights and Obligations – A challenge for party autonomy and transactional fairness* (2004).

legislators to review their consumer protection rules in the light of the developing internal market.

Whereas the supplier is given a fairly free hand to supply whatever non-misleading information he sees fit, by contrast the state is limited by internal market concerns as regards the information it can require to be supplied. Schmid cites the example of the *Axa Royal Belge SA v. Georges Ochoa Strategie Fin*[5] case where the Belgium Government had sought to rely on article 31(3) of the Third Life Insurance Directive.[6] This permits information to be required only if it is necessary for a proper understanding by the policy-holder of the essential elements of the commitment. It sought to justify a national rule that the policy inform the policy-holder that cancellation, reduction or surrender of an existing life-assurance contract for the purposes of subscribing to another life-assurance contract is generally detrimental to the policy-holder. The European Court of Justice then agreed with submissions that article 31(3) could not be satisfied by the provision as it was too general and vague. It concluded:

> 'The warning in question does not distinguish between the three options it envisages for terminating an assurance contract, namely cancellation, reduction or surrender, or specify the nature of the detriment that the policy-holder may suffer as a result of exercising those various options for the purposes of entering into a new contract. Nor does it state the criteria or the means of ascertaining the detrimental effect or otherwise of the options available to him.'

Schmid agrees that the information may be rather general and vague, but notes that at least it alerts the consumer to a genuine concern. It is certainly not misleading the consumer, simply putting him on guard.

II. MAXIMAL HARMONIZATION

This approach of the European Court of Justice in *Axa Royale Belge* seems part of a general trend in favour of maximal harmonization. It also causes concern because the issues of minimal/maximal harmonization are not being decided in the political legislative process, but rather by the courts. This was evident in the misleading advertising cases from Germany. The Misleading Advertising Directive[7] is clearly a minimum directive, but it became de facto a maximum harmonizing directive, due to the outer limits of national law being restricted by the free movement rules. The Product Liability Directive[8]

---

5 Case C-386/00 [200] ECR I-2209.

6 Directive 92/96 EC: OJ 1992 L 360/1.

7 Directive 84/450/EEC: OJ L 250/17, 1984.

8 Directive 85/374/EC: OJ L 210/29, 1985.

is another example where the courts have implemented a maximal harmonization approach in the face of article 13 of that Directive, which seemed to preserve existing national laws.[9] Again, as with *GB-Inno*, one might even agree with the actual results in those cases and yet still disagree with the underlying maximal harmonisation approach of the courts, which has potentially very far reaching and dangerous implications.[10]

In recent times the Commission has fought hard for maximum harmonization. One can fully understand why from their internal market perspective this makes sense and the frustration of harmonizing most aspects, but with irritating national divergences remaining, is obvious. However, there is a lack of confidence on the part of consumers and many Member States in Community institutions, at least to the extent that they are unwilling to entrust all policy decisions to the Community and tie the hands of the national legislators. This explains why in the Consumer Financial Services Directive[11] the Member States are left the option to maintain and introduce more stringent provisions on prior information.[12] The sting may be in the tail however, for these extra provisions must of course still be in conformity with Community law and the *Axa Royale Belge* case gives us an indication of how restrictively the European Court of Justice will view such provisions.

There has also been a vigorous debate over whether the Unfair Commercial Practices Directive[13] should be a maximum harmonization Directive. The Commission could not see the problem with a maximal harmonization approach as the Directive was intended to catch everything that was unfair; but of course when you looked into what exactly was meant by unfairness one became more nervous that the Directive might have a narrower scope than some national laws.

III. CONCERNS ABOUT MAXIMAL EC LAW

It might be worth spending some time considering why consumers and some national governments are concerned about making European law the sole source of protection. Schmid notes one problem is that these rules are created more to serve the goals of the internal market rather than more justice oriented consumer protection. That is certainly true as regards information

9 *Commission v. France* Case C-52/00, [2002] ECR I-3827; *Commission v. Greece*, C-154/00 [2002] ECR I-3879; and *González Sanchez v. Medicina Asturiana SA* Case C-183/00, [2002] ECR I-3901.

10 See G. Howells, 'Product Liability – A History of Harmonisation' in: *Towards a European Civil Code* (3ed.), (forthcoming).

11 Directive 2002/65/EC: OJ L 271/16, 2002.

12 Art. 4(2).

13 Directive 2005/28/EC: OJ L 148/22, 2005.

rules. Different rules in different Member States can impede the ability of goods and services to cross borders. This is less true of background default rules relating to product liability and the quality of goods that mandate minimum standards but not the means of achieving those levels of safety and quality. Unfair terms and fair trading laws probably fall someway in between as although their impact may be to prohibit certain terms or practices at their core they simply provide for values of fairness which are common to the traditions of the Member States.

Indeed one could argue that the EC has not been concerned enough with the internal market dimension. Background liability rules do not create direct barriers to trade and the distortions in competition they create are arguably not appreciable enough to justify intervention. Indeed some of the most probable causes of distortion in competition, like different levels of pain and suffering damages available for product liability claims, are not harmonized at all. Likewise the Consumer Sales Directive[14] improves national sales law, but does little to assist the cross-border consumer in a practical sense for it leaves the question of producer liability for another day.

There are more general concerns about the quality of the EC legislation than simply the internal market orientation. I am not simply referring to the quality of the drafting here. That would be a cheap swipe, but it is amazing to believe that all language versions have been checked over by a national lawyer linguist. Rather I refer to concerns about the substantive quality of the content independent of the internal market orientation. Part of these concerns relate to process. The Commission is in fact, contrary to popular belief, a rather streamline organization. Often the staff at the Commission dealing with an issue will be smaller than in national ministries. Yet this small Commission staff, which frequently changes, has to come to grips not only with the generic issues of the topic, but also the peculiarities of now 25 legal systems, and has to balance the consumer and national concerns against the internal market dimension. No wonder the Commission is often relieved to achieve some consensus even if the result is not ideal and bears the hallmarks of compromises and concessions inflicted in the heat of battle.

The actual forum in which those debates take place is also rather different at the European from the national level. Not only are the European procedures more opaque than at the national level, but there is also a sense in which contract law is more overtly political at the European than the national level. Contract law reform at the national level is often a matter of serious, if rather tedious, debate between lawyers. Sure questions of party autonomy versus social justice will underpin many of the contributions. Ultimately it will, however, be about making adjustments within a particular framework. At the EC level disturbances to the coherence of private law rules may be required by higher political imperative, via market integration.

---

14 Directive 99/44/EC: OJ L 177/12, 1999.

It is not unnatural for national lawyers to be sceptical that this will produce better results.

Sometimes the European legislator even comes up with quite rational rules, which simply run against the grain of national traditions. This is the case with the remedies regime in the Consumer Sales Directive. The hierarchy of remedies is fully understandable and in line with CISG, but runs counter to the UK tradition of always giving consumers the right to reject unsatisfactory goods.

Given the possible flaws in EC procedure and the possibly limited horizons of the European legislator, especially when compared to the rounded approach of national legislators and well tested procedures (at least as perceived by national legislators) it is not surprising there is some scepticism about EC laws being maximal and totally replacing national laws.

Imagine the national civil servant who has for decades tried to find the right combination of rules to tackle a subject as complex as unfair trade practices. He may have had some successes and some failures along the way. Suddenly the EC legislator says it wants to tackle the topic and in a few months proposes a formula that it believes can deal with the problem adequately for now and seemingly for always and seeks to remove the freedom of the national legislators to act. You might well understand the national civil servant's suspicions that his European counterpart is full of the enthusiasm of one new to the subject and appreciate his scepticism as to whether Europe really has found the magic formula that has evaded him for years. He might also be circumspect about the ability of the European legislator to react if it discovers it has been mistaken, given that the procedure for amending EC legislation is as cumbersome as that for adopting it.

It seems sensible to suggest that the EC should provide the minimum protection a consumer needs to participate in the internal market and to leave it to member states to decide if any extra protection is needed. If these extra forms of protection represent genuine concerns, then the only acceptable solution if harmonisation is considered essential is to harmonise at the highest level. One might, however, find that industry prefers to adapt to local conditions than to face the spread of obligations.

I hope the pendulum is swinging away from maximal harmonization at all cost being the mantra of the Commission. Indeed I feel there has been an overstatement of the benefits of complete harmonization. There will always be the risk of differential application and indeed Schmid, in the context of a European Contract Law Code, views this as desirable. Indeed it may be better to have transparent differences in laws than hidden differences in application.

IV. *ACQUIS* AS A BASIS FOR A CODE?

The *Acquis* is a series of punctual interventions in contract, often guided by the goal of market intervention, which serves to over-emphasize the role information can play and to over-promote the virtues of maximal harmonization. Is this a good place for starting discussions of a European Civil Code?

It depends. If you wanted to create the perfect contract law for Europe it would be easier to start with a blank piece of paper and fill it in with our own dreams or at least inspirations from our traditions. This is the approach of the Lando Principles[15] and the work of the Study Group on a European Civil Code,[16] whose work has sought to find common principles from the principles of the Member States' laws, together with a dash of coherence and philosophical underpinning from the distinguished lawyers involved.

Schmid views the Lando Principles as 'justice-oriented . . . without any instrumentalist flavour'. It may be that they are more coherent than the *Acquis* as they do not have to show the same practical concern for the internal market, yet they certainly reflect the values of individualism more than '*communautarianism*', albeit that the rampant self-interested individualism of the 19th century has been tempered by a more gentlemanly view of business ethics. Of course consumer protection is something outside the Principles. But the Lando Principles favour a market orientated view of contract and the cause of social justice has been taken up by another group of scholars.[17]

If instead of the perfect European contract law, you simply want there to be a European contract law then using the *Acquis* does seem a sensible starting point. The development of European contract law is in the hands of the same Commission officials who have presided over the development of the *Acquis*. If they can be persuaded that the rules of a European Contract Law Code can be found in or derived from the existing *Acquis* and that gaps can be filled by analogy or logical implication from the existing *Acquis* then this is likely to be relatively uncontroversial compared to the writing of a European Contract Law Code from scratch. Naturally there will be debates about exactly what the state of the *Acquis* is and about the extent to which particular punctual rules can be generalized. There may also be internal debates within the EC as to whether it should aim for a restatement of European Contract Law in general or simply European Consumer Law, which has been its main preoccupation to-date.

The Commission has announced it wants to establish a 'Common Frame of Reference'.[18] Its approach is likely to be to compare the results of the Lando Principles and the Study Group with those of the *Acquis*.[19] The involvement of the Community gives some authority to this project. People

15 O. Lando and H. Beale, *Principles of European Contract Law* (1999).

16 See, <http://www.sgecc.net/>.

17 The Study Group on Social Justice is organized by Martijn Hesselink.

18 A More Coherent Contract Law – An Action Plan, COM(2003) 68.

19 An *Acquis* Group has been established to consider the state of the *Acquis* in relation to European Contract Law: see, <http://www.acquis-group.org/>. The present author is a member of this group.

know that the Community has some, albeit circumscribed, legislative competence in this field. It gives the academics involved some hope that their work, which is based on both deductive and inductive reasoning, will gain some legitimacy.

Whether this is the right way forward depends upon the objectives of the exercise, which are still unclear. The work invested seems too extensive to be justified as a mere academic exercise, although undoubtedly much of value to legal education and scholarship has arisen. If the aim is to work out what contract law concepts are used in the *Acquis* and to perhaps refine them and consider if additional concepts need to be defined then this is clearly work appropriately carried on under the auspices of the Commission.

On the other hand if the adoption of a European Contract Law Code is the objective then the present form seems inappropriate. I join Schmid in his call for the work to be carried out in a more democratically accountable way. The Commission has not got the power to address all contract law concerns, only those which impact on the internal market. The current work is being undertaken by a limited number of academics – I include myself – whose work will be used by an even more limited number of officials for a yet to be determined purpose. If something approaching a European Contract Law Code is to be the outcome a far broader base is needed and the result needs to be informed by both the *Acquis* and the principles of the Member State's laws and yet freed from their shackles. It should reflect modern values of contractual justice (whatever they are determined to be) and take into account the importance of facilitating cross-border trade. It will have to address the issue of the extent to which the values of contractual justice found reflected in consumer law can be generalized, either to contracts where both parties are commercial enterprises on an equal footing or where one commercial party dominates the other.

V. WHAT SORT OF CODE?

Schmid reminds us at the start of his essay that the parlance nowadays is of an optimal instrument. If by this it means an instrument the parties opt in to, then we are only talking about a (possibly) improved version of the Lando Principles. It is even suggested they can be made the applicable law by the parties. As Thomas Wilhelmsson pointed out during the debates, if parties can choose to apply the principles of lex mercatoria and the parties to the Channel Tunnel contract can choose to opt for disputes to be determined in accordance with the principles common to English and French law, why not allow some common European Contract Law Principles to govern the contract? Whether the lawyers were wise in the Channel Tunnel contract to include the clause they did and whether many will opt for such untested rules may be debateable. There is a danger that such principles will become a kind of 'legal-Esperanto' to borrow the phrase Prof. Vékas used during his intervention.

However, the Code could become optional for Member States. Given the problems of jurisdiction within the EC Treaty it may be better to develop it outside the formal structures, as a convention that Member States can sign up to. It would be similar to the Uniform Commercial Code in the USA or a Restatement. These may be adopted by States and although local differences may emerge the law has a familiar feel so parties are happy to be governed by a system of laws whose structure, if not detail, is familiar to them. I agree with Schmid that some local flexibility is necessary and probably desirable, although over time the systems will hopefully tend to converge. Once it becomes part of Member State's law, the Code will have more standing and be more acceptable to the parties. The danger is that those countries keenest to adopt such a Code will work hardest on the project with the result that it will most likely reflect the traditions of those countries. This might ensure some hardcore States sign up, but can leave those on the outside alienated and even more determined to maintain their traditions. This is most obviously a risk with England. It has a lot to lose given the widespread adoption of English law in commercial contracts and as it has shown in relation to CISG is willing to stand outside harmonization that it does not see as being in its interest.

Schmid is right to be optimistic that if there is a European Contract Law Code it will not be stained by the domination of market integration rationales over justice among the parties. However, it still remains to be seen what the twenty-first century definition of justice between the parties is. Contract law has come a long way from the market individual values of the 19th century epitomised by the laissez-faire attitude of the contract law judges of that time and the drafters of the European Civil Codes. Consumer welfarism has indeed ruffled those principles,[20] but in a sporadic and uneven manner. It is perhaps too early to generalize new principles, certainly as general principles of contract law, rather than as principles specific to certain types of contracts. Perhaps my fear is that if a European Contract Law Code was adopted it would be a balanced, but conservative document. This might then impede more innovative developments. Schmid has noted the petrification effect of maximal harmonization. I have suggested this is a tendency for all EC law whether or not explicitly maximalist to have such effects. A convention might not be under the direct jurisdiction of the European Court of Justice, but it might be difficult for some time to argue for new principles which had not been included in this Code.

VI. BE ALERT TO THE CONSEQUENCES OF ADOPTING A CODE

We will continue to work on this European Consumer Law Code project. We have no option – the ball is rolling. The Commission normally needs to

20 The terms market individualism and consumer welfarism are borrowed from J. Adams and R. Brownsword, *Understanding Contract Law* (2000).

show some results from its labours. We should, however, take stock and think of the consequences of reaching our end point: how will the legal landscape look once that has been achieved? What role will the European Contract Law Code play in future debates? It may not be so much a codification of the past as a map for the future. At the very least we need to broaden the scope of debates to prevent a North European dominance and to bring in practitioners, industry and consumers. The law is not owned by lawyers, but merely entrusted to them to serve the needs of the community. We need to ask the community whether they would like to see this European Contract Law Code. European codifications were often seen as symbols of national identity. Such motivations are likely to be counterproductive in many parts of Europe in the context of suggesting there is a European state.

Finally, as someone with a particular interest in consumer protection, one has to be aware of the politics of this process. There must be guarantees that consumer rights will not be undermined. It may or may not be right to generalize consumer contractual values to other contexts, but any aspiration to have a common contract framework should not cause consumers to have diluted rights. Harmonization between Member States' laws and harmonization between the rules governing different types of contracts has its limits.

Part IV
Formation of Contract and Precontractual Information

Chapter 16

Formation of Contract and Pre-Contractual Information from an Italian Perspective (Final Remarks from the Perspective of European Contract Law)

Vincenzo Roppo, University of Genova

I. SCOPE OF THIS PAPER

This paper deals with information rules in contract law, and specifically with information duties between the contracting parties and with the related remedies.

The paper mainly covers Italian Law – i.e. it describes the relevant rules written in the *Codice civile* and examines the way in which such rules are interpreted and applied by both courts and scholars.

The last section covers *Acquis Communautaire*: it first describes some different patterns, according to which the *Acquis* is designed to deal with information rules and information duties, while the final part consists of some critical evaluations of it.

II. THE '*CODICE CIVILE*'

As to disclosure/information duties in the pre-contractual phase, the Italian Civil Code contains some material rules relating to all contracts in general, and some other relating to specific types of contracts.

S. Grundmann, M. Schauer (eds), *The Architecture of European Codes and Contract Law*, 283–299

1. Code Rules Relating to All Contracts in General

In this area, at least five rules should be mentioned. Only one of them expressly imposes disclosure/information duties on the contracting parties.

a. Article 1338

The contracting party who knew or should have known that the contract is not valid, and did not make the other party aware of this, is liable for damages to him/her, provided that the other party has suffered losses from relying on the validity of the contract, and such reliance is not ascribable to his/her own fault.

Four other rules do not expressly put disclosure or information duties on the contracting parties, but are nevertheless material to our problem.

b. Article 1428

If the contracting party makes a mistake, he/she may avoid the contract provided that the mistake is both fundamental and recognisable by the other party.

A mistake is 'fundamental' when it refers to the substance matter of the contract, and not to some particular, idiosyncratic interest of the party (article 1429). A party's mistake is 'recognisable' when the other party should have noticed it, by using the ordinary care (article 1431).

c. Article 1439/1

Deceit may cause avoidance of the contract, when it was of such nature that the deceived party would not have contracted, had the deceit not taken place (so-called 'determinant deceit').

d. Article 1440

If deceit was not of such nature as to persuade the deceived party to enter the contract (so-called 'incidental deceit'), the contract is not voidable; but if it convinced the party to enter the contract on different terms than he/she would have accepted had the deceit not taken place, the party may recover damages.

e. Article 1337

When dealing in view of entering a contract, the parties are required to behave according to good faith.

2. Code Rules Relating to Specific Contracts

Specific contracts involving pre-contractual disclosure or information duties are mainly sale contracts and insurance contracts.

a. Sale

Mention should be made of the complex of rules, which are contained in articles 1490–1494.

If the good sold proves to be defective, and the defects are such as to make it unfit for the purpose or to reduce its value to a significant extent, the buyer is entitled to '*garanzia*': that is, he/she may either rescind the contract, or have the price reduced (articles 1490/1, 1492/1).

However, the buyer will not be entitled to '*garanzia*':

- if the parties so agree in their contract by inserting an exclusion clause in it: but such a clause will not be effective, if the seller knew the defects and did not disclose them to the buyer (article 1490/2);
- if the buyer knew the defects at the time of making the contract (article 1491);
- if the defects could be easily recognized (noticed): but even in this case the buyer will be entitled to '*garanzia*', if the seller stated that the good was free from any defect (article 1491).

In addition to the remedies being alternatively provided under the 'garanzia' system (either rescission of the contract, or price reduction), the buyer will be entitled to damages, if the seller of the defective good does not prove that he/she was not aware of the defects, and that such ignorance was not ascribable to his/her fault (article 1494).

b. Insurance

The law provides the insurer with specified remedies, if the insured party omits to give information, or gives false/incomplete information, which is material to the former's decision to enter the contract. But a distinction is made:

- if the omission depends on the insured party's fraud or gross negligence, the insurer may avoid the contract (article 1892), and claim damages on the ground of article 1338;
- if the omission is neither fraudulent nor depending on the insured party's gross negligence, the insurer may just withdraw from the contract (article 1893).

III. COURTS AND SCHOLARS

Starting from the code rules summarized so far, the central issue is whether – apart from the cases covered by some specific duty of disclosure or information (such as the ones established by article 1338, or put on the seller and the insured by articles 1490–1494 and 1892–1893) – 'silence' may amount to 'deceit', and therefore entitles the 'victim' of omitted/incomplete information to avoid the contract and/or recover damages.[1]

1. General: Courts versus Scholars, and the Role of Good Faith in Negotiations (Article 1337)

A survey of the Italian judicial decisions and academic opinions shows that the courts are generally much more cautious, if not reluctant, in admitting that the party who was not informed by the other party about something which is material to his/her evaluation of the contract, may indeed be entitled to legal remedies, while scholars are much more generous in recognizing such material character of silence.

The current dictum of the courts is that silence 'in itself' may not amount to deceit, but only as a part of more complex frames of conduct and circumstance, showing the silent party's fraudulent intention to drive the other party into mistake.

On the other hand, scholars are more and more inclined to state that the principle of good faith in negotiations, contained in article 1337, creates a general duty for the party to disclose facts that may be material to the other party's evaluation of the contract: so that the former's 'silence' may, generally speaking, entitle the latter to avoid the contract and/or recover damages.

In the courts' dominant opinion, article 1337 does not play such an intense and general role. Many decisions (if, indeed, not all) seem to suppose that a liability for damages may arise out of article 1337 only in cases where a party's withdrawal from negotiations is unjustified (the classical cases of Jhering's '*culpa in contrahendo*'), but not in cases where the contract was concluded on improper terms – but concluded nevertheless. It's useless to say that such limitation of the rule's scope would prevent article 1337 from playing any significant role in cases where a contracting party's silence is materially at stake.

1 With reference to the various issues and problems raised in section III of this paper, see in general: De Poli, *Asimmetrie informative e rapporti contrattuali* (2002); Mantovani, '*Vizi incompleti' del contratto e rimedio risarcitorio* (1995); Grisi, *L'obbligo precontrattuale di informazione* (1990); G. Visintini, *La reticenza nella formazione dei contratti* (1972).

2. Silence as 'Incidental' Deceit

The reason why the role of article 1337 is not being emphasized so much by the courts is probably that another code rule is in existence, which may deal more specifically with liability for damages in deceptive silence cases: article 1440 on 'incidental' deceit.

Courts have no difficulty in allowing that the deceived party may recover damages on the grounds of article 1440, even in those cases where deceit consists of omitting due information. It is perhaps less difficult to admit this than to admit such cases where the deceived party may not only recover damages, but also avoid the contract.

3. Negligent versus Fraudulent Breach of Duties to Inform

Provided that some duty to inform is to be ascribed to a contracting party, another issue is whether the breach of such a duty can be material only when supported by fraudulent intention, or also when it is due to mere negligence.

By assuming that a party's silence may amount to deceit only if an element of some fraudulent conduct which aims at misleading the other party, courts clearly are in a position to give the first answer.

Scholarly opinions offer a more varied picture. Some authors share the courts' restrictive view, that there is no deceit without fraudulent intention. Others support the opposite view by arguing that silence in breach of a disclosure duty may generally amount to deceit even if depending on mere negligence. Others prefer to choose the middle ground by arguing that negligent (non-fraudulent) silence may expose the responsible party to liability for damages, but not to avoidance of the contract.

4. Misleading Silence of a Third Party

This is another issue on which a divide exists among scholars. Article 1339 provides that when deceit comes from a third party, the deceived party may avoid the contract only if the other party was aware of it. Some authors (and one judicial decision, in particular) admit that the rule may apply also to deceit consisting of silence; other authors deny this possibility.

5. The Deceived Party's Duty of Care

The core issue is to find the proper balance between one party's duty to give information, and the other party's duty to gain information by his/her own initiative.

Specific code rules assume that the party claiming remedies against the other party's deceptive silence deserves no protection, if the claimant's alleged ignorance depends on his/her own fault: when the party knowing that the contract to be entered is void does not make the other party aware of this, a liability for damages arises only if the other party's reliance on the contract's validity implies no negligence on his/her part (article 1338); and the buyer is not entitled to '*garanzia*' because of defects in the goods purchased, if such defects could be easily recognized (article 1491).

Both courts and authors agree that this requirement should be generalized, by implying the principle that the victim of the other party's silence is not entitled to legal protection, if he/she is to be reproached with his/her ignorance about material facts of the contract (that is, if he/she should have obtained the omitted information, by using the ordinary care): in this case, indeed, he/she would be the victim not of the other party's silence, but rather of his/her own negligence.

But courts and authors diverge in terms of the application of the principle in specific cases: the former usually apply it in a way which is much more restrictive and harder on the alleged victim of the other party's silence. So, let us consider the case where one party should be registered in some public register relating to the activity involved in the contract, and is not, and does not disclose this to the other unaware party. The contract may be therefore void because of infringement of a mandatory rule, but courts refuse to award the unaware party damages on the ground of article 1338 because in their opinion ignorance of a mandatory legal rule amounts, by definition, to negligence.

Most scholars strongly disagree with the belief that the evaluation of whether a party is to be reproached with his/her ignorance should not depend on an abstract and rigid criterion, such as the one by which ignorance of a mandatory rule does always amount to negligence, but rather on more flexible criteria. Two questions may be posed in this respect: was the unaware party able to find by him/herself reasonably easy access to the omitted information? Did the interested party ask the other party for the omitted or incomplete information, or not? (In this respect, the courts are ready to stress the difference between asking for information and asking for advice.)

In a more general perspective: the question of whether one party has an information/disclosure duty to the other, or whether this other party was to obtain information by him/herself according to a standard of ordinary care, is one which may be influenced by many different variables. But the different variables mainly refer to two elements which in the present analysis are: the nature of the omitted/incomplete information, and the nature of the parties involved.

6. The Nature of Information Omitted

This is an element on which Italian scholarly debate is very much focussed in order to come up with proper evaluation methods.

a. Whose Performance is the Omitted Information Referring to?

Some authors suggest that a party has in principle a duty to inform about material facts concerning his/her own performance, while he/she does not have such disclosure duty as to facts concerning the other party's performance. This standard seems quite reasonable on the elementary ground that one has much more knowledge and control over his/her things or activities than over things or activities in someone else's domain. But it cannot be absolute.

If my performance is much less expensive to me than the market average in such a way as to allow me huge profits, then I have no duty to disclose this to the other party (even if the knowledge of the circumstance would have induced the other party to offer me a lower price). It is the same perspective, according to which the buyer – as a court positively stated – has no duty to disclose to the seller that he/she has already found a third party to whom to re-sell the goods for three times the price agreed in their sale.

So, one may think that the proper criterion is rather the following: A has no duty to disclose to B facts (even related to A's own performance) if such facts just affect A's profits from the contract; but A may have a duty to disclose to B facts (even related to B's performance), if such facts are causing B to suffer losses from the contract.

This is consistent with another judicial decision. A contractor had to face unexpected difficulties and costs in performing the building work awarded, for the client had omitted to inform him about some special environmental circumstances in which the work was to be done. In principle, such circumstances affected the contractor's and not the client's performance (although they were, in a sense, related to the client's domain). The relevant point about this case is that those circumstances were material from the standpoint of the contractor's losses, and not from the standpoint of the client's profits.

b. Did the Information Omitted Imply Costs for the Informed Party to Get it, or was it Found for Free, or by Chance?

Some Italian authors appreciate the well known Kronman's theory, according to which a party has no duty to disclose information whose acquisition implied specific activities and costs for the informed party.[2] The rationale

[2] Kronman, 'Mistake, Disclosure, Information and the Law of Contract', *Journal of Legal Studies* 7 (1978) p. 1.

is not very different from the one underlying intellectual property: new information is a new 'good' from which society as a whole benefits; so the law should encourage people to spend time and resources to build new information, and this can be made by giving the discoverer a privilege on the information so discovered, that is by allowing non-disclosure; if, on the contrary, one were obliged to disclose, this would discourage future efforts to produce new information.

This rationale is often evoked in discussing the paradigmatic case of the expert and clever antiques dealer who realizes that the picture put up for sale and attributed, let us say, to an "unknown Italian painter of the early 17th century", actually is by Caravaggio; and omits to disclose this amazing discovery to the owner, so buying it at 20 or 30 times less than its real market value.

As you probably know, cases like this have been decided by French courts ('Poussin case', 'Fragonard case'), Dutch courts ('silver chantarus case')[3] and Italian courts ('dalla Quercia case', to quote just the most recent one[4]). But they were decided in different ways: sometimes by granting the seller avoidance of the contract, sometimes by denying it. In any case, such decisions have been taken mostly on grounds of mistake and unjust enrichment, rather than on grounds of deceit and pre-contractual information duties.

It is worth noting that the relationship between mistake and deceit, seen as different grounds causing the contract to be avoided, seems to show an inconsistency: with regard to deceit consisting of omitting some material information, the contract may be avoided, as we have seen, only if the victim's ignorance does not depend on his/her own ignorance; on the contrary, the victim of a mistake is entitled to avoid the contract even if his/her mistake is not excusable ('*scusabile*'): that is, even if it is to be ascribed to the victim's negligence.

A reconcilement may be found in a different extent of material ignorance in other cases: ignorance by mistake causes avoidance of the contract to a narrower extent (the mistake being required to be not less than 'fundamental') than ignorance by deceit (which is material even if misleading the victim in respect of more trivial elements).

But let us go back to the sale of some unknown art treasure. Those who refuse to admit avoidance of the contract in such cases, justify such opinion mainly with arguments related to Kronman's theory.

But let us consider the reverse case. The owner of an old, precious painting generally attributed to Caravaggio, by studying and researching harder and discovering new documents and applying more sophisticated analysis

[3] See references in Koetz, *European Contract Law, I, Formation, Validity and Content of Contracts; Contract and Third Parties* (1997) p. 180 (n. 36).

[4] Corte di Cassazione, 2 February 1998, *Contratti* (1998) p. 437.

techniques, finds out that the painting is not by Caravaggio, but most certainly by some unknown painter of his school. What, if he then sells the painting as (and at the price of) a Caravaggio, without disclosing his discovery to the buyer? His new information undoubtedly costs him time and money, and represents a progress in art criticism: but are these sufficient grounds for saying that he had no disclosure duties, and denying the seller any remedy? In my opinion, the answer should be negative.

c. Did Information Omitted Consist of Good News to the Information Owner, or of Bad News to the Other Party?

If we seek to rationalize the cases and solutions discussed above, we will find that this third criterion (although formulated in quite a rough way) is somewhat useful.

Let us start by saying, in very simple words, that information may either consist of good or bad news (good or bad, in respect of the contract's outcomes); good/bad being referred to either the party who owns it, or the other party.

When information consists of bad news for the owner, the other party has no interest in it: so there is no reason for obliging the owner to disclose it to the other party. When information consists of good news for the other party, the contract will prove better for him/her than he/she expected at the time of making it: so when he/she discovers this, he/she will be delighted at the pleasant surprise, and will not have any complaint to make against the information owner (apart from the extreme case when learning the contract's unexpected surplus value too late made him/her miss the chance of fully exploiting it). In both cases, there is no ground for a disclosure duty.

On the contrary, such a ground may be seen to apply, in principle, when information consists of good news for the party who owns it, or of bad news for the other party: in the first case, the other party's interest lies in the knowledge that something could enable him/her to negotiate a better price; in the second case, his/her interest lies in the knowledge that something could enable him/her to avoid a bad contract, or to negotiate a more convenient price.

But the two cases are to be dealt with in different ways.

When information omitted consists of good news for the party who owns it, this party should not have, generally speaking, any disclosure duty to the other; no matter if the information is related to the former's or the latter's performance; no matter whether or not obtaining the information implied efforts and costs for the owner. Let us think of the case where the clever antiques dealer buys a Caravaggio for little; or the seller makes extra-profits due to his/her very low production costs (both circumstances being ignored by the other party).

When, on the contrary, information omitted by the owner consists of *bad news for the other party*, then the information owner should have, generally speaking, a disclosure duty to the other party; no matter – once more – to whom the performance of the information is related and how the information was acquired (by suffering costs, or for free). Let us think of the cases where the contractor incurred extra-costs because the client did not disclose to him the special environmental difficulties affecting the work, or the buyer paid a very high price for the painting generally attributed to Caravaggio, because the seller did not disclose to him/her his/her personal discovery that the painting is not made by Caravaggio.

Such reasoning seems also to be consistent with the code rules providing information duties in the fields of sale and insurance contracts (*supra*, 1.2).

7. The Nature of the Parties: Professional/Non-Professional

To both courts and scholars, this is an increasingly important standard in order to assess whether a party has a duty to inform the other party of facts which are material to the latter's decision to enter into the contract.

If the party is a professional (and thus an insider of the contract's subject matter), he/she generally has more or heavier information duties than a non professional party: it will be easier for the other party to prove, on the one hand, that the professional party is liable for damages, or to avoid the contract, on the ground the he/she omitted due information; and also to prove, on the other hand, that the professional party is not entitled to avoidance of the contract or to damages, on the ground that he/she should have obtained the omitted information by him/herself, the alleged ignorance thus depending on his/her negligence.

To a very large extent, such criterion was introduced, or at least consolidated, by European contract law: mainly by the directives concerning consumer contracts. But this brings us to the next part of the present report.

IV. THE IMPACT OF *ACQUIS COMMUNAUTAIRE*: FOUR KINDS OF INFORMATION RULES IN EC LEGISLATION

As everybody knows, the European directives, mainly the ones relating to consumer contracts, provide large and complex sets of rules on information from one party to the other: namely, from the professional party to the consumer. It can be said that information – both pre-contractual and contractual in nature – represents one of the most important and peculiar, if not absolutely the most important and peculiar, feature of the European Community contract law.

This paper does not involve any analytical or critical survey of such vast material, doesn't aim to extract common principles from it, or identify specific problems and solutions. This is a work other European scholars are currently doing, and to some extent have already done.[5] Here I am just trying to outline, in an approximate way, some issues possibly related to the subject.

Let me start by questioning first of all under which perspectives EC legislation deals with information in contracts (mainly, as we have seen, in consumer contracts). My straightforward answer would be: under four different perspectives; or according to four different patterns.

1. Making Legally Binding, as terms of the Contract, Pre-Contractual Information Given by one Party, on a Voluntary Basis, Outside the Contract

Sometimes the law provides for disclosure in a different way rather than obliging the party to give specific information on this or that other subject: in this area we do not properly deal with information duties. But the party may voluntarily choose to give such information (mostly for advertising reasons: that is, on the ground that such information is presumed to make the contract more attractive to the other party). In this case, the law provides that voluntary pre-contractual information becomes contractual obligation: the party is bound to perform what he said, even if he/she said it for mere information (or advertising) purposes, with no intention of being legally bound by it.

One example may, I believe, clarify the point. The 99/44 Sale Directive provides that the seller is obliged to deliver goods which are in conformity with the contract and this means, *inter alia*, goods which 'comply with the description given by the seller', and,

> 'show the quality and performance which are normal in goods of the same type and which the consumer can reasonably expect, . . . taking into account any public statements on the specific characteristics of the goods made . . . by the seller, the producer or his representative, particularly in advertising or on labelling' (article 2.2, a) and d)).

This regulatory approach does not seem to raise particular problems.

2. A Slightly More Coercive Provision: Information Going to Become Legally Binding is Voluntary in its Origin, but not in its Content

Let's consider, as an example, Directive 90/314 on package tours. It does not put on the tour organizer or retailer any duty to make a brochure available

5 In this respect, a book published last year should be quoted: Schulze, Ebers and Grigoleit, *Informationspflichten und Vertragsschluss im Acquis communautaire* (2003).

to the consumer, containing information on the package. But where a brochure is made available, by free choice of the organizer or the retailer, the directive provides that not only 'the particulars contained in the brochure are binding on the organizer or retailer' (unless special circumstances occur, under which the particulars stated in the brochure may be changed), according to the pattern considered above; but which particulars are contained in the brochure, and how, is not the matter of a free choice by the organizer or the retailer, as the contents of it are to some extent compulsively determined by the law, by prescribing that the brochure, if made available to the consumer, 'shall indicate in a legible, comprehensible and accurate manner both the price and adequate information' on the fundamental elements of the package (article 3.1).

Unlike the one considered previously, this regulatory approach does raise a problem, which is a general problem with the EC information rules: the lack of clear and complete provisions on sanctions and remedies to be applied when some information duty is breached by the obliged party. This is because Directive 90/314 does not say what will legally happen if the organizer or the retailer gives the consumer a brochure which fails to indicate, for instance, the price or the type of accommodation.

One may think that this is left to domestic legislatures, when transposing the directive into each national system. If this actually was the EC legislature's intention, the least one can say is that it is far from being fulfilled. I do not know the state of the art in other European countries: all I know is that the Italian law faithfully follows the EC directive in providing nothing at all as to legal consequences for the breach of the considered information duty.

3. Providing Information Duties to be Turned into Contractual Terms

Sometimes the law provides that the party is obliged to give specific information, mainly relating to the nature and characteristics of his performance, in order to make it clear what the other party is entitled to expect from the contract. And the law specifies that such information must be written in the contract, thus becoming in the full sense a content of it, legally binding to the party.

Once more Directive 90/314 on package tours provides a good example: article 4 provides that 'the contract shall contain at least the elements listed in the Annex', which are all the material elements identifying the package organizer's performance (destinations, periods of stay, transport, accommodation, visits and other services, and so on).

Such a provision raises two problems.

The first problem is the same as considered above, descending from the lack of any specific provision in the Directive as to legal consequences of the informational breach: which sanctions or remedies will apply if the contract (of course, a standard form contract pre-drafted by the organizer or the retailer) does not contain some of the prescribed elements?

The second: As the informational elements to be inserted in the contract to a large extent coincide with the ones to be inserted in the brochure (provided that a brochure was given to the consumer before the contract), what happens if the contract describes a certain element in different terms than those used by the brochure in describing the same element? As both the brochure and the contract are legally binding, will the former or the latter prevail?

In this respect, other directives are better formulated. This is the case for Directive 94/47 on timesharing contracts. It provides for an informational document to be supplied by the vendor to the purchaser before the contract, and to be later transposed into contract terms (article 3.2). And it indicates which remedy is granted to the purchaser, should the contract not contain some of the information required: a longer term to exercise his/her withdrawal right (article 5.1). And it also specifies how to solve the problem arising when information in the contract is not consistent with information in the pre-contractual document (article 3.2).

4. Providing Information Duties before the Contract, with no Express Provision as to their Binding Force

Sometimes the law provides that the professional party is obliged to give specific information relating to the nature and characteristics of his/her performance, as seen above; but neither says that they are to be written in the contract as terms of it, nor that they have binding force anyway.

This time the example is taken from Directive 97/7 on distance contracts. It provides that, prior to the conclusion of a distance contract, the supplier must give the consumer clear information on various material elements of the contract (article 4), and after the conclusion such information must be confirmed in writing, while at the same time adding more information on certain other aspects of the contract (article 5). No further rule is given. In this way, two regulatory gaps are left open.

The first concerns the legal value to be attached to information given. Thus the question is: is it binding on the supplier although the directive does not expressly say so by implying a principle inherent in the *Acquis Communautaire* that due pre-contractual information turns into contractual obligation? Or is this conclusion too extreme?

The second gap concerns the legal consequences of the breach of the information duties by the supplier. Thus: what happens and which remedies are available for the consumer, if the supplier does not comply with his information duties?

V. CONCLUDING REMARKS

Finally, let me raise two points, involving an assessment of the *Acquis Communautaire* in the field of information duties.

1. The Quality of *Acquis Communautaire* in the Field of Information Duties: Achievements and Defects

In the *Acquis Communautaire* relating to information duties I recognize a precious achievement, but also identify an embarrassing defect.

The achievement is in generalizing the principle, strongly stressed by Stefan Grundmann, that precontractual information may have binding contractual force. To me, this is a good principle, capable of solving in a quite simple and sound way many of the problems that national private law systems are trying to solve in a way which is never simple, and not always sound only by using categories such as *vices du consentement*, or *culpa in contrahendo*.

But there is a problem, or a defect which lies in the provisions often failing to specify the legal consequences (sanctions and remedies) to apply when due information is not given by the party obliged to give it. This is dealt with by one full section of the recent book I quoted above.[6]

One might object that this is not actually a problem, because the gap can be easily filled either by interpreting the European directives (according – someone suggests – to the principle of *effet utile*); or by devolving the definition of remedies to domestic legislatures transposing them into national systems.

Let me disagree. In my opinion, the issue of remedies is not just an important one: it is the crucial issue in the field of legal regulation of information duties. The choice among one or another remedy is a matter of policy, involving the 'political' responsibility of the European legislature; this responsibility cannot be devolved to the scholars' interpretation. Nor can it be left to national legislatures to freely choose among the possible remedies, for this could lead to a dramatic diversity of the law with regard to an issue which, simply because it is the crucial one, requires a fair degree of harmonization. In a few words: no subsidiarity principle could justify that in one member State the remedy for breach of the same information duty is a longer term for exercising the withdrawal right, while in another State it is avoidance of the contract, or in yet another it is recovery of damages.

---

6 *Supra* n. 5. The contributions on sanctions and remedies are by Wilhelmsson, Schwintowski and Magnus.

2. Bad Influence on National Systems, and the Risk of an 'Information Mannerism'

The *Acquis Communautaire* has an influence on domestic legal systems: a good influence, if the *Acquis* turns out to be good, or a bad one, if it turns out not to be so good.

A recent piece of Italian legislation demonstrates this. A few weeks ago the Italian Parliament passed an Act regulating franchise contracts (Act of 6 May 2004, n. 129).[7] If you read the text, you will find a lot of information rules in it. For example, it provides information to be given before the contract; information to be given after the contract, during execution of it; information to be put in the contract, as a necessary part of its content; information not to be disclosed to third parties (confidentiality duties). Out of nine articles forming the text of this act, at least five deal with information rules.

Nowhere will you find significant provisions as to the legal consequences of their infringement. So my impression is that such information rules will prove as numerous and emphatic, as practically insignificant and useless. Their insertion in the law seems a sort of conditioned reflex, the passive and mechanical tribute to a trendy fashion, rather than a conscious and deliberate choice of legal policy. In a word: something phoney.

This reminds me of a category well known in the history of art: mannerism. Mannerist painters of 16th and 17th centuries felt obliged to imitate the great Renaissance masters such as Raffaello or Michelangelo or Leonardo: but in respect of their ideal models, they were – let us say the word once again – somehow phoney.

And a legislation obsessively giving nominal information rules – without defining their real legal meaning and value and impact, but just imitating what it perceives as the present fashion of European contract law – seems somehow phoney as well. This is the reason why I dare mention there is a risk of 'information mannerism'.

3. Information Rules vs. Substantive Imperative Rules?

Some scholars – among them Stefan Grundmann[8] – emphasize the role of information rules as the very core of European contract law. They fundamentally argue about two things: one in point of fact; and the other in point of policy.

---

7 Cian, '*La nuova legge sull'affiliazione commerciale*' (l. 6 maggio 2004, n. 129), in: *Le nuove leggi civili commentate* (2004) p. 1153.

8 See e.g. Grundmann, 'Information, Party Autonomy and Economic Agents in European Contract Law' (2002) 39 CMLR pp. 269–293.

In point of fact, they assume that there is a very clear trend in European contract law towards the increasing predominance of information rules (prescribing information duties and/or making informational statements legally binding) over substantive imperative rules (that is over rules directly imposing or prohibiting certain specific contents of the contract).

In point of policy, they assume that this trend is politically desirable. Information rules do not restrain the parties' freedom of contract, while substantive imperative rules do. This implies that the former are more consistent with the values of a 'private law society', based on citizens' autonomy rather than on State coercion.

My opinion is a slightly different one. And I will try to express it succinctly.

As a matter of fact, the view that considers information rules to prevail over substantive imperative rules is neither false nor completely true; it rather requires some qualification or distinction. In my opinion, information rules prevail absolutely in vertical contract regulations, that is in regulations which refer to specific market sectors (package tours, time-sharing, financial services, and so on), or specific marketing techniques (distance contracts). In fact, when dealing with specific goods or services or marketing techniques, it makes sense to prescribe specific information duties. On the contrary, it makes less sense to insist on information duties when a horizontal contract regulation is at stake. What I mean by that is a type of regulation which is not designed for contracts implying specific goods or services or marketing techniques, but to general types or categories of contract (such as sale contracts, or contracts made between a businessman and a consumer). This is the reason why the 99/44 Sale Directive and the Directive 93/13 on unfair contract terms include many more substantive imperative rules than information rules.

As a matter of policy, I share the view that in dealing with informational asymmetries and other market failures, rules which are not there to imply State coercion on the private parties' autonomy are, in principle, more desirable than rules which conversely imply such coercion. But to me this is only possible if two conditions are met.

First: rules preserving freedom of contract are technically appropriate, that is to say, they are just as fit for their purpose. And this is not the case regarding information rules in the *Acquis Communautaire*, because of their failure to provide a clear and complete system of remedies. Secondly: rules preserving freedom of contract operate in their proper fields. And where information rules are concerned, the field of horizontal contract regulation seems to be much less proper than the field of vertical contract regulation.

4. The Future of Information Rules

In this perspective, the future of information rules seems to depend on:

- whether European contract law will be able to develop a more coherent system of sanctions and remedies than it has done until now; and
- whether its future development will imply more vertical regulations, or more horizontal regulations.

Thank you very much for listening to me so patiently.

Chapter 17
Formation of Contract and Pre-contractual Information from an English Perspective

Paula Giliker, University of Oxford

I. INTRODUCTION

The duty to provide information prior to contract has often been used as an example of the divergence between common and civil law jurisdictions.[1] Indeed, in contrast to their civilian counterparts, English lawyers continue to experience difficulties divorcing the question of pre-contractual liability from the doctrine of freedom of contract. Courts will still revert to the Latin phrase 'caveat emptor' to warn buyers (and all other contracting parties) of the need to protect their own interests in the negotiation process. There are a number of reasons for this. Natural conservatism opposes any radical change from the status quo, whilst political liberalism offers a policy-based rationale against intervention. A desire for certainty also plays a significant role, requiring security of transactions and clear and predictable rules which the courts are able to apply.[2] In the words of a leading contract lawyer, 'the rule may appear to operate harshly; but if a general duty of disclosure did exist it

1 See, for example, the chapters of Professors Nicholas and Ghestin in Harris and Tallon (eds.) *Contract Law Today* (1989); Legrand, 'Pre-contractual disclosure and information: English and French law compared', *OJLS* 6 (1986) 322 and, more recently, van Rossum, 'The duty of disclosure: Tendencies in French law, Dutch law and English law; Criterions, differences and similarities between the legal systems', *M.J.* 7 (2000) 300.

2 See Lücke, in: Finn (ed.), *Essays on Contract* (1987).

S. Grundmann, M. Schauer (eds), *The Architecture of European Codes and Contract Law*, 301–319

would be very hard to say exactly what must be disclosed in any particular case.'[3] In addition to this preference for a stable regime, there are economic justifications which highlight the cost of information acquisition and the social utility of incentives promoting the efficient generation of information.[4] If one party has invested time and money in gathering information, on what basis should he or she be required to disclose this information gratuitously? If full disclosure is required, one might question what incentives exist to seek or utilize information, perhaps of great utility to society. In such circumstances, equal access to information supported by a duty to inform will not necessarily lead to the most economically efficient result.[5] By approving 'the general principle that there is no obligation to speak within the context of negotiation for an ordinary commercial contract',[6] the courts are thus led to the general rule that, in the absence of a positive act, liability will not arise.

Yet, in favouring a rigid approach, the courts must nevertheless address a number of conflicting concerns. The general rule, and the possibility of harsh results, appear less acceptable when one is faced not with commercial parties dealing at arm's length, but a consumer contract or overt bad faith. It is difficult in such circumstances to argue that the parties are simply exercising their own free choice. Equally, commentators have recognized the limitations of the economic arguments in favour of non-disclosure and questioned whether, for example, they apply where information has been obtained casually without any effort or investment,[7] although in practice such distinctions are difficult to draw.[8] Where the rule appears to permit a stronger party to manipulate a weaker party, for example where one party cannot or does not possess the means to obtain the information in question, the arguments for intervention become stronger. Such concerns are further supported by the protective measures adopted by EC law, which have made significant changes to the pre-contractual information regime, particularly in the field of consumer law.

Therefore, in contrast to the strict common law position expressed by early 20th century case law,[9] the current legal position is more complex. In addition to EC law, the courts have developed a number of exceptions,

[3] Treitel, *The Law of Contract* (2003) 390.

[4] See, generally Waddams, 'Pre-contractual duties of disclosure', in: Cane and Stapleton (eds.), *Essays for Patrick Atiyah* (1991). For an analysis on the basis of law and economics, see Kronman 'Mistake, disclosure, information and the law of contracts', *Journal of Legal Studies* 7 (1979), 1; Trebilock, *The Limits of Freedom of Contract* (1993) pp. 106–118; Duggan, M. Bryan and Hanks, *Contractual Non-Disclosure* (1994).

[5] See Nicholas, 'The pre-contractual obligation to disclose information', in: Harris and Tallon (eds.), *Contract Law Today* (1989), 185.

[6] *Banque Keyser Ullmann SA v. Skandia (UK) Insurance Co*, [1990] 1 Q.B. 665 (798) per Slade L.J., CA.

[7] Kronman (n. 4).

[8] See Trebilock (n. 4).

[9] Classically, *Bell v. Lever Bros* [1932] A.C. 161 and *Smith v. Hughes* (1871) LR 6 Q.B. 597.

which do respond to the concerns raised above and promote a protective regime contrary to the principles of freedom of contract. The English position thus lies as much with the exceptions as the basic rule. Underlying the strictures of the bright line rule are a number of measures which ensure that, despite statements to the contrary, some duties of pre-contractual disclosure do arise in English law.

II. THE BASIC RULE

As stated above, the starting point in English law is that there is generally no duty to disclose:

> 'Where parties are contracting with one another, each may . . . observe silence even in regard to facts which he believes would be operative upon the mind of the other, and it rests upon those who say that there was a duty to disclose, to show that the duty existed.'[10]

There is thus no obligation to give the other contracting party information which would influence his or her decision,[11] or to correct a false assumption on which the other party is relying.[12] In the classic example, A buys B's horse which he thinks is healthy and pays the market price for a healthy horse. He would not have purchased the animal if he had known it to be unhealthy. In the absence of any representation by B as to the health of the horse or any contractual term to this effect, A cannot avoid the contract.[13] In the words of Lord Atkin:

> 'All these cases involve hardship on A and benefit B, as most people would say, unjustly. They can be supported on the ground that it is of

---

[10] *Davies v. London & Provincial Marine Insurance Co* (1878) 8 Ch D 469, 474 per Fry J. See also *Keates v. Cadogan* (1851) 10 CB 591; 138 E.R. 234 (landlord not liable for failing to warn a prospective tenant of the ruinous condition of the premises); *Fletcher v. Krell* (1872) 42 L.J. Q.B. 551 and *Bradford Third Equitable Benefit Building Society v. Borders* (1941) 2 All E.R. 205 (211) per Viscount Maugham: 'mere silence, however morally wrong, will not support an action of deceit'. As Cohen comments, 'Continental law postulates an *a priori* limitation of freedom of action in the bargaining process, subject to excuses or justifications exempting from liability. On the other hand, the position of English law is just the opposite: it is an a priori assumption of freedom in the bargaining process, subject to special rules imposing liability': Cohen, 'Pre-contractual duties: Two freedoms and the contract to negotiate', in: Beatson and Friedmann (eds.), *Good Faith and Fault in Contract Law* (1995), pp. 30–31.

[11] See Lord Atkin in *Bell v. Lever Bros* [1932] A.C. 161 (227): 'Ordinarily the failure to disclose a material fact which might affect the mind of a prudent contractor does not give the right to avoid the contract. The principle of caveat emptor applies.'

[12] *Smith v. Hughes* [1871] LR 6 Q.B. 597, provided, of course, that no representation has been made to induce this assumption.

[13] See Lord Atkin in *Bell v. Lever Bros* [1932] A.C. 161 (224).

> paramount importance that contracts should be observed, and that if parties honestly comply with the essentials of the formation of contracts – i.e. agree in the same terms on the same subject matter – they are bound, and must rely on the stipulations of the contract for protection from the effect of facts unknown to them.'[14]

As Halson has remarked, this 'is really no more than an application of the more general disinclination on the part of the common law to recognise a duty to negotiate in good faith'.[15]

A more recent example may be seen in the Court of Appeal decision of *Sykes v. Taylor-Rose*.[16] A house had been sold to the Sykes in 2000. They subsequently discovered that a horrific murder had been committed there in the early 1980s. A young girl had been killed by the then owner, who had hidden parts of her body around the house. This had been described in graphic detail in a Channel 5 documentary, which inferred that there were still body parts existing within the property. Unsurprisingly, the Sykes moved out of the house immediately and put the house on the market. The facts of the murder were disclosed to potential purchasers and the house sold six months later for £75,000; a reduction of 25 per cent of its ordinary market value.

Certain specific duties of disclosure are imposed on the vendor of a house in English law, for example to disclose defects relating to title, but these are limited.[17] Parties, in practice, will rely on pre-contract enquiries in which vendors are expected to respond to specific questions relating to the property.[18] In *Sykes*, the vendors had been asked, inter alia, whether there was 'any other information which you think the buyer might have a right to know'[19] and had responded in the negative. The Sykes brought an action alleging that the vendors had a duty to disclose the murder which they had known to have taken place in the property. This argument was, however, rejected by the Court of Appeal. In adopting a very narrow interpretation of the question asked, the court focussed on what information a buyer *might*

[14] Ibid.

[15] Halson, *Contract Law* (2001), 31.

[16] [2004] 2 P & CR 30. See also Pawlowski, 'Things that go bump in the night', *S.J.* 144 (2000) 1166; *cf. Taylor v. Hamer* [2003] 1 E.G.L.R. 103, CA. This case received much adverse comment in the British press; *The Guardian* newspaper describing the decision as one which 'is likely to cause confusion among house-sellers and their legal advisers, and perhaps even encourage dishonesty': *Guardian*, 13 March 2004.

[17] Beale (ed.), *Chitty on Contracts* (2004) 6–152; Spencer-Bower, Turner and Sutton, *The Law Relating to Actionable Non-Disclosure* (1990), paras 7.06–7.16; although Treitel (n. 3), p. 398 finds that it is confined to unusual defects of title which a reasonably prudent purchaser could not be expected to discover: see *Molyneux v. Harvey* [1903] 2 K.B. 487.

[18] The so-called 'Sellers Property Information Form.' See Abbey and Richards, *A Practical Approach to Conveyancing* (2004).

[19] Question 13 of the standard Law Society form, which has since been withdrawn.

have a *right* to know.[20] Assuming that the purpose of the question was to enable a vendor to respond without having to resort to legal advice, the Court took the view that it was enough to respond honestly. The vendor would not be required to point to reasonable grounds for his or her answer. An answer, subjectively believed to be correct, would suffice.

On this basis, having consulted their solicitor and being informed that there was no obligation to disclose the history of the house, the Taylor-Roses could not be found to be liable. In the words of Peter Gibson L. J.,

> 'it is for the buyer to decide what enquiries to raise and in what form. It cannot be doubted that a more specific and less subjective question going to the value of the property or to the ability of the purchaser to enjoy the property could have been asked.'[21]

The negative consequences of this ruling are obvious. Solicitors will be encouraged to engage in detailed pre-contract enquiries, rendering the process more complex and increasing legal costs. This has led commentators to question how detailed pre-contract inquiries will now have to be and how to reconcile such principles with current government proposals in the Housing Bill to impose obligations on sellers to provide information packs for prospective buyers.[22] *Sykes* is nevertheless helpful in identifying a number of important characteristics of English law. Parties are expected to protect their own interests. Liability may arise for misrepresentation or in the law of tort where one party has given an incorrect answer or misled the other party, but the onus is on the buyer to formulate the questions in such a way that liability may arise. The view of the Sykes that they could not in conscience dispose of the property without disclosing its grisly past received no legal recognition; the court refusing to place this 'moral' view within a legal framework. A general duty of disclosure was not even argued before the court.[23]

20 Adopting the reasoning of the Court of Appeal in *Economides v. Commercial Assurance Co plc* [1998] Q.B. 587.

21 Para. 50. Contrast the subsequent case of *Clinicare Ltd v. Orchard Homes & Developments Ltd*, [2004] *EWHC*, 1694, in which the claimant had specifically inquired whether the property had been affected at any time by dry rot. In such circumstances, a negative response gave rise to a clear action for misrepresentation when the premises were later found to have a history of dry rot and the dry rot had, despite the efforts of the vendor, continued to manifest itself.

22 See, for example, Pawlowski (n. 16), *S.J.* 148 497. The Housing Act 2004 includes a requirement that house-sellers supply a home information pack: see Part 5, sections 148–178. Before marketing a property, the seller, or, more usually, their estate agent will be expected to prepare a home information pack of standard documents available for prospective buyers. These will be prescribed by regulations, but may include information about title, the terms of sale, the physical condition of the property and any taxes or charges payable in relation to the property: see section 163.

23 A general duty of disclosure had been argued at first instance before HH Judge Langan QC, but rejected and this finding was not appealed.

Success would thus depend on the ability of the claimant to establish liability under one of the exceptions to the general rule.

III. THE EXCEPTIONS: CONTRACTUAL WARRANTIES, MISREPRESENTATION, AND TORT

The question thus arises: when will the English courts intervene and require pre-contractual disclosure? Professor Treitel, for example, in his classic textbook lists nine exceptions.[24] Six main heads emerge, which I will examine in turn:

(1) contractual warranties;
(2) misrepresentation;
(3) tort law;
(4) special types of contract which require disclosure;
(5) custom; and
(6) statute.

1. Contractual Warranties

These mark an indirect means by which parties may choose to impose a positive obligation to disclose. If A has warranted to B that the horse for sale is healthy, then B, who purchases the horse, may sue in contract should this prove to be false. To avoid contractual liability, therefore, A would be advised to disclose all information at his or her disposal at the time of making the contract. There is a close relationship between express warranties and the law of misrepresentation which will be examined below. Whilst misrepresentation will give the party a right to rescind the contract and possibly damages, it is generally regarded as a lesser remedy to breach of contract.[25] The court, in examining a pre-contractual statement, will examine the intention of the parties in deciding whether such statements amount to a warranty,[26] although they are more willing to provide a contractual remedy

[24] Treitel (n. 3), pp. 392–400: (i) representation falsified by later events; (ii) statements literally true, but misleading; (iii) custom; (iv) contracts *uberrimae fidei*; (v) contracts in which there is a limited duty of disclosure, e.g. contracts of suretyship or guarantee; (vi) fiduciary relationship, e.g. solicitor/client, principal/agent, partners, companies and its promoters; (vii) legislation; (viii) duty to clarify a legal relationship (where A sees B acting in reliance on a view of their legal relationship which is known by A to be false); (ix) duty of disclosure in performance of a contract.

[25] See Treitel (n. 3), pp. 352–3 although he concedes that the Misrepresentation Act 1967 has reduced the force of this distinction.

[26] *Heilbut, Symons & Co v. Buckleton*, [1913] A.C. 30 (51).

where, for example, one party has greater knowledge and skill than the other contracting party.[27]

Warranties may be express or implied. It is this latter category which has, in particular, presented the courts with a means by which they may regulate pre-contractual conduct.[28] The most well known illustration of this technique may be found in the Sale of Goods Act 1979.[29] In this Act, terms are implied as to title (section 12), sale by description (section 13), quality or fitness for purpose (section 14) and sale by sample (section 15). Section 14(2), for example, provides that where the seller sells goods in the course of a business, there is an implied term that they are of satisfactory quality *unless* any defect is specifically drawn to the buyer's attention before the contract is made.[30] Such provisions indirectly impose a duty to disclose. Liability will arise unless the seller provides full information concerning the goods in question.

One sees here also the influence of the *Acquis Communautaire*. By virtue of the Sale of Consumer Goods Directive,[31] parties are given further protection where they have relied upon advertising and public statements in purchasing the goods. The United Kingdom used the technique of implied terms to implement the Directive, and amended the Sale of Goods Act 1979 and Supply of Goods and Services Act 1982 accordingly.[32] As the UK government has stated, 'We did not take the easy route of merely copying out the Directive but integrated its provisions within existing legislation to produce a more coherent result.'[33] On this basis, section 14(2) of the 1979 Act has been expanded to include public statements relating to a consumer product, which will be taken to be indicative of the quality a consumer may expect, unless, of course, the seller corrects or withdraws any false statements prior

27 Compare *Dick Bentley Productions Ltd v. Harold Smith (Motors) Ltd*, [1965] 1 W.L.R. 623 and *Oscar Chess Ltd v. Williams*, [1957] 1 W.L.R. 370. The courts will also consider the time which has elapsed between the statement and formation of the contract, the importance of the statement, and whether it was included in any formal written contract: see *Bannerman v. White*, (1861) 10 C.B.N.S. 844; *Routledge v. McKay*, [1954] 1 W.L.R. 615; *Schawel v. Reade*, [1913] 2 I.R. 81.

28 Nicolas comments that 'The characteristic Common Law instrument for the judicial development of the law of contract is the implied term' in: Harris and Tallon (eds.), *Contract Law Today* (1989) p. 170. For criticism of this approach, see Farnsworth, Can Bus, *LJ* 19 (1991) 351.

29 See also Supply of Goods and Services Act 1982.

30 s. 14 (2C). The seller is equally not liable for defects which ought to have been revealed by an examination by the buyer before the contract is made: s. 14(2C)(b).

31 Directive 1999/44/EC of the European Parliament and of the Council of 25 May 1999 on Certain Aspects of the Sale of Consumer Goods and Associated Guarantees (OJ L 171).

32 See the Sale and Supply of Goods to Consumers Regulations S.I. 2002/3045, which came into effect on 31 March 2003.

33 See DTI Fact Sheet (June 2003): <www.dti.gov.uk/ccp/topics1/facts/saleofgoods_directive.htm>.

to contract.[34] It has been noted that these provisions differ from standard disclosure requirements because the dealer will be liable even if unaware of the defects and will thus take the risk for latent faults.[35] They thus establish a protective regime in which proof of the buyer's knowledge at the time of the contract is irrelevant.

A further example of this technique may be seen with the Package Travel, Package Holidays and Package Tours Regulations 1992.[36] These again rely on implied terms to ensure that consumers are fully informed of their rights[37] or of any significant alterations to an essential term of the contract.[38] Added force is given to the duty of disclosure by the use of criminal sanctions. For example, regulations 5 (coupled with Schedule 1) and 7 prescribe information which must be contained in holiday brochures and before any contract is concluded.[39] Regulation 9 imposes an implied condition that the contract contains at least the information specified in Schedule 2 of the Regulations, and that all the terms of the contract are set out in writing or in a comprehensible and accessible form and communicated to the consumer before the contract is made.[40] This regime has been described as 'a serious sanction which should encourage organisers to keep to the rules.'[41]

In both cases, legislation has limited the parties' freedom to restrict liability by express terms of a contract, thereby providing a safeguard to consumers against the greater economic strength of the retailer. Regulation

---

[34] See s. 14(2D). These will extend to public statements by the seller or producer on the specific characteristics of the goods, including advertising or on labelling. This is subject to s. 14(2E) which excludes such statements where the seller could not have been aware of them, had withdrawn or corrected them prior to contract, or where they did not influence the decision to buy the goods in question. Note equivalent amendments to Supply of Goods and Services Act 1982, s. 4.

[35] Duggan, Bryan and Hanks, *Contractual non-disclosure*, (1994) p. 38.

[36] SI 1992 No. 3288, as amended by the Package Travel, Package Holidays and Package Tours (Amendment) Regulations SI 1998 No. 1208 which came into force on 30 June 1998. These Regulations amend the 1992 Regulations to bring the wording into line with that of Council Directive 90/314/EEC on Package Travel, Package Holidays, and Package Tours (OJ L 158/59).

[37] See Regulation 9 and Regulation 6 which provides that 'the particulars in the brochure (whether or not they are required by Regulation 5(1) above to be included in the brochure) shall constitute implied warranties', giving rise to a claim for damages if broken, unless the brochure contains an express statement that changes may be made in the particulars contained in it before a contract is concluded and changes in the particulars so contained are clearly communicated to the consumer before a contract.

[38] Regulation 12. Regulation 4 additionally prohibits misleading descriptions of the holiday, price or any other conditions. Whilst this resembles misrepresentation, by imposing strict liability for breach, it has been suggested that it would be better regarded as contractual: Beale (n. 17), 6–91.

[39] See also Regulation 8 (Information to be provided in good time).

[40] Unless the interval between the time when the consumer approaches the other party to the contract with a view to entering it renders this impracticable.

[41] Lowe and Woodroffe, *Consumer Law in Practice* (2004) p. 210.

15 of the 1992 Regulations provides that liability for personal injury resulting from the non-performance or improper performance of services involved in the package cannot be excluded and that other losses may only be limited to the extent that this is 'reasonable'.[42] Equally section 6 of the Unfair Contract Terms Act 1977 provides that, as against a person dealing as a consumer, implied terms arising from sections 13–15 of the Sale of Goods Act 1979 cannot be excluded or restricted by reference to any contract term.[43] Freedom of contract is thus subject to the protective EC consumer regime, and a mixture of civil and criminal measures mean that the retailer has a strong incentive to ensure that the consumer is fully informed of his or her rights.[44]

Such legislative measures supplement the ability of the common law to identify contractual warranties. The classic common law decision in the context of pre-contractual negotiations remains that of the Court of Appeal in *Esso Petroleum Co Ltd v. Mardon*.[45] Here a representative of Esso of some 40 years' experience in the trade had estimated the annual throughput of a newly built filling station to be 200,000 gallons by the third year of operation. Mr Mardon had relied on this figure in taking a lease of the station. Unfortunately, this figure was unduly optimistic and Mardon, despite his best endeavours, was unable to achieve any figure near this estimate. The Court found Esso liable for breach of a contractual warranty and negligent misrepresentation. A factual statement on a crucial matter made by a person who had special knowledge and skill with the intention of inducing the other party to enter into the contract would amount to both a contractual warranty and misrepresentation, entitling Mr Mardon to damages. It should be noted, however, that the warranty was not of a guaranteed throughput, but that any estimate would be calculated with due care and attention. As a result, the amount of damages awarded would be the same whether the claim was classified as one for breach of warranty or misrepresentation. Where the claimant would not have entered the contract if he or she had received the correct information, liability under both heads would be assessed with a view to placing the claimant in the position he or she would have been in had the contract not been made.[46] The basis for the claim would not affect the compensation given.

---

[42] But see Regulation 15(3): 'In the case of damage arising from the non-performance or improper performance of the services involved in the package, the contract may provide for compensation to be limited in accordance with the international conventions which govern such services.'

[43] See also s. 6(1): implied undertakings as to title under s. 12 of the Sale of Goods Act 1979 cannot be excluded or restricted.

[44] See also the provisions of the Consumer Credit Act 1974, implementing Council Directive 87/102/EEC concerning Consumer Credit (OJ L 42/48, 1987).

[45] [1976] Q.B. 801. Contrast *Howard Marine and Dredging Co Ltd v. Ogden & Sons (Excavations) Ltd* [1978] Q.B. 574, CA.

[46] The tortious measure may exceed the contractual measure if there is proof of fraud or a claim is made under s. 2(1) of the Misrepresentation Act 1967.

Therefore, both at common law and by statute, contractual warranties provide a means by which the judiciary can maintain its adherence to the doctrine of freedom of contract and yet indirectly provide consumer protection.[47] This provides an acceptable compromise, balancing the perceived need for certainty with a limited form of intervention.

2. Misrepresentation

Mr Mardon was additionally able to bring a claim for negligent misrepresentation, and this head of liability provides a further basis for liability for non-disclosure. In the absence of a broad concept of mistake,[48] which is used by many civilian systems to impose an obligation to inform,[49] English law has turned to the law of misrepresentation to provide some protection for parties misled during the contracting process.[50] Liability for misrepresentation will arise where the defendant has made an unambiguous false statement of existing or past fact which is addressed to the claimant and on which the claimant has reasonably relied. Liability is confined, however, to false statements of fact. The remedies awarded will depend on whether it was uttered fraudulently, negligently or innocently, although the Misrepresentation Act 1967 extends liability where the claimant has been induced to enter into a contract 'after a misrepresentation has been made to him by another party thereto.'[51] The law of misrepresentation illustrates a fundamental characteristic of English law mentioned above: liability will not arise unless the defendant actively intervenes.[52] Mere silence or inactivity will not give rise to liability unless the claimant can identify a pre-existing relationship with the defendant in which an obligation to disclose may arise. In practice, however, the law of misrepresentation has proved more flexible than may be anticipated. By adopting broad definitions of 'statement' and 'fact', the courts have extended liability and thus indirectly supported the existence of pre-contractual obligations, despite the general rule stated above.

47 Note also the use of the collateral warranty to circumvent the strict rules of privity: *Shanklin Pier v. Detel Products Ltd* [1951] 2 K.B. 854.

48 See *Great Peace Shipping Ltd v. Tsavliris Salvage (International) Ltd* [2003] Q.B. 679, CA.

49 For example, see the use of art. 1110 of the *Code civil* in French law: see Terré, Simler and Lequette, *Droit civil: Les Obligations* (2005), Nos 213–218.

50 In addition to other protective concepts such as duress and undue influence which target abuse of the contracting process.

51 s. 2(1). See also s. 2(2) which provides for damages in lieu of rescission in the case of innocent misrepresentation.

52 Whittaker and Zimmermann note the English courts' continuing attachment to the distinction between 'positive action (to which liability may attach) and pure omission (to which no liability will attach in the absence of special circumstances)': Zimmermann and Whittaker (eds.), *Good Faith in European Contract Law* (2000) p. 656.

a. Statement

It is well established that the claimant must show that the defendant has made a statement of existing or past fact.[53] This will exclude vague and informal sales patter, mere statements of intent,[54] and statements of opinion.[55]

Yet, in a series of cases, the courts have demonstrated a willingness to find a representation even though no statement has been made. A statement may be made orally, in writing or by conduct.[56] In the words of Lord Campbell L. C.:

> 'Simple reticence does not amount to legal fraud, however it may be viewed by moralists. But a single word, or (I may add) a nod or a wink, or a shake of the head, or a smile from the purchaser intended to induce the vendor to believe the existence of a non-existing fact . . . would be sufficient ground.'[57]

Further, the courts have been willing to infer a fraudulent misrepresentation of fact where the defendant has committed some positive act, for example, by actively concealing a defect or by uttering a half-truth which gives an incorrect impression of the facts. In *Horsfall v. Thomas*,[58] for example, the misrepresentation consisted of the seller or his workmen concealing a defect in a gun which, after being fired several times, fell to pieces. In *Dimmock v. Hallett*,[59] a vendor of land, who informed a purchaser that certain farms on the land were let at a certain rent without revealing that the tenants had given notice to quit, was found to have made a material misrepresentation, contrary to the good faith required in conditions of sale.[60]

Silence may thus, in certain circumstances, amount to a misrepresentation. Liability will extend to a 'duty to communicate the change of circumstances'.[61] Although there is no duty to correct a known mistaken

53 See Treitel (n. 3) p. 331; Beatson, *Anson's Law of Contract* (2002) p. 240.

54 *Maddison v. Addison* (1883) 8 App Cas 467.

55 *Bisset v. Wilkinson* (1927) A.C. 177.

56 *Curtis v. Chemical Cleaning & Dyeing Co Ltd* [1951] 1 K.B. 805, 808 and *Spice Girls Ltd v. Aprilia World Service BV* [2002] E.M.L.R. 27, CA.

57 (1861) De GF & J 718 at 724, 45 E.R. 1056 at 1059.

58 (1862) 1 H & C 90, 158 E.R. 813 (although because the buyer had not examined the gun, it could not be said to have induced him to enter the contract). See also *Schneider v. Heath* (1813) 3 Camp 506; *Sybron Corp v. Rochem Ltd* [1984] Ch 112 at 130, and *Gordon v. Selico Ltd* (1986) 278 E.G. 53.

59 (1866) LR 2 Ch App 21. See also *Notts Patent Brick and Tile Co v. Butler* [1886] 16 Q.B.D. 778 (solicitor 'not aware of restrictive covenants' without mentioning that this was due to the fact he had not read the relevant documents!) and *Central Railway Co of Venezuela v. Kisch* (1867) LR 2 HL 99, 114.

60 *Dimmock v. Hallett* (1866) LR 2 Ch App 21, Turner L. J. at 28 and Cairns L. J. at 31. See also *Peek v. Gurney* [1873] LR 6 HL 377 (392 and 403), HL (although the claim failed because the statements in the prospectus were not in fact directed at the claimant).

61 Lord Wright M. R. in *With v. O'Flanagan*, [1936] Ch 575 at 583 (Romer L. J. concurring).

assumption,[62] the courts have been prepared to view as fraudulent a statement previously made which is now known to be incorrect. To avoid liability, the defendant is thus forced to correct the statement prior to contract. The leading example is that of *With v. O'Flanagan*,[63] where the vendor of a medical practice, whose takings had been reduced due to his illness, was found to be liable in misrepresentation for failing to correct his earlier statement before the contract was signed. Such a decision was justified as being 'so obviously consistent with the plainest principles of equity.'[64]

b. Fact

Whilst the starting point for the courts has been to seek a statement of fact, a number of decisions have blurred the distinction between fact and intention or opinion.[65] This takes two particular forms. First, a statement of intention may be interpreted as a statement of fact as to the present state of one's mind. In *Edgington v. Fitzmaurice*,[66] for example, a prospectus which falsely stated the objectives of the company's rights issue was held to have made a representation of fact – the fact in question being the state of mind of the directors when issuing the document.[67] Secondly, a statement of opinion by someone possessing superior knowledge or skill is often construed as an implied statement that the representor is aware of facts which reasonably justify his opinion. On this basis, a statement by the owners of a hotel that it possessed a 'most desirable tenant' was taken to be a statement of fact, not opinion. In view of their position, any statement was deemed to contain an implied assertion that they knew of no facts leading to the conclusion that he was not.[68] This latter category has proved particularly helpful in practice.

62 See *Smith v. Hughes* (1871) LR 6 Q.B. 597.

63 *With v. O'Flanagan*, [1936] Ch 575. See also *Davies v. London & Provincial Marine Insurance Co* (1878) 8 Ch D 469, 475 and Hudson, 'Making misrepresentations', *L.Q.R.* 85 (1969) 524.

64 Romer L. J. (n. 63), 586.

65 For example, in *Mutual Life v. Evatt* [1971] A.C. 793, 803, Lord Diplock perceived no obstacle to the inclusion of advice and opinion within negligent misstatement and Oliver J. in *Midland Bank Trust Co Ltd v. Hett, Stubbs & Kemp (a firm)*, [1979] Ch 384 extended the action to nonfeasance.

66 (1885) 29 Ch D 459.

67 'The state of a man's mind is as much a fact as the state of his digestion': ibid. per Bowen L. J. at 483.

68 *Smith v. Land and House Property Corpn* (1884) 28 Ch D 7, 15 per Bowen L. J.: 'the facts are not equally known to both sides, then a statement of opinion by one who knows the facts best involves very often a statement of a material fact, for he impliedly states that he knows facts which justify his opinion.' See also *Brown v. Raphael*, [1958] Ch 636 and *Box v. Midland Bank* [1979] 2 Lloyd's Report 391 (misrepresentation in failed pre-contractual negotiations).

The former, however, is of more limited utility in that it does not prevent the representor changing his or her mind at a later stage.[69]

c. The Relationship between Contract and Tort Law

One further characteristic of the law of misrepresentation should be noted. By its very nature, misrepresentation draws together the laws of contract and tort. Statements which are fraudulent or negligent may be viewed from the perspective of contract law (in that, it will allow the parties to rescind a contract), or tort (in that fraud and negligence will give rise to a tortious measure of damages). The result is a hybrid action in which even if a claim is brought under the Misrepresentation Act 1967, damages will be awarded on a tortious basis.[70]

A duty to disclose may thus arise in two ways: where the defendant's false statement of fact has induced the claimant to enter a contract or where a relationship recognized in tort renders the defendant responsible for the veracity of any statement made. English law has no difficulty in accepting parallel claims in contract and tort, provided that the duty in tort is not inconsistent with any contractual relationship between the parties.[71] Even in the absence of a contractual relationship, the claimant may still be able to bring a claim in tort if he or she can establish the existence of a duty of care. This will require, in particular, the identification of a relationship of proximity between the claimant and the defendant. In the leading case of *Hedley Byrne v. Heller and Partners*,[72] for example, the House of Lords accepted that a duty of care could arise between a bank and a third party seeking information on the creditworthiness of one of the bank's clients,[73] although their Lordships would require a 'special relationship' of proximity to exist between the parties and that the recipient must have reasonably relied upon the advice given. In recent years, this 'special relationship' or 'assumption of

---

69 *BAB v. Taylor* [1976] 1 W.L.R. 13 illustrates the difficulties involved. See also *Kleinwort Benson Ltd v. MMC*, [1989] 1 W.L.R. 379, CA (free to change mind when no binding contractual promise).

70 See *Royscot Trust Ltd v. Rogerson* [1991] 2 Q.B. 297, which resolved initial confusion as to the measure of damages: see *Naughton v. O'Callaghan* [1990] 3 All E.R. 191.

71 *Henderson v. Merrett Syndicates Ltd* [1995] 2 A.C. 145, 194 per Lord Goff. Where it is not, the parties will be taken to have agreed to limit or exclude the remedy in tort.

72 [1964] A.C. 465.

73 The case overturned long-held authority to recognize liability for negligent misstatement for the first time. Until 1964, it was generally accepted that no action would lie unless the claimant could prove fraud (*Derry v. Peek* (1889) 14 App Cas 337; *Candler v. Crane, Christmas & Co* [1951] K.B. 164) or a relationship of trust and confidence between the advisor and the advisee, for example, between solicitor and client: *Nocton v. Lord Ashburton* [1914] A.C. 932. But for the disclaimer of liability, the bank would have been liable for the financial losses of Hedley Byrne, which had relied on its negligent advice.

responsibility' has been interpreted broadly[74] to invoke liability of an employer to a former employee for the negligent preparation of a reference[75] and of a solicitor to potential beneficiaries of a will.[76]

Thus, by adopting a broad interpretation of the rules of misrepresentation and using the principles of tort law, the courts have indirectly imposed a limited obligation to disclose. It is interesting to note that this obligation derives from the interaction of principles of contract and tort law. In awarding damages generally on a tortious basis[77] and stressing elements of reliance and the relationship between the parties, the principles of tort law have proved themselves helpful in mitigating the rigours of the doctrine of freedom of contract. Non-disclosure in the English context can therefore not be considered solely from the perspective of contract law.

3. Tort

Outside misrepresentation, liability in tort for a negligent failure to disclose will generally be rare.[78] There is, however, a body of authority in which the court will impose a duty to disclose in tort where the defendant has assumed responsibility for a particular aspect of the relationship.

A good illustration may be seen in the negligence case of *Al-Kandari v. JR Brown & Co.*[79] Here, solicitors representing the husband (a Kuwaiti

---

74 Whittaker, 'The application of the "broad principle of *Hedley Byrne*" as between parties to a contract', *L.S.* 17 (1997) 169 argues that this broad principle is subversive of established rules of contract law.

75 *Spring v. Guardian Assurance plc* [1994] 2 A.C. 296. See Lord Goff (at 319): 'when such a reference is provided by an employer, it is plain that the employee relies upon him to exercise due skill and care in the preparation of the reference before making it available to the third party. In these circumstances, it seems to me that all the elements requisite for the application of the *Hedley Byrne* principle are present.'

76 *White v. Jones*, [1995] 2 A.C. 207. This case has proved controversial. While a solicitor obviously assumes responsibility towards his client, it is unclear why he should assume responsibility for his work to all the possible beneficiaries of a will. See A. Haydon 'Frustration of testamentary intentions: a remedy for the disappointed beneficiary' [1995] C.L.J. 238; Hedley, 'Recovering lost legacies: *White v. Jones* in the Lords', *Web J.C.L.I* 1 (1995); Cane, *Tort Law and Economic Interests* (1996) pp. 182–186; Kerridge and Brierley, 'Will making and the avoidance of negligence claims', Conv (1999) 399.

77 Damages for innocent misrepresentation under s. 2(2) of the Misrepresentation Act 1967 remain the exception.

78 See *Van Oppen v. Trustees of Bedford College*, [1990] 1 W.L.R. 235.

79 [1988] Q.B. 665. See also *Rust v. Abbey Life Assurance Co Ltd*, [1982] 2 Lloyd's Rep 386 at 391 (aff'd [1979] 2 Lloyd's Rep 334) and Slade L. J. in *Banque Keyser Ullmann SA v. Skandia (UK) Insurance Co Ltd* [1990] 1 Q.B. 665, 798–805 (aff'd on other grounds: *Banque Financière de la Cité v. Westgate Insurance Co Ltd*, [1991] 2 A.C. 249, HL). An indirect duty of disclosure will also arise in relation to defective products. Strict liability under the Consumer Protection Act 1987 (implementing Directive 1985/374/EEC) may be avoided where the producer gives a clear warning of any possible dangers: see s. 3(2)(a) of the Act and the courts' decisions in *Worsley v. Tambrands Ltd* [2000] PIQR P95 and *A v.*

citizen) in a custody battle had undertaken to retain his passport in view of his earlier abduction of the children of the family. Due to the need to amend the passport, it had been left at the Kuwaiti embassy with strict instructions that it should on no account be given to the husband. Nevertheless, the husband succeeded in persuading the embassy staff to relinquish the passport and two days later on an access visit, kidnapped his wife and children, left his wife bound and gagged in a van, and absconded to Kuwait with his two children. The Court of Appeal, while reluctant to impose a duty on the solicitors towards the opposing side in litigation, found that this was an exceptional case. The solicitors had voluntarily assumed responsibility towards the wife and children and this would require them to inform the wife and her solicitors that the embassy had retained the passport and that they would not be accompanying her husband when he attended the embassy the following day. As Bingham L. J. stated, 'She was entitled to know from the defendants that the safeguard, subject to which access [to the children] had been ordered, was no longer effective.'[80]

Therefore in the absence of a contractual warranty or misrepresentation, a pure obligation to disclose will arise only rarely in English law. The final examples outline three specific occasions when an obligation to inform will arise: due to the special nature of the contract, by custom and by statute. This is, of course, distinct from obligations which may arise in the performance of a contract where the very nature of the contract may give rise to duties of disclosure.

4. Special Types of Contract which Require Disclosure

The most common example of a contract which, by its nature, requires disclosure is that of the insurance contract.[81] Described as a contract *uberrimae fidei* (of utmost good faith), it requires full disclosure of all facts which a reasonable or prudent insurer would regard as material[82] to his decision to enter into the particular contract of insurance.[83] The obligation is

---

National Blood Authority (No. 1) [2001] 3 All E.R. 289. Duties of disclosure may further arise in other torts, for example, a doctor will be liable for trespass to the person if he or she does not inform a patient of the risks involved in an operation: *Sidaway v. Board of Governors of the Bethlem Royal Hospital* [1985] A.C. 871.

[80] (n. 79) p. 677.

[81] See Clarke, *The Law of Insurance Contracts* (2002).

[82] Identifying which terms are material has proven to be an ongoing problem in insurance law: see, recently, *Drake Insurance plc v. Provident Insurance plc* [2004] 1 Lloyd's Rep 268, CA; *Brotherton v. Aseguradora Colseguros SA (No. 2)* [2003] 2 All E.R. (Comm) 298, CA and comment R Gay [2004] L.M.C.L.Q. 1.

[83] See *London Assurance v. Mansel* (1879) L.R. 11 Ch D 363; *Lambert v. Co-operative Insurance Society* (1975) 2 Lloyd's Rep 485. Contracts for family settlements are also treated as contracts *uberrimae fidei*: *Gordon v. Gordon* (1816) 3 Swan 400; *Greenwood v. Greenwood* [1863] 1 DJ & S 28.

mutual,[84] although litigation will usually focus on disclosure by the insured. Such a duty is deemed necessary in practice where the information on the insured risk is peculiarly within the knowledge of the insured and it would place an unrealistic burden on the insurer to obtain such information himself. Failure to disclose such facts will give a right to rescind, but not a claim for damages for breach of contract or negligence.[85]

Fiduciary relationships will additionally give rise to an equitable obligation to disclose all material facts which might affect the contemplated transaction.[86] Where a party is placed in a position of trust, he or she will be expected to act in good faith and protect the interests of the other party. Such duties may arise in a number of circumstances, for example where the very nature of the relationship implies trust, such as a solicitor/client or doctor/patient relationship, or where the relationship between the parties as a matter of fact has given rise to fiduciary obligations. Such relationships will include that of principal and agent,[87] partnerships, and companies and its promoters.[88]

A more limited duty of disclosure is required for contracts of surety or guarantee where the creditor is only bound to disclose unusual circumstances which the surety will not commonly expect.[89]

5. Custom and Statute

This final category brings together disparate examples of duties of disclosure existing in English law. There is some authority that it may arise by virtue of trade custom. For example, in *Jones v. Bowden*,[90] the court held that it was

---

84 *Carter v. Boehm* (1776) 3 Burr 1905 at 1909, 97 E.R. 1162 at 1164 per Lord Mansfield, *Banque Financière de la Cité v. Westgate Insurance Co Ltd* [1991] 2 A.C. 249 at 268 and 281 per Lords Bridge and Jauncey respectively.

85 *Banque Financière de la Cité v. Westgate Insurance Co Ltd* [1990] 1 Q.B. 665, pp. 801–802. However, this rule does not apply to all contracts requiring disclosure and much will depend on the purpose of the rule of law for which the duty of disclosure is imposed: Treitel *op. cit.* p. 401.

86 See Martin, *Hanbury & Martin's Modern Equity* (2005) Ch. 21.

87 *Armstrong v. Jackson* [1917] 2 K.B. 822.

88 Reference should be made to works on partnership and company law, for example, Morse, *Partnership Law* (2006) and Davies (ed.), *Gower and Davies: The Principles of Modern Company Law* (2003).

89 *National Provincial Bank of England Ltd v. Glanusk* [1913] 3 K.B. 335, 338; *Cooper v. National Provincial Bank*, [1946] K.B. 1, 7, although there is some authority that an employer who takes a fidelity bond by which the honesty of one of his employees is guaranteed is under a higher duty: *London General Omnibus Co Ltd v. Holloway*, [1912] 2 K.B. 72. Beatson also notes that, following *Barclays Bank plc v. O'Brien*, [1994] 1 A.C. 180, more will be expected of a bank creditor where the surety is the spouse or cohabitee of the principal debtor and the transaction is not, on its face, to his or her financial advantage: (n. 53) 272.

90 (1813) 4 Taunt 847, 128 E.R. 565.

usual in a sale by auction of drugs to state in the broker's catalogue if any damage had been suffered after transport by sea. A failure to do so amounted to fraudulent misrepresentation. Legislation has also imposed specific duties of disclosure. The classic example is section 18(1) of the Marine Insurance Act 1906:[91] "The assured must disclose to the insurer, before the contract is concluded, every material circumstance which is known to the assured, and the assured is deemed to know every circumstance which, in the ordinary course of business, ought to be known by him. If the assured fails to make such disclosure, the insurer may avoid the contract."

Such examples are limited in number and specific in character. Most significantly, the courts emphasize their isolated nature, and are careful to avoid any indication that such exceptions may collectively support a wider principle.

IV. CONCLUSION: A DUTY OF FAIR DEALING?

Despite the basic rule stated above, it may be seen that English law is prepared to derogate from this position on certain specified occasions. Whilst insurance contracts (and other contracts *uberrimae fidei*) have always been regarded as exceptional, misrepresentation and contractual warranties provide English lawyers with a limited means to enforce 'fair dealing' or 'good faith' in contractual negotiations.[92] The case of *Thomson v. Christie's*[93] is illustrative of English legal technique. Ms Thomson purchased two bronze vases described as 'Louis XV' at a cost of almost £2 million from the famous London auction house. On later discovering doubts as to their provenance, notably that they were suspected to be 19th century copies worth only £20–30,000, she brought a claim against Christie's for failing to inform her of the questionable authenticity of the vases. Jack J., as may now be expected, approached liability not in terms of a duty to disclose, but by examining the law relating to misrepresentation and negligence. Christie's had treated Ms Thomson as a special client in full knowledge that this was a new field for her and that she had never made a comparable purchase before. They would therefore be liable under both heads; the judge finding that 'Christie's gave

---

[91] Although the section, in reality, amounted to no more than a codification of the existing common law position. A more recent example may be found in the Financial Services and Markets Act 2000, which places a duty on those responsible for producing listing particulars to ensure that they contain, at the very least, adequate information to enable investors and their professional advisers to make informed decisions about the issuer and securities in question: see ss. 80 and 82.

[92] One may note the references in a number of cases to 'equity' or 'good faith' when choosing to intervene on these grounds: see *With v. O'Flanagan*, [1936] Ch 575 and *Dimmock v. Hallett*, (1866) LR 2 Ch App 21 above.

[93] [2004] PNLR 42 (QB).

what was in the circumstances an incomplete picture and Ms Thomson was entitled to a fuller one.'[94] Yet, the response to this case has been to consider it purely in the context of the potential liability of auction houses, rather than a basis for developing any general principle of liability.[95]

If we compare the judgment of Jack J. with paragraph 4:107 of the Principles of European Contract Law,[96] we may make a number of observations. The first, and most obvious, is that in terms of legal methodology, English law will start from a position of caveat emptor before considering specific exceptions. There is no general principle in favour of disclosure 'in accordance with good faith and fair dealing'.[97] The specific examples possess their own justifications. It may be information which one person is peculiarly able to know and which it would be difficult for the other party to ascertain. Alternatively, a positive assertion may have been made which requires correction, or the defendant may have actively assumed responsibility for a matter on which the other has relied. This position continues to receive academic support. Professor Waddams, for example, has maintained that whilst a general rule of disclosure is not desirable, English law should seek instead to enlarge specific exceptions to ensure that, in particular contexts, honesty is the best policy.[98] The cases do refer to matters listed in 4:107 (3) – special expertise; cost of acquiring information; ability of other to acquire information; importance of information to other party – but the approach is more consistent with case-by-case analysis than any conception of commercial morality. For example, in *Thomson*, Jack J. and the Court of Appeal are influenced by the expertise of the auction house and the fact that it had advised Ms Thomson with the aim of encouraging her to purchase the goods in question. Whilst Ms Thomson could have sought advice herself, Christie's

[94] Para. 197. Even this ground was, however, reversed on appeal ([2005] PNLR 38). May L.J. confirmed that Ms Thomson was owed a duty of care, but held that Christie's were not liable for negligence or misrepresentation by failing to warn her of minor doubts as to the authenticity of the vases.

[95] The case nevertheless received a warm welcome by the British press: see *The Times* and *The Guardian* of 20 May 2004.

[96] 4:107: Fraud:
(1) A party may avoid a contract when it has been led to conclude it by the other party's fraudulent representation, whether by words or conduct, or fraudulent non-disclosure of any information which in accordance with good faith and fair dealing it should have disclosed.
(2) A party's representation or non-disclosure is fraudulent if it was intended to deceive.
(3) In determining whether good faith and fair dealing required that a party disclose particular information, regard should be had to all the circumstances, including:
(a) whether the party had special expertise;
(b) the cost to it of acquiring the relevant information;
(c) whether the other party could reasonably acquire the information for itself; and
(d) the apparent importance of the information to the other party.

[97] 4.107 (1).

[98] Waddams (n. 4), 254.

knew that she was not in this instance taking any independent advice and was relying solely on its expertise and reputation in this matter.

Thus, whilst English law continues to reject a duty of disclosure and maintain its adherence to the values of certainty and security of transactions, one may question to what extent the exceptions now represent an underlying trend towards some concept based on a duty of fair dealing.[99] As seen above, the expansion of implied warranties, partly supported by E.C. intervention, and the generous interpretation of the rules of misrepresentation go beyond the traditional exceptions recognised by English law and suggest a gradual recognition of the limitations of freedom of contract reasoning in modern contract law. Whilst English law formally continues to object to general duties of disclosure, in practice, it is willing to accept specific manifestations of such a duty, even to the extent of imposing liability for a failure to disclose defects which the seller had no reason to know.[100] Good faith and fair dealing thus play an underlying role in challenging and modifying the classical ideals of freedom of contract and arm's length dealing.[101] As Bingham L. J. explained perceptively in 1989:

> 'English law has, characteristically, committed itself to no such overriding principle but has developed piecemeal solutions in response to demonstrated problems of unfairness . . . This may yield a result not very different from the civil law principle of good faith, at any rate so far as the formation of the contract is concerned.'[102]

The real question therefore lies with the nature of common law reasoning itself. Will English law develop beyond the particular to a general conception of a duty of disclosure?[103] As this essay illustrates, opposition to this concept may still be found both in terms of specific policy objections and the traditional inductive form of common law reasoning. This does not prevent, however, the development of a body of law which challenges such views, but until the policy heads against a general duty are directly addressed, such authority will continue, despite the growing impact of EC law, to provide a limited exception to the still-influential doctrine of freedom of contract in English law.

---

99 Or what a leading judge has extra-judicially termed a duty to fulfil 'the reasonable expectations of honest men': Steyn, *L.Q.R.* 113 (1997) 433.

100 See liability under the Sale of Goods Act 1979 above, although such liability has been described as harsh and questionable by an American commentator: see Farnsworth (n. 28), 355.

101 Kessler and Fine, '*Culpa in contrahendo*, bargaining in good faith, and freedom of contract', *Harv L* 77 (1964) 448 (401).

102 *Interfoto Picture Library Ltd v. Stiletto Visual Programmes Ltd* [1989] Q.B. 433, 439 and 445. See also Zimmermann and Whittaker (n. 52), pp. 699–701.

103 See Samuel, in: Van Hoeke (ed.), *Epistemology and Methodology of Comparative Law* (2004), Ch. 4, pp. 54–57.

Chapter 18

Formation of Contract and Pre-Contractual Duties to Inform in a Comparative Perspective

*Peter Mankowski, Hamburg University**

I. INTRODUCTION

The formation of contracts attracts less attention than the performance of contracts; remedies and damages for breach of contract capture the attention far more than the consequences of mistakes. A number of reasons can be identified why the formation of contract[1] is (erroneously) regarded as a less interesting component of contract law: First, there are fewer issues than in the field of performance and breach of contract. Secondly, some issues are not germane to contract law, but rather form part of a general law of declarations. It need not be specifically offer or acceptance when it comes down to mistake or threat (or duress). Thirdly, another set of questions still awaits in-depth discussion both in the national legal orders and in the European or UNIDROIT Principles. From those topics, the participation of third parties

* Prof. Dr. iur., Chair for Private Law and Private International Law, University of Hamburg; Director of the Seminar for Private International and Comparative Law of the University of Hamburg.

[1] On formation of contracts in EC law see Troiano, 'Formation of Contracts under EC Directives', in: Schulte-Nölke, Schulze and Bernardeau (eds.), *Europäisches Vertragsrecht im Gemeinschaftsrecht* (2002) p. 97; Pfeiffer, '*Der Vertragsschluss im Gemeinschaftsrecht*', in: Schulze, Ebers and Grigoleit (eds.), *Informationspflichten und Vertragsschluss im Acquis Communautaire* (2003) p. 103.

S. Grundmann, M. Schauer (eds), *The Architecture of European Codes and Contract Law*, 321–338

in the negotiating and drafting process has been selected for more in-depth analysis. 'Third parties' here is understood in a rather formal sense as everyone other than the contracting parties, i.e. everyone who is not himself in the formal role of a contracting party. Whether a contracting party is held responsible for, or becomes contractually bound by, the actions of such a third party is a second-tier question outside the scope of this presentation.

However, one small part of the law on the formation of contracts has been the subject of thorough legal analysis and even intensive legislation, mostly from European quarters: namely pre-contractual duties to inform. In recent years this has emerged as one of the key topics of modern-day contract law. This might reflect the increasing importance of information at the beginning era of the Information Age. On the other hand it might reflect the increasing sensitivity regarding information and the increasing value of information as a good.

One last introductory remark appears appropriate (or, even worse, necessary) in order that the reader not be misled by the title and in due course disappointed if his expectations are not met: This presentation is not a classical exercise in comparative law. It does not proceed by concentrating on the nitty-gritty of comparing section X BGB to article Y Code Civil or article Z NBW or the most recent decision of the Court of Appeal in *T v. T*. Nor is it a general report summarizing and combining national reports. A general report without the opportunity to read the national reports in advance would be futile, if not bound to fail altogether. Conversely, this presentation is comparative insofar as it circles around the yardstick for a comparison, around defining the *tertium comparationis* in substance. It boldly attempts to identify and to unveil some underlying rationales. The topics covered comprise mistake, threats (duress), participation of third parties in the negotiating and drafting process, and – last but definitely not least – pre-contractual duties to inform.

II. SELECTED ISSUES ON THE FORMATION OF CONTRACT

1. Mistake

Mistake as a legally recognized phenomenon is a common feature of European legal orders.[2] Although the legal orders vary as to the extent of such recognition and as to their respective definition of mistake, the possibility to avoid a contract on the ground of one's own error exists almost universally across Europe. The constructions might differ, but the solutions and the

2 *Cf.* for the historical development Zimmermann, *The Law of Obligations* (1996) pp. 583–620.

systematic approaches are broadly equivalent.[3] For the sake of clarity, it should be emphasized that in the present context 'mistake' means unilateral mistake and that the somewhat different issue of common or, in American terminology, mutual mistake will not be dealt with here. A mistake lies at, and undermines, the roots of a statement. Our Austrian hosts very appropriately (and with wonderful mastery of the German language) define a mistake as a '*Wurzelmangel*'.[4] Nevertheless, going one step beyond that, it appears neither self-evident nor self-explanatory why his own mistake, his own error, should allow the erring party to rescind his statement and consequently the contract. Where is the justification for such a remedy, where is the rationale behind such a bold attempt?

a. Justification for Relying on an Own Mistake

Even he who erred issued a statement. Even he who erred consented, by his own statement, to the contract. The binding force of a given word is one of the central pillars of contract law. Without it, either contract could not exist as an instrument engendering confidence or the sheer volume of safety mechanisms would make it prohibitively expensive. That the vast majority of legal orders recognise mistake and allow for consequences favouring the erring party is fact, but is not in itself a justification for undermining the fundamental values of the entire contract law system, such as the binding force of a given word.

i. Insufficiency of Protecting Free Will and of the Willensdogma

The traditional justification for favouring the erring party's interests is that a statement issued as a result of a mistake does not properly reflect the erring party's will. Congruency between that party's will and the statement is said to be lacking.[5] The error-prone statement *in extremis* was regarded as a *nullum*.[6] As long as a strict *Willensdogma* prevailed, this explanation might possibly have been deemed to suffice. In contract the required meeting of the minds (i.e. the properly expressed minds) was said to have not taken place.[7] On closer examination, however, such an assertion can be seen to be extremely questionable. To put that much emphasis on the erring party's will allows that party too many chances for opportunistic behaviour. Furthermore,

---

3 Riesenhuber, *System und Prinzipien des europäischen Vertragsrechts* (2003) p. 350; id., *Europäisches Vertragsrecht* (2003) para. 412.

4 E.g. Kerschner, *Irrtumsanfechtung* (1984).

5 *Cf.* e.g. Bork, *Allgemeiner Teil des Bürgerlichen Gesetzbuchs* (2001) para. 818.

6 D. 44, 7, 57 (Pomp.): *In omnibus negotiis contrahendis [. . .] si error aliquis intervenit [. . .] nihil valet quod actum sit.*

7 D. 50, 17, 116, 2 (Ulp.): *Non videntur qui errant consentire.*

in substance, the complex question remains unanswered – why the erring party should be allowed to externalise the consequences of his mistake and why, correspondingly, the other party should carry the respective burdens. The counter-party would hardly accept the erring party's will as a sufficient reason for the revocation of the initial statement. In any event, the erring party must not be allowed to occupy a position which enables him to become the sole interpreter of his own will, and so able to dispose of his obligations. Such partisanship would deliver a major blow to the other parties' trust in the first party's statements. Hence it would undermine an indispensable precondition for intersubjectively upheld bargains and for the efficient division of work and cooperation based on contract,[8] as it is typical for the modern world. Such subjectivity would generate counter-measures by the (prospective) counter-parties at a prohibitively high level of costs. The *Willensdogma* is idealistic. Its inherent shortcomings are obvious. Accordingly one has to look for a better reason supporting the contention that mistake nullifies, invalidates or at least allows the revocation of an error-prone statement.[9]

ii. Avoiding Superoptimal Care or a Suboptimal Level of Activity

Better reasons emerge if one considers the theoretically possible alternative that mistake-prone statements would be enforced in any event. How would a rationally acting and risk-averse party react to that? The answer would be two-fold:[10] Parties prospectively issuing statements would invest superoptimal care in order to avoid errors and mistakes at almost any cost.[11] But experience shows us that it is practically impossible to avoid errors or mistakes with 100 per cent certainty. Errors will occur. Who would claim that he 100 per cent avoids every possible lapse, however remote? Such an endeavour is simply not humanly possible. *Errare humanum est, nota bene*. No human

[8] Eisenhardt, *Allgemeiner Teil des BGB* (2002) para. 327.

[9] A comparative survey on possible remedies is provided by Kramer, 'Defects in the Contracting Process- Mistake', *Int. Encycl. Comp. L.* VII/11 (2001) paras 11/92–11/109.

[10] For the sake of clarity it ought to be mentioned that the following argument is not the least based on any preventive effect of a restrictive regulation of mistakes; *cf.* the scepticism on this other issue by Rabin, 'A Proposed Black-Letter Rule Concerning Mistaken Assumptions in Bargain Transactions', *Tex. L. Rev.* 45 (1967) 1273 (1299).

[11] Huber, 'Mistaken Transfers and Profitable Infringements of Property Rights: An Economic Analysis', *La. L. Rev.* 49 (1988) 71 (99); Wonnell, 'Unjust Enrichment and Quasi-Contracts', in: Bouckaert and De Geest (eds.), *Encyclopedia of Law and Economics, Vol. II: Civil Law and Economics* (2000) pp. 795 (801); Mankowski, 'Book review', *JZ* (2002) pp. 297 (298); Mankowski, *Beseitigungsrechte* (2003) p. 380; cf. Adams, '*Irrtümer und Offenbarungspflichten im Vertragsrecht*', *AcP* 186 (1986), 453, 486; Rasmussen and Ayres, 'Mutual and Unilateral Mistake in Contract Law', *J. Leg. Stud.* 22 (1993) 309, 334; Fleischer, '*Der Kalkulationsirrtum*', *RabelsZ* 65 (2001), 264 (280) and also Hultmark-Ramberg, 'The E-Commerce-Directive and Formation of Contract in a Comparative Perspective', *Eur. L. Rev.* 26 (2001) pp. 429 (444).

being has an absolutely perfect control mechanism. In its extreme consequence such a mechanism would also entirely suppress spontaneity, which forms an essential and not unwelcome feature of real-world human nature. Any attempt to avoid every possible error would be doomed to failure, as it could never reach its goal. On the other hand it would exceed the area of marginal benefit. Thus it would consume resources to an unnecessary extent. The party prospectively issuing a statement would have to internalize avoidance costs, which would exceed the social costs arising from correcting occurring errors.[12] Hence, superoptimal care would be applied instead of optimal care *in suis*, maximising overall welfare. Superoptimal care is no less inefficient than suboptimal care. To the contrary, it produces superfluous and thus wealth-reducing direct costs. Expenditures for superoptimal care eat into the potential surplus generated by the contract. Setting incentives for double, triple- or otherwise multiple checking is clearly inefficient.[13]

The alternative way of reacting would lead to a suboptimal level of activity.[14] Risk-averse parties would reduce their level of activity and refrain form certain activities, although pursuing and carrying out those activities would enhance and maximise welfare and general wealth. Activities enhancing general welfare should be socially encouraged. The law should by no means give incentives to refrain from such socially productive activities. The (hypothetical) loss of enhancement of general welfare resulting from not undertaking such activities at least equals the loss stemming from the insecurity generated by the legal consequences of a mistake.[15] The possibility of a revocation also reduces the risk of opportunistic behaviour where the party receiving the error-prone statement exploits detected mistakes to the other party's detriment.[16] Insecurity is the legal instrument and tool to diminish such unwanted opportunistic behaviour. Windfall profits are not secured but are likely to be taken away. Exploitation leading to unproductive, and probably[17] costly, exercises in mere redistribution should not be encouraged, but should be actively discouraged. Otherwise a perverse incentive would arise for the receiving party not to clarify detected mistakes.[18] This could also negatively effect the allocation of wealth, as the probability of misallocations would rise dramatically, if not exponentially.

12 Wonnell, 'Unjust Enrichment and Quasi-Contracts', in: Bouckaert and De Geest (eds.) (n. 11), pp. 795 (801).

13 Mankowski (n. 11), p. 380; Eisenberg, 'Mistake in Contract Law', *Cal. L. Rev.* 91 (2003) 1573 (1579).

14 Mankowski (n. 11), pp. 380–381.

15 That voidness, nullity or voidability due to mistake do not generally carry the justification that they would enhance allocational efficiency in every single transaction, does not provide an argument to the contrary; Bouckaert and Schäfer, 'Mistake of Law and the Economics of Legal Information', in: Bouckaert and De Geest (eds.) (n. 11), pp. 217 (235–238).

16 Fleischer (n. 11), pp. 264 (279); Mankowski (n. 11), 381.

17 Due to the costs of enforcement against the erring party's will.

18 Wonnell (n. 11), pp. 795 (801).

b. Avoidable and Unavoidable Mistakes

On the other hand the opposite risk, that a party alleges that it issued its statement under a mistaken belief, has to be carefully considered and, in effect, contained. An unrestricted freedom to plead mistake would make contract law implode. However, a feasible legal notion of mistake[19] and the burden of proof that a mistake in fact occurred placed upon the party pleading mistake are appropriate means of containment, especially if courts reinforce the burden of proof.[20] A restrictive notion, and a none too generous approach as to when vitiation or reversal on the ground of mistake is allowed, provide the best cure. Scepticism about allegations of a mistake and careful examination back-up such an approach.

A well-known borderline runs between avoidable and unavoidable mistakes. Many legal orders are familiar with this test, which ultimately falls back on some kind of culpa contra seipsum. In many legal orders the unavoidability of the mistake is decisive for letting the erring party off the hook of its own previous statement. From a comparative perspective, a worldwide tendency towards distinguishing along this line appears discernible.[21] The Principles clearly mirror and reflect such a trend as seen in article 3.5 (2) UNIDROIT Principles and article 4:103 (2) Principles of European Contract Law indicate.

Avoidability is closely linked to diligence costs. Insofar as an avoidable mistake ought to be internalized, a risk-averse person gets incentives to invest in diligence costs in order to avoid such a mistake. On the other hand, bearing in mind the reasons why freeing a person from his own word due to a mistake is allowed, the notion of avoidability must take into account that no superoptimal care should be exercised and that no resources should be wasted for excessive diligence costs. Once again article 3.5 (2) (a) UNIDROIT Principles prudently recognises this insofar as it excludes invoking a mistake only in the event that the declaring party acted grossly negligently and did not act diligently. Raising the threshold redefines the yardsticks and avoids the opposite danger of becoming overly restrictive. Article 4:103 (2) (a) Principles of European Contract Law employs a similar concept insofar as it refers to an inexcusable mistake. However, this yardstick is more open and thus less advisable. Generally, article 4:103 Principles of European Contract Law establishes a mixed standard with both subjective and objective elements.[22]

---

19 Comparative survey by Kramer (n. 9), paras 11/12–11/29.

20 Succinctly Farnsworth, 'Oops! Mistakes and the Law: Scepticism and Proof', *FS Peter Schlechtriem* (*2003*), pp. 465 (484–486).

21 *Cf.* for a comparative survey Kramer, *Der Irrtum beim Vertragsschluss*, (1998), paras 37–40; *id.*, 'Defects in the Contracting Process-Mistake', *Int. Encycl. Comp. L.* VII/11 (2001) paras 11/42–11/45.

22 Wolf, '*Willensmängel und sonstige Beeinträchtigungen der Entscheidungsfreiheit im europäischen Vertragsrecht*', in: Basedow (ed.), *Europäische Vertragsrechtsvereinheitlichung und deutsches Recht* (2000) pp. 85 (99); Mankowski (n. 11) p. 1128.

2. Threats (Duress)

a. Threats as Unproductive Games

Threats[23] can be seen, in economic terms, as hold-up situations.[24] They give rise to a presumption that they would not enhance and maximise overall welfare, but would only establish a redistributive zero-sum game.[25] Ordinarily, one does not have to force someone to act in his own best interests or for his own gain. He who obtains goods by way of threat might devaluate them, insofar as he might not hold them in the highest regard since he obtained them at lesser costs than he would have had to invest if the other party had been at liberty to decide. Obtaining goods by way of threat would thus not allocate goods where they are held in the highest esteem (and where they presumably would produce the highest overall wealth).[26] Even if exceptionally a positive effect of allocation can be identified, the law could not recognize the transfer: If the law recognized the transfer, inefficiency would be enhanced as a risk-averse potential victim would feel it necessary to invest in protective measures and superoptimally high protection, the aggressor would then follow suit and invest in a more aggressive potential.[27]

Additionally the institution market and the allocational function of this institution would be weakened and damaged.[28] To give effect to threats would undermine the incentives to produce and offer goods, since the producer could be forced to distribute the goods at a less favourable price which does not contain a premium for information or activity.[29] Threats, in particular latent and hidden threats, can result in a destructive power game.[30] The threatened persons could be unproductively forced into defensive measures – in such a way that resources could be wasted simply because of the possibility of the threat.[31]

---

23 Or duress in more classical terminology.

24 Graham and Peirce, 'Contract Modification – An Economic Analysis of the Hold-Up Game', *L. & Contemp. Probl.* 52 (1) (1989) 9 (11); De Geest, *Economische analyse van het contracten en quasi-contractenrecht* (1994) p. 191 following *Alaska Packers' Association v. Domenico*, [9th Cir. 1902] 117 F. 99 (101).

25 Cooter and Ulen, *Law and Economics*, (2004), 269 and also Schäfer and Ott, *Lehrbuch der ökonomischen Analyse des Zivilrechts* (2000) p. 365.

26 *De Geest* (n. 24) p. 191.

27 Landes and Posner, *The Economic Structure of Tort Law* (1987) pp. 154–156; Köndgen, '*Gewinnabschöpfung als Sanktion unerlaubten Tuns*', *RabelsZ* 64 (2000), 661 (681 *et seq.*).

28 *Köndgen* (n. 27) p. 682.

29 *De Geest* (n. 24) p. 191.

30 Heussen, in: Heussen (ed.), *Handbuch Vertragsverhandlung und Vertragsmanagement* (1997) para. 355.

31 Cooter and Ulen (n. 25) p. 269.

Additionally, in negotiations between partners of roughly equal bargaining power, threats provoke counter-threats as the opponent's preferred strategy.[32] At the very least the opponent, the threatened, would feel inclined to point out negative consequences for the threatening person, which in turn would reduce added wealth or would at least not produce additional wealth in case that the threat should be effectively realised.[33] This generates a confrontational and non-cooperative climate for the negotiation and thus causes difficulties in itself. With high probability transactions costs will rise, i.e. resources will be wasted and the overall wealth maximizing potential of the entire bargain will be reduced. Nullity, voidness or voidability of a statement by a threatened person rightly leads to the annulment of a forced transfer.[34]

b. Distinguishing Between Threats and Legitimate Bargaining Tactics

Condemning threats and sanctioning them is pretty easy. Everyone can agree on this straight away, and the rationale appears crystal-clear. But this is only one side of the coin. By far more difficult is the definition: What constitutes a threat? Or for practical purposes: how could one possibly distinguish a threat from legitimate bargaining tactics? This is the tricky one. In modern-day negotiations, an exchange of 'If you do not agree to this I will . . .' is commonplace and happens millions of times a day around the globe. Bazaar style negotiations nurture such tactics. In particular one party might be pressing for a compromise or a concession by the other party and establishes a prerequisite to its own assent. As parties are generally free to consent or not, establishing the concession by the other party as a precondition to be met is a legitimate tactic.[35] Furthermore, this does not necessarily constitute a zero sum game. In some instances, the overall welfare might be maximized and enhanced by such tactics.[36] The best effort to draw the borderline between threats or duress on one hand and legitimate tactics on the other hand is: A promise extracted as the price to cooperate in creating value is enforceable whereas a promise extracted by a threat to destroy value should be unenforceable or at least voidable.[37]

---

32 On so-called optimal threatening strategies in negotiations cf. Holler and Illing, *Einführung in die Spieltheorie*, (2000) pp. 222–226. A caveat should be added nonetheless: Those authors use a wider notion of threats which in fact includes ordinary bargaining tactics which do not constitute zero sum games, but lead to compromises enhancing the added value of the contract and are thus wealth maximising.

33 Heussen (n. 30) para. 355.

34 OLG Halle 15 September 1948, *NJ* (1949) pp. 220 (221).

35 OLG Jena 10 December 1997, *OLG-NL* (1998) 38 (40); Mankowski (n. 11) p. 368.

36 Cooter and Ulen (n. 25) p. 270; Mankowski (n. 11) p. 368.

37 Cooter and Ulen (n. 25) p. 271.

3. Participation of Third Parties in the Negotiating and Drafting Process

a. Advantages of Drafts by Neutral Third Parties

Drafts which neutral third parties insert into the negotiating process avoid a race for the relative monopoly of formulation and for agenda-setting by the parties.[38] The neutrally produced draft prevents opportunistic behaviour by the parties, insofar as the parties would otherwise try to introduce their own draft as early as possible in order to prepare the ground for the negotiation. Parties and their agents tend to pitch high and demand too much in order put themselves into a position to allegedly negotiate for reductions from the other party and thus to reach the internally intended aims.[39] Agenda setting facilitates mock concessions and the attainment of the party's own internal goals through such faux concessions. Successful agenda setting generates additional bargaining chips in the negotiations about the nitty-gritty. The other party finds itself in a position that it must make concessions in order to reduce the comparative advantage. Drafts by a neutral third party might help to structure and to focus negotiations. They allow for a level of detail and contractual provisions which would be interpreted as a sign of distrust and non-reliance if they came from either of the parties.[40] They also offer an opportunity to concentrate on the core issues. Hence they might save transaction costs by shortening the negotiations, in that they can reduce the number of rounds of negotiation by preparing a kind of level playing field. This gains more importance the more parties tend to negotiate in bazaar style. Settlement accords in insolvency proceedings, drafted by neutral receivers or '*Insolvenzverwalter*', provide an excellent example.

b. Neutrality of the Third Party as a Hidden Problem

Nevertheless, a hidden problem can be posed by the alleged neutrality of a third party. The alleged neutral might in fact turn out to be a dependent person in disguise. This is a specific principal-agent problem if the third party (the agent) acts for multiple principals who have generally diverging, if not conflicting, interests and is closer to one of the respective camps. Typically,

---

38 Walz and Fembacher, '*Zweck und Umfang der Beurkundung nach § 15 GmbHG*', *NZG* (2003), 1134 (1136).

39 Walz and Fembacher, '*Zweck und Umfang der Beurkundung nach § 15 GmbHG*', *NZG* (2003) pp. 1134 (1136).

40 Walz and Fembacher, '*Zweck und Umfang der Beurkundung nach § 15 GmbHG*', *NZG* (2003) pp. 1134 (1136).

the third party is a professional offering his drafting services. As a professional he is interested in repeat business. He is aiming for repeat business and to become the relevant agent in a number of cases. His expertise gets a higher return on investment the more often he is engaged, the more often his services are used by interested parties. If only one of the parties is a repeat customer in the respective trade or business, and the other deals with such matters at best only occasionally, the third party will be interested in establishing business links with the former. The repeat customer offers the opportunity for repeat business.

If the third party actually acts repeatedly under a contract with one of the parties, matters appear even clearer and more obvious. The most prominent example from Germany may be the '*Hausnotar*' ('house notary'). In this event the other party might feel inclined to invest more in monitoring and controlling and might check the draft produced by the third party intensely. However, the other party will have a close eye on his own marginal costs. In particular where it is a single instance for this party, investments in building up specific knowledge might not pay and will return less. Investments in monitoring costs would not produce consequential benefits. An example deliberately chosen from B2C relations: A consumer buys real estate from a commercial developer or conveyancer. The commercial party's 'house notary' produces a draft contract. Ordinarily, the consumer-buyer will not invest in having this draft checked by his own lawyer.

c. Business Organizations, Standard Setters and Standard Contracts

Up to now the focus was on cases where a particular third party got involved, chosen by the parties to develop a draft providing for an in principle individual solution. Nonetheless, third parties could become involved and exercise influence on the contents of a contract on a more abstract level too. In particular, business organizations or other standard setters can develop standard contracts, standard terms and conditions, etc., and issue recommendations to employ these in respective transactions. There is a certain appeal for the parties in this. At least it can save transaction costs which would otherwise have to be spent (if not to say sacrificed) for drafting and negotiating a concrete and individual contract. Not only costs, but also time and effort, can be saved. Additionally, the potential for rationalization regarding standard transactions can be realized. Furthermore, the parties can draw upon the experience and know-how of the business organization or standard setter. Those professionals who repeatedly do business in a market in differing roles, as buyers or sellers, appreciate this. Generally they can rely on those standards being balanced and fair to all sides of the market. A battle of forms, with its incumbent risks, is avoided and security is greatly enhanced.

At least this applies to business organizations and standard setters who ordinarily do not operate on only one side of the market and who must thus consider the interests of both sides. Many organizations offer corresponding ADR so that dispute resolution mechanisms and substantive rules conform with each other. An important example might be provided by the GAFTA (Grain and Food Trade Association) in London. Grain dealers conclude contracts with a short and conclusive reference to one of the standard contracts drafted by GAFTA, e.g. GAFTA 400.

Problems once again occur, and one may run into deep and troubled water, if the business organization represents the interests of only one side of the market, as for instance organizations of car dealers, furniture dealers or plant suppliers do. Though such business organizations are normally open about whom they represent, and in most instances the name of the organization clearly indicates that no one should expect neutrality from them. Information about the lack of neutrality is readily available. Any reliance on neutrality is destroyed even in advance, and trust must not be placed by parties on the opposite side of the market. In fact, the other party is required to find out whether there is an opposing business organization on his side of the market, or to start a battle of forms.

III. PRE-CONTRACTUAL DUTIES TO INFORM

1. Outset and Ramification

The so-called information paradigm is a true paradigm of modern contract law. Free will has its prerequisites. A decision by a person should be an informed decision. Only an informed decision can be fully binding on the person making the decision. From another perspective: Informational asymmetry can render a contract inefficient. The better informed party can attempt to benefit from its informational edge and to exploit the less informed party. Better access to information can result in quite remarkable advantages in drafting the contract. This threatens a redistributive transfer of wealth from the less to the better informed party. Neglecting possible enhancements of allocational efficiency, which are far from guaranteed, such a transfer would at best be a zero sum game, but in most instances have a negative overall outcome, as the transaction costs involved would reduce overall wealth. Additionally, the fear of being disadvantaged in a transaction due to asymmetric information might prevent otherwise mutually beneficial transactions from occurring.[41]

---

[41] Ulen, 'Information in the Market Economy – Cognitive Errors and Legal Correctives', in: Grundmann, Kerber and Weatherill (eds.) *Party Autonomy and the Role of Information in the Internal Market* (2001) pp. 98 (99).

Nota bene the daunting task consists of identifying the right scope[42] of duties to inform. There is more to it than initially meets the eye. One has to keep and maintain incentives to invest in producing, gaining and gathering socially productive information. To over-stretch duties to inform, i.e. duties to share information with someone else who does not have to invest in acquiring the information in question, would be tantamount to wiping out such incentives, as investing in information could become unattractive. That would reduce the socially desirable level of investment in information. Many gems of information would not come to light. The fear of freeloading would overshadow everything and become both deterrent and dominant. He who invests in information wants to get a premium from this, an information rent. If he has to, and more if he is forced to, share valuable information, the benefits to him of obtaining costly information might disappear. Accordingly, the law should aim to discourage freeloading and to protect the incentives for acquiring and collecting information.[43] Hectolitres of ink have already been spilled on the topic, and it appears virtually impossible to add something both sensible and innovative. Nevertheless some aspects which have not yet been the focus of attention deserve a closer and more thorough investigation than they have received so far.

2. Protecting Investment as a Paramount Approach

The first and foremost point of discussion circles around the protection of investments. It closely mirrors the related question to what extent investment in information should be encouraged by awarding an information rent and, in turn, to what extent freeloading ought to be deterred. An information rent could be seen as a return on *investment*. Investment broadly is an efficiency-based justification to withhold information.[44] Article 4:107 (3) (b) European

---

42 A second task consists in identifying the right remedies; on this aspect Magnus, '*Rechtsfolgen im Acquis communautaire*', in: Schulze, Ebers and Grigoleit (eds.), *Informationspflichten und Vertragsschluss im Acquis communautaire* (2003) p. 291; Storme, 'Information Requirements and Remedies in the Principles of European Contract Law', in: Schulze, Ebers and Grigoleit (eds.), *Informationspflichten und Vertragsschluss im Acquis communautaire* (2003) p. 231; Wilhelmsson, 'Private Law Remedies against the Breach of Information Requirements in EC Law', in: Schulze, Ebers and Grigoleit (eds.) *Informationspflichten und Vertragsschluss im Acquis communautaire* (2003) p. 245; Schwintowski, '*Informationspflichten und effet utile*', in: Schulze, Ebers and Grigoleit (eds.) *Informationspflichten und Vertragsschluss im Acquis communautaire* (2003) p. 267.

43 van den Bergh and Lehmann, *GRUR Int. 1992*, 588 (593); Mankowski (n. 11) p. 316; *cf.* also Kronman, 'Mistake, Disclosure, Information, and the Law of Contracts', *J. Leg. Stud.* 7 (1978) 1 (13 *et seq.*); Fleischer, *Informationsasymmetrie im Vertragsrecht* (2001) pp. 281 and 283.

44 Fleischer (n. 43), pp. 992–993.

Principles of Contract Law recognizes this insofar as it tentatively denies a duty to inform if the informed party has invested time or money in acquiring the information. The paramount question should be formulated as to when an investment is substantial enough to justify rent-seeking by the investor, i.e. the person having acquired and now holding the information. Part of the answer can be found in a rather arcane area of EC law:[45] The *sui generis* right[46] generated by the Database Directive[47] purports to protect not the collection of data as such but the investment in such collection. It can serve as a model for an 'investment paradigm'. Unfortunately it does not define an exact or proper threshold, but rather establishes an open standard as 'substantiality' of the investment. However, one point of utmost importance should not be overlooked: The Database Directive recognizes the 'sweat of the brow',[48] i.e. personal effort, expertise and time, as items which can both be protected and which are worthy of protection. This recognition of non-corporeal, but nevertheless substantial, (and by no means immaterial) investments is a quantum leap forward and a progression not to be neglected. It can easily be generalized and transcribed into the law of duties to inform. Regrettably, this insight only forms part of the solution and stops far short of being comprehensive. But it certainly constitutes a first step in the right direction and is not ill-founded. Tentatively this is recognised in article 4:107 (3) Principles of European Contract Law where the costs a potentially obliged person incurs in acquiring the information feature amongst the factors which could help decide whether a duty to inform exists or not.[49] However, judges are not called upon to determine something like a *iustum pretium* since the argument is on one hand simpler and starts on the other hand with the question whether there should be a duty to inform or whether the better reasons point against establishing such a duty in the particular case. The partial concept advocated here is an open one and does not require that the threshold be fixed exactly.

---

45 *Cf.* more elaborately Mankowski (n. 11), pp. 317–320.

46 *Cf.* only OGH November 27, 2001, *GRUR Int. 2002*, 940, 941 – Gelbe Seiten; LG Berlin 8 October 1998, *CR 1999*, 388, 389, *AfP (1998)* pp. 649, 651; Vogel, in: Schricker (ed.) *Urheberrecht* (1999), Vor § 87 a UrhG ref. 20; Köhler, '*Der Schutz von Websites gemäß §§ 87 a ff. UrhG*', *ZUM 1999*, 548 and 551f.; Kotthoff, in: Dreyer, Kotthoff and Meckel, *Urheberrecht*, (2004), § 87a UrhG ref. 3.

47 Directive 1996/9/EC of the European Parliament and the Council of 11 March 1996 on the legal protection of databases, OJ L 77/20, 1996.

48 Gaster, '*Sui-generis-Recht der Datenbankrichtlinie*', in: Hoeren and Sieber (eds.), *Handbuch Multimedia-Recht*, (looseleaf, 1999), Ch. 7.8 ref. 70 (December 1998).

49 *Cf.* Grigoleit, '*Irrtum, Täuschung und Informationspflichten in den European Principles und in den Unidroit-Principles*', in: Schulze, Ebers and Grigoleit (n. 42) pp. 201 (214).

3. Peculiarities of Duties to Inform in B2C Relations?

To ask whether a party with a possible duty to inform may withhold information due to a justified protection of his investments, at first sight fits badly with the prevailing approaches, which mostly concentrate on the other party. We are almost trained to take the stance of the less informed party when talking about duties to inform and to turn to the other party only for a controlling check whether this other party's interests are unfairly affected or diminished by fostering the less informed party's cause. The focus on duties to inform owed to consumers in EC law has added to this slightly one-sided perspective. B2C relations however have the specific difference that the better informed party is a repeat player in a (potential) multitude of contracts of the same kind whereas the consumer as the less informed party is not. This specificity singles out B2C relations at least to some extent. A second peculiarity of B2C relations might be observed: Consumers are less likely to exploit businesses and professionals. This applies to both the individual consumer and to consumers in their role as the opposing demand side of the market. By the very nature of the relationship and the quasi-natural distribution of the respective bargaining power amongst the parties, the inherent danger of exploitation and freeloading is dramatically reduced. Enterprises simply do not allow consumers to exploit them on a regular basis. Ultimately, if the law forced upon them a too extensive duty to disclose, they could refrain from concluding contracts which would eat too much into their expected surplus, or into their contractual gain. But such an extreme solution is not even remotely required, nor would it be realistic. The vast majority of duties to inform that enterprises have to accept concern types of information which do not allow for freeloading. How could information about the effective rate of interest[50] put the bank customer applying for a loan, or anyone else, in a freeloader's position? This information might enhance the customer's ability to compare the offered conditions to the conditions the bank's competitors would offer. But this is not freeloading. In a functioning and perfect market the bank would advertise its conditions. Hence, the duty to inform only makes good shortcomings and malfunctions of the market. It prevents exploitation by the better informed party and does not allow the possibility of opportunistic behaviour by the less informed party. Another example: How could revealing one's proper address and identity – as 'forced' upon businesses under article 4 (1) (a) Distance Selling Directive[51] and article 5 (1) (a),

[50] Art. 4 (2) (a) Council Directive 87/102/EEC of 22 December 1986 for the approximation of the laws, regulations and administrative provisions of the Member States concerning consumer credit, OJ L 42/48, 1987.

[51] Directive 97/7/EC of the European Parliament and the Council of 20 May 1997 on the protection of consumers in respect of distance contracts, OJ L 144/19, 1997.

(b) E-Commerce Directive[52] – possibly give rise to freeloading? How could this possibly constitute an investment that could deserve protection? In my humbly submitted opinion you could run through the entire catalogue of duties to inform contained in the EC Directives in the same manner, and would not come up with different results. Put them to the test to see whether the information which must be disclosed enables freeloading or deserves protection since it was derived by a substantial investment. Only very few exceptions might be found. Hence, those duties to inform attracting most attention today are not exceptions to the general approach, but to the contrary hidden confirmations. The peculiarities of B2C relationships provide ample explanation why those duties to inform can be formulated as rules (and sometimes rigid rules at that). Consumer law provides the prime examples of unequal bargaining power whereby the better informed party could exploit the less informed party. It provides the prime example for social benefit stemming from duties to inform. It provides the prime example for balancing informational asymmetry. This is only paradoxical at first sight; consumer law supports and confirms the general approach. Major lobbying by multinational or larger enterprises to adapt their practices as to information policy as mandatory disclosure rules in order to drive smaller businesses out of the market by the margin, cannot be identified in this regard and might generally not be that relevant as an obscuring factor.[53]

4. Duty to Disclose Information Acquired Without Specific Investment?

Yet another question might be prompted by an approach placing reliance on protecting investments: Can we on the other hand draw a conclusion *e contrario* that information acquired without substantial investment, in particular by chance or literally *en passant*, never deserves protection and is always subject to disclosure? To reach such a conclusion would be bold and rash, way too rash.[54] Accidentally acquired information might not trigger

---

52 Directive 2000/31/EC of the European Parliament and the Council of 8 June 2000 on certain legal aspects of information society services, in particular electronic commerce, in the Internal Market (Directive on electronic commerce), OJ L 178/1, 2000.

53 But *cf.* Hopt, 'Disclosure Rules as a Primary Tool for Fostering Party Autonomy – Observations from a Functional and Comparative Legal Perspective', in: Grundmann, Kerber and Weatherill (n. 41) pp. 246 (263).

54 Trebilcock, *The Limits of Freedom of Contract* (1993) p. 113; van Rossum, 'The Duty of Disclosure – Tendencies in French Law, Dutch Law and English Law: Criterions, Differences and Similarities between the Legal Systems', *Maastricht J. Eur. & Comp. L.* 7 (2000) pp. 300 (315 *et seq.*); Mankowski (n. 11) pp. 324–325. But *cf.* Kronman, 'Mistake, Disclosure, Information, and the Law of Contracts', *J. Leg. Stud.* 7 (1978) 1 (14); Eisenberg, 'Disclosure in Contract Law', *Cal. L. Rev.* 91 (2003) pp. 1645 (1656–1661).

protection for previous investments, but is not worthless and is possibly valuable. Though a comparative sentence might be tentatively put forward that the probability of a burden to share information is inversely proportional to the level of investment. Or formulated the other way round: The higher the investment the higher the threshold for establishing a duty to inform; the lesser the investment the higher the likelihood of a duty to inform. However, an equation 'no investment = duty to inform' would go way beyond this. The minimum caveat would be to weigh the informed party's information rent against the costs the other party would have to incur in order to acquire the same information.[55] This might heavily influence, for instance, the outcome in the case that a producer of goods acquired information about the goods produced and their quality in the process of production itself whilst the other party would run into high marginal costs to get the same information and is only a small scale market player.[56] That some profit could still remain for the informed party even if he had to disclose, provides in itself no sufficient justification for establishing a duty to disclose.[57]

At least one should very carefully investigate whether in fact the information was acquired casually and without underlying investment. One must have regard to general investment building up know-how (e.g. market knowledge), as distinguished from specific investment in particular information. Even though, as far as general investment is concerned, no concrete figure naming an exact amount of money can be relied upon (as opposed to specific investment which can quantify the amount invested), acquiring information did not occur by chance, but purposefully and not without costs related to it. Mathematicians and economists might break down appropriate portions of general investment attributed to the concrete information in question. General investment might not be small and insignificant.[58] An investment in better knowledge about markets and market information must not be discouraged by establishing a respective duty to share the acquired information.[59] That would give rise to opportunistic behaviour and freeloading. To the contrary, incentives for building up socially useful and potentially welfare-enhancing knowledge and information ought to be maintained.[60]

[55] Mankowski (n. 11) p. 325.

[56] Cf. Magoulas, '*Zur ökonomischen Analyse des Konsumentenschutzes*', in: Magoulas and Simon (eds.), *Recht und Ökonomie beim Konsumentenschutz und Konsumentenkredit* (1985) pp. 23 (32); Mankowski (n. 11) p. 324.

[57] *Contra* Eisenberg (n. 54) pp. 1645 (1660).

[58] *Contra* Eisenberg (n. 54) pp. 1645 (1658).

[59] *Giesen*, 'Case note on BGH 28 April 1971', *NJW* (1971), pp. 1795 (1797 *et seq.*); Mankowski (n. 11) p. 316.

[60] Rehm, *Aufklärungspflichten im Vertragsrecht* (2003) pp. 61–62.

5. A Journey to the Boundaries of Human Recognition

In modern times – and once again reverting to EC consumer law – statutory duties to inform, although only recently established, have already been challenged by the opposite notion of informational overkill. Human rationality is bounded, and a single person's ability to process information is limited.[61] Rising amounts of information might counterproductively hamper the decision making process; it does not guarantee that a better informed and consequently a better decision will be made.[62] Consumer psychology has shown us many things about the boundaries of human recognition.[63] Not even EC law can stretch those boundaries. Nevertheless it puts them to the test by compelling enterprises to transmit rather complex information. The complexity is derived both from the quality and the sheer quantity of information required to be produced. This does, however, apply more to the regulations based on the complexity of the type of contract regulated (consumer credit, timeshare) than to the regulations purporting to overcome situational deficits (doorstep selling, distance selling).[64] However, duties to inform not based on statute but derived and developed from written rules can reflect this. They are directly related to specific information. They urge the better informed party only to disclose *relevant* and material information.[65] They do not demand over-disclosure. Leaving out some minor detail of the information to be disclosed would not amount to a relevant breach of the duty to inform.[66] The

---

61 Groundbreaking and seminal Simon, 'Rational Choice and the Structure of the Environment', in: Simon, *Models of Man: Social and Rational* (1957) pp. 261 (270 *et seq.*); *cf.* also Kahneman, 'New Challenges to the Rationality Assumption', *JITE* 150 (1994) p. 18; Conlisk, 'Why Bounded Rationality?', *J. Econ. Lit.* 34 (1996) p. 669; Kreps, 'Bounded Rationality', in: Newman (ed.), *The New Palgrave Dictionary of Economics and the Law, Vol. I* (1996) p. 168; Korobkin and Ulen, 'Law and Behavioral Science: Removing the Rationality Assumption from Law and Economics', *Cal. L. Rev.* 88 (2000) pp. 1051 (1075–1102).

62 Simon, 'A Behavioral Model of Rational Choice', *Quart. J. Econ.* 199 (1955) pp. 69 (87); Fleischer, '*Vertragsschlussbezogene Informationspflichten im Gemeinschaftsprivatrecht*', *ZEuP* (2002) p. 772; Ebers, '*Informations- und Beratungspflichten bei Finanzdienstleistungen: Allgemeine und besondere Rechtsgrundsätze*', in: Schulze, Ebers and Grigoleit (n. 42) pp. 171 (180).

63 *Cf.* in particular Kind, *Die Grenzen des Verbraucherschutzes durch Information – aufgezeigt am Teilzeitwohnrechtegesetz* (1998) and also e.g. Wein, 'Consumer Information Problems – Causes and Consequences', in: Grundmann, Kerber and Weatherill (n. 41) p. 80; Ulen, 'Information in the Market Economy – Cognitive Errors and Legal Correctives', in: Grundmann, Kerber and Weatherill (n. 41) pp. 98 (106–127); Haupt, 'An Economic Analysis of Consumer Protection Law', *German L.J.* 4 (2003) pp. 1137 (1142–1144); Wendlandt, '*Die Timesharing-Richtlinie, das BGB und die Privatautonomie – "realistisch betrachtet"*', *VuR* (2004) p. 117.

64 For a classification and an in-depth analysis of the respective rationales *cf.* Mankowski (n. 11), pp. 222–243.

65 *Cf.* only Fleischer (n. 43) p. 985; Grigoleit (n. 49) pp. 201 (215).

66 Mankowski (n. 11) p. 323.

legislator searching for abstract and more general solutions is far more likely to overcompensate. Courts will take proper account of the limits of information if called upon to define a duty to inform in a particular case. On the other hand, abstract duties to inform which can be taken ex ante as guidelines (as opposed to judge-made rules developed *ex post*) might offer an opportunity to reduce the complexity of information by standardization.[67]

[67] *Cf.* Ebers (n. 62) pp. 171 (180).

Chapter 19

Pre-contractual Duties to Provide Information and Their Violation from the Perspective of Polish Private Law – Selected Issues

Fryderyk Zoll, Jagiellonen University Cracow

I. INTRODUCTION

The provisions of the Polish civil law do not explicitly impose any general duties on the parties to a contract to furnish the other parties with information prior to the formation of the contract. This situation is quite common in the continental private law systems in Europe.[1] The lack of such provisions opens the field for scientific discussion on the existence and extent of such pre-contractual duties. Today we live in times of progressive deconsolidation and decodification of the continental legal systems (despite ongoing attempts to renew, codify and consolidate the law).[2] The consistency of the system is evaporating, gradually leaving growing gaps. Polish law feels such pressures strongly, given the number of internal and external transitions pressing upon it.

The Polish civil law includes a number of provisions that directly or indirectly govern a duty to provide information to the other parties at the

1 For the comparative overview see Lando and Beale, *Principles of European Contract Law* (2000) p. 256.

2 On the notion of 'decodification' see Bellomo, *The Common Legal Past of Europe* (1995) pp. 27–29.

S. Grundmann, M. Schauer (eds), *The Architecture of European Codes and Contract Law*, 339–358

stage before the contract has been concluded. These disparate provisions do not seem to be guided by any governing concept or principle. They differ in complexity and clarity with regard to establishing a duty to provide information and regarding the sanction for a violation. Some provisions state specifically that one party is to provide information in particular situations and clearly provide for the consequences of omission of pre-contractual information.

The following discussion divides the Polish law relevant to the duty to provide pre-contractual information into four 'circles'. The first 'circle' encompasses legal provisions which appear to be clear but, upon further examination, raise a number of questions as to whether such clarity is apparent or real. The second 'circle' concerns provisions of law that specify pre-contractual information to be provided, but contain no express sanction for a violation. The third 'circle' refers to legal duties to provide information pertinent to a contract, but it is not clear if these provisions apply only after the formation of the contract or if their scope of application is broader. The fourth 'circle' concerns the grey area of missing legislation and the question whether general principles of law or general clauses like good faith should be invoked with regard to pre-contractual information. I will also address the question whether additional duties to provide pre-contractual information should be derived by analogy from existing law.

In my article I will review these four 'circles' regarding Polish law on pre-contractual duties and will seek to determine their borders and content. In addition I will discuss possible sanctions and remedies for the violation of these duties. The reader should realize, however, that Polish law has little doctrine and jurisprudence on this topic. Hence this text is in many ways speculative. It is likely however that Polish law will soon face these problems.

The division of the article into four 'circles' is an imprecise one. The borders between the 'circles' that are determined by the 'clarity' of the legal provisions are not strict. For instance, it can be disputed whether the provisions that I put in the first circle are sufficiently precise and autonomous to be in that category. The structures of the circles, however, help us to understand the problems regarding pre-contractual duties to provide information. I do not seek to identify all possible provisions of Polish law that may be relevant, but rather to present those most representative of the structure of Polish law on this topic.

II. THE FIRST CIRCLE – PROVISIONS OF LAW IMPOSING DUTIES TO PROVIDE INFORMATION AND SANCTIONS FOR THEIR VIOLATION

The majority of European directives imposing certain duties to provide pre-contractual information on one party establish a sanction for the violation of these duties. The main instrument in combating such violations is an extended right of withdrawal from the contract – limited by time in the Distance Contract Directive,[3] or with unlimited time to withdraw in the Distance Financial Services Directive[4] and the Doorstep Selling Directive.[5] One of the remedies against misleading or false information also can be the incorporation of the misleading information into the contract itself, which determines the scope of the legally enforceable obligations of the entrepreneur, e.g. the Package Tour Directive.[6]

The Polish legislature implemented these directives by using a wording which is close to that in the directives. Therefore the Polish Law had to regulate a duty to furnish sufficient information supported by a cooling-off period, during which the consumer can withdraw from the contract if the other party violated its duties to inform. Only in the case of doorstep selling the directive was not properly implemented. Article 4 of the Polish Statute on Protection of Certain Consumer Rights[7] provides that, if a consumer fails to receive written notice of the right to withdraw upon entering a sales contract, the consumer may withdraw from the contract within ten days after he or she receives the required information. This right, however, expires three months after the performance of the contract. The latter restriction is a violation of the directive. A similar provision in German law was found to be a violation by the ECJ.[8]

The Polish legislation on distance contracts implements two pre-contractual duties for professional parties imposed by directives – first a duty to provide 'prior information' (article 4, section 1 of the directive and article 9, section 1 of the Statute on Protection of Certain Consumer Rights) and second a duty to give a written confirmation. Like the directive in article 6, section 1, the Polish Statute imposes a sanction if the seller fails to provide the required information in the proper form. Article 10, section 2 delays the commencement of the period in which the consumer may exercise the right to withdraw from the contract. This wording from the directive and the Polish law provides this sanction only for failing to provide the written confirmation. But it remains unclear what the consequences of the violation of the duty to provide information prior to the formation of the contract are. In

3 Directive 97/7/EC of the European Parliament and of the Council of 20 May 1997 on the protection of consumers in respect of distance contracts, OJ L 144, 1997, pp. 19–27. See art. 6, s. 1.

4 Directive 2002/65/EC of the European Parliament and the Council of 23 September 2002 concerning the distance marketing of consumer financial services, OJ L 271, 2002, pp. 16–24. See art. 6, s. 1.

5 Directive 85/577/EEC of 20 December 1985 to protect the consumer in respect of contracts negotiated away from business premises, OJ L 372, 1985, 31. See art. 5, s. 1.

6 Council Directive 90/314/EEC of 13 June 1990 on package travel, package holidays and package tours, OJ L 158, 1990, pp. 59–64. See art. 3.

7 *Ustawa o ochronie niektórych praw konsumentów*, 2 February 2000, Dz. U. No. 22, position 271.

8 ECJ, 13 December 2001, C-481/99. See van Huffel, '*Das Europäische Vertragsrecht zwischen Mythos und Realität*', in: Eiselberg (ed.), *Europäisches Vertragsrecht* (2003) pp. 23–24.

the case of the directive, this only means that the national legislature has to deal with this problem on its own. But the Polish national legislature has not met this challenge.[9] Therefore, it is necessary to determine what consequences the entrepreneur has to face if he fails to provide the information required under article 9, section 1.

In the majority of cases, the violation of the information duty under article 9, section 1 of the Statute on Protection on Certain Consumer Rights will be combined with a violation of the duty to provide a written confirmation, but it is not necessarily so. The standard written confirmation may be provided properly, but a duty of prior information under article 9, section 1 may still be violated. The duty to provide this prior pre-contractual information is not formalized by the Directive or by Polish law. It is difficult to verify whether the entrepreneur has complied with it, because also unrecorded pre-contractual information may be sufficient. The violation of this prior duty however does not influence the consumer's right of withdrawal. The lack of a specific sanction for the violation of the information duties, however, is not seriously detrimental from the consumer's point of view. Although he may have decided to enter a legal transaction without the information that he should have been provided with, he still has an opportunity to change his mind, based on the later written confirmation. He can withdraw from the contract according to the general rules. In some situations, this remedy of withdrawal may be insufficient. It may then be possible for the consumer to use other remedies in the usual private law arsenal. I will discuss these general remedies in the context of the 'second circle' of rules governing pre-contractual duties.

A slightly different solution is given by the Polish law concerning distance financial services. According to article 16d, a consumer is authorized to withdraw from the contract in the case of a professional party's violation of duties arising from article 16b, section 1-3 of the Statute. Article 16b, section 1 of the Statute imposes pre-contractual duties to provide information (at least at the moment of making a proposal for the conclusion of the contract). Section 3 governs the duty of the confirmation of the information. This duty is also determined a bit differently from in the regulation on distance contract. Generally the confirmation needs to be provided before the formation of the contract and only in exceptional situations can a confirmation subsequent to the conclusion of the contract be sufficient. As mentioned above, the Polish legislature made full use of the authorization given by article 11 of the Distance Financial Services Directive. In case of violation of the information duty, the consumer may cancel the contract at any time, free of charge and without penalty. Even if the entrepreneur has provided a proper confirmation of the information, the consumer still may withdraw from the contract. In such a case, the proper confirmation does not compen-

[9] Łętowska, *Ustawa o ochronie niektórych praw konsumentów* (2000) p. 55.

sate for the lack of pre-contractual information. The function of the provision for pre-contractual information and the written confirmation are not the same. A consumer relies on the completeness of the pre-contractual information when making his decision whether to enter the legal transaction at all. After the formation of the contract, when some other decisions in connection with the contract may have been made, it may not be easy to cancel the contract. If the consumer had received all the proper information, the consumer might have declined to enter the contract at all.

Pre-contractual duties of information and confirmation of this information should be treated similarly to regulation of distance contracts and distance financial services. Because the directive on distance contracts is a minimum regulation (article 14), a national legislature is authorized to adopt a sanction of extended right of withdrawal also for the violation of the pre-contractual duties in distance contracts and should make use of this competence.

The Polish Statute on Protection of Certain Consumer Rights in all three fields of regulation (Doorstep Selling, Distance Contracts and Distance Financial Contracts Directive) does not explicitly set out the consequences for providing false information. False or misleading information could be given as prior information or by means of the written confirmation, or both could be false or misleading. (Of course such confirmation is not required in the case of Doorstep Selling.) It is not clear what the consequences are when the data contained in a written confirmation is incorrect. There are two possible interpretations. According to the first option such false confirmations do not meet the requirements of the statute and should not be treated as confirmations at all. According to the second option the misleading confirmation can still be considered a confirmation and the consumer is not provided with the extended period to cancel (in case of distance contract) or without time limits (under the regulation of distance financial services). I think the first is the better interpretation. False or misleading prior information and confirmation of such information cannot meet the requirements of the statute. For instance, a part of the required information is the right of withdrawal (article 9, section 1, No. 6, article 16b, section 1, No. 9 of the Statute on Protection). False or misleading information on this issue may cause the consumer to forgo making use of the right to withdraw from the contract. Therefore, if an entrepreneur provides such misleading information it cannot be treated as the fulfilment of the information duty and triggers the Statute's remedies for omitted information (like extended right of withdrawal).

A different system has been adopted in the Statute on Consumer Credit. The Consumer Credit Directive[10] prescribes certain duties to provide information to the consumer in article 4. Although this information needs to be

[10] Council Directive 87/102/EEC of 22 December 1986 for the approximation of the laws, regulations and administrative provisions of the Member States concerning consumer credit, OJ L 042, 12 February 1987, pp. 48–53.

included in a written credit agreement, it can be treated as a duty of pre-contractual information. The idea is to equip a consumer with knowledge which allows an assessment of the prospective contract of credit. The directive, however, does not provide a remedy for the violation of these duties. It requires only that the Member State creates sufficient effective regulation to ensure that consumers will not be deprived of the protection granted by this directive (article 14, sections 1 and 2).

In consumer credit, the Polish legislature uses a conventional means of consumer protection, a 'cooling-off period'. An extended right of withdrawal for the consumer is also used in this context as a tool against violation of the information duties, but only with a quite limited scope of application. According to article 11, section 1 of the Polish Statute on Consumer Credit, a consumer may cancel a contract if he was not informed at the time of contract formation about the ordinary right of withdrawal. The consumer has ten days to exercise this right after receiving proper notice of the right of withdrawal, but this option expires three months after conclusion of the contract. The main instrument of combating the violation of information duties is found in article 15, section 1 of the Statute on Consumer Credit. In the case of infringement of these duties, the Statute converts the credit contract into 'gratis credit' – a credit without interest and other costs. This provision in the original version of the Statute simply enforced such conversion without additional conditions or requirements. This harsh provision for credit institutions has been amended – the consumer needs to declare to the credit provider his intention to pay back the principal without interest. This amendment is very ambiguous. It is disputed whether this requirement for the consumer's declaration is necessary for the conversion of the credit. It is relevant in a case when a part of the credit has been paid with interest, according to the contract, before the consumer noticed the violation of the information duties. Could he or she claim a repayment of the already paid interests and costs or does the consumer's declaration affect only future payments? One part of the doctrine deprives the necessity for a consumer's declaration of any legal gravity.[11] The effect of the conversion into credit without costs and interests comes about automatically and an express declaration of the consumer has only a declarative value. The second part of the doctrine takes a less consumer-friendly position. Following this concept under the amended Statute, the consumer cannot reclaim interests and costs already paid. His or her declaration has an effect only *pro futuro*.[12]

---

[11] Pisuliński, '*O nowelizacji ustawy o kredycie konsumenckim*', *Monitor Prawniczy* 19/2003, p. 878; Włodarska in Pisuliński, *Komentarz do ustawy o kredycie konsumenckim* (2004) p. 357.

[12] Rusinek and Włodarska, '*O zmianach w kredycie konsumenckim*', *Prawo Bankowe* 10/2003 p. 47. Włodarska in her commentary mentioned above has changed her view and took the first position.

The second solution seems to be more convincing. The original text of the provision was intolerably harsh for the credit institutions. A simple mistake in formulation of the information could lead to loss of any interest for extending credit. For instance, an unintentional mathematical error in the calculation of interest, printed in form documents, could result in major losses for the credit institution, even if the actual error was insignificant with regard to what consumers were supposed to owe. This might harm not only the lending institution but also consumers if insolvency were the result. The provision should allow for the assessment of the gravity of the infringement in the decision to apply a sanction. Not all information required to be provided under the Consumer Credit Statute has the same degree of importance in the consumer decision-making process.[13] The original sanction could apply, not only for pending credit relationships but also, in cases where the credit has been paid back completely. Hence it is understandable that a legislature tried to reduce the harshness of this provision. It is another question whether a proper means has been used to achieve this goal. The current system is to the disadvantage of the consumer – if he or she has not learned about the violation by the credit provider, either because the consumer did not notice the error or omission in the documentation provided or because he or she was not aware of the existing law. The legislature was trying to ameliorate the situation of the credit institutions by exploiting the lack of knowledge of the consumers. The new construction also does not give the judge the discretion to vary the sanction according to the seriousness of the violation of the credit provider's information duties. Article 15, section 1 of the Polish Consumer Credit Statute shows the conflict of the values behind the statutes, leading to ambiguity about the meaning of this provision.

The regulations mentioned above belong to the consumer law. The duty to provide pre-contractual information is established as one of the basic instruments to diminish the imbalance of knowledge between professionals and consumers. But the legislature is trying also to diminish the imbalance of the knowledge in another direction – to protect a professional institution. Such imbalance is significant for the banking and insurance sector. The clients (who are not only consumers) often have knowledge relating to their own sphere or business, which can influence very strongly the decision of the banking or insurance institution. Therefore, the legislature imposes certain pre-contractual duties of information also on this type of client. Thus, such laws governing the insurance relationship belong to the first circle – the violation of the duty to provide required information is met by a specific sanction prepared by the legislature for this case. The banking law regulation, however, is incomplete – I will describe it briefly in the 'second circle'.

The construction of the duty to provide information in insurance contracts differs from that provided in consumer law. According to article 815

[13] See Włodarska in Pisuliński, *Komentarz do ustawy o kredycie konsumenckim* p. 352.

§ 1 of the Civil Code, a prospective insurance client is obliged to provide the insurance company with all information known by the prospective client, which is requested by the insurance company in the form of the offer or other writings. The client is not obliged, at least according to the language of the statute, to provide any information unless asked about it. If the client did not answer the question, but the contract has been concluded, the omitted questions are considered immaterial – the client's omission does not have negative consequences for him.[14] If the client has provided untrue information to the insurance company, the insurer is freed from the liability arising from the contract (article 815, § 3 of the Civil Code).[15]

This has been only an overview of selected problems in regulation of duties to provide pre-contractual information. There remains the question of whether these regulations, which are to some extent 'complete' in imposing a duty and providing sanctions for violation, can be supplemented by remedies in the general civil law, such as those concerning fraud or tort. I will address this issue later. First I will turn to the possible application of provisions in the 'second circle': regulation prescribing pre-contractual duties of information which provide no sanction for violation.

III. THE SECOND CIRCLE – 'INCOMPLETE REGULATION' IMPOSING INFORMATION DUTIES BUT PROVIDING NO SANCTION FOR VIOLATION

In connection with various private law provisions, the legislature imposes pre-contractual information duties without specifying sanctions linked directly and specifically to these duties. The reasons for such 'incompleteness' in the regulation are various. The legislature does not try to create leges imperfecta. It treats the general sanctions provided by the legal system for the case of breach of law as sufficient. The rules of private law may provide remedies, but also the violations of law may trigger action by the administrative authorities of the country. I, however, focus on private law remedies rather than the possibility of public law sanctions.

The provisions of the Polish Civil Code concerning contract formation were recently amended.[16] The legislature was trying to incorporate the Principles of European Contract Law and the Vienna Convention into Polish law.[17] With these changes, some provisions of the E-Commerce Directive have been incorporated into the General Part of the Civil Code dealing with

14 Ogiegło in Pietrzykowski, *Kodeks cywilny*, Vol. 2 (2003) p. 477.

15 See Czech in *Kodeks cywilny*, Vol. 2 (2005) p. 562. Also Decision of the Polish Supreme Court, 28 March 2000, II CKN 895/98, LEX No. 50715.

16 Dz. U. 2003, No. 49, position 408.

17 See for example Liebscher and Zoll in Liebscher and Zoll, *Einführung in das polnische Recht* (2005) p. 114.

the formation of the contract (article 66 and subsections). Article 66[1], § 2 imposes on a party making an electronic offer a duty to inform the other party 'clearly and comprehensibly' on certain issues related mostly to the legal and technical matter concerning this mode of communication. This information needs to be provided also when inviting the other party to make his or her own offer or enter the negotiations. This Polish provision is a quite faithful implementation of article 10 of the E-Commerce Directive.[18] In transactions between professionals, these pre-contractual information duties may be excluded by the parties (article 66[1], § 3 of the Civil Code – following article 10, section 1 of the E-Commerce Directive). They do not apply in cases of e-mail or similar types of private communication (article 66[1], § 4 CC; see article 10, section 4 of the E-Commerce Directive). The Code does not provide any kind of express sanction related to the violation of the information duties arising from article 66[1], § 2 CC.

I now will review four possible avenues for finding a remedy in the general institutions of private law for violation of pre-contractual duties to provide information. If such violation causes damages, a remedy might be found in the law of tort and breach of obligations (article 415 and subsection CC and article 471 and subsection CC). The contract also might be nullified under fraud law. A lack of specific information related to the technological aspects of the contract using electronic means could result in the total lack of the animus obligandi – the electronic declaration may be treated in such a situation as not serious and not leading to the formation of the contract. The first three possibilities above are not exclusive – to some extent there is a possibility for the parallel application of them. The Polish law does not recognize the French rule of '*non cumul*'.[19]

Liability for damages for both tort and breach of obligations are based on the general clauses (article 415 CC for torts and article 471 for breach of obligations). Article 415 CC resembles article 1382 of the French Civil Code: 'whose fault fully caused damage to another person is obliged to compensate'. According to article 471, a creditor may claim compensation from a debtor if the creditor suffered damages caused by the breach of obligation, unless the debtor is not responsible for the breach. The notion of fault in article 415 CC is used in the old-fashioned sense of 'fault in an objective sense', which simply means a violation of the law, and 'subjective fault' or *mens rea*. Because the Polish law did not adopt the principle of '*non cumul*', there is a need to define the situations that are pure fact patterns of the breach of the obligation, pure tort cases, and those which can be both. These distinctions are important in the case of the information duties arising from

---

18 Directive 2000/31/EEC of the European Parliament and Council of 8 June 2000 on certain legal aspects of information society services in particular electronic commerce in the Internal Market (Directive on electronic commerce) OJ L 178, 17 February 2000, p. 1.

19 Czachórski in Radwański, *System prawa cywilnego*, Vol. 3, part 1 (1981) p. 700 and sub.; Liebscher and Zoll in Liebscher and Zoll, *Einführung in das polnische Recht*, p. 254.

article 66[1], § 2 CC. Is this violation a violation of law in the sense of article 415 CC, is it a case of breach of the obligation, or maybe both? The answer to these questions touches the central problem of the place of pre-contractual duties of information in a legal system. Both general clauses – article 415 and article 471 CC – require a sort of violation of law. Certainly also a breach of contract is a violation of the law, because the law requires a correct performance of the obligation. But not every breach of obligation could be classified as a tort if the statutory distinction between both regimes is to remain reasonable. The Polish doctrine, therefore, distinguishes between absolute and relative unlawfulness.[20] The first is required to meet the conditions of the tort, the second for the breach of obligation. If the violation touches only an obligation in relation to the other party, it is only a breach in a sense of article 471 CC. If the violation is independent from the breach of the obligation, infringing rules serving the public, then the general unlawfulness may constitute a tort. It is quite clear that the distinction mentioned above is far from being precise – like the distinction between public and private law in the famous definition of Ulpianus.[21] It gives only an indicator that a breach of obligation in relation to another party is on its own not sufficient to constitute a tort. A tort requires an additional 'evil'.

It is an open question how to qualify duties arising from article 66[1], § 2 CC. These duties ensure the security of a contract which is made by using electronic means. They aim to protect a client, most of all a consumer, against risks connected with the use of modern technology in communication between people. The legislature is trying to ensure that citizens are not surprised by the effects of electronic means of communication. The security of the internet and other technological means of communication are an essential condition for their quick development. The duty of information seems to be established, not only to protect an individual interest of the client in the undisturbed performance of the obligation, but also to protect the confidence of the public in the security of the technology of communication. An additional argument here could be the imperative character of these duties in relation to the consumer. For these reasons, a violation of the duties to provide pre-contractual information in the case of article 66[1], § 2, CC seems to fulfil the requirements of unlawfulness in the sense of article 415 CC (tort).[22] In such situations the claim can be based on both grounds – articles 415 and 471. In the second case, article 66[1], § 2 CC is an independent source of the obligation Also this thesis is not an indisputable one. It is really a relationship in the sense of article 353, § 1 CC: 'In the obligation a creditor may claim a debtor to perform and a debtor bears a duty of performance?' According to article 66[1], § 2 CC, an entrepreneur, who makes an electronic

[20] Czachórski in Radwański, *System prawa cywilnego*, pp. 700 *et seq.*; Bobrzyński, Liebscher and Zoll in Liebscher and Zoll *Einführung in das polnische Recht*, p. 254.
[21] Ulpian, D.1,1,1, 2 – see Max Kaser and Knüttel, *Römisches Privatrecht* (2003) p. 38.
[22] Machnikowski in Gniewek, *Kodeks cywilny. Komentarz*, Vol. I (2004) p. 262.

offer or undertakes the other handlings mentioned in § 3, needs to provide information, even if the other party does not ask for it. The structure of this duty according to article 66[1], § 2 CC does not mean that the client can enforce this pre-contractual duty of information. When the information has not been provided, the dispute typically commences after the contract was concluded. It is hard to imagine that the client can by judicial means enforce this duty of information before the parties entered the contract. But this practical observation does not prevent the quantification of the relations between parties as an obligation in a sense of article 353, § 1 CC. A client has an enforceable right to be informed and the other party needs to comply with it. There are sufficient elements of the obligation. Therefore, a client generally has a right to claim for damages in a case of a violation of pre-contractual duties arising from article 66[1], § 2 CC based on the provisions on torts and breach of obligations. Remedies in torts and breach of obligation may be cumulative.

A client whose right to be informed has been violated also has another remedy to enforce his right. According to the article 86, § 1 CC, a party who lacks required information because of fraud may cancel the effects of the party's declaration of the will ('relative nullity' of the juristic act). The requirements for fraud also can be satisfied when the error was caused by the omission of the party (or third person under condition of article 86, § 2 CC) in providing the information. In such a case, it is an essential condition that the party who failed to provide information had a duty to provide such information.[23] Article 66[1], § 2 CC is a sufficient source of such duty. In such a case, the omission in informing must cause an error by the other party or support an already existing error. This error must be an essential one, such that the party would not have otherwise contracted. The effects of the declaration of will can be erased within one year after the party has learned about his own error (article 88, § 2 CC). If the party made use of this right, the transaction is void. This, however, does not exclude a claim for damages according to the provisions governing torts (article 415 CC and subsections).

One additional possibility for a remedy in a case of the violation of the pre-contractual duty of information can be found in the from of article 66, § 2 CC. Article 66 concerns the technological aspects of the formation of the contract (article 66[1], § 2, No. 1 CC), the legal effects of the confirmation of the offer's reception (article 66[1], § 2, No. 2 CC), or the languages in which a contract may be concluded (article 66[1], § 2, No. 5 CC). These duties to inform should assist the client in understanding the legal meaning of the person's declaration given by using electronic means of communication. Very often people forming internet contracts are not conscious that their 'click' can be understood as a declaration of will in the sense of article

[23] Radwański in Radwański, *System Prawa Prywatnego*, Vol. 2 (2002) p. 409. Liebscher and Zoll in Liebscher and Zoll *Einführung in das polnische Recht*, p. 133.

60 CC. Hence, it is possible to argue that a failure to provide adequate pre-contractual information should render a person's declaration not legally binding.[24] I think however, that such a general conclusion cannot be adopted. This requires an evaluation from the perspective of the addressee of the declaration (articles 60 and 65 CC). Under certain circumstances, the lack of information may be taken under consideration as one of the arguments against a declaration of will. A generalization and automatic extension of denying the binding nature of the declaration would be contrary to the experience of life: certainly a number of reasonable people do not need any special information to understand a process of making contracts by electronic means of communication. Denying the seriousness of their declaration of will would be against their interests and against their express intent. Fraud provisions provide sufficient protection when a party to a contract is uninformed and the contract should be declared void.

Another characteristic provision in the second circle, imposing pre-contractual duties to furnish information without a specific sanction, is article 69, section 2 of the Banking Law. This is a more general provision than those rules in the Consumer Credit Statute mentioned above. Article 69, section 2 applies to all credit contracts, without limitations of the Consumer Credit Statute. The provision of the Banking Law concerns not only the consumer but all possible clients of the bank. Its scope of application is narrower than the Consumer Credit Statute because article 69, section 2 of the Banking Law applies only if the credit institution is a bank. It serves a similar goal as the Consumer Credit Statute, transparency of credit contracts, but the Banking Law does not provide direct sanctions from the private law perspective. This provision determines, according to its language, a mandatory content of the credit contract. This formulation is misleading. The credit contract in the language of this provision should be understood as a document to be turned over to the client. It would not be enough to have this information in a separate document. Article 69, section 2 does not specify a minimum content of the contract of credit. Therefore, in a case where some required information is omitted from a credit contract, it does not influence a formation of the contract as such. But of course the lack of a specific sanction leaves open the issue of the consequences of the violation of the duty arising from the article 69, section 2. This situation is not comparable with the issue regarding article 66^1, § 2 CC, which was discussed above. The required information based on article 66^1, § 2 CC serves as an improvement in the client's knowledge about using modern technology in the context of contract making. It is not information about the contract itself. In article 69,

24 Łętowska considers and rejects such options in the case of pre-contractual duties of information in distance contracts in *Prawo umów konsumenckich* (2002) p. 282. See also Wejman, *Wzorce umów na stronach www i w poczcie elektronicznej, Transformacje Prawa Prywatnego* 4/2000, pp. 45–47.

section 2 Banking Law, it is information concerning the content of the contract of credit. The possible sanction for the omission of including certain information into a contract of credit could be the lack of the incorporation of certain terms into a contract. Article 69, section 2 of the Banking Law should be treated as part of the law on standard terms. The vast majority of credit contracts are formatted by using standard terms. The general conditions for the effective incorporation of standard terms into a contract are laid down under article 384, § 1–4 CC. The basic condition is the handing over of the standard terms to the client, which could be replaced under certain conditions by providing an opportunity for easy access to the content of the terms. The dominant opinion is that also in the case of handing over the terms, it is necessary to also provide easy access to the content of the terms.[25] A violation of a duty to provide certain information, arising from article 69, section 2 of the Banking Law, should be understood to be a violation of the conditions of incorporation of the standard terms into a contract by denying easy access to the content of standard terms. Outside of the standard terms issue the practical problems with article 69, section 1 Banking Law are rather hard to imagine.

As mentioned under the second section of this paper, the Banking Law also establishes duties of bank customers to provide pre-contractual information to the bank. According to article 70, section 1 of the Banking Law, a credit applicant is obliged, upon request of the bank, to provide the information and documents necessary to evaluate his or her creditworthiness. The Banking Law does not provide a sanction for violation of this duty, but the obvious sanction is the denial of credit to the applicant who fails to provide such information. If the information provided by a credit applicant was misleading or false, the bank is authorized to terminate the contract according to article 75, section 1 of the Banking Law, not because the information was false but because of the actual financial situation of the credit recipient. Providing false information about one's financial situation certainly constitutes a fraud under article 86 CC, if it is intentional,[26] and it is a tort under article 415 and sub CC.

These selected examples show the diversity of problems with provisions of law regarding pre-contractual duties in the 'second circle'. It is not possible to provide a general answer regarding the sanctions which should apply following a violation of these duties. The solution does not only depend on the specific nature of these duties and their function from the perspective of the parties but also on the public interest perspective regarding compliance with these duties.

---

[25] Łętowska, *Prawo umów konsumenckich*, pp. 314–315; Liebscher and Zoll in Liebscher and Zoll, *Einführung in das polnische Recht*, p. 121.

[26] Molis in Zoll, *Prawo bankowe. Komentarz*, Vol. 1 (2005) p. 703.

IV. THE 'GENERAL SANCTIONS' IN CASE OF THE 'FIRST CIRCLE' REGULATIONS

It is also doubtful whether remedies arising from the central institutions of private law can be applied to the pre-contractual duties belonging to the 'first circle'. As mentioned above, the regulations of this group are to some extent only apparently 'complete': the legislature provides a specific duty of information and a specific, especially 'designed' sanction for a violation. The 'completeness' of these regulations raises the question of the possibility of an additional application of the 'general' sanctions, mentioned in the third section of this paper, such as compensation for damages, based on regulation of torts or breach of obligation, further fraud, etc. As in the case of the regulation from the 'second circle' it is not possible to provide a single answer to this question. The duties to provide pre-contractual information are manifold and there is a diversity of the provided consequences for the failure to provide the required information.

As discussed above, article 15, section 1 of the Consumer Credit Statute punishes violations of the duties to provide information named by this Statute with a conversion of a credit into a free credit. This sanction combines a dissuasive effect for the credit institutions with compensation for the consumer. Violation of the duty to provide the information specified in a Consumer Credit Statute should not cause damage beyond relief from the obligation to pay interest and costs of credit. The benefit of free credit puts a consumer in a much more beneficial situation than he or she could expect in the market. The cancellation of the credit contract based on a fraud would be also more detrimental to the consumer than the sanction from article 15, section 1. Only in one instance might the rights to cancel the contract according to the regulation of fraud (article 86 CC) be more beneficial to the consumer. This is the issue mentioned in Section II of this paper regarding the controversy about the meaning of the current formulation of article 15, section 1 of the Consumer Credit Statute. Even if this provision was to be construed such that the consumer, when he has paid the interests and costs of a credit, cannot demand reimbursement of the interests and other costs, a declaration that the credit contract was void under article 86, § 1 CC would nevertheless allow this consumer to ask for reimbursement of interests and other costs based on principles of unjust enrichment (article 405 CC). It should be noted that not every violation of the duty of information constitutes a fraud. To be fraud, the violation must be intentional, not only negligent, and the omission must be subjectively essential, having influenced the consumer's decision to enter the contract. In such situations, it is possible to apply a remedy arising from the provisions concerning fraud.

In the case of the other three consumer regulations, discussed in Section II (doorstep selling, distance contract, distance financial contract), the question on possible further sanctions cannot be resolved generally. The specific sanction in all these cases is an extended or unlimited period to withdraw from the contract by the consumer. If the violation concerns information about the right of the consumer to withdraw, the existing specific sanction of the extended right to withdraw seems to be sufficient. The consumer will not suffer any kind of damage if he can still withdraw from the contract. The problem starts if the time to withdraw has passed. The time limitation to withdraw from the contract, even if there was a violation in providing information concerning this right, is determined in the case of distance contract (article 10, section 2 of the Statute on Protection of Certain Consumer Rights) and doorstep selling (article 4 of this Statute). In the second case, the limitation is not binding because of the lack of conformity with the directive (*Heininger* ECJ case). In the case of the distance contracts, it could be that because of the prescribed period of the time, despite the violation of the information duty, a withdrawal is no longer possible (three months after delivery or after formation of the contract in case of services – article 10, section 2 of the Statute on Protection of Certain Consumer Rights). But even in this case it is difficult to imagine a fulfilment of the conditions for fraud. If there was no information on the right to withdraw, even if this omission was intentional, this lack cannot be subjectively essential – a consumer, who entered a contract without knowledge of his right to withdraw, cannot claim that had he known his rights, he would not have entered into the contract. But even when the right to withdraw from the contract has expired without the consumer being aware of the right, the consumer can still claim damages based on breach of the obligation (article 471 CC) or tort (article 415CC). The tort remedy is more open to question because of the previously mentioned dispute as to whether the violations of the duty to provide pre-contractual information qualify as an 'absolute unlawfulness'. In general pre-contractual duties should not receive more protection than contractual duties. In the case of consumer law, however, the duties established to protect consumer interests, because of their weaker position, are a part of the public policy system which aims to globally improve the position of consumers in the market. Therefore, in the case of a violation of information duties established in the interest of the consumer, the provisions of tort may apply. The possibility to claim damages (based on article 471 or 415 CC), because of the lack of information on withdrawal rights, would however be more theoretical – it would be quite difficult to quantify damages and it would usually be an amount unworthy of the judicial action.

In the case of other duties to provide (or confirm) a pre-contractual information arising from article 9 or 16b of the Statute on Protection of Certain Consumer Rights, the violation may cause different consequences than discussed above: torts, breach of obligations or fraud, or even a simple error (article 84 CC). In some more exceptional cases, a failure to provide certain information also can mean that certain contractual clauses have not been effectively incorporated into the contract, according to article 384, § 1–4 of the Civil Code (usually it will be a situation of contract making with the use of standard terms). This last case could be if a consumer has not been informed of certain additional fees (article 9, section 1, No. 3 and article 16b, section 1, No. 5 of the Statute on Protection).

If the right of withdrawal from the contract has not expired, it does not mean that the consumer's right to claim damages cannot be established. It depends on the further characteristics of the information which had to be given or was given wrongfully. If for instance pre-contractual information describes the essential features of the offered goods in a misleading or untruthful way (violation of article 9, section 1, No. 2 of the Statute on Protection), a consumer could make a choice from a range of existing rights. The consumer can claim rights arising from article 8 of the Statute on Special Aspects on Consumer Sale (implementation of the directive on Certain Aspects of the Sale of Consumer Goods and Associated Guarantees), because the description of the features of the offered good plays an important role from the point of view of the evaluation of the conformity of the goods with the contract following the article for of the Consumer Sale Statute. A consumer also can make use of article 471 CC (breach of obligation) and claim for compensation of damages. As mentioned above, tort provisions also may apply. The existence of the ordinary right of withdrawal does not preclude a consumer from using other remedies.

The regulations in the 'first circle' are also 'incomplete'. The existence of a 'specific' remedy does not prevent a person, whose right to receive certain information has been violated, from making use of other 'general remedies'. In some cases, however, the specific remedy makes the use of a 'general remedy' pointless. The kind of general remedy depends on the specific nature of the violated duty to provide 'pre-contractual' information.

V. THE 'THIRD CIRCLE' – PRE-CONTRACTUAL OR CONTRACTUAL DUTY OF INFORMATION?

Recently the legal system has tended to develop detailed specific duties to provide information. In this way, the legislature is seeking to protect a weaker party, and trying to ameliorate the typical intellectual handicap of the consumers or others, who have deficits in knowledge about relevant circumstances of the contract. This strategy of protection, however, is not a new one. The legislature saw a need to equip the typically uninformed party with certain information, which would enable him to benefit fully from the contract. The most important example of this regulation is article 546, § 1 CC. According to this provision, a seller is obliged to inform a buyer about all necessary circumstances related to legal and factual aspects of the goods being sold. The language of this provision treats this duty as one arising from the contract. The question whether this provision also covers pre-contractual duties is not discussed in Polish doctrine. No judicial decisions discuss this question. There are arguments for a broadening of the scope of application of article 546, § 1 CC. The information, which is to be provided according to article 546, § 1 CC, is much more useful before a person makes a decision on entering a contract than if the person received the information just after the conclusion of the contract. It would be nonsensical to say that a seller is obliged to inform a buyer about such legal obligations in relation the object of a sale, such as a lien, only after the contract has been concluded. The legal situation of a good to be sold is perhaps the most important information needed before entering a contract. For this reason it would be difficult to accept a thesis that article 546, § 1 CC concerns only the duties after formation of the contract – a buyer needs such protection, at least to this same extent, before the contract has been made.[27] Hence, I think that article 546, § 1 CC covers also the pre-contractual duties of the seller.

The scope of application of article 546, § 1 CC is much broader than merely the field of the contract of sale. It applies directly to all kinds of contracts and refers to the regulation of the contract of sale. This is the case in the contract of exchange (article 604 CC) and contract of delivery (article 612 CC).

In all these cases, taking into account the argument mentioned above, it should be accepted that the duties to provide information in all these contracts also cover the pre-contractual stage. In the case of a contract of exchange, these duties affect both parties. Both parties have specific knowledge of their own goods, which are to be exchanged.

In the case of the aforementioned contracts, a violation of the pre-contractual duties should be treated in the similar way to the violation of the contractual obligations according to article 471 CC. Such violations, consisting of the delivery of misleading or false information, may constitute a liability based on statutory warranty according to article 556 and subsection of the Civil Code (lack of the features whose existence has been assured by the seller – article 556, § 1 CC).

The intentional omission of the provision of such information, or delivery of false information, may also constitute a fraud. In such case, it is also possible to admit the 'absolute unlawfulness' and accept a tort (article 415 CC).

VI. THE 'FOURTH CIRCLE' – IS THERE A PRE-CONTRACTUAL DUTY TO PROVIDE INFORMATION IN POLISH LAW IN SPITE OF THE LACK OF EXPRESS STATUTORY PROVISIONS?

This short and incomplete review of the first 'three circles' of regulation of pre-contractual duties shows a diverse and somewhat disparate system of

[27] See Zoll, *Die vorvertragliche Informationspflichten im polnischen Recht – eine Frage des Bestehens einer generellen Verpflichtung zur Erteilung der vertragsrelevanten Informationen*, *Krakauer – Augsburger Rechtstudien 2* (2006) pp. 228–230.

pre-contractual duties of information. There are a variety of diverse sanctions related to the violations of these duties. Many of the provisions on pre-contractual information are found in consumer protection laws, or are based on a similar consideration of protecting the typically weaker party. The chosen legislative technique of numerous specific regulations raises, almost automatically, the question as to whether, in the case of the lack of express regulation of pre-contractual duties, the existence of such duties should still be accepted based on such legal reasoning as an analogy. It is also a question whether a general duty to provide pre-contractual information can be settled just by the principle of good faith.

This diversity of the regulations prevents the formulation of just one answer on the question of admissibility of analogy from the rules expressly determining pre-contractual duties. The core of the regulation determining pre-contractual duties is the consumer regulation or the regulation based on similar ideological concepts – protection of the weaker party of the contract. In the case of the regulation of the 'first circle', the main idea behind the system of protection is the prescription of detailed, specific information which is to be provided to the client, backed up by a severe sanction if the provisions are violated, also if the violation was not intentional (but was at least negligent). The extreme example of this system is a Consumer Credit Statute with its article 15. In these cases extending an information duty by way of analogy would be highly dangerous. The existing regulations charge the entrepreneur with a duty to prepare special forms, containing required information. The entrepreneur, in organizing his business, must be certain that he complies with the legal requirements. Consumer law should avoid expansive interpretation, establishing additional requirements and limiting the freedom of the entrepreneur. Otherwise an entrepreneur cannot determine when his business is in compliance with the law. It cannot be the aim of the legal system to cause permanent uncertainty whether a contract has been definitively concluded, or whether there is a right to claim a payment or not. In the standardized, typical legal transaction, it could only cause unnecessarily high costs to the economy. Therefore, an analogy from the consumer rules on information should not generally be accepted. This does not mean that an analogy in determining the existence of a pre-contractual duty of information should always be excluded. A typical provision which could be a basis for an analogy, could be the already discussed article 546, § 1 CC. This provision is based on a presumption that a seller should have much broader knowledge of a good to be sold than a buyer. The seller is treated in such situations as the cheapest source of information. Because of his or her experience with the former use of the good, or because of the seller's professionalism, he should know about all features relevant to the buyer without having to incur additional costs. As I have mentioned, the provisions on the contract of sale have a broader scope of application – the Code Civil refers to them in cases of mutual contracts with the obligation to transfer a title. These same interests and values could also be found in other kinds of contracts, where there is not a provision governing the contract of sale in article 546, § 1 CC, for instance a tenancy contract (article 659 and subsection CC), a contract of employment (article 627 and subsection CC), or direct leasing (article 709^{18} CC). There could be different reasons why in these cases an express regulation on pre-contractual duties is missing. For example, in the case of certain kinds of direct leasing (for example a 'sale back leasing'), a leasing provider certainly has less information concerning the good than the client. If the legislature did not provide enough specific regulation on this issue, it would be unreasonable to make a general reference to article 546, § 1. In the case of a contract of employment it also may depend on many diverse circumstances – it is difficult to make a standard assumption on the knowledge of the parties. But in the cases of these two contracts, there are certainly situations where the positions of the parties (imbalance of information detrimental to the client) reflect the situation imagined by the legislature in case of article 546, § 1. In a case of the rental contract, it is rather typical that the owner of the rented good has a lot of specific information related to the object. Looking at the 'program' of the legislature, and the way in which it balances interests, the application of analogy should be justified in these cases.

In Polish doctrine there are some arguments for a general duty to provide pre-contractual information.[28] These duties are part of the general principle of loyal behaviour during the process of negotiation. One can look for the source of the general duty to provide pre-contractual information in the so-called 'principles of the social cohabitation'. This general clause, formulated under the old regime, should be interpreted today as a requirement of good faith. A number of provisions contain such a requirement: article 5 (defining the borders of the subjective right – the Polish version of the construction of abus de droit, resembling the formulation of article 2 of the Swiss Civil Code) or article 353^1 CC (defining the borders of the freedom of contract) or article 354 (containing the general provisions for performance of obligations, resembling article 242 of the German Civil Code). Despite the great importance placed on the principle of good faith in the Polish civil law, this principle generally has not been considered a basis for legal action. Article 5, regarding good faith, is usually considered a basis for a defence but not for a right to action.[29] Otherwise the system of 'good faith' would be an alternative system of subjective rights, concurring with the system of positive law. Such an extension of the concept of 'good faith' cannot be accepted.[30]

[28] Łętowska, *Prawo umów konsumenckich*, pp. 215 *et seq*. See also for a more sceptical position Radwański in Radwański, *System Prawa Prywatnego*, Vol. 2, p. 409.

[29] Wolter, Rola zasad współżycia społecznego w nowych kodeksach, *Nowe Prawo* 11/1964, pp. 1040–1043; Liebscher and Zoll in Liebscher and Zoll, *Einführung in das polnische Recht*, p. 141.

[30] See Zoll, *Die vorvertragliche Informationspflichten im polnischen Recht* (2005) (forthcoming).

VII. CONCLUSION

I do not think that the Polish legal system contains a general principle regarding pre-contractual duties to provide information. Most of the provisions of law concerning pre-contractual duties are very specific and offer no basis for further generalisation. An analogy may be drawn from some less specific regulations, such as article 546, § 1, but it is advisable to remain sceptical of the tendency to broaden these duties.

Chapter 20
Option and Pre-Contract*

Ana Giménez Costa and Esteve Bosch Capdevila, University Rovira i Virgili (Tarragona)

I. INTRODUCTION

The option is among the most widely-used tools in modern legal transactions. In the world of the property market one frequently hears talk of an option on purchasing a particular property, or in the business sphere of stock options, and even in the sporting field, of the option of acquiring the rights to some footballer.

The option consists of the parties agreeing to the conditions under which a particular piece of business is to be done, at the same time agreeing that this business going ahead is to be decided by one of the parties, in such a way that the holder of the option or optee may, as they see fit, impose the execution of the business or not. The party granting the right must abide by the optee's decision.

While the option has on occasion been used for the purposes of a guarantee, sometimes concealing a *pactum comisorium*,[1] the option may also serve perfectly lawful purposes, such as the following:

* This paper is included in the Research Plan BJU2003-06718-C02-02, '*La nueva regulación de los derechos reales en el derecho civil catalán*', of the Spanish Ministry of Education and Technology, the main researcher of which is Professor Dr. Pedro del Pozo Carrascosa.

1 The option used as a guarantee may indeed conceal a *pactum comisorium*. If, in the case of an obligation that is not met, the creditor/optee is allowed to obtain the good of the debtor under guarantee by exercising the option and without having to pay anything, or by paying a much-reduced fee, the similarity between this situation and that of a *pactum comisorium* is clear: the creditor may acquire the goods under guarantee, so, if the value of the goods is much greater than the amount owed, the detriment to the debtor is obvious.

S. Grundmann, M. Schauer (eds), *The Architecture of European Codes and Contract Law*, 359–372

- granting the optee a period of reflection as to whether or not to proceed with a particular piece of business;
- allowing the optee to raise the money they need to afford the acquisition; or
- attempting to take advantage of a possible appreciation in the value of the good which is subject to the option.[2]

As may be appreciated, the option is established in the interest of the optee, as it is only the conceder who is bound by it. This involves a significantly advantageous situation for the former; whereas the conceder is generally compensated by the payment of a price to constitute the option.[3]

Widespread use of the option in professional practice has not, however, been accompanied by a significant number of measures within the pertinent legal regulations governing it. On many occasions this has led to a situation of legal insecurity. Many countries' civil codes, following the example of the French civil code of 1804 (article 1589), have simply and in a very brief way regulated the promise of sale.[4]

Nevertheless, in modern codes, or in modern revisions of traditional codes, it is increasingly common to see the option regulated.[5] This is the case, among others, with the 1963 Guatemalan civil code (article 1676 *et seq.*), the 1984 Peruvian civil code (article 1419 *et seq.*) or the 1998 Argentinean draft civil code (article 936). Perhaps the most comprehensive regulation of the option is to be found in one of the so-called regional civil law procedures, that of Catalonia. This region, on the path towards approving its own civil code, has enacted a special law regulating the so-called rights of acquisition, including pre-emption, redemption and the option.

The above-mentioned codes have placed regulation of the option within the framework of the pre-contract; this is correct, though it is not the only possibility, as the example of Catalan civil law will show.

At a Conference such as this one, devoted to the formation of the contract, it is logical that study of the option be limited to the option qualified as a pre-contract; Catalan regulations in this area will be taken as a starting point, but attention will also be paid to other comparative legal models.

---

2 In professional practice, the so-called 'mediatory option' is fairly common. This is characterized by circumstances in which the holder of the option is in theory an intermediary who does not wish to exercise the option but to take advantage of the value afforded by the right to the option in order to transfer it to a third party, who is the one who exercises it. The justification for this 'mediatory option' lies in the intrinsic value of the right of option if this allows one to acquire a good at less than the real price.

3 This price may consist of a lump sum or a periodic sum, or even a non-monetary consideration.

4 Among others, art. 1451 of the Spanish civil code; arts 1710–1712 of the Quebec civil code.

5 One exception is the Quebec civil code, which, in arts 1710–1712, and following the French civil code, regulates only the promise of a contract.

II. THE PRE-CONTRACT

The pre-contract has been defined in various ways. Mention is made of a 'preliminary' contract (article 934 *et seq.* of the Argentinean civil code), a 'promise' of a contract (article 1674 *et seq.* of the Guatemalan civil code and 419 of the Portuguese civil code) or a contract 'preparatory' to a further contract (article 1414 *et seq.* of the Peruvian civil code, or article 2243 *et seq.* of the Mexican civil code), among other formulations. There is some agreement in terms of doctrine and in the codes which regulate the institution in that by means of the pre-contract the parties undertake to sign a future contract, in the sense that a binding obligation exists for the parties. Thus, article 1414 of the Peruvian civil code states that through the obligation to contract, the parties undertake to make a definitive contract in the future. However, the relationship between pre-contract and definitive contract has raised many doubts and several theories have been put forward. While some authors see the pre-contract as being different from the definitive contract, so that the latter cannot exist until the parties have once again given their consent, others identify the pre-contract with the definitive contract, in the sense that the statement of the consent needed for the definitive contract to exist is already to be found in the pre-contract, and for this reason the parties need not give their consent again.

The first of these two theories would fall within the classic approach which situates the pre-contract within the phase of forming the contract, and fits in better with the descriptions mentioned above of the pre-contract as a 'preliminary' or 'preparatory' contract, or a promise of a contract. According to this theory, in the pre-contract there is still no contract, but simply an obligation to formulate one if one of the parties decides to do so. If the other party were to refuse to give their consent to the definitive contract, application might be made to a judge to enforce such consent and only out of this consent would the definitive contract be established.

However, if the pre-contract already includes all the essential elements of the definitive contract, a further contract need not be signed. Therefore, according to the second theory, which is the one we support, the definitive contract blurs into one with the pre-contract, in such a way that contractual consent has already been granted in the pre-contract. In fact, the pre-contract involves the existence of a contract with all its essential features, the efficacy of which depends on the will of the two parties. Where such a will exists, no new agreement is necessary to ensure that the contract becomes effective, as it is already fully laid out in the pre-contractual agreement. On the other hand, one cannot talk of a pre-contract if some essential feature remains to be determined; this would require a new agreement between the parties. The pre-contract must include all the features which would be incorporated in the definitive contract; the lack of any of its features is no impediment to the existence of a pre-contract – neither would it be for that of the definitive contract – if the said feature may be deduced through the application of 'self-construction',[6] the law, accepted usage or good faith.[7]

Therefore, it is not that the pre-contract establishes the whole of the 'basis' or principal framework of the future contract, but it does include all the features which are to make up the definitive contract. What distinguishes it from the definitive contract is that, while the pre-contract includes the necessary requirements for the contract to come into operation, this does not occur for the moment – and may never occur – but awaits a further voluntary action by one of the parties.

Subjecting the effectiveness of the contract to the will of the parties appears to allow the pre-contract to resemble a contract that is subject to an optional condition by the parties, such that the contract will come into effect when one of them feels it to be appropriate. The execution of the option or the pre-contract depends on the fulfillment of the condition previously imposed on the contract. Under this theory of the condition the notion of a pre-contract becomes superfluous.

However, while the parallel between pre-contract and contract subject to an optional suspensive condition is certainly evident, there are also considerable differences between them:

(1) If the contract is conditional, fulfillment of the condition will bring about retroactive effects, which must not exist in the pre-contract.[8]
(2) The definitive contract cannot be said to exist until the pre-contract is executed, while in the case of the conditional contract, the contract exists while the condition is still pending. The pre-contract in itself is not identical to the definitive contract – though in terms of content it is – but it is 'transformed' into the definitive contract.

This means that the figure of the pre-contract has its own autonomy, and attempts should not be made to assimilate it to other institutions.

The definitive contract is the result of some preliminary negotiations leading to the pre-contract which, if the party or parties so desire, will become the definitive contract. However, the pre-contract is not situated in the stage of the preliminary negotiations but is in fact the result of such negotiations. As a consequence of these negotiations a contractual content is established. This is the content of the pre-contract and may become the content of the definitive contract. The pre-contract implies the existence of a type of clause in the contract that conditions its efficacy to the will of the parties involved.

6 'Self-construction': a way of filling in holes in the contract by extrapolating the principles from the civil procedure governing it.
7 Art. 1451 of the Spanish civil code, which deals with contract of sale, mentions only object and price as elements that must be determined.
8 In the Spanish civil code, this is governed by art. 1120.

Figure 1: Stages of Contract

III. THE OPTION AS PRE-CONTRACT

The 'entry into force' of the pre-contract and its transformation into the definitive contract remain in the hands of the parties. Depending on whether both parties may demand this 'entry into force', or whether only one of them may do so, this is a case either of a bilateral promise or of unilateral promise. We call the unilateral promise, in which only one of the parties is obliged, an option. In fact, the option consists of a form of pre-contract distinguished by the fact that the binding obligation exists for only one of the parties, but not for the other, so that the former is the only one who can demand the execution of the contract. That is to say, the option is a form of pre-contract characterized precisely by the fact that the contract's entry into force may only be demanded by one of the parties, with the other dependent upon the decision of the former. While the optee may exercise their right and execute the contract – though they may not be obliged to do this by the other party – the conceder remains subject to the decision made by the holder of the right of option. Otherwise, the option has all the features of the pre-contract.

Figure 2: Pre-contract and Option

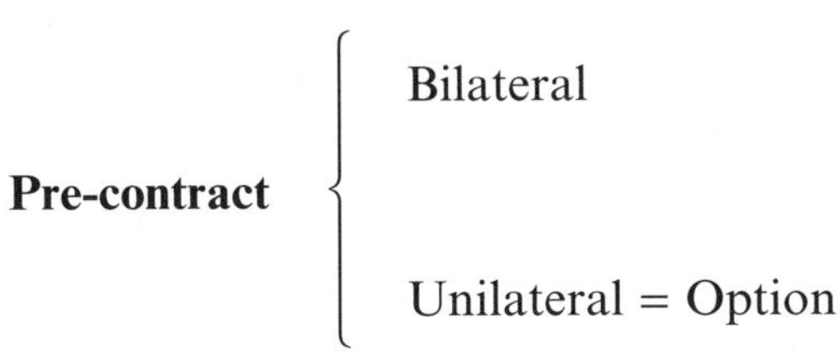

The few civil codes that have so far regulated the pre-contract follow this scheme, which considers the option as a form of pre-contract. The Peruvian civil code of 1984, for example, after regulating the so-called 'commitment to contract' in articles 1414 to 1418,[9] regulates the option contract in article 1419, stating that within this type of contract, one of the parties is bound by its statement to make a definitive contract in the future, and the other party has the exclusive right to make it or not. The Mexican civil code[10] and the Portuguese civil code[11] also follow this scheme, but perhaps the clearest code in this respect is the Guatemalan civil code, whose articles 1674 to 1685 regulate the promise and option; article 1675 states that the promise of contract may be unilateral or bilateral, and article 1676 states that the unilateral promise is the stipulation that one person makes in another's favour, granting them the option to acquire a thing or a right under agreed conditions and for the time agreed.

IV. THE CIVIL LAW MODEL IN CATALONIA – THE DISTINCTION BETWEEN PERSONAL AND REAL OPTION

Catalan civil procedure contains fairly complete regulation of the option, but structured in a way which is different from anything hitherto seen. Within the process of codifying Catalan property law,[12] Law No. 22/2001 (referred to hereinafter as LSSDA), dated 31 December 2001, regulates in articles 19 to 35 the rights of pre-emption, redemption and option.[13]

It may be surprising that, although provision is made for such rights being of a personal or a real nature, their regulation is to be found in a law governing various real rights, and not in the field of contracts. This may be

[9] Defined in art. 1414 which states that, because of the commitment to contract, each party obliges the other to draw up a definitive contract in the future.

[10] The Mexican civil code in arts 2243 to 2247 regulates the promise of contract; art. 2244 states that the promise to contract, or the contract preliminary to another, may be unilateral or bilateral.

[11] Arts 410 to 413 of the Portuguese civil code regulate the promise-contract, and also provide that it may be unilateral or bilateral.

[12] Catalonia is currently immersed in the codifying phase of its civil code. This should culminate in the complete publication of its own civil code, which will be different from the Spanish civil code. For reasons relating to competence, however, this process of codification is not without controversy: the central government maintains that, in accordance with art. 149.1.8 of the Spanish Constitution, certain civil matters are exclusively their own competence.

[13] The extremely fast codification process of Catalan civil law will mean that sectorial laws regarding civil matters, one of which is the LSSDA, will be repealed when the books of the Catalan Civil code are successively approved. Options in Catalonia will therefore no longer be regulated as a single concept and by a single law (the LSSDA), but by two books of the Catalan civil code. The option with real nature will be regulated by the Fifth Book, which deals with property and limited real rights, and the option with personal nature will be regulated by the Sixth Book, which deals with obligations and contracts. The LSSDA will maintain its importance, however, for having contributed to the construction of a general theory on options.

due to the peculiarities of Catalan civil procedure, which for the moment does not govern all civil institutions, but only the right of succession and numerous institutions of family law and real property rights. On the other hand, regulation in the contractual field is virtually nonexistent,[14] partly due to the conflicts of powers with the Spanish state that this would involve. It may therefore be said that in Catalan law the option is not regulated within the pre-contract because no suitable framework exists to regulate it.

In Catalan law 22/2001 (LSSDA) the option may be, as we have stated, of a personal or a real nature. It may also have its origin in a contract, in some other type of instrument *inter vivos*, or in an act *mortis causa* (article 23 LSSDA). The 'pre-contractual' option is therefore just one among the different forms that the option may take in civil procedure in Catalonia: when the option is to be one of a personal nature, it comes into existence by means of a contract.

Consequently, in Catalan civil law, the option is not always a pre-contract, and the pre-contract is not always an option.

The distinction between the real and the personal option is important. Apart from other aspects which are more of detail, such as, for example, the form of constitution,[15] or the maximum duration of the right,[16] the basic consequences of the distinction between real and personal options are as follows:

(1) The personal option may be exercised by the optee only as regards the conceder, while the real option may be exercised *erga omnes*.
(2) The general rule is that the personal option cannot apply to third parties, the exception being cases where the personal option is entered in to the Register (and, though this is arguable, also where the third party shows bad faith). On the other hand, the real option, resulting from property publicity, always applies with respect to third parties.
(3) While the exercise of a right of acquisition of a real nature supposes the acquisition of a thing (article 29.1 LSSDA); on the other hand, the exercise of a right of acquisition of a personal nature suggests demanding the fulfilment of an obligation to hand over the object (article 30.1 LSSDA). Therefore, the difference lies in the consequences of exercising the option: the immediate effectiveness of acquisition of the thing if the option is real, or the ability to demand fulfilment of the obligation to hand over the object if the option is personal. In the real option the

[14] Only a few specific contracts are regulated. One example is that which regulates the exchange of land for future development (Law 23/2001 of 31 December 2001).

[15] The real option requires the agreement of the parties in this respect, the public instrument and entry in the Register of Property (art. 20 LSSDA). Therefore, if nothing is said in this respect, the nature of the option will be personal.

[16] Greater for the real option (ten years on immovable property, five on movable property), as opposed to four years for the personal option (art. 25 LSSDA).

acquisition is not contractual, and in consequence *traditio* is not necessary; on the other hand, the exercise of the personal option supposes the transformation of the pre-contractual option into a contract, which will lead to the same consequences as the perfection of any contract: that the obligations may be demanded, but not necessarily the acquisition of the property, which in Catalan law also requires the *traditio.*[17]

V. THE SYSTEM GOVERNING THE OPTION OF A PERSONAL NATURE

Below is explained, in a highly systematic manner, the system governing the option of a personal nature, taking as a starting point its regulation under Catalan civil procedure. This system, which we deduce from the Catalan regulations on the matter (Law 22/2001: LSSDA), could serve as a model for other civil codes or as a proposal for a European Code of Contracts.

1. Capacity

The conceder will need the capacity to make the definitive contract. This is because the consent given by the conceder to establish the option is sufficient for the perfection of the definitive contract and the consent does not have to be given again. On the other hand, the optee will only need the general capacity to make contracts, because the contract's entry into force requires the optee to re-express his will. However, if the option is established onerously, the optee will require the capacity to have the object given in consideration.

2. Object

The object of the option can be extremely varied. Examples are premises, land, flats or other types of accommodation, shares (the so-called stock options), and rights to the services of professional sportsmen.[18]

In addition to the requirements for any object in any contract (that its existence is possible and that it is licit and determined),[19] the object of the right represented by the option must be identifiable. Given that the contract

[17] Art. 609.2 in fine of the Spanish civil code, suppletorily applicable to Catalonia.

[18] In fact, in the world of sport it is fairly common for clubs to deal in the rights to acquire or recover the services of certain players. What determines whether the option is exercised or not are the player's progress and the financial situation of the club that holds the option.

[19] Arts 1271 to 1273 of the Spanish civil code, suppletorily applicable to Catalonia.

only produces obligational effects, the option right may be future goods (e.g. flats in a building still under construction), as is expressly outlined in art. 21.2 LSSDA. In this case, the option may be exercised even though the good is a future one.

3. Form

The option may be constituted by means of a separate contract, or as an agreement forming part of another contract (article 23.II LSSDA), as occurs for example when renting with a purchase option.[20] Furthermore, also in accordance with article 23 LSSDA, the option may be constituted by transfer (the owner transfers the right of option to another person), but also by division (the owner transfers ownership to a person and at the same time constitutes a right of option to the benefit of another) or reservation (the owner transfers ownership, but reserves the right to recover the thing sold). The latter method represents the so-called *pactum de retrovendendo*, which in reality constitutes a re-purchase option, and in consequence its regulation should fall within the framework of the right of option, and not as an agreement added onto the contract of sale, as is the case in the majority of civil procedures, including Catalan.[21]

The act of constitution must meet and include a series of requirements (article 24 LSSDA):

- if the right of option was set up against payment, the agreed charge for setting it up;
- the address of the owner of the good, so that they may be notified if the optee exercises the option;
- the duration of the right;
- if the acquisition was against payment, the consideration set for acquiring the good.

However, we understand that it must be required that all the conditions under which the alienation is to take place be listed.[22]

Unlike the case of the real option, the LSSDA does not require that the contract establishing the right to an option be entered in a public instrument or Register of Property. However, as is outlined in article 1674.2 of the Guatemalan civil code, this promise of a contract should be given in the form demanded by the law for the promised contract, as a consequence of the identification of the pre-contract with the definitive contract.

---

[20] Art. 1677 of the Guatemalan civil code establishes the same.

[21] Catalan law attributes real nature to this pact and regulates it in arts 326 to 328 of the Compilation of the Civil Law of Catalonia.

[22] As in the case of the Peruvian civil code in art. 1415.

If the option is stated in a private document and subsequently it is wished to enter it in the Register of Property, and the conceder refuses to sign the contract, a Judge may substitute this consent by issuing the corresponding public instrument (article 1683 of the Guatemalan civil code).

4. Maximum Duration

The right of personal option involves a considerable burden for the conceder, who is obliged not to alienate the good. As a measure to protect them – the conceder may be described as the weaker party in the contract – there is a clear need for the law to set a maximum term for the right of option: the conceder cannot be indefinitely subject to the uncertainty that goes with knowing that the optee can at any moment exercise the right to option. The period fixed by the LSSDA is four years (article 25.2), though this may be subject to successive renewals that obviously require the agreement of both parties and which may not be for longer than four years each.[23]

It must be borne in mind that, as stated above, the duration of the right is a necessary requirement in the act of constitution, for which reason if no duration is set then the right shall be null and void.[24]

5. Transferability of the right of option

Given that this transmission involves the transfer of the status of party to a contract, it is logical that it should require the consent of the other party, that is, the conceder.[25] This is laid down in article 28.2 LSSDA, by virtue of which, for the optee to transfer their right, they must be expressly empowered to do this.[26]

Voluntary transfer may be expressly authorized in the original title of the right to acquisition, or in a later process. A general transfer or a specific act of transfer may be authorized. If the transfer has taken place without

23 In art. 1681 of the Guatemalan civil code the period is shorter: two years if the option covers immovable property and one if it affects movable property; on the other hand, art. 1423 of the Peruvian civil code does not appear to set a maximum term, but simply a period of one year in cases where the parties have not set the term.

24 On the other hand, other regulations rule that if the parties do not fix a term, this will be the maximum allowed by the law (art. 1682 of the Guatemalan civil code), or a subsidiary legal period is fixed (art. 1423 of the Peruvian civil code).

25 Art. 1421 of the Peruvian civil code, 412.2 of the Portuguese civil code and 1678 of the Guatemalan civil code.

26 This need for authorization, which as we have said is proper for the personal option, is also required by art. 28 LSSDA when the option is of a real nature, which is not so proper, given that the general rule is that real rights covering property are freely alienable.

the consent of the conceder, the acquirer cannot oppose the exercise of the option right before the conceder.

6. Obligations of the Conceder during the 'Pending' Phase and Consequences of its Non-fulfilment

The obligations of the conceder of a right of option while it has not been exercised, are not expressly stipulated in the LSSDA, though the following conclusions may be drawn as to its general regulation:

(1) The conceder has a duty of 'material' care of the thing, in the sense that they may not damage it but must keep it so that, should the optee exercise the option, it should be in the same state as it was when the option was constituted.
(2) Furthermore, the conceder is subject to an obligation of a negative nature, which consists of not carrying on any legal activity which might impede the exercise of the option; they are therefore obliged not to alienate or otherwise encumber the thing covered by the option.

Article 30.3 LSSDA lays down the consequences of non-compliance by an owner as a result of having transferred the thing covered by the option to a third party; the precept states that if the object is legally in the possession of third parties, compensation for damages is necessary. Three situations may be distinguished:

(1) There can be no doubt that if the third party is in good faith and has made a valid acquisition, they will not be affected by the optee's right of option, and the latter will only have the right to insist on the conceder's liability for damages arising from their non-compliance.
(2) If the right to option was shown in the Register of Property – which is possible under Catalan and Spanish law in accordance with article 14 of the mortgage regulations – the right of option may be invoked against the third party, whether they knew of the existence of the said right or not. This does not mean that the optee can exercise their right of option against the third party, which they could only do if the option were of a real nature, but that the said option will affect them insofar as the alienation could be reversed, the thing returned to the conceder and the right of option exercised in respect of the conceder.
(3) The most disputed case is when the right of option is not entered in the Register, but the third party acquires the goods in bad faith, knowing of the existence of the right of option. Doctrine is divided in this respect, but the opinion we believe to be the most correct – though it is not the one which adheres most closely to the letter of article 30.3 LSSDA – is that which considers that the third party, despite being supported by the Register, is not protected, in such a way that the alienation could also be reversed in this case.

7. Requirements for the Exercise of the Right of an Option

In addition to meeting any other requirements which may have been stipulated, the optee is obliged to notify the owner, authentically and reliably,[27] of the exercise of their right (article 31 LSSDA). This is currently the only right the owner of the object has: the right to be informed that the option is being exercised and therefore that the contract has come into effect.

8. Effects of the Exercise of the Right of Personal Option

Article 30.1 LSSDA establishes that the exercise of a right of personal option has the following consequences:

(1) Compliance with the obligation to hand over the object may then be demanded. While the exercise of the option constituted with a real nature gave rise to the acquisition of the ownership of the object, the personal option only gives rise to the obligation to hand it over. The exercise of the option formalises the contractual relationship between the conceder and the holder of the right, so that both must fulfil their obligations: the conceder must hand over the thing, and the optee must pay the price; as with any contract, the formalisation of the contract only creates obligations for the parties.
(2) The optee is obliged, if appropriate,[28] to pay the price. Unlike in the case of the real option, payment of the price is not a requirement for the exercise of the option,[29] but an effect of this exercise.

9. Annulment and Rescission of the Contract Resulting from Exercise of the Option

Procedures, such as the Catalan one, that allow contracts to be contested, and also rescinded due to *laesio ultradimidium*, raise the important matter of determining the moment when the contract is deemed to be formalized. This is in order to begin calculation of the periods of contest or, in the case of rescission due to damage, to fix the fair price for the good. As we said, this is an important problem that, from the dogmatic perspective, is hotly disputed

[27] Notification should normally be made by means of a notary, but any other way that attests its content would be admissible.
[28] Acquisition may be free, in which case no price is to be paid.
[29] Arts 29.2 and 32.1 LSSDA demand; for the real option, payment of the price for the exercise of the option; the justification for the difference in comparison with the personal option is that in the case of the former, its exercise makes the optee into the owner of the thing; on the other hand, as we said, if the option is personal, its exercise only confers the right to demand that the thing be handed over.

and there are arguments in favour of both possibilities, i.e. to choose the moment at which the option is agreed or to choose the moment at which it is exercised. The controversial nature of this problem demands that the codes expressly reach a decision on the matter, but this has not happened in Catalan civil law.[30]

Perhaps the most correct solution would be to consider that, since the contract is formalized when the option is exercised, this is the moment that should be taken into account when calculating the fair price and beginning the calculation of the time periods. The exception to this general rule would be when one wishes to contest the contract because of a defect in the consent of the conceder. The conceder does not give new consent for the formalization of the contract since he has already given it when the option was first established, so that is the moment when the period for annulling this consent should begin.

VI. CONCLUSIONS

The case of the option is a further example of the usefulness of comparative law in proceeding to regulate an institution. Different models of comparative law – among them that of Catalonia – must be used in order to copy their successful points and avoid repeating their errors, with the aim of achieving a form of regulation which is as correct as possible.

The option is actually one of the tools that could be most useful in any future European Code of Contracts because the various national legislatures would be more receptive to introducing new concepts – for example, the option – than modifying already regulated contracts.

It is correct and laudable that the parties can configure the option to be of a real nature or of a personal nature depending on their interests.

The personal option must be situated within the scope of the pre-contract, which in turn must be separated from preliminary negotiations and therefore from the stage of formation of the contract, and included within the scope of general effects. The real option, on the other hand, lies within the framework of limited real rights, specifically within the so-called acquisition rights.

The so-called *pactum de retrovendendo*, which many codes regulate as an agreement additional to the contract of sale, is no more than an option constituted through reservation, for which reason it must be regulated within the option.

---

[30] French Law No. 49-1509, of 28 November 1949, on the other hand, clearly laid down the criterion for evaluating the time of the exercise of the option, with the incorporation of a new art. 1675.2, stating '*En cas de promesse de vente unilatérale, la lésion s'apprécie au jour de la reálisation*'.

Any attempt to regulate the option should clearly establish the moment at which the contract is made in order to determine the fair price for the good and establish the moment to begin calculating the period for the rescission or contest of the contract resulting from the exercise of the right to option.

Chapter 21
Discussion Report

Mr Baumann referred to Mr Roppo's demands for the introduction of uniform jurisdictional measures and wanted to add to this the idea of a harmonization of procedural law along the lines of the harmonization of material law. Other areas of law, which he specified, needed to be harmonized as well. Homogeneity of procedure must be safeguarded through an extensive adaptation of procedural issues.

Prof. Collins introduced two heresies into the discussion. The first is that an idea had entered legal thinking in Roman times and has stayed there ever since, namely the idea that somehow the contract that the parties had made didn't really exist, which is actually a fiction. He referred to nullity or voidness because of problems in the formation of the contract, a mistake, fraud, duress, some sort of argument of that kind. In his view this whole doctrinal development was very unfortunate and the most important question is whether in a European code it should be repeated. He proposed that these cases should be solved by imposing a duty to pay (substantial) compensation, but the contract itself should be left intact. The second heresy Collins named is that lawyers have a much richer vocabulary – especially when it comes to different terms for 'information' – than economists so economists need to learn from lawyers for a change, as they should learn to distinguish between various types of information.

Following these remarks Prof. Micklitz pointed out that the duty of information in EU consumer regulations mentioned by one of the earlier speakers was producing the result that contracts were being standardized. Neglecting the duty of information was not penalized with any sanctions on the EC level. He then raised the question whether there should be a sanction as well if consumers did not make use of their information rights. He concluded his remarks by saying that presumably EU law was going to generate new distribution patterns between party autonomy and responsibility.

S. Grundmann, M. Schauer (eds), *The Architecture of European Codes and Contract Law*, 373–374

Prof. Mankowski commented on the issue concerning consumers who failed to exercise their information rights. He suggested that it may in fact be this type of behaviour which makes duties of information, which would otherwise be too onerous, tolerable in practice. As far as standardized elements in contracts are concerned he expressed strong opposition to sweeping generalizations.

Dr. Calliess advocated a flexible system with a formalistic approach keeping the redistribution and allocation of profits as simple as possible.

Private Law in European Context Series

1. M. Bussani and U. Mattei (eds.): *The Common Core of European Private Law*. Essays on the Project. 2002 ISBN 90-411-2004-1
2. S. Grundman and J. Stuyck (eds.): *An Academic Green Paper to European Contract Law*. 2002 ISBN 90-411-1853-5
3. M.W. Hesselink: *The New European Private Law*, Essays on the Future of Private Law in Europe. 2002 ISBN 90-411-1962-0
4. M. Bussani: *The Common Core of European Private Lae*. 2003 ISBN 90-411-1852-7
5. H. Collins (ed.): *The Forthcoming EC Directive on Unfair Commercial Practices*. 2004 ISBN 90-411-2224-9
6. S. Grundmann and D. Mazeaud (eds.): *General Clauses and Standards in European Contract Law*. 2005 ISBN 90-411-2432-2
7. M.W. Hesselink (ed.): *The Politics of a European Civil Code*. 2006 ISBN 90-411-2410-1
8. S. Grundmann and M. Schauer (eds.): *The Architecture of European Codes and Contract Law*. 2006 ISBN 90-411-2530-2